I0814027

CCCC STUDIES IN WRITING & RHETORIC

Edited by Stephanie Kerschbaum, University of Washington

The CCCC Studies in Writing and Rhetoric Series (SWR), established in 1984, supports research that explores how writing, rhetoric, and literacy are currently and have been historically taught, learned, practiced, and circulated within communities, whether in colleges, workplaces, or neighborhoods, in local, national, digital, or international contexts. The series also focuses on supporting a broad range of projects that accurately represent the diverse identities of teachers, learners, administrators, and researchers involved in writing, rhetoric, and literacy, addressing the cultural, social, political, and material realities that define their work. Work published in SWR seeks to identify and resist the inequities and forces of oppression that shape the teaching of writing, rhetoric, and literacy as well as to intervene in them. The series aspires to be global both in scope and reach and is dedicated to the use of digital technologies that ensure its publications are accessible and available to a national and international audience.

All SWR volumes try in some way to inform the practice of writing teachers, students, or administrators. Their approach is synthetic, their style concise and pointed. Complete manuscripts run 50,000–60,000 words, or about 150–200 pages. Authors should imagine their work in the hands of writing teachers, including those at two- and four-year colleges and universities, in dual enrollment programs, and in a wide range of extra-institutional and/or non-US-centered pedagogical contexts. While writing teachers may be a primary audience, the series aims to be accessible and engaging to broad audiences of those who are interested in how we make our ways with language and literacy.

SWR was one of the first scholarly book series to focus on the teaching of writing. It was established by the Conference on College Composition and Communication (CCCC) in order to promote research in the emerging field of writing studies. As our field has grown, the research sponsored by SWR has continued to articulate the commitment of CCCC to supporting the work of writing teachers as reflective practitioners and intellectuals.

We are eager to identify influential work in writing and rhetoric as it emerges. Authors are encouraged to submit proposal queries to share questions and project concepts ahead of submitting a formal proposal. Project proposals should clearly situate the work in the field, showing how the research being developed and shared intervenes in and engages conversations hosted by the series and/or in writing, rhetoric, and literacy studies. Prospective authors are asked to indicate how the project extends, redirects, and/or reshapes ongoing conversations about writing, rhetoric, literacy, and their teaching. Proposals should include an overview of the project and its stakes, a brief annotated table of contents, a market analysis of comparable/related work published in the last 5–7 years, and a sample chapter. They should convey the project's conceptual and/or empirical archive/data set and how the text's arguments emerge from the archive/data. If the project involves human subjects, please indicate IRB approval. We welcome work that originates outside of the academy and collaborations among authors who experiment with form and knowledge-making practices. The series does not accept unrevised dissertations.

For more information, visit https://cccc.ncte.org/cccc/swr/submissioninfo.

Memoria

Essays in Honor of Victor Villanueva

Edited by

Asao B. Inoue
Arizona State University

Wendy Olson
Washington State University Vancouver

Siskanna Naynaha
California State University, Dominguez Hills

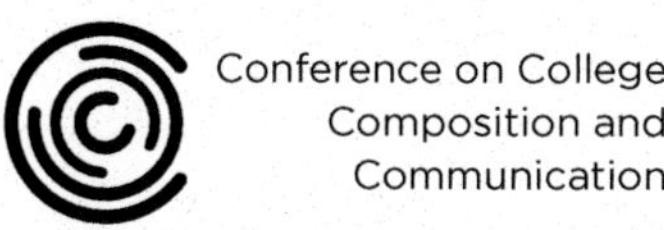

National Council of Teachers of English
340 N. Neil St., Suite #104, Champaign, Illinois 61820
www.ncte.org

Staff Editor: Cynthia Gomez
Manuscript Editor: Bonny Graham
Series Editor: Stephanie Kerschbaum
Interior Design: Mary Rohrer
Cover Design: Pat Mayer
Cover Photo: Victor Villanueva

ISBN 978-0-8141-0182-7 (paperback); ISBN 978-0-8141-0183-4 (ebook);
ISBN 978-0-8141-0184-1 (PDF)

Library of Congress Control Number: 2024935241

CONTENTS

INTRODUCTORY MATTERS

Asao B. Inoue, Wendy Olson, and Siskanna Naynaha

THE PURPOSE OF THIS COLLECTION IS twofold. First and foremost, it is an encomium to Victor Villanueva, the scholar, rhetorician, teacher, editor, mentor, and friend. In the field of rhetoric and composition, it is hard to find anyone more respected and beloved than Victor. We, the editors of this collection (Asao, Wendy, and Siskanna), were Victor's graduate students at Washington State University during the early 2000s, right after he had served as chair of the Conference on College Composition and Communication. He was also the chair of each of our dissertation committees, and over the years, Victor has continued to mentor and guide each of us in profound ways. Like so many rhetoric and composition scholars across the country and even around the globe, we each owe Victor so much because he's given us and the field so much.

The second purpose for this collection is to introduce folks new in the field to Victor's scholarship and mentorship, particularly graduate students who may know less about him and his work. So this collection offers an introduction to him as a mentor and to his scholarship around *Memoria* and the study of rhetoric and racism. We envision this collection to be a first step toward learning more about what Victor's scholarship still offers today's graduate students, and it provides an understanding of just how prescient his work still is to those studying race and racism and teaching writing in college settings.

VICTOR'S HISTORY IN BRIEF

Victor was born in 1948 in Brooklyn, a Puerto Rican in New York—Nuyorican, as he likes to say, to the core. He tells his own story in literally award-winning detail in the book considered by many to be his seminal work, *Bootstraps: From an American*

Academic of Color, and he does so with greater acuity and verve than we could ever hope to match here. Published in 1993, *Bootstraps* earned Victor both the National Council of Teachers of English's Richard A. Meade Award for Research in English Education (1994) and the David H. Russell Award for Distinguished Research in the Teaching of English (1995). While he expresses gratitude for the accolades he received for *Bootstraps* over the years, saying he "wouldn't have had a career without it," Victor notes that it was really his way of reckoning with the profession and speaking to folks in the field who, like him, identified as people of color and did not see themselves or their experiences reflected in the disciplinary discourse on language and literacy.

Victor has received many additional awards over the decades that define his storied career, including Rhetorician of the Year from the Young Rhetoricians' Conference in 1999. In 2008, he was the first ever recipient of the NCTE Advancement of People of Color Leadership Award. He has called being chair of the Conference on College Composition and Communication (CCCC) in 1999 one of the highlights of his career, and in 2009 he was granted the CCCC Exemplar Award for "years of service as an exemplar for our organization represent[ing] the highest ideals of scholarship, teaching, and service to the entire profession." And there are more. Many more. In fact, it wouldn't be quite right to say that Victor's professional awards and recognitions are innumerable, but it wouldn't be far off the mark either.

Since receiving his PhD in English with an emphasis in rhetoric and writing from the University of Washington in 1986, Victor has held academic posts at different institutions, but his longest tenure was at Washington State University, where over the years he served variously as director of composition, Department of English chair, associate dean, director of American studies, and director of the Writing Program. In his time at WSU, he received the Martin Luther King Distinguished Service Award (1999); the Sahlin Faculty Excellence Award for Research, Scholarship, and the Arts (2005); Mentor of the Year in American Studies (2009); and Most Supportive Faculty Member (1998 and 2010). His mentorship is legendary, as the pieces in this collection demonstrate. And a thread runs through all of Victor's recognitions, honors, and awards: his commitment to scholarship as teaching and teaching as scholarship. In his own words, though, the true legacy Victor will leave: "It's you, my students. It's true. I really love y'all."

WHAT'S IN THIS COLLECTION

Following this short historical overview, we include two chapters that serve as an introduction to Villanueva and some of his most influential publications. Each of these introductory chapters discusses the "best of" his work from the perspective of Olson and Inoue. While we've tried to cover his most influential publications between the two chapters, it is also true that what is meaningful to each of us in terms of Villanueva's published work often coincides. There is complementary overlap in these two chapters, yet we engage the texts from our individual perspectives and experiences. In "On Engaging Tradition and Change with Victor," Olson focuses on three broad themes that develop from Villanueva's scholarship and inform the field for her: the history and legacy of critical pedagogy in our field, thinking through political economies of rhetoric and composition, and rhetorics of racism. In "Languaging from My Roots in Victor," Inoue focuses his selection and discussion on what he considers the most important works for teachers and scholars new to the field. These introductory chapters reflect our thinking on these works and their contributions at this moment in our lives. At the same time, we've also thought mostly about readers who may be new to Villanueva's scholarship and ideas, and so framed our discussions with this primary audience in mind.

Key to both chapters, it is worth noting, is Villanueva's emphasis on Antonio Gramsci's understanding of hegemony as rhetorical. Born in Italy's Sardinia in 1891, Gramsci was a student, worker, writer, and social activist. Arrested as a political prisoner by Mussolini's government in 1921, he died in prison in 1937. Appreciated for his emphasis on political praxis, Gramsci's primary influence on Western Marxism is his theory of hegemony. Gramsci's theory complicates previous Marxist definitions of hegemony, which focused on coercion and force, expanding it to include how hegemony often functions as ideological consent. We see Gramsci's influence on Villanueva's work as he focuses on how hegemony thus functions and circulates rhetorically. We see this influence in his discussion of cultural and critical literacy, the academy, and his lived experiences as an academic of color in *Bootstraps* (1993); in his analysis of how racism circulates as common sense in "On the Rhetoric and Precedents of Racism" (1999); and in his reflection on reclaiming memory in and as rhetoric (as dialectic) in "*Memoria* Is a Friend of Ours: On the Discourse of Color" (2004). We highlight these three publications here, as they are most often referenced and considered by contributors in the collection.

In the rest of this volume, we've organized the contributions into three sections. The first and second sections, "*Memoria* of Rhetoric" and "*Memoria* of Mentoring," contain full chapters that explore various aspects and influences of Villanueva's scholarship, teaching, and mentoring. In some instances, they discuss the ways that Villanueva's scholarship opened up avenues of research. In some cases, the authors explain the various ways that Villanueva has mentored as author, as teacher, as editor. Sometimes they do both. The last section, "*Memoria* of Relations," contains a series of short works that center on Villanueva from unique perspectives. These pieces are meant to be creative and reflective contributions that honor his impact on the field and its scholars and teachers at the individual and personal level. They provide meaningful insight into Victor the person.

The first section, "*Memoria* of Rhetoric," assembles chapters that speak to how memory/*Memoria* has been taken up in the field of rhetoric and composition, and how the contributors consider the importance of Villanueva's influence and impact on such current efforts. In "'as it flashes in a moment of danger': Reflections on *Memoria*, Colonialism, and Rhetoric," John Trimbur focuses on Victor's critical understanding and performative enactment of *Memoria*, with particular attention to his insistence that memory, as a rhetorical and political practice, is "more than recollection." In doing so, he illustrates that while Victor draws, as he says in

"*Memoria* Is a Friend of Ours," on "personal discourse, the narrative, auto/biography" as a "necessary adjunct to the academic," the exigence of *Memoria* has burst through these genres, producing a new political-rhetorical register in US college composition capable of releasing the past from the oppressive grip of its finished histories and making available its emancipatory resources. He posits that Villanueva's published work, in its main lines of development, explores the invention of rhetoric on the periphery, as a weapon of the subaltern in the war of positions between colonizer and colonized. In contrast to the austerity of the Anglo-American plain style, he argues, Villanueva's writing is marked by the heightened presence of the author, the intensity of its reader–writer interactions, and its associative conversational logics.

In "Re-Collecting Chicanx Collective Memory," Miriam L. Fernandez addresses the concept of collective memory, which is present across several of Villanueva's written works. In doing so, she analyzes a few significant narratives in the Chicanx collective memory via personal memories, photographs, and analyses of select texts. Looking back at her experiences during a series of trips to Mexico City, she discusses how she has been both recipient and participant of collective memory. Certain memory places in Mexico represent important collective memories for Chicanx, yet their physical locations make them difficult to access without time and money. Born in Mexico, but still an outsider with a limited understanding of certain political and cultural nuances, Fernandez speaks to this common experience among Chicanx no matter which side of the border they were born. The framework through which she looks at collective memory is based on her subjectivity as a Chicana.

In "'Home Is a Funny Thing': Critical Race Theory Home and Abroad," Catherine Prendergast uses Victor's subdefinitions of *funny* to reflect on how our collective "home" has changed in the last few decades. Positioning her own ethnographic research from 1992 to 2003 in post–Soviet Slovakia as a jumping-off place, she reflects on how the fates of two countries where she feels at home—the United States and Slovakia—have switched utterly. On a recent visit to Bratislava, she found everything she used to find "funny" about 1990s Slovakia—the shortages in stores, the inability to leave the country, the mistrust of the post office—have become normal now in the United States. In the meantime, Slovakia has embraced a liberal democracy and blossomed socially and economically, with its citizens moving freely throughout a world that Americans, in 2020, were barred from. Drawing on inspiration from Villaneuva's complex notions of "home," she argues that whatever our critical work, we have to move from a stance of ironic detachment to horrified citizen—that this is not a rhetorical posture so much as an ingrained sense of being. It is a life- and career-long commitment to humility, to reconciling that there is always here, and vice versa.

In "Anticolonial Critique, Decolonial Directions, and Making Space for Américan Rhetorics," Christa J. Olson examines the ways in which US-based study of Latin American rhetoric owes its nature to Villanueva's efforts and commitments. Olson highlights three specific orientations that Villanueva provided for the study of Américan rhetorical history. These orientations, she argues, have made the subfield what it is and point toward work yet to do. They are fundamental and expansive: (1) Villanueva ensured that rhetorical scholars looking toward Latin America went through, not around, the realities of colonial violence; (2) his model required subsequent scholars to linger in—not skirt—racialization; and (3) he built frameworks that connected Latinx and Latin American rhetorics without collapsing them, implicating all of us residing in the hemisphere within Américan complexities. In the remaining words of her chapter, Olson expands on these foundations, showing how they might ground new projects and facilitate further engagement.

In "Re-membering '*Memoria*': The Value of the Personal within Academic Discourse for Our Contemporary Moment," Laura Gray-Rosendale seeks in large part to champion and revisit Villanueva's essential essay published in 2004, "*Memoria* Is a Friend of Ours: On the Discourse of Color." Modeling her chapter on the beautiful and creative format of Villanueva's own essay, her piece moves in and out of her own personal experiences and narrative as well as various academic discourses, making the case for the need to revitalize the personal as foundational to the history and theory of rhetoric, particularly in our contemporary historical moment. She argues that, more than ever, what we need, in light of the COVID-19 pandemic, increasing economic unrest, climate change, domestic terrorism, MeToo, Black Lives Matter, and our discipline's—as well as all of higher education's—radical destabilization, is a weaving together of the personal and the academic. Gray-Rosendale's chapter demonstrates this weaving.

In the next chapter, "Corporeal Composition: *Memoria* and the Discourse of the Body," Victoria Houser draws on Villanueva's "*Memoria* Is a Friend of Ours: On the Discourse of Color" to explore what Victor's call to invite memory holds for our scholarship and teaching in two ways. First, she examines how the invitation to memory has been practiced in the field of rhetoric and composition. Second, she practices this invitation, including her own memories and narratives as a young scholar teaching and writing in the field.

In the closing chapter of this section, "Personal and Collective Memory as Shadow Work," Romeo García draws from Villanueva's scholarship to theorize the potential of collective memories as shadow work toward rhetorical decolonial praxis. Sharing his own memories and experiences from growing up in Texas' Lower Rio Grande Valley (LRGV) through graduate school, alongside reflections on Villanueva's work and other decolonial theorists, he reflects on the haunting of racism in the United States and academia. His discussion foregrounds the role of Villanueva's influence on his own stories-so-far as a Brown(ed) academic and the possibilities of new stories for both the field of writing and rhetorical studies and himself.

The chapters in the second section, "*Memoria* of Mentoring," speak to the importance and legacy of Victor's mentorship of both individuals and the field. In "Cuentos de Mi Historia con Nuestro Hermano Victor Villanueva: Fictive Kinship to Support Writers of Color Addressing Racism," J. Paul Padilla explores the importance of fictive kinship from writing teachers like Victor to support students of color who address matters of racism sympathetically in academia. He considers the importance of fictive kinship through an understanding of the challenges faced by writers of color, the challenge of teachers and administrators to provide genuine kinship to writers of color who address racism, and ideas for teachers and administrators in light of Victor's retirement.

In the next chapter, "On the Rhetoric and Precedents of Representation: Following Villanueva in Challenging Disciplinary and Institutional Racism," Morris Young takes up Villanueva's "On the Rhetoric and Precedents of Racism" as a central reflective text. He reflects on whether much has changed in our broader society as racial violence and other acts of hatred have only increased in frequency and intensity, and in our educational institutions where the COVID-19 pandemic has only exacerbated issues of equity and access and made highly visible the barriers that still exist for students when they enter seeking the promise of education only to find that privilege remains a premise. In engaging with Villanueva, Young reminds us that what Villanueva called for more than twenty years ago remains a constant struggle that we must undertake to transform our rhetorical present and future.

In "Antiracism, *Zhuangzi*'s Happy Wanderer, and Overcoming the Crusades," Robert Eddy centers on Villanueva's scholarship on rhetorics of racism and how it speaks to Victor's mentorship and care for others. Eddy uses Zhuangzi's figure of the happy wanderer, who has "the unique ability to heal," to illustrate and discuss Villanueva's work and influence in Eddy's own life. He explains that Villanueva performs a kind of "dance, of being 'playful and disciplined, imaginative and profoundly realistic' but always attempting to study and open up with those who follow their natures in balance and peace."

In the next chapter, "Dandole Gas: Un Profe con Sangre del Fil," Octavio Pimentel writes in Spanish and English as he intermixes the complexities and ganas that Villanueva's "The Block" (from *Bootstraps*) provided for him as he struggled and faced obstacles in an academic field that oftentimes does not want to understand people like himself—a Brown academic. Pimentel illustrates, like Villanueva, how racism functions in both our K–12 school system and higher education in the US. In doing so, he demonstrates the ongoing reach of systemic racism in our culture and society.

Following Pimental's chapter, Lauren Rosenberg's "Writing with Victor" draws from Villanueva's essay "Hegemony: From an Organically Grown Intellectual" to share her story of his extraordinary mentoring while they collaborated on her book. She illustrates how he has encouraged generations of scholar-writers to examine ways that hegemony can be countered, often through ordinary acts such as changing one's literacy practices. Her chapter blends reflection and analysis, storytelling and critique, creative and theoretical lenses, in the ways Victor showed her to do when they worked together as editor and author in an extended conversation on the politics of literacy education.

In the final chapter in this section, "Villanueva and We: Breaking Precedents of the Rhetoric of Racism," Ana Milena Ribero and Aja Y. Martinez provide a counterstory as allegory/fantasy that sends them back in time to a fictionalized late-1990s context, placing them in conversation with Victor on the precipice of his crafting "On the Rhetoric and Precedents of Racism." As they invoke this counterstory method, they transport their audience back in time to a coffee shop in the late 1990s where they encounter Villanueva mulling over ideas that will serve as his precedent-breaking response to a reviewer's rejection of his concepts. They have crafted characters to voice their perspectives in conversation with Villanueva, whose words and concepts, represented as dialogue in this essay, are directly extracted, quoted, paraphrased, and cited from his words within the landmark article. In doing so, the authors invite their readers to join the dialogue, hear their voices, see their gestures, and perhaps imagine themselves taking a seat at the table.

The third and final section, "*Memoria* of Relations," includes short works that provide individual reflections that invite readers to see and experience Villanueva from the authors' various vantage points and experiences with him. These vignettes present snapshots that embody and honor the *Memoria* and mentoring that Villanueva enacts and what it represents for the authors. Contributors of this section include the following:

- "How We Know," Jessie Eulalia Padilla
- "Family," Mitzi Ceballos and Wyn Andrews Richards
- "Of Mentors and *Memoria* and Rhetorical Houses in Need of Fixing," Asao B. Inoue
- "Footprints to Follow," Sherwin Kawahakui Ranchez Sales
- "Blown Away," Tiffany Rousculp
- "Embodied Engagements," Stephanie L. Kerschbaum
- "Gracias, Viejo," Siskanna Naynaha

Fittingly, we close the collection with these snapshots, these personal histories. Collectively, they share, show, and represent the legacy of Victor's imprint on the field and on multiple generations of teachers and scholars. One story at a time.

Chapter I

On Engaging Tradition and Change with Victor

Wendy Olson

> Hegemony will not be countered in one semester or in one quarter or two. We cannot deny students' economic desires nor our own economic needs. But we can begin the dialectical process necessary to counter hegemony. We can play out our contradictions as deputies of hegemony and as subversives, agents of tradition and, with our students, potential agents of change. We can follow Gramsci's example: promoting critical dialogue within a cultural literacy.
>
> —Villanueva, *Bootstraps: From an American Academic of Color*

LIKE MANY OF THE CONTRIBUTORS to this collection, I became aware of Victor Villanueva's work through *Bootstraps: From an American Academic of Color. Bootstraps* represents much for me and my identity as an academic. It introduced me to Victor's work and what scholarship can do. It gave me the confidence to think that maybe I could do this work as well, to continue on as an academic and make it my life's work. It familiarized me with Antonio Gramsci, his contributions to Marxist philosophy, his theory of hegemony, and his history and some part of his lived experience. As demonstrated in this chapter epigraph, Victor's reading of Gramsci in *Bootstraps* (as well as elsewhere in his work) distills key concepts, such as Gramsci's notion of hegemony, in tangible ways. Victor illustrates the significance of the processes of hegemony—not just what it is but also the messiness of how it works and why it matters—and he applies that in particular to our discipline and disciplinary concerns. We see that in his discussion of cultural literacy as dialectic. *Bootstraps* helped me make sense of the politics of education as a first-generation student and scholar, aiding me in the development of my scholarly and teacherly self. Victor became a mentor to me through *Bootstraps*, even before I met him in person three years later in Pullman, Washington. This is what his scholarship does: it teaches and it mentors in ways that make sense in our day-to-day realities.

Victor's work, and *Bootstraps* especially, engages significant and needed questions about our field and our teaching practices, all the while attending to the material. His scholarship asks us to reflect on and engage our own experiences, assumptions, and worldviews, as well as those of our students. It guides and trains us to honor our students while also challenging them to see and understand how language functions and influences worldviews in ways that we don't often register but that are nonetheless significant. His work asks us to consider the impact of rhetoric on our collective lived experiences. These impacts include, of course, the material realities and effects of racism, economic crises, civic discourse, and educational policies, among others.

Entering my MA program in English studies at Western Washington University, I was introduced to literacy studies by Donna Qualley, the director of composition at the time. It was then, too, that I became aware of composition and basic writing as fields of study. As a first-generation female student and a white working-class Appalachian, I was drawn to the politics of literacy and writing instruction. I decided to focus my MA thesis on literacy narratives, and Donna, who also served as my thesis director, suggested that I read *Bootstraps*. This was in 1998. In 2002, after two years of teaching composition at three different two-year colleges in the Pacific Northwest (and running a basic writing program at one of those institutions for the latter year), I entered the PhD program in rhetoric and composition at Washington State University. By that time, I had read more of Victor's scholarship and had attended a talk or two of his at the Conference on College Composition and Communication Annual Convention. I was grateful and felt fortunate when Victor agreed to direct my dissertation. That was a little more than twenty years ago.

As a working-class academic, I was interested in working-class issues. I was interested in race, too. Literacy studies, cultural studies, critical race theory, Marxism, feminist theory—these were my interests (still are). It was through Victor's reading of Gramsci's work in *Bootstraps* that Gramsci's work began to mean something to me, and I was able to bring these interests together in a way that made sense via rhetorical theory. To clarify, I was introduced to Gramsci in an Introduction to Theory course during my first semester as a graduate student at Western, by way of a reading of Raymond Williams's "Base and Superstructure in Marxist Cultural Theory." It was required reading. I'll confess, though, that I didn't remember much from that initial reading or the discussion. I remembered that it was a thick text. After reading *Bootstraps*, though, I returned to Williams's article. It was one of those a-ha moments. Victor brought me back to this text, helped me to unravel Gramsci and his work, to contextualize his work and see the significance of it in the context of rhetoric and composition, in the context of education, in the context of my own lived experience.

Victor is drawn to Gramsci because Gramsci's theories reflect his lived experience: "[T]o tell of Antonio Gramsci is to tell of a life dramatically affected by the hegemonic forces he sought to oppose" (*Bootstraps* 122). Victor's focus is on Gramsci's definition of hegemony and its relation to rhetoric. Hegemony, for Gramsci, is "domination by consent," domination that functions ideologically (123). Victor's reading of Gramsci in *Bootstraps* succinctly articulates how Gramsci's notion of common sense illustrates such processes, how common sense, for example, functions rhetorically as hegemony: "the common sense consists of the commonly held conceptions of the world held by various cultures, a culture's ways of seeing and believing. These are carried and transmitted by discourse" (124). In his theory of hegemony, Gramsci complicates the traditional Marxist notion of "false-consciousness" by illustrating how mass consent circulates through common sense in civil society. And in doing so, Victor explains, Gramsci articulates an epistemic view of language in his understanding of hegemony. This connection clicked for me—a way to better see and understand the complications of ideology manifest in my working-class upbringing, a way to better understand the sometimes contradictory beliefs and values I lived and witnessed around me. It also gave me a way of talking about the role of language and persuasion in these meaning-making processes and configurations of worldviews.

Here is Williams, working-class Welsh academic and socialist writer, on Gramsci. Gramsci's hegemony, he writes,

> supposes the existence of something which is truly total, which is not merely secondary or superstructural, like the weak sense of ideology, but which is lived at such a depth, which saturates the society to such an extent, and which, as Gramsci puts it, even constitutes the substance and limit of common sense for most people under its sway. (458)

Williams reads Gramsci's notion of hegemony as a way to rearticulate the dynamic and ever-changing processes of social formation. Hegemony is plural, continuously "active and adjusting" in ways that maintain domination, Williams affirms (459). As such, hegemony contains internal conflict. That is, hegemony must be repeatedly constructed in a struggle of competing discourses; consequently, it must dominate by popular consent through common sense.

And here is Victor, translating and contextualizing for rhetoric and composition. While hegemony is "virtually watertight," he explains, "there is leakage": "hegemony must shift" (*Bootstraps* 126). Within the competing, contradictory activity of hegemony, counterhegemonic practice can happen, the process by which emergent or oppositional cultures might rise to challenge the dominant culture. To be sure, these moments are fleeting, and more often than not they are co-opted. That's the dialectic between tradition and change. And this dialectic is also why we should care about hegemony as scholars of rhetoric and composition and teachers of writing. These processes, while eventually risking and often succumbing to incorporation into the dominant culture, illustrate an avenue by which individuals can move within the collective to push toward change, if not total transformation. We call this movement agency in twentieth- and twenty-first-century theory talk. And equally important: Victor describes counterhegemony as "a matter of individual and collective will—an active rhetorical practice" (126). And such practice, while fundamentally rhetorical and thus tied to meaning making, must also move beyond it. Consequently, both consciousness raising via rhetorical awareness and material change might, just might, effect hegemonic change. That's the dialectic of tradition and change toward a possibility that counters hegemony.

Victor's reading of Gramsci provided me with the means by which to better understand how Gramsci's notion of hegemony provides the backbone for a contemporary Marxist rhetorical theory and its affinity with rhetoric. Gramsci's notion of hegemony complicates either/or debates concerning base and superstructure in Marxist philosophy by moving toward a both/and notion of how ideology works. That is, in adopting Gramsci's understanding of ideology as hegemonic processes, the messiness of the production and processes of meaning making through a rhetorical lens is uncovered. This understanding opens up the possibility of acknowledging materiality as a process, yes, but also as a reality. This possibility is realized in Gramsci's notion of counterhegemony, as Victor relates in *Bootstraps*. It is also essential, I'd argue, as a framework for thinking through what we do as academics and teachers.

As illustrated in *Bootstraps*, a predominant thread of Victor's scholarship reads as a dialectic engagement with Gramsci in a twentieth-to-twenty-first-century, US-situated context. "Of all of the leftists," Victor reminded me recently, "his work made the most sense to me." This engagement with Gramsci echoes throughout Victor's work, functioning as a generative arc that evolves his articulation of his own work as a scholar, teacher, and mentor. It provides a framework for his politic of the personal made public, a scaffold for Victor's conception of the dialectic relationship between tradition and change (signifying his ongoing conversation with

Freire as well as Gramsci): "Tradition and changes in tradition" ("Considerations" 633). This dialectic of tradition and change lives, too, in the legacy of Victor's work. It lives in the dissertations he has directed and the students he has mentored, in the scholarship he has responded to and shepherded to publication, and in the teachers and scholars he has supported and encouraged into the discipline. In the select overview of Victor's work that I address below, I take up this engagement: what it means to me as a scholar and teacher, and what I see as its importance as a historical touchstone for folks new to our field.

ON CRITICAL PEDAGOGY

> Hegemony exploits traditions. The American Freireista can at least provide a way for students to discover those traditions that are in need of change. We can have students discover the traditions that form the foundations of the academy while simultaneously promoting and instigating change in the ideologies that shape the academy. Tradition and change for changes to the traditions.
>
> —Villanueva, "Considerations for American Freireistas"

In my reading of Victor's work, I see this early piece as an important reflection on the role of critical pedagogy in the history of composition studies. Published in 1991, in "Considerations for American Freireistas" originally appeared in *The Politics of Writing Instruction: Postsecondary* edited by Richard Bullock and John Trimbur and was reprinted in the first edition of Victor's *Cross-Talk in Comp Theory* in 1997. In it, Victor provides a nuanced critique of the application of critical pedagogy in the academy broadly and in the writing classroom more specifically. He speaks to the messiness of praxis in a first-year composition classroom when attempting a pedagogical approach borrowed and informed by Paulo Freire's philosophy of critical pedagogy.

Victor calls out his purpose in this text upfront:

> I will argue that to achieve a pedagogy that aims at more than mere reform we must begin by acknowledging the unlikelihood of dramatic revolutionary change in the most immediate future. I will argue that less dramatic but no less revolutionary change might come about by our becoming more aware of the workings of hegemony. (623–24)

His call to do so, he explains, is in response to classroom trends that tend to reduce politics to discussion of cultural differences and/or discussions on social injustices, discussions attempting a counterhegemonic pedagogy that is often not realized for the students it is intended for and for whom it is directed.

In many ways, "Considerations for American Freireistas" and "Hegemony: From an Organically Grown Intellectual" can be read in conversation—in cross-talk—with each other. In "Hegemony," Victor's focus is on providing an overview of Gramsci as a historical and political figure, his definitions of *hegemony* (ideological domination by consent that is carried through discourse) and *counterhegemony*, the cycling through hegemony and counterhegemony toward new hegemony, and the role of the organic intellectual. In doing so, Victor takes up the then (but also ongoing and regenerating) US debate surrounding cultural literacy and critical literacy, referencing Gramsci's notions of education as a kind of "critical cultural literacy": "a dialectic among students, a dialectic between student and teacher, between lived experiences and official ideologies" (30). Victor's emphasis on and defining of dialectic as pedagogical practice asks us to consider the *how* in supporting critical literacy practices in introductory writing courses. This understanding of the politics of literacy education, the need for fostering a critical literacy, and the relationship of both to the teaching of writing, is key, I would argue, in the development of a writing pedagogy for first-year composition.

In "Considerations for American Freireistas," Victor puts this dialectical approach into practice, arguing for a "classroom composition that confronts tradition with change" (623). In doing so, he reflects on the field's attention to critical pedagogy at the time and provides a needed critique of critical pedagogy in practice. Freire's definition of critical literacy is developed in response to what he sees as a passive and problematic educational model. Critiquing what he defines as the "banking concept of education" (73), Freire proposes instead a critical pedagogy that embraces a dialectical problem-posing concept of education (86). A primary appeal of Freire's pedagogy as adopted within composition studies is the acknowledgment that language mediates our understanding of ourselves and our world. And to be sure, this is a powerful appeal for teachers of writing. At the same time, Victor encourages writing scholars and teachers to think through how they embrace and employ this critical pedagogy, particularly in the adoption and adaptation of Freire's work into a US context in American colleges and universities.

For American compositionists, too, Freirean critical pedagogy alludes to the importance and significance of writing classes as sites where mediation, thus agency, might take place. Freire's pedagogy, however, evolved organically out of his own lived experience of working with Brazilian fieldworkers. In contrast, American followers of Freirean pedagogy often start with the theory of critical pedagogy by applying it to their classrooms. This distinction, as Victor points out and I agree, creates complications for praxis. It raises the issue of what the relationship between theory and practice is, between the theoretical and the material, and how it manifests in particular classroom contexts. For all teachers, but especially new teachers, it is important to reflect on and think through this dilemma, which is always inherent in praxis and the application of pedagogy to the classroom.

So, in "Considerations," Victor speaks to this dilemma of praxis, to the paradox of critical pedagogy and its implications in a US higher education context. For example, within the hegemony of the university, the university professor is able to critique inequality and even to work against it through critical pedagogy. In fact, the university has historically often sanctioned this work in the classroom—though not so much lately. The irony is, though, that this critical pedagogy scholarship, while rooted in social justice and liberation, sometimes also acts as cultural capital—intellectual capital—in the educational system. This unintended complicity runs the risk of undermining the project of critical pedagogy—and its most recent manifestation, social justice pedagogies. Consequently, the work of social justice pedagogies in the context of higher education can sometimes produce the kind of "changes without change" that Victor identifies.

Although some might argue that critical pedagogists just need to rectify this inconsistency, the situation is a bit more complicated than simple hypocrisy. Victor's reading of Gramsci in "Rhetorics Is Politics" offers a way of thinking through this contradiction within liberatory education. Victor articulates how the complicity of academics happens:

> We are subject to what Antonio Gramsci describes as a "directive hegemony" . . . which he describes as a hegemony that allows academics to struggle against coercive ideologies as long as basic systems are not too seriously threatened. With a directive hegemony, efforts tend toward reform, reforms that make token changes that can seem substantial. Reform tends to amount to what Gramsci calls "revolution-restoration" . . . changes without change, affirmative action quotas, say, more color in traditionally white positions while the basic inequalities remain. (329)

Here, Victor speaks to the paradox of critical pedagogy and the implications of that paradox more broadly, suggesting that we as educators can make use of the contradictions within hegemony. As he explains, Gramsci complicates notions of ideology and hegemony in positing that hegemony must be repeatedly constructed in a struggle of competing discourses; consequently, it must dominate by popular consent. Because of these competing and contradictory discourses, Victor proposes a dialectic between tradition and change in the classroom affords the possibility of change or, in Freire's language, transformation ("Considerations" 624).

In my own teaching, I take Victor's critique of critical pedagogy seriously. I see the potential for a critical pedagogy that is inherently rhetorical at its core. I am pulled toward critical pedagogy, not only because of its affinity with the rhetorical, but also because it strives to make the politics of education explicit in the classroom, positing that education should be a transformative experience for both students and teachers. As a teacher, I attempt to put this Freirean ideal of education as transformation into practice through the dialectic of tradition and change that Victor proposes. Employing this kind of pedagogical praxis is always a negotiation and never easy, yet I strongly believe that such a student-centered approach is valuable. It honors what students bring to the classroom, and it requires teachers to participate as learners as well, reflecting on their own positions, motivations, and practices.

And as a teacher of writing teachers, I use these readings and critiques by Victor as an introduction to the history and legacy of critical pedagogy in our discipline in our graduate program's contemporary composition theory course. My approach to the course emphasizes ways in which theories of composition have developed both historically and concentrically—that is, in dialect with other theories and against the backdrop of social and material change—in order to better understand the scholarly debates, contentions, and contradictions that have shaped composition studies as a field. A foundational tenet of my approach to the course, informed by my training with Victor, is the assumption that effective pedagogies must be theoretically and historically informed. We discuss how the theories we are reading about might complicate and inform not only how we construct our syllabi, assignments, and daily activities, but also our overall developing and evolving philosophies of teaching writing. For new writing teachers, engagement with this introduction to critical pedagogy through Victor's work provides a valuable theoretical and historical context for looking back, as well as for looking forward and for situating contemporary social justice and antiracist pedagogies within our field and teaching practices.

ON RHETORIC AND POLITICAL ECONOMY

Let me put it this way. The role of rhetoric, according to Burke, is the demystification of the ideological. The role of

> political economy is the demystification of relations tied to the economic. If we're to understand where we are and what is happening to us—and maybe even affect it—we need the tools provided by both.
>
> —Villanueva, "Toward a Political Economy of Rhetoric (or a Rhetoric of Political Economy)"

Published in 2005, Victor's "Toward a Political Economy of Rhetoric" appears in *Radical Relevance: Toward a Scholarship of the Whole Left* edited by Laura Gray-Rosendale (also a contributor to this collection) and Steven Rosendale. A political economy of rhetoric, according to Victor, provides an avenue for investigating the relationship between the rhetorical and the material in our lives, a way to both recognize and unveil potential gaps between what we know through language (the rhetorical and the ideological, as noted previously) and the reality of our day-to-day living as material beings caught up in an economic web of existence. Such a view of economics, it is important to point out, does not reduce human existence merely to the economic. It does not, in other words, return conversations concerning materialism to a basic economic determinism, to a simplified cause–effect relationship between the base and the superstructure, in Marxist terms. What it does do is recuperate cultural materialist conversations from the slippery slope of postmodernism. That is, in arguing for a political economy of rhetoric, Victor recognizes the complexity of the cultural sphere, yet he also makes explicit the need to not divorce it from material conditions.

To clarify this significance, a mapping of potential Marxian theories of rhetoric might sort out into two distinct patterns regarding the relationship between base and superstructure in a contemporary Marxist rhetorical theory. One approach, as characterized by Kenneth Burke (*Rhetoric*) and Louis Althusser, posits ideology, the superstructure, as an obstruction to real knowledge—that is, the truth of the economic base. Another approach, as illustrated by V. N. Vološinov and Michel Foucault, complicates the relationship between the base and the superstructure, but in doing so tends to conflate the two in a way that underdetermines the importance of the economic base and thus some notion of reality and existence as fixed outside of cultural production. Traditional Marxist theory assumes a process of consciousness that posits humans as subjects within their worlds in a way that is impossible in many postmodern-informed theories. In these postmodern theories of discourse, the nondiscursive consciousness is subsumed by the discursive.

Focusing on the relationship between rhetoric and political economy, Victor attends to this predicament. He suggests that we need an avenue for investigating the relationship between the rhetorical and the material in our lives, a way to both recognize and unveil potential gaps between what we know through language (again, the rhetorical and/as the ideological) and the reality of our day-to-day living as material beings caught up in an economic web of existence. A political economy of rhetoric, he proposes, might assist in this process by allowing for "the demystification of the relations tied to the economic" ("Toward" 58). Victor argues that our current conversations about the rhetorical nature of the cultural are necessarily limited. Contrary to our scholarly professions that such work exposes ideological constructs, he suggests that such work does in fact more often than not maintain ideological mystification:

> we cannot discuss the ideological and thereby the rhetorical reproduction of beliefs about gender, race, class, age, nation, religion, or any other of the axes of difference—without a grasp of how such axes are embroiled in the economic. In short, rhetoric is tied to political economy, if the work of rhetoric is the demystification of the ideological. (64)

Political economy, Victor points out, "is concerned with the whole configuration of power and economy. When that power is not coercive, then political economy is concerned with the rhetorical and the economic" ("Toward" 58). As an area of study, political economy complicates mainstream assumptions about the economy, namely, positivist assumptions about economic laws and methodology. According to Charles Sackrey and Geoffrey Schneider, theories of mainstream economics are too narrow because they do not address the effects of noneconomic influences on the economy (96). In contrast, political economy affords an approach that recognizes an interdependent relationship between economics and society, including social and political factors that might not be reduced to something measurable for an economic equation but that nonetheless materially impact the economy. Political economists "believe that human nature is pliable and conditional, rather than fixed" (111) and as such it is people, not natural law, who create economies. Political economy also attends to the cultural and hegemonic processes that shape and inform the economy—the role of the rhetorical, that is.

Victor's argument that we need to better understand political economy is valuable for our work in rhetoric and writing studies for multiple reasons. Here are a few illustrations of that value. One, it assumes a material relationship between economics and aspects of culture, such as, in the case of our discipline, the impact of cultural notions around literacy and language on lived experience. This analytic framework deconstructs cultural myths concerning the naturalness of language and literacy generally—and academic discourse specifically—by revealing literacy education as a political economy. It provides a framework for mediating and interpreting the relationship between ideologies of literacy and literacy standards in accordance with the rise of capitalism.

Two, to fully explore the intertwined politics of literacy education and capitalism, political economy allows for an analysis of not only cultural materialism but also historical materialism. A historical mapping or understanding of what Deborah Brandt identifies as literacy acceleration and accumulation and its potentially destabilizing impact for literacy learners, for example, is something we need to better understand as teachers of writing, if our role, as it should be, is to help students negotiate literacy economies within schooling and postsecondary education.

Three, the relationship between rhetoric and political economy provides a framework for thinking through how we address and talk about racism. "We know there is a connection between racism and the relation between power and money" Victor writes, "but being engaged with rhetorical political economists of the past could help us rethink the present" ("Toward" 59). A rhetoric of political economy, then, constitutes an important framework for situating our disciplinary knowledge and investigating hegemonic processes within our field as well as through the lens of our field. Through theories of political economy we can more fully investigate the junctions where rhetorics of education, economics, politics, and philosophy—as well as rhetorics of race, gender, and class—intersect with history and materiality to construct the institutionalization of literacy and writing instruction. And in doing so, we are better positioned to make good on our promises to students.

ON RHETORICS OF RACISM

> So here we stand. The new racism embeds racism within a set of other categories—language, religion, culture, civilizations pluralized and writ large, a set of master tropes (or the master's tropes).
>
> —Villanueva, "Blind: Talking about the New Racism"

Racism is a predominant theme in Victor's scholarship, and his analyses of rhetorics of racism are vital to our field's development, its growth, and critical reflection. As illustrated in the quote above and as informed by Gramsci, political economy, and critical race theory, Victor's work here looks to reveal how race operates rhetorically in the context of history and economics, how structural racism continues, and what it does and should mean to us as a field, as teachers. He examines, in other words, how racism functions as a political economy. In doing so, he asks us to recognize and become aware of the ways in which our courses, our teaching, our programs, our scholarship—our discipline and subdisciplines—are inevitably embedded within the arc of US racial formation. Important work. Necessary work.

In his 1999 *CCC* article "On the Rhetoric and Precedents of Racism," Victor asks us to prioritize the "depth of trouble" that is racism in our field: "[A]s priorities go, racism seems to have the greatest depth of trouble, cuts across most other bigotries, is imbricated with most other bigotries, and also stands alone, has the greatest number of layers" (648). He speaks to the distinct manifestation of racism for people of color in the US, addressing, in conversation with critical race theorists, the problem of multiculturalism in this context: "[E]thnicity and the cultural plurality suggested by multiculturalism appeal to common sense in ways that can address racism—and sometimes they do, maybe often—but without tugging at its hegemony with the kind force so many of us would wish" (650). What he is getting at here is that contradiction within hegemonic processes, how we produce, again, "changes without change," even with the best intentions. Here too Victor is unpacking how the discourse of racism alters, how language shapes and carries ideology via commonsense conceptions such as "multiculturalism," inadvertently sustaining domination by consent. So here we stand: the language of new racism established, embedded, and circulating via civic discourse, the processes continuing to sustain racism through civic society.

Victor continues this analysis of new racism in his article "Blind: Talking about the New Racism," taking up how new racism manifests rhetorically through figures of speech. He illustrates how language carries ideologically (whether we recognize it or not) to maintain racism and stereotypes via these rhetorical devices. In doing so, he takes up Kenneth Burke's "Four Master Tropes," illustrating how these master tropes—metaphor, metonymy, irony, and synecdoche—operate in the discourse of new racism. A hegemonic manifestation of reform without change.

To illustrate the importance of how racism functions rhetorically, here's a bit more context. In contrast to old racism, new racism, as defined by folks such as Barker, Balibar and Wallerstein, and Winant, talks of the cultural rather than the biological. As Winant describes, World War II marked the move to a new racial order. Of the Civil Rights Movement, he writes,

> [T]here was a price to be paid for civil rights reform: it could take place only in a suitably deracialized fashion, only if its key provisions were articulated (legislatively, juridically) in terms compatible with the core values of U.S. politics and

> culture: individualism, equality, competition, opportunity, the accessibility of "the American dream," and the like. (173)

While overt discrimination was sanctioned in the old racial order, as we know, this new racial order denies racism through a new common sense. This common sense reads the Civil Rights Movement as the historical point where folks of color "made it," where racism finally ended, and equality began in the United States.

As Victor describes,

> though racism has always been tied to language, has always had to be sold rhetorically, the rhetoric has changed, the tropes are different more often than not. There's been a tropic shift in the topos of racism. And we aren't keeping up. So we don't know how to engage, don't know if to engage. (11)

Of significance, we can see how these same tropes continue to play out in the US today—particularly with respect to political, cultural, and civic debates. And in what Kemal Dervis describes as the "post-Trump reconstruction of America," we can see, too, the intermingling reemergence of the tropes of old racism (briefly buried, perhaps, but not forgotten). Collectively, these tangled discourses circulate and manifest in real-world and material implications that negatively impact the lives of people of color, including through racial disparities, trauma, and violence. These are realities that we must attend to in our classrooms, that we must acknowledge as impacting the lives of our students, our colleagues, our community members.

With this framework of how rhetorics of racism function as master tropes, Victor provides an accessible tool for undergraduate students to use to perform rhetorical analysis. I have assigned "Blind" in composition courses as a way to introduce students to both how rhetoric functions through rhetorical devices and why it matters. It is an activity and assignment that clicks most of our outcome boxes for composition courses: rhetoric as meaning making, language and/as power, genre and rhetorical awareness, real-world problem posing, composing as social processes, etc. It engages students, too—meets them where they are and invites them into the conversation and analysis. It also enacts Victor's pedagogical principle of "tradition and changes in tradition" through dialectic teaching: Victor is in dialogue with Burke, and the students are in dialogue with Burke and Victor. It is one classroom strategy for doing our work, I'd suggest, that also productively takes up Victor's call to address racism in our teaching and in our classrooms.

So I'll close with this bit. We are not, by and large, bad people. We are, generally, good people attempting to do good work. Such work can't happen, though, so long as we remain satisfied with the stories we tell ourselves about ourselves. This is true for all of us, to be sure, and for us white folks, most definitely. As such, this is a confirmation and gentle nudge, the likes of which Victor might provide at the end of a classroom lecture or in response to a question posed at a keynote presentation at a conference. *Do the work. Do this work. Make it matter.* This message, I think, is a crucial element of Victor's legacy: he reminds us of this ongoing dilemma and the need for this work, our work. He pushes us to understand that if we want to be able to perform any kind of counterhegemonic work, we must first be able to recognize the depths to which we are spoken by the dominant hegemonic forces we are immersed within, racism especially. And he mentors us on how to do this work, how to keep up and keep on with this messy labor of love.

> Nagging questions that guide: How do nice people abide by and maintain not nice things, like a system in which certain groups are consistently relegated to the bottom of the structure in disproportionate numbers? How is ideology transmitted rhetorically? How can more oppressive ideologies be countered in the rhetorical enterprise, which includes the teaching of composition?
>
> —Villanueva, "'Rhetoric Is Politics,' Said the Ancient. 'How Much So,' I Wonder"

WORKS CITED

Althusser, Louis. "Ideology and Ideological State Apparatuses." *Contemporary Critical Theory*, edited by Dan Latimer. Harcourt, Brace, Jovanovich, 1989, pp. 61–102.

Balibar, Etienne, and Immanuel Wallerstein. *Race, Nation, Class: Ambiguous Identities*. Verso, 1991.

Barker, Martin. *The New Racism: Conservatives and the Ideology of the Tribe*. Junction Books, 1981.

Brandt Deborah. *Literacy in American Lives*. Cambridge UP, 2001.

Burke, Kenneth. "Four Master Tropes." *Kenyon Review,* vol. 3, no. 4, 1941, pp. 421–38.

———. *A Rhetoric of Motives*. U of California P, 1969.

Derviş, Kemal. "The Post-Trump Reconstruction of America and the World." Brookings Institution, 19 Jan. 2021.

Foucault, Michel. "The Discourse on Language." *The Archeology of Knowledge and the Discourse on Language*. Pantheon Books, 1982, pp. 215–37.

Freire, Paulo. *Pedagogy of the Oppressed*. 30th ed., Continuum, 2000.

Gramsci, Antonio. *Selections from the Prison Notebooks of Antonio Gramsci*. Edited and translated by Quintin Hoare and Geoffrey Nowell-Smith. International, 1971.

Sackrey, Charles, and Geoffrey Eugene Schneider, with Janet T. Knoedler. *Introduction to Political Economy*. 3rd ed., Dollars and Sense, Economic Affairs Bureau, 2002.

Villanueva, Victor, Jr. "Blind: Talking about the New Racism." *Writing Center Journal,* vol. 26, no.1, 2006, pp. 3–19.

———. *Bootstraps: From an American Academic of Color,* National Council of Teachers of English, 1993.

———. "Considerations for American Freireistas." *The Politics of Writing Instruction: Postsecondary,* edited by Richard H. Bullock and John Trimbur, Boynton/Cook, 1991, pp. 247–62. Rpt. in *Cross-Talk in Comp Theory: A Reader,* edited by Victor Villanueva Jr., National Council of Teachers of English, 1997, pp. 621–37.

———. "Hegemony: From an Organically Grown Intellectual." *Pre/Text,* vol. 13, no. 1-2, 1992, pp. 18–34.

———. "On the Rhetoric and Precedents of Racism." *College Composition and Communication,* vol. 50, no. 4, 1999, pp. 645–61.

———. "'Rhetoric Is Politics,' Said the Ancient. 'How Much So,' I Wonder." *Writing Theory and Critical Theory,* edited by John Clifford and John Schilb, Modern Language Association, 1994, pp. 327–34.

———. "Toward a Political Economy of Rhetoric (or a Rhetoric of Political Economy)." *Radical Relevance: Toward a Scholarship of the Whole Left,* edited by Laura Gray-Rosendale and Steven Rosendale, SUNY P, 2005, pp. 57–65.

Vološinov, V. N. *Marxism and the Philosophy of Language*. Harvard UP, 1973.

Williams, Raymond. "Base and Superstructure in Marxist Cultural Theory." *Contemporary Literary Criticism: Literary and Cultural Studies*, edited by Robert Con Davis and Ronald Schleifer, 3rd ed., Longman, 1994, pp. 454–66.

Winant, Howard. *The World Is a Ghetto: The Making of a New World Racial Order*. Basic Books, 2002.

Chapter 2

Languaging from My Roots in Victor

Asao B. Inoue

It is sometime late in 1999. I'm talking to Victor on the phone about going to Washington State University to get my PhD in rhetoric and composition. I'm nervous. I'm twenty-nine years old.

"Dr. Villanueva?" I say, unsure as to how to address him and concerned that I might offend him if I don't show proper deference.

"Just Victor," he says in a friendly way, "I don't need to be called 'Dr.' to be respected."

How we reference one another publicly and in private is important, isn't it? Mom, mommy, ma, dad, daddy, da. Bro, bruv, bra. Grandma, granny, nanna. Dr. So-'n-So, or Ms. So-'n-So, or hey you. In this chapter, I use "Victor" to reference Victor Villanueva, both as the embodied academic mentor-father I know in real life and as the author I read in his texts. I use Victor's first name because it feels inauthentic, wrong even, to call him by his last name, as if I don't know him as Victor, as if all this stuff is just some academic exercise and not a dozen different ways I make my life. Sometimes to show respect, you show familiarity. You call the person by their name.

I'm also trying to make my discussion of his scholarship match the relationship I have with the man I know in the flesh. When I read Victor's words, it is always a personal practice, even the very first time I did so, before I knew him, before the phone call, which I remember very well (I'll explain that later). I am always reading Victor, not Villanueva. I am always reading him off the page by feeling his words in my life, my teaching.

Now, if you were to ask me what the most important published works by Victor are, ones that a new writing teacher or someone studying rhetoric and race today should read, I'd say at least these pieces:

- "Hegemony: From an Organically Grown Intellectual" (1992)
- *Bootstraps: From an American Academic of Color* (1993)
- "Maybe a Colony: And Still Another Critique of the Comp Community" (1997)
- "On the Rhetoric and Precedents of Racism" (1999)
- "*Memoria* Is a Friend of Ours: On the Discourse of Color" (2004)
- "Toward a Political Economy of Rhetoric (or a Rhetoric of Political Economy)" (2005)
- "Blind: Talking about the New Racism" (2006)

There are other important scholarly contributions I could list, such as *Cross-Talk in Comp Theory*, which went through four editions (1997, 2003, 2011, 2024), the last two coedited with Kristin Arola. The first edition of that collection I cut my teeth on as a teacher. There's also *A Language and Power Reader: Representations of Race in a "Post-Racist" Era* (2014), coedited with Robert Eddy (a contributor in this collection), and there's *Language Diversity in the Classroom: From Intention to Practice* (2003), coedited with Geneva Smitherman. My point is, I can't talk about everything he's done. There's much that Victor has done that matters to me and my teaching. Out of necessity, I'm gonna be very selective about what I discuss in this chapter, what I think someone newer to Victor should pay initial attention to.

Below then are my responses to just a few of Victor's works, the ones that seem most salient to me at this moment in my life. Of course, my responses are seasoned with my own experiences in the academy and the world. For instance, I can't help but have in the back of my mind recent events that seem relevant: two mass shootings in communities of color, one in Buffalo and one in Uvalde, Texas. I'm also thinking about my own struggles as a former associate dean of academic affairs, equity, and inclusion at my university, and my recent experiences publicly leaving the Council of Writing Program Administrators (CWPA)—I'd been a member for more than fifteen years—calling for them to do real antiracist work in their organization because of the toxic white supremacist culture pervasive in it.[1] Needless to say, these few works by Victor still teach me things, give me words to reflect with.

What I won't do is summarize Victor's scholarship; instead I'll move through these texts in chronological order by their publication dates, offering some context, drawing out a few key ideas that seem salient, and responding in my way. I hope this shows just how vital he has been to me, my teaching, and my antiracist assessment work.

"HEGEMONY: FROM AN ORGANICALLY GROWN INTELLECTUAL" (1992)

For me, this article is the foundation on which everything else in my scholarship and teaching is built, so I'll have more words related to it than the others, even *Bootstraps*. Hegemony is the place I start, or assume. It's how racism and white supremacy are made and understood. Understanding hegemony in a nuanced way is how antiracist assessment ecologies are made. I hear Victor's discussion in this article in most of my interactions with him over the years, but especially in grad school, where he was my dissertation advisor. He also happened to be in the office across the hall from mine in the Avery building on campus, just at arm's reach from my desk.

One takeaway from this article is that hegemony is "essentially rhetorical" (20, 24). That's what Victor says in the article, but he does it by first showing us Antonio Gramsci, not just ideas and words from his *Prison Notebooks*, but by revealing first an embodied, real Gramsci, one who was born in southern Italy and goes to school in Turin. He shows us Gramsci who is in bad health and drops out of college, then works as a journalist for the radical newspaper *L'Ordine Nuovo*, then leaves it and forms the Italian Communist Party. He travels to Russia and France, marries "Giulia Schuct in 1923, a Muscovite of Austrian heritage" (19). He has two sons with Schuct, but Gramsci is jailed by Mussolini before he can really know either boy. Gramsci never leaves jail. He dies there, deteriorating slowly and painfully, his teeth falling out, contracting tuberculosis, over eleven years.

The point is, Victor starts with Gramsci the man with flaws and weaknesses, not Gramsci the powerful theorist or revolutionary Marxist. What I take from this move of Victor's is the importance of embodying our theories and theorists so that we can better understand the conditions that made such ideas, rhetoric, and people. Rhetoric is an embodied practice, not just words well formed, or disembodied texts with no originators. Rhetoric is people in particular places, dealing with particular material problems. In classrooms this is how we might better learn rhetoric, or languaging, as I usually say. We should work to keep it embodied.

Victor's discussion of Gramsci focuses on hegemony as rhetorical, a languaging in the world that participates in larger social structures that we consent to. I use this idea in my teaching. That is, I try to pose questions with my students about the politics of language and its judgement, about the hegemonic in all of our languaging and in the standards used against us. I don't usually use the word *hegemony* with undergraduates, a word I learned from Victor. I find other ways to get the idea across.

Hegemony is just a reference to the process of historical, cultural, racial, social, and political conflict that works from the consent of those it oppresses. It ain't just a rule, a policy, or a dominant ideology. Hegemony is structural in nature yet uneven in its consequences and control. So we can always point to places, things, people, incidents that seem counterhegemonic. Hegemony is the conditions of rule that don't seem like ruling conditions. Thus, we consent, often out of narrow self-interest, not out of larger interests of the community, nation, group, etc.

The term is also a way to investigate the determined nature of all kinds of systems or structures that end up making conditions that favor a dominant group. In *Marxism and Literature*, Raymond Williams offers a way to understand "determinism" as both a "setting of limits" and an "exertion of pressures" within society (87). Further, hegemony, Williams says, is "always a process . . . a realized complex of experiences, relationships, and activities, with specific and changing pressures and limits" (112). And so the hegemonic has a determined nature to it.

In my classrooms, we focus on conditions that make for our consent to habits of white language (HOWL)—that's the hegemonic. HOWL are the habits that get reproduced and valued in the academy as if they are the only ways to communicate, critically think, cite sources, argue ideas, make meaning, analyze, narrate, etc.[2] But HOWL require white supremacist conditions to participate in and reproduce white language supremacy, even as HOWL are a constituent of those conditions. So having a list of what HOWL typically look like isn't enough for classrooms. When we discuss HOWL, I'm always reminding both teachers and students that it's not simply the presence of a few habits in the list that make for white language supremacy. Antiracist languaging ain't about eradicating HOWL from our practices. It is about how HOWL are circulated in the assessment ecologies, how they make conditions of languaging, how they rank or punish people for languaging in the ways they do. So we are back to hegemony, the historical conditions of conflict that make our languaging.

Hegemony, then, is a way to understand the cultural and ideological clash of groups that always happens in any society, and often happens through language, stories, folktales, narratives, scripts, and common sense, as well as acts done or accomplished, monuments to events and people, holidays, and other celebrations. But in all of the hegemonic, there is language that describes and explains and celebrates and names. Victor taught me this. This means language is part of the ways the hegemonic naturalizes the methods of our oppression. The writing classroom, from this view, becomes central to an already racialized language revolution.

Language is part of the hegemonic, which makes language learning in school a paradoxical practice, one that can be critical and colonizing, creative and coercive. That's the paradox I hope my students face. In my own language learning, I was colonized, while paradoxically that historical process engendered my own critical, revolutionary, antiracist orientation to language, one I'm still working on. How do you do one without the other in our schools and colleges today? I mean, how do you learn to language criticality without some degree of language colonizing? Again, our conditions present us with paradoxes. This has been a lesson I've come to through revisiting Victor's work on hegemony and racism.

Languaging is also how revolutions work, how they get started or continue. Through languaging that explains oppression and racism, for instance, we make present the things we must overcome, the things we can come together around and collectively fight against. But languaging is also the ways in which we make agreements, judge or get judged by others, as well as form our collective or individual understandings and critiques of what the hell is going on around us and why. This means languaging is how we consent to things that are counter to our own interests. It's how we harm ourselves in acts of helping. I'm rehearsing much of what Victor explains about Gramsci (20–21), that languaging (rhetoric) is also the way we represent many of our values and ideals that form the grounds of consent to conditions that we otherwise would not agree to, conditions of oppression, of racism, of white language supremacy.

I'm always looking for ways in my courses to pose questions about hegemony that would give Victor a smile. He enjoys a good turn of phrase, making words do things that are surprising, twisting their meanings, then poof! Magic. It's really Gorgian rhetorical prestidigitation—I wish I had a non-Western reference for this, but I don't. That's my own colonized languaging. So I ask my students to ask questions about language and its judgement from the languaging they provide, that is, from their writing and the feedback they get on it from their colleagues in the course. This problem posing of languaging is really inquiring about hegemonic languaging, what we have consented to as natural, right, and preferable in languaging and its "standards," or our genres, or our conventions and style guides. These are the habits of language, HOWL and others, that we should notice, name, and question. It's really Freirean problem posing, which is another thing Victor showed me (more on that later).

So Victor's explanation of hegemony helps me present the aroma of the hegemonic to my students for their sniffing. This sniffing out of hegemonic language might start with thinking through the politics of my use of "Victor" instead of the conventional "Villanueva" in this writing. Or it could be the way I spell *judgement* with an extra *e* and not *judgment* because I want a visual reminder that judgements always come from judges (so the "judge" stays in the word), reminding ourselves that our references to judgements are references to people making judgements. This can lead us to ask: Who are the judges making such judgements about language and people? How are they racially organized? What conditions afford such racialized judges the ability to judge in the ways they do and get away with it? Who have we consented to as the primary judges in our world when we accept *judgement* without the *e* without the judge doing language? What happens when we just have judgments? That's hegemony. That's the naturalizing of the things outside of the natural. Accepting judgements without judges is consenting to ideas and language without noticing the racial and other politics of that languaging.

My students and I might also consider Robin Wall Kimmerer's discussion in *Braiding Sweetgrass* of her own languaging from her Potawatomi cultural roots. Kimmerer is an Indigenous botanist, and she capitalizes plant names that typically are not in science writing. She explains that the conventional rules of capitalization that leave out plants and animals "expresses deeply held assumptions about human exceptionalism, that we [humans] are somehow different and indeed better than the other species who surround us" (385). Of course, Kimmerer understands that humans are not better, not higher in some imagined, Western, white hegemonic hierarchy. She realizes that participating in this kind of capitalization language practice participates in white, colonial settler, hegemonic languaging that harms our world. It is a way that consent is made one letter at a time in our languaging. And the next thing you know, we don't question the hierarchy of being that rationalizes environmental destruction, or unsustainable living practices, or the human-made eradication of another species from existence.

Much like Victor's move to start with an embodied Gramsci, my examples of sniffing out hegemonic languaging and posing questions about them illustrate how Victor has helped me find ways to embody language teaching. We start with ourselves, our own languaging and histories. But I would not have gone to Gramsci first to learn about hegemony or revolutions. Gramsci is just too hard to read, at least for me back then at the age of thirty when I was first encountering these ideas. What I also mean is that my problem posing is not simply about raising questions about the social and existential nature of language and its judgement. It is about coming to understand our relationship with words and how they create our values, our experiences of our worlds, and our consent to our conditions. It's about how our languaging lives and grows in our bodies.

It's also about realizing that if we consent to the hegemonic language, say of HOWL, we also have options to resist or counter it. I mean, how do structures that build our consent to racist outcomes in our world come to be the conditions of our lives? How is it that we are left with a horrible, catastrophic decision to make: Choose your own self-interest or choose that which sustains your world? Why must that choice be an either-or? Sounds dramatic, doesn't it? Recent events, global climate change, mass shooting after mass shooting, our inability to do anything substantive about white language supremacy in schools, colleges, and our academic disciplines, all say otherwise to me. What I understand is that white hegemony is maintained, determined.

What I hope you can hear in what I'm saying is that antiracist teaching of language is often teaching the paradoxes of language politics and its judgement. If we can feel the paradoxes in the choices around language that we offer students, we may realize that antiracist teaching in a language class isn't about finding racists, or blaming people, or criticizing a text for its inability to notice its own whiteness. It's about understanding the conditions that make such texts participate in racist languaging and the white hegemonic practices they do. This means, first, making present our conditions that we consent to, making present our limits and pressures. Making white hegemony present for questioning means we make our conditions more present for questioning. And it is our conditions that need changing if we think we are going to eradicate racism or address white language supremacy.

Doing this kind of languaging hegemony work with students attempts to open spaces to make future "concrete revolutions" and not simply "passive revolution." This is what I hope my class can be. I want learning languaging to be the grounds for concrete revolution. These terms are Gramsci's, ones Victor explains and applies to more contemporary issues of racism:

> Gramsci calls seemingly radical hegemonic shifts "passive revolution" or "revolution-restoration." Civil rights protests lead to affirmative action. Minorities and women are granted greater access to America's bounties. But there are no structural changes that would remove basic inequities, no "concrete revolution." And the changes are accepted. Revolution restoration or passive revolution (passifying revolution, more like) is accepted not because people are unaware of exploitation. We're aware. We know. We know that others gain wealth and power at the expense of our labors. We accept because self interest prevails. As long as interests are met, and as long as general senses of morality and ethics are assuaged, consent continues to be granted. Hegemony survives. (22)

So hegemony feeds on self-interests. Hyperindividualism. Shit. That sounds like a damned-if-you-do-damned-if-you-don't kind of choice. But Victor has always been optimistic. If I called him today and asked, I imagine he'd say something about the younger kids coming up, how more of them today are smarter and more revolution-conscious, how more of them are aware of the systemic critique. I share that sentiment, and the smile that I know Victor would have with the words. I think he'd also agree that more people today are more aware of the fact that we get tricked into consenting to our own exploitation, or that sometimes we don't get a chance to deliberate on such structures or policies or laws. They just happen to us, all wrapped up in false news, deep fakes, and lies.

I suppose we should be careful of passive revolutions we accomplish too. As Victor says, these are conditions that "passify" us. A pacifier, something put into our mouths to shut us up, words that are meant to sooth and calm us, but do not—cannot—sustain us, feed us. Pacifiers block your mouth, your language maker, your food acquirer. Pacifiers silence you. What's the old Latin phase for consent by silence? *Qui tacet consentire videtur* ("silence gives consent"). Passive revolution sucks. That is, when we are pacified, we suck and suck, but no milk is ingested. I'm thinking about the ways we accept small, insignificant changes to our learning outcomes in order to be more "inclusive" or "equitable," adding a few more authors of color in course reading lists, or asking about the "preferred interests" (not required interests) for new hires around antiracist teaching. All are pass(c)ifying conditions that maintain white hegemony. I'm also thinking about the maintenance of HOWL and white language supremacy in our standards and ways of judging our students, things that many argue are in the interests of our students, especially our BIPOC students, because they'll need those language habits for their futures, which isn't a lie but it ain't the full truth either. We gotta prepare them, we tell ourselves, for a racist and white language supremacist tomorrow by fitting into that racist hegemonic system. Pass(c)ifying conditions. Restoration of the status quo. Restoration of white language supremacy in our classrooms.

To avoid such pass(c)ifying conditions, curricula and assessment practices need to make conditions for concrete revolutions. *Concrete*, a word signaling a new foundation, antiracist structures. Victor raises the issue of curriculum in the article too. He says that "[a] curriculum that conceives of empowerment as enabling access to the middle class is fundamentally traditional, no matter the doffs of the hat to women's studies, minority literature, multiculturalism. At bottom, there is still hegemony" (29). So the preparation argument I hear so often, the one I gestured to earlier, is really one that builds consent for the elite white hegemonic status quo, for participation in white language supremacy. So empowerment ain't about access to some illusory middle class, whether we are talking about it in economic, cultural, or linguistic terms, but these are always tangled together. The writing curriculum, as I hear Victor tell me, can be about making conditions out of pedagogical concrete and rhetorical rebar that question and redefine what student "empowerment" means, how empowerment can be sustainable and ethical and joyful.

Now, I added that last term, *joyful*. I believe joy is a necessary component of all good, critical, and lifelong learning, even the hard shit, even when we are talking about oppression, colonialism, and racism. In fact, we need it most there because the details are so depressing. But Victor is a good model for this too. Just read the chapters in this collection. Joy is in Victor's smile, laugh, and demeanor. He comes to this work with a joyful spirit. He's my model for that—or maybe, I've taken him as such. Find your own.

I remember my first conversation with Victor on the phone, the one I reference at the beginning of this chapter. I was a faculty member at Chemeketa Community College in Salem, Oregon. I was one year from tenure. I was considering going back to grad school, getting the PhD, and working with Victor. I asked him if he'd work with me if I went to WSU, moved to Pullman. He said, "Yes, of course." And he chuckled a bit, and I swear I could hear his smile in his words. And this was a serious conversation. I was not sure I wanted to uproot my growing family and leave our secure situation at that time. I was conflicted. I needed to hear his voice. He was the main reason I applied to WSU in the first place. I don't think I could have labeled this at the time as learning with joy, but now it's pretty clear. I needed joy in learning as much as I needed some Gramsci and Victor, and some counterhegemonic concrete.

About learning and the teachers who cultivate it with students, the kind of learning I needed back then, the kind I think I try to engender today, Victor says this:

> Economic necessity, at the very least (keeping a job, gaining tenure, getting promoted), guarantees a degree of compliance. No matter our good intentions, we are pulled by contradictory forces the hegemonic against the subversive. [. . .] In essential, hegemonic terms, we are no different from

> our students. As our status as workers becomes more apparent and as we come more in contact more potential intellectuals from non traditional backgrounds, we find ourselves in a potentially decisive moment. The moment is right for America's intellectuals in traditional academic roles to help organic intellectuals recognize themselves as such and to begin to fuse with them creating Gramsci's new intellectuals.
>
> This is not to say that we would convert our classrooms into political propaganda pits. The war of position is a protracted war. Hegemony will not be countered in one semester or in one quarter or two. We cannot deny students' economic desires nor our own economic needs. But we can begin the dialectical process necessary to a counter hegemony. We can play out our contradictions as deputies of hegemony and subversives, agents of tradition and, with our students, potential agencies of change. (31–32)

The paradox I hear in Victor's identifying of the learning conditions in language classrooms is what I'm striving for all the time. I just found that the crucial hinge in the classroom to do this work, to make new intellectuals, means we have to cultivate antiracist assessment ecologies (see Inoue, *Antiracist*). Assessment is the key. Judgement is the key. There's no way around it. Language is judgement, always. And judgement is assessment in classrooms, but not always—or it doesn't have to be. Language participates in the rhetorical. Rhetoric is hegemonic, and if we're doing it right, counterhegemonic too.

I'm moved to offer a poem that comes directly from my present reading of Victor's article. It's called "Hegemony Is a House."

Hegemony
is a house built on personal contradictions.
It means that the critically conscious
    are critically guilty,
    and seemingly hypocritical.
It means limits and boundaries
that feel like freewill,
but are really

predetermined preferences
that feel like ourselves
and feel good in our bones.
It all works better
when the system doesn't have to point a
gun or order people to do or think things.
It lets people
point guns at
themselves, do and
think things
it wants them to do and think.

Hegemony convinces people
that their oppression isn't oppression at all.
It's Sunday afternoon football games,
and going out to eat after church,
or watching the latest action film, or playing an innocent video game
made of killing and collecting
electronic representations
of real-life people and things
that aren't real, but feel like it.
It's conspicuously choosing
the choices given to you.

Hegemony is a system
that makes you feel bad
and inadequate for what it doesn't provide.

It's like blaming the tennis player for where the baseline is located,
or that you only get two chances at serving for each point.
Only the hegemonic sets up its rules
in order to benefit those who make rules.
In such places,
a few make rules and systems
to perpetuate the things, conditions, and world they want
to keep and pass on to their kids.

This is all called fairness:
merit,
hard work,
and always-receding delayed gratification,
    or should we say, deleted gratification,
    gratification never meant to be realized,
    only dangled in front of so many,
    a rhetorical ponzi scheme,
    played by those who only give
    the oppressed words,
    and try to convince them
    that they are not oppressed
    but free, free to be poor,
    free to do whatever they want.
There is much oppression in the freedom
that only words make.
These are our values
that devalue.

Putting aside
the abstraction of "the middle class,"
what I think is left in the world,
    the real, material world,
is our languages,
our stories,
and the common senses
we tell ourselves.
But be careful.
Everything is paradoxical
when you drill down.
A word is hegemony made personal.
And our stories help us
consent to an unfair and racist world
by offering us,
    teachers and intellectuals,
a slice of really nice pie.

Sure, the pie can do things,
and it's awfully sweet and tasty,
but language is paradoxical.
How is access to the middle class,
whether abstract or real,
not also becoming an agent of
white supremacy,
becoming the beautiful agent of racist systems
made syrupy sweet?
Are we not merely offering future opportunities and success
in inopportune and anti-successful systems
    in our classrooms?

Hegemony
is a house built on personal contradictions.
It's the sweet taste of almost there.

Once we've bitten into
the delicious and comforting pie,
we can't help but eat it all,
    gobbling it down,
    and asking for more from the system
    and those who made it.
But how exactly are the systems made
that make our hunger for more pieces of pie?
And in our classrooms, we try to help our students,
    especially those coming from places
    and groups who have not
    had a taste of the pie yet,
    get their tastes.
But it's all just the same old pie.
And the result?
Rotten teeth and diabetes.
And it's all our fault,
and their fault,
and the system's fault.
And it's all we can do,

even as we resist.
You gotta live, right? You gotta pay the bills
and be happy, right?

Hegemony
is a story-house built on personal contradictions.
It's metonymy and synecdoche.
It's white supremacy made in us all.

BOOTSTRAPS: FROM AN AMERICAN ACADEMIC OF COLOR (1993)

It doesn't escape me that Victor and I were both the same age, forty-five years old, when we published the books we each are most known for. For him, that's *Bootstraps* in 1993. For me it's *Antiracist Writing Assessment Ecologies* in 2015. Their publications are twenty-two years apart. I don't know if that means anything, but it's a nice number, a double two, two twos. Lots of things come in twos in my life. I'm a twin. I'm a Gemini. I've had two first names in my life. I have two sons. Twenty-two years.

I first read *Bootstraps* in 1998 on my own. No class. It wasn't assigned to me. I was called to read it, I suppose. I don't remember why. I don't even remember how I knew about it. I was not in grad school. I'd been out for several years. I was a full-time, tenure-track faculty member at Chemeketa Community College. I was busy teaching and becoming a father. I was living in Monmouth, Oregon. I was expecting our first son.

My first reading of *Bootstraps* was a mix of confusion and excitement. I didn't understand everything, especially the Marxist stuff, even though now it all seems so clear, so well expressed. I even use bits of the book in my courses with undergraduates. Victor's explanation of Paulo Freire's *conscientização*, or "conscientization," or "critical consciousness," is particularly helpful to my students and me. The Portuguese word is often difficult to pronounce. Freire was initially resistant to translating the term because, as Donald Macedo explains, "the arrogance of English monolingualism . . . constitutes a type of deskilling experienced by most English speakers," who expect translations of such concepts into English.

I mean, not translating the word is part of the point of critical pedagogy, isn't it? Our words are our worlds, to draw on Freire's own formulation (Freire and Macedo). Don't take my world and translate it into your words and call it the same thing. Here's how Freire explains the word–world connection:

> Reading the world always precedes reading the word, and reading the word implies continually reading the world. As I suggested earlier, this movement from the word to the world is always present; even the spoken word flows from our reading of the world. In a way, however, we can go further and say that reading the word is not preceded merely by reading the world, but by a certain form of writing it or rewriting it, that is, of transforming it by means of conscious, practical work. For me, this dynamic movement is central to the literacy process. (Freire and Macedo 35)

It is in the practice of his conscientização that I find the word–world connection opened up as a critical languaging process. In my courses, I try to offer the original Portuguese term to my students when we discuss it. I break the word up into two sections of three short syllables each. Six syllables total. It's the best I can do with the Portuguese word. Phonetically pronounced, it is CON-SEE-IN-JAH-SAH-SOW. But I also show students the Elmo video. Yeah, there's a YouTube video that uses Elmo from Sesame Street to give a lesson on conscientização (Gough).

In his description of Floyd, an African American poet and teacher, Victor explains Freire's conscientização. As a practice, you start with the individual's personal experience and then reflect on it, which leads to generalizing out, out into the world, into the structures of society and language. In effect, this is good antiracist assessment practice with students if the focus is on our words, our languaging that leads us to our historical conditions that afford our languaging.

As explanations go, I haven't found a cleaner one anywhere. And while Victor doesn't say so, the practice of critical consciousness, of conscientização, is not just about posing questions about our world or language; it is an antiracist problem posing of judgement through language. Victor explains the practice:

> Critical consciousness is the recognition that society contains social, political, and economic conditions which are at odds with the individual will to freedom. When that recognition is given voice, and a decision is made to do something about the contradiction between the individual and society's workings against individual freedom, even if the action is no more than critical reflection, there is *praxis*. The way to arrive at critical consciousness, for Freire, is through *generative themes*. Generative themes are critical assessments of *limit-situations*, the myths that maintain the status quo. More simply put, Freire would have students look at their individual histories and cultures and compare those histories and ways of being with what they are led to believe is their place in the world, making the contradictions between their world views and the official world views explicit. This is the dialectic between the subjective and the objective, the stuff known from within and the stuff from external forces.
>
> Freire juxtaposes two philosophical schools, the existentialism of a Jean-Paul Sartre and the structuralism of a Louis Althusser, to arrive at the heady term of *problematizing the existential situation*. Simply put, existentialism says that the essence of being human is individual freedom. Structuralism says that there are social, political, and economic systems in place that keep us from changing the way things are, systems that keep us from fully exercising our freedom, systems that we see as "natural:" The way out of these systems is through the *problematic*, by questioning the things we don't normally question, questioning just how natural the "natural" is. Freire would have his students look to themselves, their own experiences, in order to question. (54)

The experiences we start with in my writing courses are our experiences of others' texts, of their languaging, of our own languaging. We use the feedback we already generate to help us pose problems about language and its judgement that makes present the two competing interpretations of the world that Freire juxtaposes: our individual languaging habits and our historical languaging conditions that afford each of us our languaging.

This posing problems about our languaging affords us chances to notice our language conditions, to notice how natural something like "clarity" is in a paragraph. We notice how much we've come to accept conditions in our lives that pressure us to see "good writing" or "logical organization" as particular habits of language because our languaging has been limited, bounded by particular language conditions. But in classrooms, the conditions are always white language supremacy, that is, habits of white language (HOWL) as standards, all of which we've taken on to some degree, come to believe as neutral language habits. In other cases, some of us have used such standards to judge ourselves as inadequate because of our differences from that HOWLing. If we can notice the limiting conditions, the structural, of our lives in this way, then we can also notice the ways our choices and agency are pressured in certain directions by our conditions. These explorations, I think, are the grounds for a languaging revolution.

"MAYBE A COLONY" (1997)

Victor has done more to help me think through my theorizing and practicing of antiracist writing assessment ecologies, and this article is another example of it. "Maybe a Colony" was published a few years after *Bootstraps*. In it, Victor says:

> When we demand a certain language, a certain dialect, and a certain rhetorical manner in using that dialect and language, we seem to be working counter to the cultural multiplicity we seek. And I think that means that we will have to rethink the whole thing. (183)

Demanding a single standard of language in our writing courses is not just denying students' rights to their own languaging; it participates in the historical white supremacist practices of colonizing people of color by colonizing their tongues. It's the first rule of ruling, isn't it?

Control information by controlling the language of information. You control people's language and you control their thoughts and desires too. It's the lesson of hegemony all over again. A few pages later, Victor labels this racialized colonizing of tongues:

> And America's people of color feel that colonialism, a legacy from histories of colonialism, histories that often affect our self-perceptions, histories that can affect how we are regarded. Those effects, the ways in which we people of color conduct ourselves in response to the ethnocentricity which has its roots in a colonial history, is *internal colonialism.* (186)

Internal colonization is a difficult lesson for many students to figure out what to do with. I get it. It's a paradox. *There are colonies in all of us.* . . . I mean, not in the colonizers, of course. But then, we're really talking about colonizing conditions, not colonizers. To explain this, it's easier to tell you a story.

The boy of color, maybe he's Chicano or Puerto Rican, maybe Inuit, maybe he's Black or Vietnamese or Hmong, sits at his desk, doing what he thinks must be college in the US. He reads the Standardized American English words. He has written something for the colonizer, who will grade him by how much he can show how colonized he is. He wants badly to use these words toward his own success, a success the words afford, so others have told him. He also wants to do good things in a world made of colonies. But he knows deep in his belly that somehow there will be a problem with his version of the words asked of him. There's always something that amounts to not enough, not quite right, not yet white.

And of course, he wants to learn this language. He wants to be a languageling like his white teacher. She's nice when she's not grading his words. But those words are the keys to the gates, or so he's been told over and over and over. The words are not just truisms floating in his environment. They don't have lips anymore. They just feel true because, well, look around you. The boy doesn't question that truth anymore. Why, when the consequences seem so clear and obvious?

Deep in his belly, he knows that he will never match up, not because he lacks some ability or willpower, or some urge to do and be and talk and become something else in the world, but because he is made of other stuff, of other people and experiences and words and places than what his teacher asks of him or assumes. And the colonizing conditions don't give a shit about those other people, experiences, words, or places. The rubric, the standard, the grading scale don't give two fucks about how he feels or how the words feel like gravel and glass in his mouth.

The teacher can see her colonizing gestures only as teaching and helping and doing good. That's how she defines teaching and helping and doing good: holding standards, or rather, holding standards against students. The paradox is that the teacher does teach and help and do good, while also doing the opposite of these things. The paradox is that the teacher doesn't wanta be a colonizer either, doesn't wanta sit in conditions of colonizing anymore than the boy of color does. And yet, here they are, sitting in it.

Teachers usually say, just do like I do. Try to be like me, so that you can succeed, as if success was being them only, as if success defined by a racist system is a worthy goal to put in front of your face and bow to. Be me, the teacher says, and you too can get by. The boy can only nod. What else can he do? He ain't got no power, ain't got no language of power.

And the boy asks himself as he sits in the classroom waiting for the "it's-not-quite-right-not-quite-white" response from the teacher: Is it her feelings and intentions that make her think she is teaching and helping me only? What's wrong with me? Why can't I just be like all these white people around me? Why must help always hurt, always take away as it gives? The boy does not know how to do the languaging so that the teacher will accept it unconditionally. The colonizing conditions just won't let him.

What the boy knows is that his lips will be smacked every time he speaks or writes from himself, from his past and his places. He has to learn not to use his own words. Every time he uses his mom's sweet and sour words, his tongue will burn and crack. In the white space of the language classroom, he can either stand up and be smacked in the mouth for the residual, sticky word-places of his nurture, or he can help the teacher by smacking his own mouth and wiping the honey from his lips, pretending that it didn't taste good until it doesn't taste sweet anymore, until there is only the memory of its taste.

It is these kinds of conditions that make me ask as a teacher: How do we make antiracist assessment conditions that do not internally colonize, that do not make colonies inside all of us? And it comes out of Victor's words about a colony.

"ON THE RHETORIC AND PRECEDENTS OF RACISM" (1999)

A few years later, Victor makes another offering to me and my classrooms. He writes it at roughly the age I am today. Victor explains:

> Now as I try to think of how this profession can improve on its multiculturalism, do more than assuring that people of color are represented in our materials, more than assuring that people of color are read and heard in numbers more in keeping with the emerging demographics of the nation and the world, I remain tied to the belief that we must break from the colonial discourse that binds us all. What I mean is that there are attitudes from those we have revered over the centuries which we inherit, that are woven into the discourse that we inherit. (656)

A bit later, he says:

> We don't look to the South. Freire came to our attention only after he became a member of the faculty at Harvard. We tend to get our Great Thinkers from Europe, and too often only after our literary brothers and sisters, themselves too many and too often still quite literally an English colony, have discovered them. [. . .] Break precedent! We are so locked into the colonial mindset that we are now turning to the ex-colonials of Europe to learn something about our own people of color. There again, I'm grateful for the insights. But

> what are the ex-colonials of the U.S. saying, the ex-colonials of our hemisphere, now caught in neocolonial dependency? (658–59)

Break precedent? That's what antiracist writing assessment ecologies attempt to do. I mean, to break precedent—the metaphor is one of cracking something into two halves, like a board or a cinder block, like concrete—you gotta apply pressure in the right conditions. But breaking concrete is hard work. To look to other languagelings for our language teaching and learning ain't as simple as just looking toward them. I'm speaking of the act of looking toward something else itself. Hegemony makes conditions that form habits that keep our heads not turned. How do we get turned (I'm tempted to use the Black English here, "turnt")? Our habits are hard to break, even harder than concrete. That's why they are habits, part of the habitual.

How does a writing teacher break precedent from their racist and colonial training, from the white language supremacy of the discipline of writing studies, rhetoric, of schools and course outcomes, of programs of study built over decades, over centuries? How do we break our own precedents, the ones in our bones, the ones we wear like a shirt we never take off, or maybe one we cannot take off? Precedents that are made flesh, tattooed on us. If the colonial and white supremacist discourse binds us, makes us, gives us authority, allows us to be critical and authoritative, then what happens when we unbind, unravel, undo all that we are, all that binds us? What if the tattoo becomes skin itself? For me, I wonder, at fifty-three years old: Is there anything left behind my own white (supremacist) mask, behind my HOWLing?

Of course there is. And maybe my mask ain't all that white. But it takes time, and opportunity, and trying, and failing, and being willing to not give an antiracist fuck about what white hegemony thinks or will do. These things are not easy to impart onto students, not easy habits to acquire when you are busy trying to pay the rent. Unbinding ain't easy. Gettin turnt ain't easy either.

And we all contain multitudes, to quote a famous white guy (Whitman). We are paradoxes. We are all consubstantial to the colony and to those lands and places not inside the colony's walls. Now, how the hell do I teach that to a 20-year-old? How do I help people who have spent a lifetime binding themselves with white cords, tied very tightly, so much so that if they are loosened, we will all be undone, or so we think? How do I tell someone who cannot imagine our world undone, untied, a world some might call freer?

I am in a classroom, my first classroom. I'm maybe twenty-three. It's the very first day of the quarter, my very first few minutes as a real teacher with real teacher responsibilities. And I write a question on the blackboard, which is a real chalkboard with actual chalk, and then I ask them to write. Respond to these words I've written. I sit on the table in front of the classroom, like a real teacher, surrounded by twenty-five students, real students who are all around eighteen years old. I write with them. I don't remember a single face, just that they were all around me, writing. And I was writing on a yellow pad of paper. This real experience was intoxicating. I ask them to write. They write. I sit pleased, waiting to hear what they have written, and ready to respond.

As I write this experience now with these words, with this colonizing rhetoric, from my own precedents, I remember thinking in that moment, being taken back a year or two to one of my models, a teacher who was good at this kind of thing. He would write a question on the board and invite us to write. Just write and keep writing, he would say. It doesn't matter what you say or how you say it. What matters is that you have a response, and it will all be okay. And it was all okay. I wrote. And I was invited by my own inner urges to speak my written words to the class. And it all felt good in my mind's eye looking back then and now. That was learning. In that first class, I am now that teacher offering that learning, I think, or becoming him, a white, male authority, only I'm not white like that first mentor.

I'm also not aware at that moment in that first classroom that I am reenacting a whitely stance toward words and ideas. I am unaware that I am not that white teacher. I cannot be. I am unaware of the ways I can easily reproduce white language supremacy in my own classroom without even realizing it. I think I'm the good teacher, and I am, and I am not. I have no other precedents but those given to me, those laid before me in my own writing classrooms like a picnic lunch on a crisp, clean, freshly ironed, white cloth.

And what makes all this more difficult is that my own classroom, that first one, is also my precedent. I mean, what else do you do in writing classrooms? You write. You read. What is there to do but write and read and talk? How is that racist? But if we take our lessons from Victor and Gramsci on hegemony, we should probably ask: How are those conditions *not* racist? How do they counter the status quo, how do they question the white language supremacist conditions we already live in?

In my first classroom, we didn't talk about the ways the discourse I asked of my students and that I used to respond and grade with was a particular kind of discourse with a particular history with bodies in time and space. It contains a politics—or rather, it participates in a set of relations to groups of elite, heteronormative, monolingual white people and white places in the world. We ignored that those groups and places are racialized and classed, that they are set into hierarchies that seem so natural and normal to us all, even when they hurt us. We just assumed language was language and people and their histories were other things, divorceable from our learning. We assumed that language could be disembodied. But people, their conditions, and their languaging are a permanent marriage, till death do us part.

Back then, I just took it all for granted because it felt like good teaching, felt like my precedents, but I wasn't much older than my students, and I was still in the process of being colonized. I wasn't turnt. I was looking soberly forward at HOWL. I returned that colonizing to my students. I rehearsed it. They would have been upset if I'd done something different. They'd have questioned my authority, said I wasn't teaching them right, that is, teaching them how to be more white.

I mean, most of my students were white and middle class. Most didn't work while attending school. Most were from Oregon. It's easy to ignore the racial politics of languaging and judgement when you have only one kind of languaging around you every day. It's easy when you think there's only one way to be clear or persuasive, to reflect and read a word, because your conditions have only presented a limited set of ways and pressured you in a direction that seemed, in the moment, to be natural.

So Victor makes me ask: How do I look South when I may not know where South is, or that there is a South to look toward? Our habit, the one in our bones and veins, is to look West, so much so that we think everyone can only look West, that when we are asked to look toward some place, the West is all we understand as a location to look toward. The act of looking equates to seeing the West. The South is just babble, confusion, nonlogic. Or it isn't even an understandable direction. Directions are only things in the West.

How do we break such habitual precedents when breaking seems so inconceivable? I mean, we do not have a word or action or practice for breaking the precedents of our own languaging, do we? What's the word for putting a complex puzzle together by throwing the pieces out the window? Perhaps our most durable precedents in the conditions of racism are the paradoxes we must language and live through. My knowing how to explore these questions with my students, even if I'm still learning, is a legacy I am grateful to have gotten from Victor. It's understanding hegemony as embodied languaging and the conditions that make such habits. It's assessment in classrooms that is really conscientização. It's Turnt Theory, an erotic, excited, revolutionary buzz in the classroom that breaks old concrete and makes new language structures that revolutionize in new concrete ways, even as we must paradoxically pay our rent.

NOTES

1. You can read about this on my blog, where some of the action happened and I posted my experience in an Executive Board meeting (Inoue, "Why I Left the CWPA").

2. I have offered versions of HOWL in previous publications: Asao B. Inoue, *Labor-Based Grading Contracts: Building Equity and Inclusion in the Compassionate Writing Classroom* (27, 278–79); Asao B. Inoue, "Classroom Writing Assessment as an Antiracist Practice: Confronting White Supremacy in the Judgments of Language" (399–400); and Asao

B. Inoue, *Above the Well: An Antiracist Literacy Argument from a Boy of Color* (22–28).

WORKS CITED

Freire, Paulo, and Donald Macedo. *Literacy: Reading the Word and the World.* Bergin & Garvey, 1987.

Gough, Zachary. "conscientizacao and praxis." *YouTube,* 19 Dec. 2015, https://youtu.be/njoJ0VRbYzc. Accessed 30 May 2022.

Inoue, Asao B. *Above the Well: An Antiracist Literacy Argument from a Boy of Color.* WAC Clearinghouse/Utah State UP, 2021.

———. *Antiracist Writing Assessment Ecologies: Teaching and Assessing Writing for a Socially Just Future.* WAC Clearinghouse/Parlor Press, 2015.

———. "Classroom Writing Assessment as an Antiracist Practice: Confronting White Supremacy in the Judgments of Language," *Pedagogy,* vol. 19, no. 3, Oct. 2019, pp. 373–404.

———. *Labor-Based Grading Contracts: Building Equity and Inclusion in the Compassionate Writing Classroom.* WAC Clearinghouse, 2019.

———. "Why I Left the CWPA (Council of Writing Program Administrators)." *Infrequent Words,* 18 Apr. 2021, https://asaobinoue.blogspot.com/2021/04/why-i-left-cwpa-council-of-writing.html. Accessed 29 May 2022.

Kimmerer, Robin Wall. *Braiding Sweetgrass: Indigenous Wisdom, Scientific Knowledge, and the Teachings of Plants.* Milkweed Editions, 2013.

Macedo, Donald. "The Centrality of Conscientization in Critical Pedagogy." *Handbook of Critical Approaches to Politics and Policy of Education,* edited by Kenneth J. Saltman and Nicole Nguyen, Routledge, 2022, n.p. https://www.routledge.com/Handbook-of-Critical-Approaches-to-Politics-and-Policy-of-Education/Saltman-Nguyen/p/book/9780367702700. Accessed 29 May 2022.

Villanueva, Victor, Jr. *Bootstraps: From an American Academic of Color.* National Council of Teachers of English, 1993.

———. "Hegemony: From an Organically Grown Intellectual." *Pre/Text,* vol. 13, no. 1-2, 1992, pp. 17–34.

———. "Maybe a Colony: And Still Another Critique of the Comp Community." *JAC,* vol. 17, no. 2, 1997, pp. 183–90.

———. "On the Rhetoric and Precedents of Racism." *College Composition and Communication,* vol. 50, no. 4, 1999, pp. 645–61.

Williams, Raymond. *Marxism and Literature.* Oxford UP, 1977.

SECTION I:
MEMORIA OF RHETORIC

AS ONE WAY TO THREAD THE chapters of this section together, we offer readers a few themes and questions in this short introduction. Complementing the brief summaries of each chapter that we include in the introduction, here we make some connections and pose questions for readers to consider as students and scholars of rhetoric, writing, and rhetorics of racism in light of Victor's influence on these areas as a shaper of the field.

Most of the chapters in this section center their discussions on Victor's influential essay, "*Memoria* Is a Friend of Ours: On the Discourse of Color," published in *College English* in 2004. In the essay, Victor argues that we all might reclaim and remember the centrality and importance of the rhetorical office of *Memoria*, memory, while also saying early on, "Memory simply cannot be adequately portrayed in the conventional discourse of the academy" (12). In one sense, this section's chapters demonstrate the reclaiming of *Memoria* in the study of rhetoric over the last twenty years and Victor's role in this revitalization. The chapters also demonstrate how powerful, even seductive, *Memoria* can be to all of us as we constitute ourselves in and through language, through rhetoric.

In the opening chapter, John Trimbur reminds us of a fuller trajectory of the term *Memoria* that Victor has worked from and invokes. *Memoria* is Mnemosyne, the "ancient mistress of time and memory of the past, and the mother, by Zeus, of the nine Muses, the patron deities of artistic inspiration and the craft knowledge of poets, musicians, dancers, and historians" (p. 57). Trimbur argues that Victor is practicing *Memoria* as more than simply memory of the past, but as Mnemosyne. In this way, perhaps readers might think of *Memoria* as a shadowy character in the section's chapters, one next to Victor himself, and one that Romeo García recasts as "shadow work" that responds to the racism in our world in the final chapter.

Trimbur illustrates the *Memoria* that Victor calls upon by discussing the backward-facing gaze of the Angel of History in Walter Benjamin's "Theses on the Philosophy of History." This figure, as Trimbur explains, was inspired by the painting *Angelus Novus* by Paul Klee. The *Memoria* that Victor reveals to us, in Trimbur's view, is deeply historical and works from excavating and digging at the past. Thus, we might ask ourselves in times when we hold *Memoria's* hand, when we write, reflect, read, or remember: What is being dug up?

Of course, *Memoria* is more than an individual remembering the past and learning about it, or even from it. Miriam L. Fernandez's chapter considers the ways Victor's work contributes to and calls her to re-collect "Chicanx collective memory." This is not memoir work in the way Laura Gray-Rosendale's chapter explores the term later in this section, but historical work made through recognizing *Memoria* around us in physical structures. Fernandez associates collective memory with marginalized groups, subaltern collective memory that functions next to larger "dominant national memory" (p. 73). In this framing, one might think of collective memory as the materials and methods for counterhegemony. Thus, *Memoria* is exemplified in a collision of ideological and rhetorical forces experienced in a variety of uneven ways by different individuals in particular material places. *Memoria*, as Fernandez shows, is a site of historical, personal, material, and rhetorical intersections that hold and conjure meaning. She labels this intersection "memory places," and recounts her own trips to Templo Mayor in Mexico City, showing personal photographs and discussing the history and rhetoric on display at the site. In these ways, *Memoria* is a recasting of the past, which Fernandez illustrates as the past made present.

In these first two chapters, the *Memoria* that Victor has reintroduced to the field, and perhaps to our classrooms, is backward facing, historical, and personal. It is memory, and processes of excavation of that past that simultaneously look forward. *Memoria* is also a place, not just the figurative topos students of rhetoric learn about, but the "memory places" that Fernandez walks through, takes pictures of, ruminates over, connects and feels separated from. It is a place of counterhegemonic power, perhaps. Our places, our classrooms, our essays, our homes and neighborhoods participate in *Memoria*, and we might do well to ask about that and its significance, to see and feel her shadow. We might let such memory places that embody the figure of *Memoria* move us to explore more of ourselves and histories, our biases and pedagogies, our habits of language, and the always *otherwise* that might confront harmful hegemonic conditions in the present.

Exploring and excavating her own past, Catherine Prendergast goes back to Bratislava, Slovakia, a place she's been several times in her life, teaching, decades earlier, but at this recounting, it's a wedding in 2019. The place and people are different, changed, no longer a socialist country but one transformed into a capitalist one, yet *Memoria* is there around every corner. *Memoria* also offers her a way to ruminate on Trumpism and capitalism and their deep roots in racism, lessons from an earlier generation of critical race theorists, and of course, from Victor. In one sense, similar to Gray-Rosendale's and Victoria Houser's chapters later in the section, Prendergast invokes *Memoria* as method, as a way to excavate and understand the present with the past. Such chapters beg us to ask and reflect on the following: How do we, as individuals in communities, negotiate such colliding memories evoked by places and narratives around us? How do we engage with *Memoria*, our complicated friend, when we do our research, when we teach our students, when we move around in the world?

Moving out to a disciplinary view, Christa J. Olson enacts *Memoria* as she traces the influences that Victor has epitomized and pushed in Américan rhetorical history, as well as the larger field of rhetoric and composition, over the last few decades. Those influences deal with encouraging scholars to address colonial violence, confront racialization, and maintain the complexities in Latinx and Latin American rhetorics. Olson is looking back, *Memoria*-style. In doing so, she illustrates how *Memoria* as a method might also contribute to disciplinary critique, reclaiming, and reimagining.

Next, Laura Gray-Rosendale connects *Memoria* to memoir, to personal work. She illustrates *Memoria* as a driving force in Victor's and her own life, as a way toward writing itself, writing her memoir, writing of the personal and academic together, of confronting past traumas and perhaps healing. She traces a theme that builds in this section's chapters that we might pose as a reading question: If *Memoria* is looking back in order to look forward, remembering in order to change, heal, and recover history, then how does *Memoria* become practice for us all in a world that doesn't ask us to do this? How can we as readers, as scholars, as students, as teachers embrace *Memoria* as a teacher and a healer? Is it dwelling in the memory places that Fernandez discusses? Does it start with memoir work, with digging up our own histories, connecting them to larger ones and the structures that make them?

Similar to Gray-Rosendale's focus on memoir, Victoria Houser considers the way Victor's thinking about *Memoria* invites a "corporeal" politics in her own teaching and scholarship. She resists the false mind–body dualism in most academic traditions, saying that "Villanueva's call to revitalize memory in rhetoric and writing studies opened academic writing to the potentiality of bodies and lived experiences as central elements of scholarly composition" (p. 151). In effect, Houser puts flesh onto *Memoria.* She argues in various ways throughout the chapter, always staying connected to her body learning with Victor, for what she calls "the corporeality of *Memoria.*" In her conclusion, she says: "We must write what lives inside us—inside our memories and inside our bodies—because as brilliant and meaningful as academic exercises can be, they are not the point of this business" (p. 160). While we each might answer what the point of our business is differently, Gray-Rosendale links whatever that answer is to real bodies that feel, get hungry, that sweat. *Memoria* lives inside our bodies. Thus, we might add to Fernandez's memory places the corporeal place of our own bodies. How might our own bodies be places of memory? How might we teach in our writing courses, or read or write, with an understanding that *Memoria* is a corporeal memory and a material one around us?

In the final chapter of this section, Romeo García offers a rumination on the nuanced way he has taken up *Memoria* as a scholarly project, recasting it as "shadow work." He begins historically and structurally but demonstrates how such shadow work is a part of his own life trajectory, responding to the racism he and his family experienced at every step of his education. What he recounts is a corporeal *Memoria*, one that is about his Brown skin and how others hear his English. He explains that such embodied *Memoria* is about "*stories-so-far* and *possibilities of new stories*" (p. 189). It's also about memory places, homes, cities, and neighborhoods. A central figure in García's theorizing is his grandmother, whom he cites and listens to carefully. She asks, "¿qué ves?" | "¿qué oyes?" | "¿entiendes?" | "¡entiendes!" *Memoria* is fully corporeal and fully history and fully rhetorical. For García, *Memoria* leads him to ask questions of constitution, of how we get made in rhetoric, in our lives, through racism, and in his case, through the shadow work that constitutes his responses to racism. And so this closing chapter might encourage us to ask: Who does this kind of shadow work that García recounts? How might shadow work be different for others than it is for ourselves? Perhaps one way to engage these questions is to first engage with *Memoria*, our friend.

Chapter 3

"as it flashes in a moment of danger": Reflections on *Memoria*, Colonialism, and Rhetoric

John Trimbur

ONE OF VICTOR VILLANUEVA'S CENTRAL messages is about how rhetoric springs, in the past and present, from sources in the colonies, as an expression of lived experience at the edge of empire. Villanueva enables us to envision how rhetoric takes shape in the historical predicament of the early rhetoricians—Corax, Gorgias, Protagoras—in Sicily and Thrace, at a remove from the Athenian metropole, where the exigencies of imperial expansion, the rise and fall of homegrown tyrants, the threat of war and disputes over land played out in the realm of new language practices. Rhetoric is formed, in the political imagination, through struggles over diplomacy, ownership, the means of livelihood, forms of knowledge, language, and rhetorical footing. Villanueva's published work, in its main lines of development, explores the invention of rhetoric on the periphery, as a weapon of the subaltern in the war of positions between colonizer and colonized. The ancient Sophists loom over Villanueva's critical examination of colonialism, a tutelary presence linking the pre-Socratics to the politics of Nuyorican poetics.[1]

Villanueva is speaking, it must be emphasized, not from a postcolonial standpoint but rather from the Puerto Rican diaspora on the mainland and the actually existing, multisite colonies of the United States offshore. The conditions of speech—what Walter Mignolo calls the "locus of enunciation" (114–16)—are geohistorical in character, the result of a settler colony on the North American continent that turned, by the end of the nineteenth century, into a settler empire with its own internal and external colonies: the tribal reservations on remnants of conquered Indigenous land; the Mexican possessions in California and the Southwest and Spain's territories in the Philippines and Caribbean, seized in the wars of 1846 and 1898; the unassimilable Chinatowns, citizenship denied by the 1882 Chinese Exclusion Act; the annexation of the Kingdom of Hawai'i and other Pacific Islands; the Black Belt in the Jim Crow South, where a majority Black rural proletariat emerged from plantation slavery after Emancipation. According to Villanueva, the differences between immigration and colonization are crucial to the formation of historical destinies. Assimilation sets the outer limits in the metropole for the colonized relative to immigrant groups, including those who came as refugees and outcasts, uprooted and impoverished by events like the Highland Clearances in Scotland, the Great Famine in Ireland, pogroms in Russia and Poland, and the massive dislocations of a half century of two World Wars. The difference, as Villanueva says, is that the "immigrant enters; the minority is entered upon" (*Bootstraps* 29). Differing degrees of assimilation are apparent in the civic belongingness accorded to immigrants from Europe (even if sometimes grudgingly in the anti-Semitic, anti-Catholic world of White Anglo-Saxon Protestant America) while setting barriers to the full politico-rhetorical standing and socioeconomic participation of people of color, the caste-like minorities who remain, Villanueva says, "not quite American" (28).

The geohistorical coordinates of Villanueva's rhetorical investigations of colonialism are located not outside but at the margins of empire, starting in the borderlands of the Western classical tradition of Greece and Rome—in the Sophistic rhetorics that came from Sicily and the northern frontier in Greece, from Asia Minor at the time of the Second Sophistic circa 230 CE, from Byzantium and the Arab peninsula, and from the 700-year Moorish occupation of Spain. For Villanueva this genealogy reveals the roots of a way with words in Arabic and Spanish prose traditions that were recontextualized in the New World, localized as a creole modality distinct from the neo-Aristotelian rhetoric and the Anglo-American plain style that have dominated US college composition.

Defying Aristotle's separation of the disciplines, the Sophists and their descendants merged the arts of philosophy, rhetoric, and poetics, highlighting language play and the power of style. In contrast to philosophical notions of universal truth, the Sophists believed that knowledge was provisional, contingent, and pluralistic, set at the level of human experience (e.g., Protagoras's "man is the measure of all things"), not by Plato's ideal forms or Aristotle's logical categories. Villanueva maps out a rhetorical style that foregrounds voice and dialogue, in contrast to the logocentrism of mainstream essayist literacy, relying on the mutual involvement of writers and readers rather than the effacement of the author, the "divorce," according to David Olson, that enables text to be autonomous—to reduce the need for interpretation and to speak for itself.

Rather than the austerity of the Anglo-American plain style, Villanueva's writing is marked by the heightened presence of the author, the intensity of its reader–writer interactions, and its associative conversational logics. The rhythms of dialectic animate the prose with the back and forth (and sometimes overlapping) movement of people talking—writers and readers, the colony and the colonizer, past and present generations. Villanueva's prose is the soundscape of the Puerto Rican diaspora inside the academy, with the voices of poets, including Victor Hernández Cruz, Sandra María Esteves, Martín Espada, and Luis J. Rodriguez, alongside the scholarly citations.

As is well known, the Sophists advocated uses and powers of language that were disparaged by Plato and his followers, and then marked in modern times at the popular level as "sophistry," the verbal deceptions of politicians, pundits, conspiracy theorists, and ad writers, to get people to buy things they don't need or vote for political candidates who don't represent their interests. In the commonsense understanding, complaints about people who act like "sophists" index something unseemly and dishonest, lower class, on a moral scale far below the eloquent integrity of Quintilian's "good man speaking well." The truth is that the Sophists challenged the aristocratic monopoly of rhetoric by selling their unruly arts to ordinary people. For a price, they offered to teach the rhetorical skills needed in the courts and the polis to those, like themselves, on the margins, foreigners, provincials, and former slaves, *metics* who held some civic standing but who could never be full citizens of Athens.

The Sophistic threat to respectable rhetoric—the very idea that language can enable you not so much to trick people as persuade them to imagine the unthinkable—helps illuminate its radical appeal to colonial modernity. If anything, the Sophistic practices of paradox, antithesis, contradiction, metaphor, hyperbole, satire, and irony seem to anticipate "arts of the contact zone," such as *jaibería* in Puerto Rico, the subversive complicity and evasive, nonconfrontational forms of rebellion named after the mountain crab *jaiba,* who advances by moving sideways. In Villanueva's version, Sophistic rhetoric points ahead to strategies of mimicry that withhold consent, that use the colonizers' own terms and representations to de-identify with the values of an assimilation that is already thoroughly racialized and thereby never fully forthcoming to colonized people of color. For the colonized, Sophistic rhetoric offers not so much a point of entry as a means of self-defense, the conjuring of hidden transcripts, seditious histories, and counterknowledges to offset the hegemonic rule of colonialism.

What I believe Victor Villanueva has developed from these Sophistic antecedents—and what I wish to trace in this essay—is a unique politico-rhetorical register in US college composition. As Villanueva says in "*Memoria* Is a Friend of Ours: On the Discourse of Color," "[p]ersonal discourse, the narrative, the auto/biography" are "a necessary adjunct to the academic" (17). Villanueva's blurred genres are memoirist in style (i.e., in how they call for and occupy readers' attention) but collective rather than individualist in execution and effect, producing innovations in academic writing that employ memory to personalize the political and politicize the personal. To put it another way, Villanueva's writing constitutes a radical experiment within the means of rhetorical production to restore "*Memoria* as the mother of the muses" and revalue it as "the most important of the rhetorical offices" (16). For Villanueva, *Memoria* possesses the capacity, auto/biographically and auto/ethnographically, to reoccupy historical time, to release the past from the finished histories of the victorious metropole and make it available instead as an emancipatory resource, a convolution of forces in the hands of the colonized that are overdetermined, contradictory, and unresolved.

VILLANUEVA AND PLATO: MEMORY AND DIALOGUE

The importance of memory to the Greeks is personified in myth by the archaic divinity Mnemosyne, daughter of Uranus (Heaven) and Gaea (Earth), who appears in Hesiod's *Theogony*, like Prometheus, as part of the generation of Titans that predate the Olympian gods. Mnemosyne was the ancient mistress of time and memory of the past, and the mother, by Zeus, of the nine Muses, the patron deities of artistic inspiration and the craft knowledge of poets, musicians, dancers, and historians. With the rise of rhetoric, memory and the arts of remembrance shed some of their mythic aura when they were systematized, at the level of technique, as one of the five canons in Cicero's *De Inventione*, along with invention, arrangement, style, and delivery.

In the oratorical culture of the classical curriculum, the training of memory was an indispensable part of rhetorical education. A long history of techniques to enhance retention in oratorical performance stretches from the Classical era through the Renaissance to the seventeenth century and the Early Modern period, the mnemonic devices Frances A. Yates famously traces in *The Art of Memory*. But there is more to memory in the rhetorical tradition than memorization. For rhetoricians, memory also signifies the ability of rhetors to extemporize, to compose in real time by drawing on available formulas, poetic rhythms, and figures of speech, a performative repertoire that can be studied and mastered, not unlike the oral-formulaic methods of the bards and poets of preliterate traditions or the blues musicians of Black vernacular culture. The power of memory, moreover, extended to the subject position of the audience in the rhetorical features that establish attention and make a discourse memorable, that makes it resonate and linger in the imagination.

Villanueva notes that memory, compared to the other canons, is often ignored in modern rhetorics of writing or, like delivery, treated as an afterthought from the era of oratory and left relatively underdeveloped conceptually ("*Memoria*" 16). There are, to be sure, refracted traces of memory in US writing instruction—for example, in the invention strategies where memory is both the target of brainstorming (the noun form of memory as a storehouse of knowledge) and the assaults designed to prompt remembering (the verb form of memory as action); or in the arrangement of old and new information into reader-friendly memory structures that produce the sensation of coherence; or in the search of databases and the use of citation in the memory systems of the research paper. (Readers will no doubt call to mind other instances of memory in composition pedagogy.) I mention these mundane, often unmarked uses of memory in teaching writing as a backdrop, to highlight the audacity of Villanueva's attempt to radicalize our understanding of memory, to unsettle its routine meanings and reinvigorate its neglected powers.

To summon his project, Villanueva performs a linguistic sleight of hand, a kind of word magic that turns the Anglophone lower case noun *memory* into *Memoria*, in its Latinate form, italicized to highlight its origins outside English, capitalized as a proper noun, and gendered feminine, like Mnemosyne and her daughter Muses. As a starting point, Villanueva says that "there's something to Plato's notion of memory as more than recollection," something in the reciprocal exchange of the Platonic dialogue that goes beyond simple access to the storage facilities of memory, something more creative and generative of understanding. For Villanueva, Plato "is maybe the coolest of the philosophers because of the resonance of the dialogue" and the way it leans "on a written discourse that approximates orality as a means toward arriving at Memory" ("*Memoria*" 16). For Plato, as we've been taught, Memory's destiny is to transcend the phenomenal world by recognizing the nonmaterial forms that constitute the true essence of things and states of being. Genuine learning, as opposed to mere perception, is really a matter of remembering, or *anamnesis*, the reawakening through dialectical interchange of the innate knowledge humans already possess of the ideal forms, that's inborn as a function of the human soul.

Among the affordances that the Platonic dialogue offers, Villanueva notes, are the "possibility for humor, the clear presence of all three points in the rhetorical triangle and the often unspecified dimension which is context" ("*Memoria*" 16). These features make up some of the rhetorical equipment, Villanueva suggests, that one needs to gain rhetorical footing—the differential, unequally distributed capacity to be recognized and make oneself understood— and to have voice in the dialogue between colony and metropole, the past and the present, the living and the dead. Villanueva's link to Plato is a telling one, about how memory is activated dialogically through an exchange of voices that sets the soul—which is really the human imagination—in motion. Still, for all his appreciation of Plato, Villanueva's notion of *Memoria* operates unequivocally in historical time, not the timeless philosophical present of the ideal forms. For Villanueva, memory's meanings are worldly, incomplete, and constantly changing, not transcendental or eternal. As Fernandez notes in the next chapter, it is unfinished work. Villanueva ultimately upends Plato by locating the dialogue not in the peripatetic philosophical space of Athens but across geohistorical scales, in the asymmetric stratified orders of meaning making that link the colony and the metropole, in the material world of European invasion and Indigenous self-defense.

This dialogue is set, for example, in the opening pages of Villanueva's "On the Rhetoric and Precedents of Racism," in the late fifteenth century, when an "Incan philosopher-rhetorician . . . enters into dialectical interplay" (645) with the Franciscan missionary Father Valverde. The Incan's discourse concerns "five preeminent men" the missionary has told him he ought to know: God ("three and one, which are four, whom you call the creator of the universe"); Adam ("the father of all men, on whom they piled their sins"); Jesus ("the only one not to cast sins on that first man, but he was killed"); the pope; and Carlos, the king of Spain. The rhetorical situation, in the most immediate sense, involves the payment of tribute to Carlos, which the Incan rhetorician, following an exposition of the facts (the *narratio*), rejects (the *dispositio*), saying the Spanish king "was never lord of these regions and whom I have never seen" (the *refutatio*). In a broader sense, the Incan rhetorician's dialogue moves translocally across semiotic spheres and orders of indexicality, appropriating the mythic and real characters the missionaries have introduced (the "five preeminent men") in order to recontextualize them as objects of inquiry in an Indigenous rhetoric that lays bare the contradictions and inconsistencies of the Spanish account of invasion, and resists, in a situation of military occupation, acquiescence to the status and subjectivity of being conquered.

Along similar lines, Villanueva presents a second example of Indigenous rhetorics, in this case a delegation of Aztec *tlamatinime*, or trained philosophers, who addressed Franciscan missionaries in Mexico in 1524, employing a "rhetoric called the flower-and-song (*in xochitl in cuícatl*)" ("On the Rhetoric" 647). As in the Incan dialogue, the rhetorical situation is shaped by conquest: "Since we have handed over all our power to you," the *tlamatinime* say, "*if we abide here, we will remain only prisoners.*" Nevertheless, they say, "We refuse to be tranquil or to believe as truth what you say, even if this offends you" (647). There may be no reversing the conquest, but, as the Incan rhetorician and the Aztec *tlamatinime* demonstrate, the presence of *Memoria* provides the means for the vanquished to make new uses of Indigenous knowledge systems and refuse to accept the hegemony of Spain's epistemic regime, as warranted in the discourses of the ancestors:

> You have said that we do not know the lord-of-the-intimate-which-surrounds-us, the one from whom the-heavens-and-the-earth come. You have said that our gods are not true gods. We respond that we are perturbed and hurt by what you say, because our progenitors never spoke this way. (647)

Villanueva's treatment of the Incan and Aztec rhetoricians' encounters with Franciscan missionaries ends rather abruptly, with his cryptic summary comment on the two events that there was no "multiculturalism there, no cultural hybridity possible" (647). The section closes on a preemptive note, naming (but not really explaining why) two terms (*multiculturalism* and *cultural hybridity*) often invoked in discussions of colonialism and its legacies that don't fit or aren't possible, and, in any case, by implication, should be left out of our understanding of the Indigenous rhetoricians' dialogue with empire.

My guess is that the lack of explanation is in fact the point here, a maneuver on Villanueva's part meant to stop readers in their tracks, to divert them from the normalized uses and unthinking reproduction of the terms *multiculturalism* and *cultural hybridity*. There is an implied warning, I think, against presentism, a caution not to dissolve the late-fifteenth- and early-sixteenth-century dialogues of Indigenous rhetoricians with the Spanish authorities into contemporary categories, whether as part of a celebratory rainbow nation pluralism, on one hand, or the indeterminate fluidity of ludic postmodernism, on the other. I can imagine Villanueva worrying that readers under the cosmopolitan influences of a globalized elite will miss how the presence of *Memoria* ("our progenitors never spoke this way") constitutes the grounds to hold the Spanish invaders accountable—to delegitimize the claims of the conquest, withholding consent to the hegemony of empire even when overrun militarily by imperial forces.

VILLANUEVA AND BENJAMIN: *MEMORIA* AND THE ANGEL OF HISTORY

Villanueva's notion of *Memoria* resembles in certain key respects Walter Benjamin's Angel of History, which appears in "Theses on the Philosophy of History," Benjamin's final essay, completed in the spring of 1940. Inspired by the Paul Klee painting *Angelus Novus*, the Angel of History, Benjamin writes, looks "as though he is about to move away from something he is fixedly contemplating":

> His face is turned toward the past. Where we perceive a chain of events, he sees one single catastrophe which keeps piling wreckage upon wreckage and hurls it in front of his feet. The angel would like to stay, awaken the dead, and make whole what has been smashed. But a storm is blowing from Paradise . . . [that] irresistibly propels him into the future to which his back is turned, while the pile of debris before him grows skyward. This storm is what we call progress. (257–58).

As is true of the Indigenous rhetoricians in Peru and Mexico, a sense of melancholy pervades Benjamin's essay. The Angel of History's inability to change the past and his reluctant backward entrance into the future are marked no doubt by the historical moment of the essay amid the mounting disaster of fascism and the Nazi occupation of France, where Benjamin was in exile, hoping to flee to the United States. It is hard not to feel the threat of escape routes being closed off and the looming presence of Benjamin's death by suicide.

But there is also another level of melancholy present, I think, that comes with the Angel's revelation that history is an escalating catastrophe. The wreckage that piles up from the past figures for the Angel as "one single event" that thrusts us into the future, not a progressive chain of events whose meaning unfolds like a "March of Time" newsreel. The Angel of History has seen living proof that there "is no document of civilization which is not at the same time a document of barbarism" (256). As Benjamin insists, whatever critical edge the idea of progress once had in modernity's break with divine right and the feudal past, it has been used up and is now exhausted, just another name for the winds of disaster that propel the Angel of History, against his will, into the future. This is why the Angel is facing backward—and why memory/*Memoria* matters.

What follows is that for *Memoria*—as Benjamin's backward-looking Angel of History anticipates—time is not an "empty homogeneous" space but rather is saturated with dialectical meaning, bent and shaped by what Benjamin calls a "secret agreement between past generations and the present one." The sense of temporality is vertical, layered, and overwritten, like a palimpsest, a congestion of voices rather than the horizontal distribution of time in a linear sequence. This is the "*weak* Messianic power" each generation is endowed with, a "power," Benjamin says, "to which the past has a claim" (254). For Benjamin, appeals to the future—to look ahead as the doctrinaire Marxists of the old school did, staking everything on the historical inevitability of socialism's triumph—risk breaking the pact between past and present, defaulting on the debt owed to the past and its claims to the attention and allegiances of the present. This debt, Benjamin holds, cannot be settled cheaply by deferring it teleologically to the future. Eliding the claims of the past on behalf of a redemptive future ignores the accumulative wreckage so evident to the backward-looking Angel of History. As Benjamin notes, such a denialism caused the Social Democrats to lose their nerve, to forget the "hatred" and "spirit of sacrifice" that are the working class's greatest strengths, the qualities of unreconciled class consciousness that are "nourished by the image of enslaved ancestors rather than that of liberated grandchildren" (260).

For Benjamin it is not "man" or "men" in some generalized sense of the human spirit but "the struggling, oppressed class itself" that "is the depository of historical knowledge" (260), the seat of revolutionary memory/*Memoria.* Instead of heralding a redemptive future about to unfold, *Memoria* and the Angel of History face backward because they signal the end of the old order, the culmination of past suffering rather than the beginning of a new era. This is the final act of the international proletariat, the ultimate mission of "the last enslaved class." The plot centers on the revenge of the Angel of History/*Memoria*, with the multitudes of empire cast in the role of the "avenger," who, Benjamin says, "completes the task of liberation in the name of generations of the downtrodden" (260). The motive force is not so much a utopian vision of the social future but the direct redress for the wreckage of history, with the power to close the book on the claims of the past.

For Villanueva the past's claim on *Memoria* is rooted in the dialogical "connection between narratives of people of color and the need to reclaim a memory." Villanueva notes the importance of *Memoria*'s backward-facing gaze and the "need to reclaim a memory . . . of identity in formation and constant reformation . . . as well as formed through the generations" ("*Memoria*" 12). And yet, for Villanueva, the politico-rhetorical work of *Memoria* is not identical to reclaiming memories of identity: such recollections are indeed necessary but not sufficient to register the full weight of the past and what the present owes it. There is another dimension, Villanueva says, the "need to reclaim and retain the memory of the imperial lords, those who have forcibly changed the identities of people of color through colonization" (12; see also Benjamin).

To avenge the "enslaved ancestors" requires not just the recognition of the pluralistic identities of the oppressed—an affirmation of Indigenous knowledge and vernacular tradition—but a political economy that comes to terms with the meanings and effects of colonial power, its systems of knowledge, divisions of labor, and extractive modes of production.[2] The backward-facing gaze of the Angel of History, like that of *Memoria*, is fixated on the past because its piled-up wreckage is the enemy's base of operations, the source of its sovereignty, and a reminder of its coercive force and its morbid symptoms. If, as Benjamin puts it, "the Messiah comes not only as the redeemer, [but] he comes as the subduer of Antichrist" (255), then, for *Memoria* and the messianic generation of the oppressed and exploited, the ability to defeat and dismantle colonialism requires a strategic understanding of the enemy, how it rules by force and how it has invaded the consciousness of the colonized.

VILLANUEVA AND GRAMSCI: "PESSIMISM OF THE INTELLECT/OPTIMISM OF THE WILL"

As Benjamin says, to "articulate what is past does not mean to recognize 'how it really was.' It means to seize hold of a memory, as it flashes in a moment of danger" (255). Benjamin and Villanueva's understandings of revolutionary memory/*Memoria* converge where the past makes its claim on the present, where the issue is not just the recollection of events but an unblinking recognition of the memories that the dangers of the present have summoned up as necessary. The politico-rhetorical mission of *Memoria* is not, in the first instance, a matter of reanimating voices that have been silenced but of bringing to consciousness the lived experience of the past that is needed to abolish the existing order. What this means is that memory is not so much inherited from the ancestors, passed down, like a keepsake, from generation to generation. Rather, memory must be seized according to present necessity, "as it flashes in a moment of danger," in the kairotic instant when memory's meanings become suddenly available to consciousness, to be decoded and analyzed, through the struggles of the oppressed and exploited.

It is all too easy to accommodate the existing order—to suppress the barbarity of civilization's every act—by a kind of willful naïveté that, as Benjamin describes it, expresses "amazement that the things we are experiencing are 'still' possible in the twentieth century" (257). There is, in other words, a powerful desire to normalize the current state of affairs by making the disasters of history—the massacres and genocide, the use of rape and torture as state policy, the cruelty of leaders like Hitler and Trump, the atavistic racism and xenophobia of fascism and white nationalism—into aberrations rather than inherent structural features of the system. Consent to the moral authority of empire depends in part on the psychic relief that comes from the ruled believing that the inevitable atrocities of the rulers are accidental. In contrast, the role of revolutionary memory/*Memoria* is to broadcast what Benjamin says the "tradition of the oppressed teaches," namely, that "the 'state of emergency' in which we live is not the exception but the rule," the actual ground of our historical existence (257). The task is to resist explaining away the wreckage of the past as an unfortunate mistake or temporary anomaly. The work of revolutionary memory/*Memoria* is instead to amplify the state of emergency, to crank up the felt sense of crisis, and to "wrest," as Benjamin puts it, "tradition away from a conformism that is about to overpower it" (255). In this light, Villanueva's *Memoria* amounts to a seizure from below—an appropriation by the popular forces of the means of producing and circulating the meanings of the past.

The politico-rhetorical workings of *Memoria* "as it flashes in a moment of danger" can be seen in the quick historical overview of Puerto Rico in "*Memoria* Is a Friend of Ours." Villanueva uses the "common saying among Puerto Ricans and Cubans—*Te doy un cuento de mi historia*" (I'll give you a story about my history)—to frame a short impressionistic chronicle that begins a thousand years before the Europeans arrived, with the Indigenous Arawak inhabitants of the island, who were colonized by a Taino offshoot. "Then came Columbus," Villanueva recounts. "And then Ponce de León. Then the priests" ("*Memoria*" 17)—who were followed in succession by Indigenous revolts, smallpox deaths, the Atlantic slave trade, gold and silver mines, and the surreptitious trade with pirates by the African and Indigenous people who escaped Spanish rule in the remote interior of the island. Decades, centuries, even millennia flash by in memory. The *jaibería* of maroon subversion and the "plural manifestations of the entire universe insert themselves" in the *créolité* of the Caribbean. Postwar migration creates Nuyorican colonies in Brooklyn, the scene of Villanueva's boyhood, and the other boroughs of New York City. "I assimilate," Villanueva says. "And I don't. But I know how to seem to be—*jaibería*—and I have the memory—the memory provided by the stories told" (17).

So what exactly *is* that memory? What *is it* that Villanueva, the Angel of History, and *Memoria* all seem to know? There is the knowledge, to be sure, about personal origins—about "who I am, from where, playing out the mixes within" ("*Memoria*" 17). This level of knowledge feels tentative, about states of existential seeming and double consciousness. At the same time, however, there appears to be an older knowledge that *Memoria* accesses, that comes from deeper sedimented layers of archaeological and historical time, with "an ancestry dating back before the Europeans" (17). In this regard, *Memoria* operates through the metaphor of excavation, as an extractive activity that digs, the deeper the better, into the past to discover unsuspected treasures buried far below the surface. This is probably the dominant understanding of how memory and memoirist writing work.

There are, however, other ways of understanding *Memoria* that elucidate more fully its multiple and sometimes contradictory manifestations, how "it flashes in a moment of danger." We might see *Memoria*, that is, not as the autochthonous legacy of the past, with deep roots in native soil, but rather as an emergent force in the dialogue from the periphery that demystifies the governing logic of the center, that aims to settle the accounts of the "enslaved ancestors" in the present. This view of *Memoria* shifts the framework from individuals digging genealogically into the past to recover personal and collective identities to the struggles between classes and class fractions, colonizers and the colonized, the periphery and the center, to control the production and circulation of memory in a wider war of positions for political and epistemic hegemony. This ideological warfare, the battle over consciousness between the oppressed and the oppressor, is always lurking, I think, right at the edge of Villanueva's *Memoria*, in the moments of dialogue when the claims of the dead occupy the attention of the living.

Villanueva has found himself in a complicated politico-rhetorical situation, playing off the twin Gramscian modalities "pessimism of the intellect/optimism of the will." Their dialectical interdependence is ever-present in Villanueva's writing, in the way, for example, he problematizes the overly simplistic optimism in "celebrations of cultural multiplicity" by "looking at the combat zones as well as the kinder contact zones" ("Maybe" 189) while avoiding, at the same time, the totalizing ontological vision of social death found in some variants of Afropessimism. To my mind, Villanueva, of all contemporary rhetoricians, keeps butting up against the opacity of history and keeps living, in the unfinished way we must, with the unresolved (and unresolvable, really) tensions in rhetoric's work of demystifying the ideological. I admire Villanueva's reluctance to insist on closure, his willingness to say, "So here is where the essay runs out, limping to a halt. I don't have a conclusion. All I have, I hope, is the beginning of a conversation" ("Maybe" 189). This is hardly the tight formulaic ending of the academic essay that summarizes, calls for further research, or recontextualizes the issues in a wider frame of reference. It's instead the language of dialogue that opens the essay to readers' participation, inviting them into the conversation that activates *Memoria*—and that extends beyond the essay, with the backward-facing Angel as a companion, into the maelstrom of history.

Of all contemporary rhetoricians, it is Villanueva, I think, who best understands Walter Benjamin when he says, "Only that historian will have the gift of fanning the spark of hope in the past who is convinced that *even the dead* will not be safe from the enemy if he wins. And the enemy has not ceased to be victorious" (255). There is a double making at work here, in which a spark of hope is set alight by the conviction that "*even the dead*" need to be defended from the enemy. For Benjamin—and I think for Villanueva too—such solidarity with the dead is based on the lived experience of a troubled history that is overdetermined, contradictory, and unfulfilled in the present, where teleology has failed, the dead remain unsafe, the enemy keep winning, and the "enslaved ancestors" wait to be avenged. The situation seems desperate, but it is precisely because of this desperation, not in spite of it, that *Memoria*, as Villanueva puts it, "calls and pushes us forward" ("*Memoria*" 19). *Memoria* may well be "a friend of ours," as Villanueva says, but it is not necessarily a joy or a comfort. It is rather the inescapable bond between past and present generations, the joint recognition of history's mounting catastrophes, the vendetta sworn on the graves of the ancestors—and the only imaginable means of lighting the spark of revolutionary hope that "flashes in a moment of danger."

NOTES

1. See Villanueva (*Bootstraps* 77–88) for his account of Sophistic rhetoric.
2. For more on his views on political economy, see Villanueva ("Toward").

WORKS CITED

Benjamin, Walter. *Illuminations.* 1955. Translated by Harry Zohn, Schocken Books, 1968.

Mignolo, Walter D. *Local Histories/Global Designs: Coloniality, Subaltern Knowledges, and Border Thinking.* Princeton UP, 2000.

Olson, David R. "Writing: The Divorce of the Author from the Text." *Exploring Speaking-Writing Relationships: Connections and Contrasts*, edited by Barry M. Kroll and Roberta J. Vann, National Council of Teachers of English, 1981.

Villanueva, Victor, Jr. *Bootstraps: From an American Academic of Color.* National Council of Teachers of English, 1993.

———. "Maybe a Colony: And Still Another Critique of the Comp Community." *Journal of Composition Theory,* vol. 17, no. 2, 1997, pp. 183–90.

———. "*Memoria* Is a Friend of Ours: On the Discourse of Color. *College English,* vol. 67, no. 1, 2004, pp. 9–19.

———. "On the Rhetoric and Precedents of Racism." *College Composition and Communication,* vol. 50, no. 4, 1999, pp. 645–61.

———. "Toward a Political Economy of Rhetoric (or a Rhetoric of Political Economy)." *Radical Relevance: Toward a Scholarship of the Whole Left,* edited by Laura Gray-Rosendale and Steven Rosendale, SUNY at Purchase, 2005, pp. 57–65.

Yates, Francis A. *The Art of Memory.* Routledge and Kegan Paul, 1966.

Chapter 4

Re-Collecting Chicanx Collective Memory

Miriam L. Fernandez

THROUGHOUT THE TIME WE HAVE known each other, Victor Villanueva and I have had many conversations about the intersections between memory, rhetoric, and race. We have often made sense of these concepts from our personal experiences, noting the similarities and differences in our distinct identities. He is an American-born Puerto Rican from Brooklyn, a high school dropout, a veteran, a respected professor who teaches in a primarily white institution, and a theorist who has shaped our collective understanding of how race and racism function within rhetoric and composition. I am a Mexican-born Chicana raised in California's Central Valley, a traditional student who went from high school to BA, to MA, to PhD, and now assistant professor at a Hispanic Serving Institution. Although we both speak Spanish, our Spanishes sound different—a fact that has never stopped us from fully understanding each other.

We are drastically different from each other in significant ways but, because of our experiences as Latinx in the United States, we also share a collective identity. We are both racialized even though we lack a discrete racial identity, both of us a product of the "uneasy mixes of races that make for no race at all yet find themselves victims to racism" (Villanueva, "*Memoria*" 17). We are both read as white or white-adjacent or, as Villanueva explains it, "[t]hose of us who are light-skinned don't pass for white; we're just not automatically sorted into the appropriate slot" (14). We inhabit a liminal space between the privileged and the racialized. Outside of our cultural differences as Puerto Rican and Chicana, we also share a collective memory that forms the foundation of our shared identity: racialized people in the United States.

Collective memory can offer marginalized groups a reprieve from the darkness of racism, stereotypes, isolation, and the general feelings of exclusion that can permeate our lives. Groups of people with historical or present-day connections to displacement, genocide, racism, and more face a reality marked by loss: histories erased; kinships severed; lands seized; languages silenced then forgotten. Villanueva, for example, often looks to the collective memory of Puerto Rico's Taíno past to trace both loss and survival. We know little about the lives, customs, and rhetorics of the Taínos, so Villanueva focuses on the memory that lives on through language ("Rhetoric" 15). He traces words such as *yucca, tobacco, hurricane, canoe, hammock, potato,* and *baseball* to their Indigenous origins. He shows us that a memory of the Taíno—the people, their language, and their ways—lives on even after colonization has erased, suppressed, and killed what once was (19). Many of our memories are fragile and faint, haunting yet hopeful. How often have we touched, spoken, or seen some remnant of our past and not known it? How many of us will resort to analyzing our DNA, hoping to fill the gaps left by colonialism and slavery? The history is tragic, painful, and violent, but collective memory is about preserving our ways of being and knowing to prevent further cultural loss.

The concept of collective memory is present across several of Villanueva's written works. In his article "'I Am Two Parts,'" Villanueva argues that collective memory "help[s] to establish the genre of a movement, the pattern or form—a conditioning causality 'decisively contributing to shape social life'" (488). For Villanueva, collective subjectivities lead "to that utopian hope of a successful program . . . [where] we all get a real chance at making change even as we understand multiple traditions" (492). Collectives, which can exist only when people recognize a collective memory, are vehicles for political and social change (488). Like Villanueva, I believe that collective memory is a powerful tool against oppressive social systems. Why else would conservatives in this country be waging a rhetorical war against critical race theory if it weren't that they fear the inherent power of critical memory?

My experience of collective memory tells me that as much as memory liberates, it can also restrain; as often as it subverts dominant oppressive institutions, it just as often can become subservient to those same institutions. As a Chicana well-versed in the Chicanx collective memory, I see the beauty and power of the memory we have constructed. I also see the ways that aspects of our collective memory retain a certain sexism and racism. This contradiction within our collective memories is what Villanueva struggles with as he reflects on that liminal position of being "in a truly fine place, yet so far from home" ("'I Am'" 482). He writes about the struggles of leading when one is "holding onto the traditions of the academy while trying to change the traditions so that those of us who are perforce othered can be more than 'recognized' or 'accommodated'" (485). Like Villanueva, I struggle with this contradiction and how it plays out in dominant institutions like the university. I also struggle with how this contradiction plays out within Chicanx and Latinx communities. Within our communities of color, the contradictions of memory that liberates and memory that restrains threaten to fracture our collective subjectivity and create obstacles to our collective causality.

Victor's attention to memory is a theme taken up by a number of contributors to this collection. In this section, John Trimbur addresses Victor's emphasis on memory as historical and dialectical, Laura Gray-Rosendale speaks to the powerful role of memoir and the personal in academic discourse, and Romeo García engages collective memory as hauntings. My goal here is to engage with and cross-talk with Victor's work on collectives and memory. I do so by focusing on the rhetorical workings of collective memory as an unfinished text. To see collective memory as an unfinished text privileges the process of construction rather than the product that has been constructed. In other words, it shifts the focus from what is currently remembered by the collective (the product) to how and why we remember (the process). Roger C. Aden et al. introduce the term *re-collection* to emphasize the ongoing rhetorical activity of collective memory. They argue, "[P]laces of memory are *not* finished texts, but sites of re-collection in which individuals and groups selectively cull and organize re-collected versions of the past that are (not) shared by others" (313). In this context, collective memory becomes a series of do-overs, a dialogue between past and present guided by the collective as they choose what values to privilege and maintain. If we recognize that collective memory is an unfinished rhetorical construction, we can use that knowledge to continue to shape our shared memory in better and more productive ways.

As an interdisciplinary concept, collective memory has been applied in varying ways and thus requires some unpacking. In the simplest of terms, collective memory is a shared group memory. Barbie Zelizer explains that "collective memory comprises recollections of the past that are determined and shaped by the group . . . [and] presumes activities of sharing, discussion, negotiation, and, often, contestation" (214). Collective memory is constructed through rhetorical activity because it is shaped by communicative acts (discussion, negotiation, contestation) that are inevitably influenced by sociopolitical interests. Since any social group can compose and maintain a collective memory, and because the term is also used to describe the broader national memory, the term encounters both flexibility and inconsistency. To avoid confusion, I use *dominant national memory* to refer to a greater national shared memory (from both the US and Mexico) and *collective memory* to refer to the memory shared by marginalized groups within the United States. This is consistent with Villanueva's use of collective memory to refer to folks of color. Villanueva names his primary collective community as "Americans of color, the traditionally excluded Latinos y Latinas, African Americans, Asian Americans, Pacific Islanders, and American Indians, all of us who became a part of the United States by way of colonialism and the individuated colonization that is slavery" and notes that his secondary community is found in the academy ("'I Am'" 484). Given my own identity and background, I primarily focus on Chicanx group memories to analyze how collective memory is always in construction and how that construction is always rhetorical.

In what follows, I analyze a few significant narratives in the Chicanx collective memory via personal memories, photographs, and analyses of select texts. Looking back at my experiences during a series of trips to Mexico City, I discuss how I have been both recipient and participant of collective memory. Certain memory places in Mexico represent important collective memories for Chicanxs, yet their physical location makes them difficult to access without time and money. I realize, then, the privilege of my experiences with these trips to Mexico City, which were squeezed in during school breaks and partially funded by research grants. My fluency in Spanish and the fact that I lived in Guadalajara as a young child also made it easier for me to navigate Mexico City. Even though I was born in Mexico, I am still an outsider with a limited understanding of certain political and cultural nuances—a common experience among Chicanx no matter which side of the border they were born. As a result, the framework through which I look at collective memory is based on my subjectivity as a Chicana.

I realize, too, that there is something of a contradiction in using the individual experience to make sense of collective memory. Yet memory is personal, and the personal complements the scholarly (Villanueva, "*Memoria*" 14). As Villanueva explains, we need the personal to make sense of memory because "[m]emory simply cannot be adequately portrayed in the conventional discourse of the academy" (12). Additionally, Aden et al. make the case that "the re-collections of individuals are products of their interactions with groups; thus, patterns of memories will emerge from among individuals who reveal their cultural moorings" (324). Although my experiences are not representative of the collective, they can be helpful in understanding how collective memory is co-constructed by individuals within that collective. I do not intend for this analysis to be the final word at the end of a conversation. I intend for it to be one voice in a discussion started by Villanueva's ("'I Am'") exploration of collective subjectivity. I invite readers to reflect on how they have engaged with these or similar memory places and add to this conversation by bringing awareness to other memory fragments that mean something to their sense of collective identity. Collective memory is, after all, a collaborative construction.

TEMPLO MAYOR: MEMORY PLACES AS SPATIAL ARGUMENTS

In Mexico City, behind black metal gates, the ruins of an Indigenous religious structure lie exposed like an open wound on the earth. These ruins are what remain of a great city that belonged to the people known as the Mexica (commonly known as the Aztecs), the people who migrated from Aztlán in the eleventh century and built the city of Tenochtitlán in present-day Mexico City (Mundy 26–27). Templo Mayor, or Hueyi Teocalli in Nahuatl, was once a grand pyramid in the city of Tenochtitlán. It was a unique architectural structure with twin temples at the top, one for the god Huitzilopochtli and one for the god Tlaloc (Mundy 30). Today this archaeological site serves as a memory place for many Mexican and Chicanx people alike. Memory places refer to the spaces where "collective memory is emplaced, in sites both physical and imagined," and "where individual members of the remembering collective experience—and interact with—the rhetorical representations of the past" (Aden et al. 312). Dickinson et al. explain that memory places are objects of attention and desire that present themselves as markers of collective memory and are unique in that they are rooted in touristic practices (25–26). A play on words between memory *places* and memory *palaces* suggests a dialectical rhetorical relationship. Memory places are extrinsic rhetorical constructions crafted by others; memory palaces are intrinsic rhetorical constructions crafted by the self. Both function as forms of cultural knowledge as memory places convey social or cultural identities, and memory palaces "established synthetic connections between individual memories and cultural knowledge or historical records" (Vivian 289). Both leave a lasting "impression."

People from all over Mexico and other parts of the world visit Templo Mayor for various reasons. I visited because I wanted to experience being in a place that has a special significance to my present cultural identity. Aden et al. explain that when we enter "a site of re-collection, then move through and between places within the site, we quite literally sense a place by taking in what surrounds us" and ultimately the physical experience of a memory place "help[s] concretize our memories" (320). My experience of Templo Mayor was multilayered. As a Chicana, I was emotionally invested. As a scholar and rhetorician, that emotional experience was often interrupted by self-reflection and interrogation of why I felt what I felt or thought what I thought.

The first time I stepped into the archaeological site, I was overwhelmed as I stood over the ruins of the former Mexica religious temple. As I made my way around, I came to a spot with a clear view of both the ruins and the cathedral nearby (Figure 4.1). In front of me was a different manifestation of familiar contradictions: The height of the cathedral contrasting with the depth of the archeological site. The ornateness of the church against the now-colorless ruins. The grandness of my religion's church casting its shadow on the ruins of the Mexica religious temple.

I felt sadness thinking of all the violence, the loss of life, and the painful changes to the Indigenous culture that the people went through. I felt curious about how the Mexica lived before the conquest and wondered what their city might have looked like before the Spaniards took over. And I also felt, or imagined, a sense of connection, knowing that what transpired over Tenochtitlán had some impact on who I am today. I wondered if I had Mexica heritage. I wondered about my ancestry. I imagined myself as a product of Indigenous survival. I ignored the colonizer as part of my heritage even though I was born in the lands he took, even though I speak his language and practice his religion too.

Most of my experience during my first visit was dominated by my imagination and the tensions within my identity. In addition to wondering about Templo Mayor's connection to me, I had mixed feelings about being in Mexico (was I a tourist? a researcher? a Mexican citizen?). Villanueva recounts a similar tension when he reflects on his position in academia, speculating over "the contradictions of this supposed leader—me—a leader of color who leads in overwhelmingly White institutions, still doing what I can to lead others of color, though maybe less *lead* than advise. And the advice concerns more of these fine places so far from home, where we are most often welcomed but not often understood. So

Figure 4.1

I slip into memory and self-appraisal" ("'I Am'" 482). Whether in the workplace, the home, or amid travel and cultural exploration, the contradictions follow. My imagined connections to Templo Mayor certainly heightened my awareness of these contradictions because I was conscious of (or perhaps looking for) some ancestral connection.

Since Templo Mayor is primarily a self-guided experience, visitors can walk around the archaeological site and the attached museum in whatever way they prefer. This freedom allows visitors to interact more strongly with the memory place by relying on an internal dialogue between what they see and the "other discursive fragments of memory that they bring to the interpretive process" (Aden et al. 323). My first visit was strongly guided by the discursive fragments I brought with me (my studies on the Spanish conquest and my collective identity) because I struggled to make sense of the location. Along the path that allows visitors to circle the ruins, various placards in Spanish and English help provide context for what visitors see. Yet, even with these pieces of information, the site can be difficult to read accurately because the placards are not numbered (thus lack suggested order), and the information was at times hard to follow because the ruins are broken and without a clear form. During my first visit, I failed to understand that the broken pieces I was walking past were all part of one structure that was expanded by building over the previous one. I had read the placards, but I had difficulty making sense of what I was reading after a long day of travel on a hot day. I misunderstood the site and thought that only the covered area was the main temple and assumed that other parts were remnants of the old city. It was lost on me how large the original temple was when the Spaniards first came upon it. By extension, I also limited my imagination of the size of the original city. After my first visit, I researched more about the site. After reading Barbara Mundy's *The Death of Aztec Tenochtitlan, the Life of Mexico City,* I picked up on the many nuances I had missed during my first visit.

In many ways, the first visit failed in terms of understanding the site, but it succeeded in terms of emotional effect. Although I had misunderstood the site, I still felt connections to the memory place. The emotional impact was tied to my sense of cultural identity and to my academic studies. I thought about important moments in the history of this place: Moctezuma being held as hostage by Cortés, the unprovoked massacre of Indigenous people that took place during a religious celebration, the Mexica rebellion that followed, and so on. A year later, I went back to Mexico City, this time bringing my parents to Templo Mayor to share the experience with them. During the second trip, my experience of Templo Mayor felt like a collective meaning-making experience. My parents and I collaborated in piecing together various fragments: the information on the placards, the ruins in front of us, the information I had read since my first trip, the history they knew, and other stories we had. All three of us found the experience culturally enriching, although I imagine that we experienced it differently. For example, my mother shared how surprised she was that she had not known about this site before. For her it was a bad reflection on Mexican education and public memory. She then reflected that even if she had been aware, she likely would not have been able to afford the trip. I constructed my experience of Templo Mayor as a kind of mythical "going home," a cultural experience based on my subjectivity as a Chicana. My parents, who grew up in Mexico and lived there until their mid-twenties, seemed to experience it from the perspective of Mexican history, Mexico's education system, and the connection between opportunities for cultural enrichment and poverty in the country.

While the lack of guidance in Templo Mayor can present numerous opportunities for collective meaning making, it also offers opportunities to reinforce myths, stereotypes, and misinformation that visitors might bring with them. Although the space does not provide too much guidance in how visitors should move around the site, a few elements function to support a particular narrative of the Mexican nation's Indigenous heritage. In other words, certain rhetorical choices physically inscribed for visitors offer them one way of understanding the cultural significance of the memory place. This is especially evident with four historical quotes inscribed upon two large walls across from the entrance. Dickinson and colleagues explain that all memory places incorporate additional memory techné such as "words, inscribed and/or spoken, as part of an interpretive program" and that these elements complicate how visitors experience the memory place (29). The quotes inscribed over the archaeological site and their arrangement persuade visitors to experience the memory place through narratives of patriotism and nationalism. The result is that the patriotic or nationalist perspective diminishes and downplays the complicated history of colonialism that the site embodies.

On the first wall, there are three quotes originating from the sixteenth century. The first quote is from Hernán Cortés, the middle quote is by Bernal Diaz del Castillo, and the final quote is by Fray Motolinía. The first two quotes, both from Spanish conquerors, provide details about Tenochtitlán before its destruction and focus primarily on the beauty and greatness of the city. The quote from the Spanish missionary Toribio de Benavente, commonly known as Motolinía, focuses on the aftermath of conquest when the "seventh plague was the building of the great city of Mexico." The quote communicates (in my opinion, ambiguously) that some Indigenous workers died "when they fell from high" and other Indigenous people were crushed when "the buildings that were being taken apart in one area to build on another area" fell on the workers. Since the quote focuses on aspects of construction and uses the verbs *taken* and *fell* (tomaban y caían) to allude to the death of the Indigenous workers, I experienced the quote as an unclear text. I searched for the original source in *History of the Indians in New Spain* by Motolinía and found an interesting rhetorical choice: the inscribed quote is missing key text.

The inscription at Templo Mayor begins by naming the construction of Mexico City as a plague, describes how packed the streets were with workers, then recounts accidents that cost them their lives, and finally moves on to the Indigenous people buying and bringing materials. In Motolinía's translated complete quote, with bold text to indicate the omitted sections, he states:

> In the construction some were crushed by beams, others fell from heights, others were caught beneath buildings which were being torn down in one place to be built up again in another; **especially did this illicit when they tore down the principal temples of the devil. Many Indians died there, and it was many years before they completely demolished the temples, from which they obtained an enormous**

> **amount of stone. The custom of this country is not the best in the world,** for the Indians do the work, get the materials at their own expense, pay the stonemasons and carpenters, and if they do not bring their own food, they go hungry. (Motolinía 41)

While the omission does not affect the overall narrative or general information, it softens the visitor's perception of what the site represents. These rhetorical choices essentially hide colonial violence from the visitor's perception. This is a problem. As Villanueva argues, we "need to reclaim and retain the memory of the imperial lords, those who have forcibly changed the identities of people of color through colonization" ("*Memoria*" 12). Hiding colonial violence provides an incomplete picture of our histories. The full text communicates not only the (presumably) accidental construction deaths, but it also reminds us that the Spanish were forcing the people to tear down their own religious sites and that there was an increase in deaths during that time, perhaps a symptom of a greater cultural pain. We are also reminded that the religious ruins were mined for materials to build colonial structures, and we are even presented with Motolinía's own criticism of the working conditions for Indigenous people. The choices of which quotes to use and which parts of the original text to omit suggest ideological persuasion through rhetorical intervention.

A final quote provides stronger evidence that the memory place is marked by the ideology of the nation. The final inscription, an excerpt from an Independence Day speech given by the Mexican journalist Ignacio Ramírez in 1861, appears as a stand-alone quote physically and historically separated from the first three (see Figure 4.2). Although we can question the choices behind the first three quotes, they mostly make sense given that each one references the memory place. The Ramírez quote, on the other hand, does not fit the context of the memory place. Ramírez is not focused on either Tenochtitlan or Templo Mayor, he speaks more than one hundred years after the fall of the city, and the speech was performed in a different location in Mexico City.

Figure 4.2

Although it is outside of the context of the memory place, the Ramírez quote provides an ideological frame with which visitors can experience Templo Mayor. The quote, pictured in the right-hand image of Figure 4.2, translates to:

> Where do we come from? Where do we go? This is the double problem whose resolution individuals and societies seek without respite. . . . [T]he germ of yesterday encloses the flowers of tomorrow; if we become infatuated with being pure Aztecs, we will end by the triumph of a single race only to adorn with the skulls of the others the temple of American Mars; if we insist on being Spaniards, we will voluntarily rush into the abyss of the reconquest, but no! Never! We come from the town of Dolores, we are descendants of Hidalgo and we were born fighting like our father for all the symbols of emancipation and like him, fighting for such a holy cause, we will disappear from the earth. (Figure 4.3)

The only connection between the quote and Templo Mayor is the topic of Mexican racial heritage as Aztec and Spaniard. I see two main ideological threads with this quote. The first has to do with the placement of the inscription and the ideal of historical continuity. Read in succession, the four quotes present a narrative that first tells of the Spaniards encountering the great Indigenous city (blatantly skipping over the violent conquest) to the destruction of that city in order to build a new one, and ends with the Mexican people contemplating their relationship to the past and deciding that their loyalty is to the nation.

The succession of the narrative in the quotes mirrors our concept of history as a continuous narrative. This is a rhetorical effect that allows the arrangement of the quotes and the information included (or omitted) to present the colonization of Indigenous nations as a necessary precursor to the independence of the Mexican nation. Two separate historical events—related but ultimately distinct—are presented in a cause-and-effect relationship. Visitors, many of whom are Mexican, are persuaded to see the independence of the Mexican nation as the victorious ending to the past colonial violence. Thus, when Ramírez's quote is read in succession, it functions as an epideictic celebration of the nation for breaking free from colonial rule.

The second ideological thread comes by way of reading the Ramírez quote as part of a larger spatial argument. Dickinson et al. state that "memory places are also arranged in various spatial orientations that give rise to how they communicate or inculcate memory" (29). The final quote, if memory serves, is the closest to the entrance of Templo Mayor and slightly more visible (Figure 2). If the archaeological site is read like a spatial argument, then the final quote works as the main claim that states: "The Mexican citizen cannot be loyal to either the Aztec or the Spaniard, he must be loyal to the nation." Ramírez presents the search for a racial or cultural ancestor as dangerous to the Mexican nation. Loyalty to the Spanish part of us will lead us to fall into the "abyss of reconquest," while an infatuation "with being pure Aztec" will lead the Mexican nation to the "triumph of a single race" as we "adorn [our temples] with the skulls of the others." As an argument for why we ought to leave behind past cultures and racial identity, Ramírez relies on dangerous stereotypes of the Mexica as violent idol worshippers who relied on human sacrifice. Spatially, the site supports the claim with evidence in the form of a nearby structure of stone skulls (Figure 4.3).

The stone skulls offer another discursive space of contested meanings. On the one hand, the archaeological site simply explains that the stone skeletons are a tzompantli altar with an "interior [that] contained a spectacular offering, including representations of musical instruments, along with puma and wolf skeletons and other elements." Additionally, the placard explains that the "building is located on the north side of the Great Temple, symbolically alluding to the region of the dead known as Mictlampa, according to Mexica cosmovision." On the other hand, the strength and endurance of the stereotype of Indigenous violence is likely to dominate the more neutral presentation of the tzompantli altar. Most people have heard something of the violence associated with the Mexica. For example, a cursory search for "Templo Mayor" on Google's search engine includes within the first four hits a BBC article by Jonathan Glancey titled "The Templo Mayor: A Place for Human Sacrifices"

Figure 4.3

with a synopsis that reads: "The pinnacle of Aztec architecture was a vast religious building—with a blood-soaked history." When we are presented with practices of death and violence from a different culture, especially an Indigenous one, these acts are contextualized from a discourse of Western progress and are thereby presented as examples of primitive violence. To me, the association of the Mexica with human sacrifice does not seem so different from death penalty practices in the United States. Is executing a person to "restore justice"—a concept personified by a blindfolded woman holding a sword and a balance—all that different from the Mexica executing a person for good rains and good fortune? I'm certain many people will say "yes, they are different," but to me, the difference is primarily that our practices of death and violence are presented within a familiar ideological framework that we comprehend and accept.

Ramírez viewed Mexicans as divided between their racial and cultural past and their newfound nationalism. The speech, given in 1861, was only a few decades after Mexico had gained its independence. Thus, when he urges the people to shed their racial identity for a nationalist one, it is because pockets of the population wanted a different direction for the nation and the possibility of Spain regaining control was far more real. In fact, months after the speech, France invaded Mexico and took political control for the next few years. This context is entirely absent from the inscription at Templo Mayor. As a stand-alone quote, visitors are reminded to admire and celebrate their nationality and patriotism over questions of race or heritage. The problem with this is that Mexico is not made up of one unified race or one consistent racial mixture. Race and racism are real issues that need to be confronted. Paradoxical then, or perhaps fitting, that the space that celebrates Indigenous history presents visitors with a spatial argument that prioritizes nationalism over racial identity. Although the ruins themselves, coupled with Motolinía's words of colonial violence and general public knowledge of the conquest, do highlight the tragedy that took place, Ramírez's quote shifts the emphasis from an Indigenous history to a Mexican national history.

The memory place thus contains multiple competing narratives and influences visitors in different ways depending on the discursive fragments they arrive with. Memory places tend to "value and legitimate some views and voices, while ignoring or diminishing others" (Dickinson et al. 29). Since the discourse presented in Templo Mayor has the potential to influence the Mexican national identity as well as the Chicanx cultural identity, it is important that we understand how rhetoric functions within collective memory. Memory places like Templo Mayor are not straightforward educational sites, and they don't just provide information so visitors can learn about history. Instead, memory places "emerge from the intersections of official and vernacular cultural expressions" (Bodnar 13). Every aspect of the presentation of a memory place is negotiated by people and shaped by those people's ideologies. For Chicanx who visit this site, it is important we be aware of how nationalist or patriotic perspectives may color our experience and how our own collective memory will influence how we navigate such a space. Ultimately, any experience of a memory place, whether physical or imagined, is an opportunity for rhetorical action by the person who engages with the memory.

RE-COLLECTING AZTLÁN AND RHETORICAL CLAIMS TO THE LAND

In the previous section, I recalled my engagement with a memory place significant to the Chicanx collective memory and then analyzed how the site's physical composition is an emplaced rhetoric that persuades visitors to experience Indigenous ruins as an extension and celebration of Mexican nationalism. The point of this analysis is to provide evidence that collective memory is a continuous rhetorical construction. Through the discursive fragments and frameworks we carry, we interact with external discourses of memory. The dialogue between memory discourses leads to individual (and collective) conclusions about the significance of that memory. We gauge the memory's authenticity, we decide what the reconstructed past means to our present and future, and ultimately, we choose whether we will reject, accept, or revise the claims that memory presents. What does this mean for Latinx, for people of color, and what connection does it have to Villanueva's ("'I Am'") reflections on the collective subjectivity of leaders of color?

The short answer is that our collective memory is a rhetorical construction that is always in progress. Our collectives have choices to make about what the future of our collective memory will be. We can continue doing what we have been doing and trying to advance a unified singular version of our past, or we can build a collective memory where complexity and contradiction thrive. When Villanueva writes about collective memory, subjectivity, and causality, he argues for "a collection of collective subjectivities" as a response to the struggles we face when we try to navigate the experiences that come from being racialized and marginalized by dominant ideologies ("'I Am'" 492). Villanueva contextualizes his role as a leader of color in academia from a familiar liminal space, "attempting to break from the Subjective that is wrestling with the Collective. I am a White person of color, a Latino, a Puerto Rican, *and* an academic in all the traditional ways" (483). Villanueva finds an answer to the problem by going back to memory and back to collective subjectivity (488). Here, he relies on Domingues, who explains that social realities are "*processes* in which individuals and collectivities are from the very start, in an *ontological* sense, entangled in interactive interplays" (48). Domingues argues that collectives with varying levels of (de)centering interact with (and can change) social life (42). The belief that collectives can function only when they are strongly centered (acting in unison) is an incorrect assumption since decentered collectives can have as much impact (45). So, when Villanueva reflects on his experiences and concludes "that as a member of collectivities with their subjectivities, their own decenteredness, [he] can be organic, traditional, maybe even 'new'" ("'I Am'" 491), he argues for finding empowerment in the contradictions and complexities of a "collective code-meshing, a subjective meshing . . . [where he is] at home . . . with the language ways of the streets from which [he] came and the streets on which [he] walks now" (491). Villanueva presents a productive way to move our collective memory forward.

From my perspective, Chicanx struggle with decentering even though we are a diverse group with many different experiences. Chicanx in the 1960s and 1970s participated in diverse social movements with a variety of goals and actions. Holland et al. would likely categorize the various Chicanx social movements as a decentered approach, "seen not as relatively unified actors, but, as multiple sources of cultural discourses attempting the everyday actions of movement participants" (97). Nowadays we tend to remember this period as "the Chicano movement." It is a simple shorthand way to remember that time and many Chicanx are aware that "the movement" is defined by distinct groups with various goals. However, the shorthand of "the Chicano movement" has secondary rhetorical effects. It has the effect of erasing the diversity of the larger historical group and reinforcing the assumption that the collective has had one unified and continuous goal. The problem with imagining that the collective has a singular unified goal is that it runs the risk of supporting exclusionary tactics when subgroups are perceived as threatening the collective vision. Chicana feminists, for example, were historically regarded as a threat to the goals of the primarily male-led student movement in Southern California. Even today, Chicanx excuse and maintain sexist, racist, and homophobic narratives and actions by relying on that tired excuse that someone is acting outside the goals or values of the collective.

The desire to unify the collective under one set of values with one definition is evident in the collective's use of the imagined memory place of Aztlán. Aztlán offers a useful rhetoric that engages with broader narratives of Chicanx displacement but also falls back on limiting narratives. Emma Pérez explains, "If diaspora . . . is a 'history of dispersal coupled with myths and memories of a homeland,' where 'alienation in the host country' often fosters a 'desire for eventual return' while a collective memory reconstructs the alienated group's history . . . then Chicanos/as are appropriately diasporic" (78). Pérez links the need for the mythic homeland of Aztlán to a diasporic subjectivity among Chicanx. There are many terms that try to describe this Latinx experience: a diaspora, an internal exile, an internal colonialism, or, as Villanueva calls it, a "colonial consciousness among the still colonized Latinos" ("Maybe" 187). Latinx in the United States often feel the weight of second-class citizenship, of the constant political narrative that points to us like an invading hoard that threatens the nation. Latinx are often treated as perpetual immigrants, while our Spanish, a dominant language, is minoritized just because we dare to speak it. At the same time, our proximity to whiteness affords some of us the ability to escape.

Whether I am in the United States or in Mexico, a part of me always feels that my unique mix of Mexican and US American makes me not quite Mexican and not quite American. Many Chicanx share these feelings, although they may present in different ways. For example, some have a strong desire to know Mexico because it represents an origin—the place where we, or where our parents, or grandparents, or great grandparents, were born. For example, Bernadette Calafell opens one of her essays with "I prepare to return to a home that I do not know but that continues to define me. Mexico City awaits me. Here I will come face to face with the women of my cultural past. Marina, Guadalupe, Frida" ("Pro(re-)claiming" 44). Yet, as Alicia Gaspar de Alba writes, many Chicanx experience a displacement from Mexico too. She explains that "many Chicana and Chicano writers who have made that journey [back to Mexico] have discovered . . . that Mexico is not the homeland after all but a foreign land in which they are perceived as 'gringo wannabes' and 'sellouts' to their Mexican culture" (91). Even within the US, Mexican communities are often perceived or perceive themselves as different from Chicanx communities. Calafell explains that "Chicanas/os are often viewed as *pochos,* inauthentic, or American to Mexicans who might ridicule their desire to a precolonial past" ("Disrupting" 186). Although some people see little difference between the subgroups of a larger collective, those differences exist and are often tied to economic, educational, and social opportunities. Calafell writes that some Mexican American communities have "the desire to distance [themselves] from Mexican communities as a way to establish citizenship in the eyes of the dominant culture" ("Pro(re-)claiming 186). This is similar to the different opportunities that are afforded to stateside Puerto Ricans as opposed to those on the island and vice versa.

For the Chicanx collective, one form of dealing with the perpetual sense of homelessness we often experience in both the US and Mexico is to reach back to recover memories of when our imagined ancestors were peacefully at home in the land that is now the United States. Sometimes this is accomplished by recalling that much of the Southwest once belonged to Mexico or by recalling Aztlán, the Mexica's ancestral home, believed to have existed somewhere in that same Southwest region. These two memories are closely linked and accomplish the same thing. Both scenarios present Chicanx as having legitimate claims to being in the United States because they can point to ancestral ties that predate land ownership by the US nation. Villanueva writes that our colonial histories "affect our self-perceptions, [these are] histories that can affect how we are regarded" ("Maybe" 186). Most of the time, our colonial histories tend to put us at a disadvantage, but when the Chicanx community reclaims the memory of Aztlán, it flips the script and provides a rhetorical claim to the land where we stand, a counterargument to the racism we experience.

Yet our construction of Aztlán often carries exclusionary narratives that can perpetuate troublesome ideas. The memory of Aztlán that we have constructed tends to be male-centric and excludes other Indigenous languages and communities. Mexican and Chicanx do not simply equal Aztec and Spanish. This is not like Puerto Rico's history with the Taínos. Puerto Rico is significantly smaller than Mexico, and so the island's Indigenous histories are more straightforward—primarily a Taíno population. Mexico, on the other hand (including former Mexican territories), has been home to a multiplicity of Indigenous populations that are culturally and linguistically distinct. Yet we continue to make a choice that privileges one narrative and erases the complexity of our histories. Memory is not neutral, so our constructions of mythic memory places tend to reflect the same biases that we carry. Villanueva explains that "we need to think of subjectivity in terms of power—the powers we are subjects *of* and the powers we are subjected *to*" ("'I Am'" 485). Whitlinger similarly argues that "collective memory is structured and maintained by asymmetrical social relations" (650). We live in a sexist, racist, homophobic (to name a few) world, and these discourses make their way to the constructions of our shared memories. As Trimbur explains in the previous chapter, *Memoria* is at the center of "the battle over consciousness between the oppressed and the oppressor" (p. 67). As participants in our collective memory, it is our responsibility to analyze how our choices to remember and forget certain aspects of our past affect our present and shape our future.

I think back to my trip to Templo Mayor. I think back to how the memory place was inscribed by such a limited history: Spaniard meets Aztec, Spaniard conquers Aztec, Mexicans are born. And I wonder how different that is from the Chicanx collective memory we have crafted for ourselves. But then I think about our collective condition, the way that our histories have been erased. I think about what a struggle it is for me to locate positive memories of Mexicans, Chicanx, or Latinx in the United States. Tragedies and losses are all that come to mind: lost battles, lost lands, a plane crash carrying thirty Mexican workers, Mexican women sterilized against their will. When our access to celebratory memories is so limited, we are left with limited choices. So we pull from Mexican history—the events, the people, the documents—and we take with us some of that nationalist dominant ideology that tries to hide the racism and sexism.

Although we struggle with the contradictions, the contradictions can be a place of rhetorical potential. What might it look like for us to recognize "two sets of memories—and more—memories that are me and memories that are us, even different 'usses'" (Villanueva, "'I Am'" 491–92)? This is what I imagine. I imagine recognizing that Spanish is both a dominant language and a marginalized language. I imagine celebrating the Mexica past while acknowledging that I do not fully understand that past and that it does not belong to me. I imagine acknowledging how racism has affected me and my family while opening my eyes to how my communities and I perpetuate racism within and outside. I imagine learning from others about the interesting memories I know nothing about while sharing the memories I do know. "*Memoria* is a friend of ours" (Villanueva, "*Memoria*" 19), but she is not an uncomplicated friend.

WORKS CITED

Aden, Roger C., et al. "Re-collection: A Proposal for Refining the Study of Collective Memory and Its Places." *Communication Theory*, vol. 19, no. 3, 2009, pp. 311–36.

Bodnar, John. *Remaking America: Public Memory, Commemoration, and Patriotism in the Twentieth Century*. Princeton UP, 1992.

Calafell, Bernadette. "Disrupting the Dichotomy: 'Yo Soy Chicana/o?' in the New Latina/o South." *Communication Review*, vol. 7, no. 2, 2004, pp. 175–204.

———. "Pro(re-)claiming Loss: A Performance Pilgrimage in Search of Malintzin Tenépal." *Text and Performance Quarterly*, vol. 25, no. 1, 2005, pp. 43–56.

Dickinson, Greg, et al., editors. *Places of Public Memory: The Rhetoric of Museums and Memorials*. U of Alabama P, 2010.

Domingues, José Maurício. "Collective Subjectivity and Collective Causality." *Philosophica*, vol. 71, no. 1, 2003, pp. 39–58.

Gaspar de Alba, Alicia. *[Un]framing the 'Bad Woman': Sor Juana, Malinche, Coyolxauhqui, and Other Rebels with a Cause*. U of Texas P, 2014.

Glancey, Jonathan. "The Templo Mayor: A Place for Human Sacrifices." *BBC*, 27 Feb. 2015, https://www.bbc.com/culture/article/20150227-a-place-for-human-sacrifices.

Holland, Dorothy, et al. "Social Movements and Collective Identity: A Decentered, Dialogic View." *Anthropological Quarterly*, vol. 81, no. 1, 2008, pp. 95–126.

Motolinía, Toribio. *History of the Indians of New Spain*. Translated and edited by Elizabeth Andros Foster, Greenwood Press, 1973.

Mundy, Barbara E. *The Death of Aztec Tenochtitlan, the Life of Mexico City*. U of Texas P, 2015.

Pérez, Emma. *The Decolonial Imaginary: Writing Chicanas into History*. Indiana UP, 1999.

Villanueva, Victor, Jr. (2017). "'I Am Two Parts': Collective Subjectivity and the Leader of Academics and the Othered. *College English*, vol. 79, no. 5, 2017, pp. 482–94.

———. "Maybe a Colony: And Still Another Critique of the Comp Community." *JAC*, vol. 17, no. 2, 1997, pp. 183–90.

———. "*Memoria* Is a Friend of Ours: On the Discourses of Color." *College English,* vol. 67, no. 1, 2004, pp. 9–19.

———. "Rhetoric of the First 'Indians': The Taínos of the Second Voyage of Columbus." *Rhetorics of the Americas: 3114 BCE to 2012 CE,* edited by Damián Baca and Victor Villanueva, Palgrave Macmillan, 2010, pp. 15–19.

Vivian, Bradford. "*Ars Memoriae,* Collective Memory, and the Fortunes of Rhetoric." *Rhetoric Society Quarterly,* vol. 48, no. 3, 2018, pp. 287–96.

Whitlinger, Claire. "From Countermemory to Collective Memory: Acknowledging the 'Mississippi Burning' Murders." *Sociological Forum,* vol. 30, no. 1, 2015, pp. 648–70.

Zelizer, Barbie. "Reading the Past against the Grain: The Shape of Memory Studies." *Critical Studies in Mass Communication,* vol. 12, no. 2, 1995, pp. 214–39.

Chapter 5

"Home Is a Funny Thing": Critical Race Theory Home and Abroad

Catherine Prendergast

FEW PEOPLE USE THE WORD *funny* as much as Victor Villanueva and use it to mean so many different things. If you know Victor personally, you know that he is funny in the most conventional sense. At conferences you can hear his full belly laugh long before you see him; when you follow the sound to the man himself, you're greeted by a wide grin.

But "humorous" is not always what Victor means when he uses the word *funny* in his writing. In a recent reflection on racism in the United States, he observed, "home is a funny thing" (Bailie et al. 198). For people of color in the United States, he points out, the notion of home is always determined by centuries of colonialism and control. Other contributors in this collection, including Miriam L. Fernandez, Christa J. Olson, and Romeo García in this section, also address this intertwined legacy of racism and colonialism. Victor's estrangement from Puerto Rico, the pressure in the 1950s to assimilate as linguistically white, and the ongoing nightmare that is colonialism all make the notion of "home" a vexed one. So, when he says, "home is a funny thing," he means not a humorous thing. In fact, the meaning of *funny* in this context is closest to "nearly intolerable."

Yet Villanueva owns this complex picture of his identity. "I'm okay about being an American. I'm never not okay with it, really.

I just wish that racism wouldn't be so damned entrenched in this society" (Bailie et al. 199).

That racism is so damned entrenched in America has been amply demonstrated during Victor's long career countering it. In his 1993 seminal work, *Bootstraps: From an American Academic of Color*, Victor identified the structural, engrained nature of racism long before the recent 1619 Project drew attention to the mainstream media's attention to it. Nicole Hannah-Jones, one of the authors of the 1619 Project, has just been denied tenure at the University of North Carolina at Chapel Hill—a high-profile incident of backlash against scholars doing the recovery project of making the history of people of color in America visible.

So, once again, critical race theory (CRT) has emerged as the target of white rage. I say "again," because Derrick Bell, one of CRT's founders, wrote an article titled "Who's Afraid of Critical Race Theory" in 1995, a full generation ago. What had been in the 1990s a more coded culture war against multiculturalism has in the post-Trump years blossomed into a full-throated white panic. Fox News is blaring the dangers of CRT on all their shows. Legislation banning the teaching of CRT in schools has advanced in multiple states, despite few knowing what critical race theory is (Asmelash; Metz). We are witnessing a chilling assault on any attempt to discuss—never mind repair—the harms of whites upon people of color in America. Yes, racism is damned entrenched.

As a white woman, I do not feel that I can fully participate in the project of *Memoria* that guides this volume. I am here because my early work, based on CRT, was cited and cheered by Victor (Prendergast, *Literacy* and "Race"). I had been drawn to CRT during my graduate education in theories of literacy. Critical race theory filled in for me the gaps in my coursework, which at the time was focused on binaries: orality versus literacy and social versus cognitive. Rather than stark binaries, CRT introduced me to contradictions. It explained the deepest contradiction of the United States: its foundation on the principle that all men are created equal, and its crystal clear record of failing to live up to that principle in its actions. CRT didn't strike me as theory at all but rather a rigorously empirical project. In very long, footnote-laden law review articles, critical race theorists examined every word of key civil rights court cases and their impact. They combed over property values to demonstrate the influence of redlining. They counted how many white students actually moved into formerly Black schools. And based on this evidence, CRT rejected the prevailing definition of *racism* as individual intentional aberrant acts of harm and concluded that racism was normal in America: the feature, not the bug.

I found Derrick Bell's notion of "interest convergence" most compelling to explain movements in literacy history. Bell argued that historically whites conceded rights to Black citizens only when it was in their own interest. *Brown v. Board of Education* happened, Bell maintained, not because whites suddenly woke up to the inhumanity of segregated schools, but because America needed to appear more equitable to fight Soviet expansion in nonwhite nations during the Cold War (Bell, "*Brown*"). The idea of interest convergence—that whites act out of self-interest rather than virtue or sympathy—flies in the face of the popular, almost sacrosanct narrative of racial reconciliation: that sufficient sacrifice on the part of Blacks will finally spur whites to dismantle structures of inequality. It's nearly apostasy to say no amount of Black sacrifice will compel whites to do that. But it's historically accurate.

So, if critical race theory is a theory, it is only so in the sense that the theory of evolution is theory. That is, its conclusions are based on overwhelming—and mounting—evidence with no evidentiary-based counterexplanation.

My second book was not about America. It was an ethnographic study of English language learners in Slovakia (Prendergast, *Buying*). It told the story of how an Eastern European country, fresh out of Soviet occupation and socialism, embarked on a massive project to learn English with the goal of assimilating into capitalism and the world economy. I will own now, this book was designed to get me out of the cornfields of the Midwest for a semester and take me back to a place that to me felt quixotically more to me like "home": Bratislava, Slovakia.

It's still impossible to escape the "damned entrenched" nature of American racism, even when you leave the country. I remember in 1992, when I first taught English in Bratislava with my graduate school friend Rebecca, hearing my high school–age students talk about what Black Americans were like. I would then give them a lesson in history and stereotypes and ask them how many Black people they had ever met (which I knew to be zero, because in most cases, we were the first Americans our students had ever met). Their stereotypes were a combination of homegrown xenophobia and Western media. We soon learned that there were tensions between ethnic Hungarians and ethnic Slovaks in our classrooms that were complicating our attempts at "get to know you" group activities. As it turns out, socialism is a lot like American democracy: despite all the stated commitments to equality, it seems racism and ethnicism keep humming along.

Otherwise, the differences between America and Slovakia circa 1992 were stark. In Slovakia, there was no Diet Coke. There were no plastic bottles of any kind. Pizza was made with ketchup and edam cheese. When we pointed out that this was disgusting and not pizza, our friends would call us "Rozmaznaní Američania": "Spoiled Americans."

I rolled with it. It was true.

Yet more than any one thing you "couldn't get" like jeans or orange juice, the weirdly "public" focused socialist system had made a hellscape of the public sphere. I don't remember anyone smiling on the streets back then. Nobody talked in public on the trams or trains. Or even talked. It's hard to explain this pervasive affect (and I do mean *affect*, not *effect*) of late Soviet-occupied states to people who haven't experienced it. Remember that languishing feeling we all had during the pandemic? When we were loath to leave our homes and, when we did, were on our guard wondering who could be trusted to act responsibly? When we worried a casual interaction might kill us? Now imagine that going on for decades. That's what Slovaks had to do. In 1992, Rebecca and I had to do it only for a summer. Sitting in the "dietetic canteen" where we used to eat pork and cabbage at a table with sullen construction workers,

I forced my usually garrulous self to be as quiet as everyone else in the room. I never felt more American in my life.

In 1994, I taught English in Bratislava again. We returned because we missed the friends we had made there in 1992, but most of all we missed the people we had come to call "our family": four generations of women living under one roof. Our landlady (generation 3) had taken us in as boarders because as a single parent she needed the extra income to raise her children: a 5-year-old daughter (Lenka—generation 4) and her baby brother. I often marvel how my life would have been different if we had stayed in another home, with unsympathetic or distant people. I wonder at the chemistry that strengthened our bonds in 1992, and again in 1994, and again in 2003 while I was doing research for my book. All this led to an email I got in 2007 from Lenka, who was then college age. She asked, would I want an au pair for my son? And so, for the summer of 2008, she lived with my family. This brings us to the near present. In 2019, I woke up to a Facebook message from Lenka, who was then in her thirties. She was getting married in November, she told me. Rebecca and I bought tickets immediately.

Little did I know that this trip would take me down a rabbit hole of busted binaries. I was about to experience the collapse of East and West, past and present, home and abroad, and with it, the damned entrenched nature of racism.

The day before the wedding, Lenka's brother picked us up at the bus station in Bratislava and took us to the family compound (it is cheaper in Slovakia to build on to the main house to accommodate relatives rather than to buy new properties). We were given the apartment previously occupied by a recently deceased relative. Our fridge had already been stocked with all the Slovak foods and drinks they knew we missed in America.

Because we are family, we are put to work immediately. We're not even one hour in the house before we are helping the bride's mother prepare the *chlebíčky*—tiny open-faced sandwiches with their artful collages of ham, cheese, and gherkins—for the celebration the next day. So far so good.

But nobody had warned us that a proper Slovak wedding starts in the afternoon of one day and ends the morning of the next. It kicks off with close relatives and friends visiting the bride's family. We sit as an accordionist plays polkas and sings folk songs while Lenka, beautiful in her dress, dances and greets everyone. When there is no longer a square inch to move around in, the party moves out to the garden where there is more singing and the arrival of friends begins. The groom's sister is tasked with pouring out shots of *slivovica*. She carries a wooden board holding six shot glasses that are used again and again by each party member (are you seeing how prepandemic this all is?). Another woman follows with boxes of small cakes. The bride and groom sing along with the accordionist while facing each other, and the guests hoist their cakes or shot glasses to toast the couple.

Then it's time for the traditional wedding skit designed to lovingly humiliate the groom. I ask Babka (grandmother, generation 2) what is going to happen, but she's not sure, because the groom is from a different part of the country and every region has its own version of this tradition. This skit involves the groom's friends coming by and telling him that they can build him a house for his new bride, but first he must buy the wood. Then he must buy a saw. Then he and his bride are obliged to cut the wood in half with a flimsy saw that is impossible to control. Imagine wearing a full bridal gown, trying to saw a piece of wood to the hilarity of your friends and relatives. They tried and of course failed. Finally, the groom is forced to pay his friends to saw the log in half for him (he has to first pay for a real saw, of course), and the skit is over. Pulling money out of the groom is a frequent theme of these skits. (This one is preferable to what my older friends in Slovakia experienced, when two women of the wedding party dressed up as peasants and would arrive at the reception holding a baby, accusing the groom of having previous obligations he had failed to provide for.)

We board the coach bus the family leased to go to the "Coronation Church" downtown, so named because members of the Austro-Hungarian royalty were crowned here when the Ottoman Empire got too close to Vienna. The church ceremony is very meaningful for the family, many of whom were denied one under socialism. After the ceremony and photos (and more cake), we board the bus again, bound for a banquet hall in the woods out of town. The guests sing and drink the whole way. When we arrive, we are not allowed to cross the threshold of the hall before the couple. The proprietor gives Lenka and her husband a plate to smash on the ground. The number of pieces it crashes into is said to equal the number of children they will have. It breaks into an alarming number of pieces. The couple are then given a broom and dustpan to sweep it up. That task completed, Lenka is carried by her husband over the threshold, and we are allowed to enter.

At the formal dinner (at which the couple must consume food using only one place setting and a joint bib), I get to socialize with many of Lenka's extended family and friends. I have previously seen some of them only on Facebook. Her best friend is now working in Spain. Her cousin's husband tells me he has to leave the festivities early because he has a meeting in Dubai the next morning. Lenka's brother, whom we have known since he was in a pram, is now a software developer in a modern building in downtown Bratislava. He's with his girlfriend, who works for an NGO helping corporations to support sustainability initiatives. They met in the Netherlands when he was studying abroad for a master's degree.

All these people are the children of parents who were not allowed to leave their country. That they can pursue high-paying and fulfilling careers is good news. But if you know someone who has lost a corporate job in America in the last ten years, it's quite possible it was outsourced to one of the people at this wedding.

The dance floor floods after dinner. There are coed dances, men-only dances, and women-only dances. This part reminds me of American Jewish weddings I've been to, and no surprise, as we are just west of the Pale of Settlement, that most western region of the Russian Empire, a region where Jews were forced to live during the reign of Catherine the Great. Around midnight, the dance floor clears for the arrival of professional dancers in folk costume. Lenka was part of this folk-dance troupe, so joins in a dance about matrimony that they've been hired to do at other weddings. This time she gets to play the bride. In the dance, she is given the choice: surrender her "maidenhead"—the garland of flowers on her head—or allow one of the men to cut her entire head off with an ax.

She chooses to lose the garland, which is to be replaced with a modest bonnet like the ones her mother and mother-in-law are wearing. The two older women fasten the bonnet on Lenka's head. Figurative maidenhead dispensed with, the men of the troupe teach the groom how to dance.

At 1 a.m., a buffet feast is rolled out to fuel the guests through the night. The rest of the evening differs little from American weddings—drinking and disco dancing—save that it goes on until 6 a.m. Rebecca and I make it until 3 a.m., and since my pidgin Slovak is at this point slurred, Lenka's brother tells the bus driver how to take us home.

We wake the next morning on the thirtieth anniversary of the Velvet Revolution, the day Czechoslovakia officially expelled its Russian occupiers and began its transition from socialism to capitalism. Everyone is nursing hangovers. We take a group portrait of the family sitting in chairs and reclining on the couch, raising peace signs in the air. "Slovaks celebrating the anniversary of the revolution," they all joke.

But Rebecca and I can't wait to see how the Old Town, the area of the city just down the hill from our family's house, has changed. We walk past the parliament building and the old fortress that is now the presidential palace. Heading farther down centuries-old stone steps that skirt the steep hillside, we arrive next to the Danube and at an unusual sight: a memorial for the synagogue that was destroyed on that spot during Soviet occupation. An exhibit tells the story of the Jewish quarter, which has now all but vanished. Contrary to the myth that the Soviets eased existing tribal animosities, in fact they exacerbated them, in this case by deliberately flattening the synagogue and much of the Jewish quarter to build a modern bridge across the Danube. The Coronation Church was spared—barely. The elevated off-ramp runs within feet of it, and the vibrations from the road threaten its stability.

Rebecca and I walk from the church to the grocery store, outside of which in 1992 we would line up to wait for a basket; the matron at the door would stare us down lest we attempt to enter the store without her handing us said basket, as it was her assigned life's job to do that. The store is now a high-end café where we are greeted in English and seated at a free table near stylish women with small dogs on their laps and teenagers giggling over their coffees. It's the thirtieth anniversary of the Velvet Revolution, and people are being blissfully bourgeois, drinking coffee and chatting with one another like it's just another day.

Frankly, given what I've seen of the place over the years, that's fabulous.

When we get to the edge of Old Town and arrive at SNP Square (Náměstí Slovenského Národního Povstání, named to honor the Slovaks who risked their lives in World War II to overthrow their Nazi occupiers), we see another memorial. This one is dedicated to Ján Kuciak, the 27-year-old journalist who, with his girlfriend, was murdered in 2018 by hit men hired, it is still suspected, by government agents who wanted to thwart his investigation of political corruption. As a reaction to his murder, in 2019 Slovakia elected anti-corruption prosecutor Zuzana Čaputová as president. Yes, Slovakia, a country for not even one hundred years, elected a woman as president before the United States of America did. The memorial for Ján consists of a photo of him and his girlfriend in a frame on the ground, surrounded by hundreds of votive candles, presumably left there by people who have come to pay their respects.

We decide to head across the square to check out Stará Tržnica—the Old Market. In 1992 we used to shop here for onions and walnuts, sold by old women and men who had lugged their wares to town in the hopes of earning more than they would in their village. By 2003 the market had broadened into sandwich shops and SIM card vendors. But we didn't know what to expect from the market of 2019.

We see a crowd of people by the entrance. In our memory, the market closed early, so this itself surprises us. There's a sign outside advertising an event hosted by the Central European Forum. The name of the event is "Verejnosť proti Strachu," or "The Public against Fear." This phrase is an allusion to the organizing call from the Velvet Revolution against Russian occupation in 1989: "Verejnosť proti Násiliu" or "The Public against Violence."

We walk inside. The hall is wide open, with no stalls and no food at all. Near the entrance are displays of photos from the Velvet Revolution of 1989. At the front, a Black woman is on a stage speaking in English to the crowd. It is Nigerian author and MacArthur "genius" fellow Chimamanda Ngozi Adichie. Adichie was recently lambasted in the US for being a "TERF," or "trans-exclusionary radical feminist," but here she is well received. She warned the audience not to fall too in love with their newly elected woman president lest the backlash become severe the moment she, inevitably human, makes a mistake.

As Adichie talks, my eyes scan the audience. I spot *New Yorker* columnist Masha Gessen toward the side of the venue. I've been somewhat obsessed with Gessen since reading her magisterial *The Future Is History: How Totalitarianism Reclaimed Russia.* Published in 2017, it charts Putin's rise, and helped guide me through what to expect in the Trump years. Gessen is wearing all black and holds her jacket slung casually over one shoulder.

Here is where the rabbit hole fully opened up for me. Russian lesbian thinker–icon, uber-intellectual Masha Gessen is about to speak to us in the market where we used to buy walnuts from old ladies. I feel as though a rip in the fabric of time and space has just opened up. I lean over to Rebecca, who is studying the photographs, and say, "We're staying."

Gessen takes the stage as part of a panel. The other speakers include American David Graeber, one of the instigators of Occupy Wall Street whose most recent book, *Bullshit Jobs,* rails against the new feudalism of the modern workplace. Graeber is said to have coined the phrase "We are the 99%." The third speaker is Bulgarian political scientist Ivan Krastev.

The panelists begin by talking about the current corruption in so many governments all over the world. Gessen notes that corruption is not always illegal. She argues that it is corrupt yet legal in America to have the "entire political system constituted on the basis of financial contributions—the entire political system." She offers that the primary system elevates candidates in each party who have raised the most money. "The most bribes," Graeber adds.

Well, the Slovak moderator says, then how did the Western system go wrong? "Mm, capitalism?" Gessen offers. The crowd applauds. We are definitely not in 1989 anymore.

Ivan Krastev has a different view of the transition from socialism to capitalism. "In 1989 the hopes were highest everywhere." He argues that the things that went wrong were also things that went right. Allowing people to cross borders, to leave the Soviet boundaries for the first time, was good. Of course, it led to outsourcing and anti-immigrant backlash. But he worries that by just saying it all went wrong, we play into "apocalyptic discourse in which basically nothing can be done."

Gessen counters that for gays and lesbians, 1989 wasn't all that hopeful. "Everyone was dying of AIDS, and LGBT people had no rights outside of Scandinavia." Autocrats today, however, want to turn the clock back on rights for homosexuals as a populist gesture aimed at those who feel that everything was better in the past. When Putin suggests that there were no queers in Russia during Soviet times, that they were all imported for the West, he is selling an imaginary of the past—a unified, homogenous Soviet past.

Krastev agrees that populists today instill anxiety in those who feel in some nebulous way that they don't like the way the world is going, even if their own life is materially better (as in Eastern Europe in most cases it is). "And this is different from fear," he argues. "Fear is when you exactly know what you fear." Fearful people are quiet, but anxious people are loud. "Anxiety is producing so much noise and hatred"—the hate speech of the internet, Krastev argues. Gessen agrees that anxiety makes someone a minimally functioning member of society—someone who goes to work, comes home, gets drunk, but never causes any trouble. She says that Russian TV, where people are screaming at each other constantly, amounts to "state manufacture of anxiety on a daily basis."

Graeber is arguing that Fox News in America is no different in that regard, but his microphone has started squeaking, so he is distracted by wrestling with the batteries. Meanwhile, Gessen discusses the inefficacy of the Democrats to counter autocratic populism because they offer themselves only as "technocrats"—

mere government functionaries without any clear moral vision.

Graeber, microphone fixed, agrees. "If you look at what happened with Obama and Trump, Obama ran as a visionary. I mean 'hope,' 'change,' all those dreamy looking posters. . . . He ran as a guy who would have a vision, but it never occurred to people to ask what that vision was, which turned out to be nothing. Personal power. So he ruled as a technocrat. People were so angry and felt so betrayed and frustrated that they took this utter nihilistic reaction to that" (Imaginácia).

Some people applauded. I booed. People looked at me. I looked at them right back. In that moment, I had gone from being starstruck by this event to being deeply disturbed by it. I was ratcheting myself back up the rabbit hole at a furious pace.

It occurred to me that not once in this whole conversation about the world's problems had the word *race* been mentioned. *Hate*: check. *Immigration*: check. *LGBT*: check. But *race*, never. There was no recognition that white supremacy was on the rise. And there was certainly no recognition that the election of a Black president in a country that had since even before its founding thought hard about how to keep Blacks subjugated might have had something to do with Obama's being replaced as president by the man who called for him to show his birth certificate.

Beyond what was said on stage, the entire event began to irk me. It had a strange air of ironic detachment. It presented itself as an art piece, carefully curated for our entertainment, from the Black fashions worn by the speakers to the blown-up black-and-white photo of police descending on a protester as the stage backdrop. And we in the audience were doing our part to participate in the detachment. In 2019 Bratislava, we could safely absorb the congenial atmosphere as we contemplated the world burning, peruse old photos of people standing in front of tanks, appreciate this cosmopolitan display of ideas by globe-trotting intelligentsia, and buy something at the merch table as we exited.

A couple of days later, I was back in the United States. Over the next six months, I watched my home become, as Villanueva would call it, a "funny" thing. America spiraled into an uncontrollable pandemic, made worse by Trump's actions and inactions. Suddenly, Americans were for the first time in generations faced with shortages, quarantine orders, and restrictions on travel; all those things that have long been happening "somewhere else" were now happening at home. During this time, David Graeber died tragically at the age of fifty-nine in a Venice hospital of necrotizing pancreatitis, perhaps COVID related, perhaps not.

Professors became a target of the right wing. I was put on right-wing Turning Point USA's Professor Watchlist of left-leaning professors, surprisingly for my book about Slovakia, not for my book about race. "In the book titled, *Buying into English: Language and Investment in the New Capitalist World,* Prendergast states that English is the first language of capitalism" (Professor Watchlist). They also cited my tweet, "Do you realize the entire reason we don't have socialism is because of racism."

Two of my most beloved Slovak friends, the ones who first dubbed us "Rozmaznaní Američania," began spouting the Kremlin versions of QAnon conspiracy theories and sang to me their praises of Trump. When I complained that Trump was putting immigrant children in concentration camps, they asked me, what's wrong with that?

That was the moment a friendship of twenty-five years died.

Then the world watched the US erupt at the release of the video of George Floyd being murdered by grinning police officer Derek Chauvin. And the violence of police upon Black bodies continued as if nothing had happened.

White supremacy at this point threatens to break America in two again. Even as I write this, a policy think tank has released a statement of concern by one hundred scholars of democracy who warn that if we do not act to counter rampant voter suppression laws, our next election will be neither free nor fair. It will be a coup (New America). Voter suppression laws have emerged as a direct response to those Black voters who in 2020 successfully deprived Trump of a second term.

This is the crucial point that Graeber and Gessen and too many commentators today have missed: People might influence elections with money, but they do it because of race. Racism is globally created, circulated, marketed, and sustained. It is here, there, and everywhere.

Just as the critical race theorists had told us it would be, a generation ago.

WORKS CITED

Asmelash, Leah. "Florida Bans Teaching Critical Race Theory in Schools." *CNN*, 10 June 2021, www.cnn.com/2021/06/10/us/critical-race-theory-florida-ban-trnd/index.html?utm_term=link.

Bailie, Brian, et al. "Reflections on Racism and Immigration: An Interview with Victor Villanueva." *Reflections*, vol. 8 no. 2, 2009, pp. 197–208.

Bell, Derrick A., Jr. "*Brown v. Board of Education* and the Interest-Convergence Dilemma," *Harvard Law Review*, vol. 93, no. 3, 1980, pp 524–25.

———. "Who's Afraid of Critical Race Theory." *University of Illinois Law Review*, vol. 4, 1995, pp. 893–971.

Gessen, Masha. *The Future Is History: How Totalitarianism Reclaimed Russia.* Riverhead Books, 2017.

Graeber, David. *Bullshit Jobs: A Theory.* Simon & Schuster, 2019.

Imaginácia proti strachu. Conference, Central European Forum, 17 Nov. 2019, Bratislava, SK. *YouTube*, https://www.youtube.com/watch?v=V_MNb09uv7M&t=25s. Accessed 10 June 10 2021.

Metz, Sam. "Nevada Schools Reckon with Race, Triggering Polarization." *Associated Press*, 11 June 2021, https://apnews.com/article/government-and-politics-nv-state-wire-nevada-race-and-ethnicity-racial-injustice-6185b8f9c5b56e1fa1347b7f4a203a52. Accessed 10 June 2021.

New America. "Statement of Concern: The Threats to American Democracy and the Need for National Voting and Election Administration Standards." *New America*. 1 June 2021, https://www.newamerica.org/political-reform/statements/statement-of-concern/. Accessed 10 June 2021.

Prendergast, Catherine. *Buying into English: Language and Investment in the New Capitalist World.* U of Pittsburgh P, 2008.

——— (@cjp_still). "Do you realize the entire reason we don't have socialism is because of racism. OK done." *Twitter*, 12 Aug. 2020, https://twitter.com/cjp_still/status/1293601731415343116.

———. *Literacy and Racial Justice: The Politics of Learning after* Brown v. Board of Education. Southern Illinois UP, 2003.

———. "Race: The Absent Presence in Composition Studies." *College Composition and Communication*, vol. 50, no 1, 1998, pp. 36–53.

Professor Watchlist. "Catherine Prendergast." *Turning Point USA*, https://professorwatchlist.org/professor/catherineprendergast. Accessed 19 June 2021.

Villanueva, Victor. *Bootstraps: From an American Academic of Color.* National Council of Teachers of English, 1993.

Chapter 6

Anticolonial Critique, Decolonial Directions, and Making Space for Américan Rhetorics

Christa J. Olson

"We cannot seriously study the history of rhetoric and communication in the United States while bracketing out the impact of Latina/os and Latin America on this history," wrote René De los Santos in 2012. "This conclusion," he continued, "is not new" ("La Ola Latina" 321). Even though scholars in Latinx studies, Latin American studies, and American studies had been situating the United States in a larger hemispheric context for decades (and Latinxs and Latin Americans had been doing so for far longer), in 2012 such thinking was actually alarmingly "new" for many scholars in composition and rhetoric. Latinx ways with words began to find purchase in the field in the late 1990s and early 2000s as scholars pondered postcolonial rhetorics, multi- and translingual writing, and the broader intersections of language, literacy, race, and power. Racist frameworks, habitual whiteness, and racialized understandings of English often tried to relegate Latinx scholars and ways with words to the margins. They, undaunted, made those margins and borders the center.

Even with those shifts and recenterings, Latin America—with its vast landmass, long history, and powerful present—was still barely on the horizon for composition and rhetoric in the early 2000s. When, in 2005, I expressed interest in learning from Latin American rhetorical histories, I was met with interest but also confusion. How would I do such a thing? Who would guide me? As a graduate student and then early career professor, I spent a lot of energy explaining how a scholar of Latin American visual rhetoric could belong in writing studies and an English department. I spent a lot of time figuring out who I could learn from. As a white woman with US citizenship, I also got the benefit of the doubt; I brought an "exotic" field of study into the room without changing the room's predominant color or otherwise upsetting the established order of things. Still, even as white privilege cleared my pathways, the larger discipline's take was clear: Latin America was niche, and even if Latin American rhetorical histories were interesting, they had very little to do with (US) American rhetorical history.

But scholarly frames were starting to shift in that moment, and I had the opportunity to be among the first scholars whose work positioned Latin American rhetorical history as crucial, not ancillary, to rhetorical studies in the United States. It is ironic but not at all coincidental that many of the first US-based scholars to make our names via Latin American rhetorics are white. Implicit and explicit habits of white supremacy made it easier for white-presenting scholars like me (who hold unquestioned access to US citizenship and wield recognizable disciplinary credentials) to make the case for an "other" America. Colleagues of color who had already been making similar arguments about Latin American rhetorics in conference panels, in manuscripts, and on the job market often met more outright resistance and dismissal. That fact means that it would be very easy to tell a whitewashed story of the emergence of scholarly attention to Latin American rhetorical history from within the United States. For this reason, it feels essential to me to not just avoid whitewashing the scholarly conversation but to firmly root the memory of this scholarly story in the work of Américan academics of color.

Though it is necessary to acknowledge whiteness and access to disciplinary citizenship as powerful factors in how scholarly conversations develop, my purpose in this chapter is to decenter those factors and instead foreground another disciplinary story and set of memories. That story about how América Latina matters to US rhetorical studies begins well before the 2010s. Those memories follow routes "of color." And one good way to follow those roots and routes is to look at the scholarly and mentoring career of Victor Villanueva. Villanueva did not set out to be the ur-figure for Latin American rhetorics in the United States, and he will likely demur, even now, from this characterization. But starting from Villanueva makes sense. Now, I understand: for a long time, Villanueva had other disciplinary and intellectual work to do and wasn't actually focused on Latin America. However, over the decades and even when he was focused on other things, Villanueva's work included nurturing both rhetorical conversations and human rhetoricians who found themselves at the confluence of American, Latinx, Indigenous, and Latin American studies. And so, in many ways, US-based study of Latin American rhetoric—including my own—owes its nature to Villanueva's efforts and commitments. He directed us toward an "Américan" rhetoric that could, as De los Santos says, "re-imagine rhetoric and rhetorical studies in the United States as part of a larger hemispheric history of communicative practices and interactions" and position rhetoric in the United States as "part of a larger *American* hemispheric endeavor" (De los Santos, "La Ola Latina" 322).

Victor Villanueva wasn't single-handedly responsible for the emergence of that Américan orientation within rhetorical studies, but there can be no doubt that he played a crucial role, contributing material, building connections, and fostering opportunities. His publications, from "Maybe a Colony" to "Colonial Memory and the Crime of Rhetoric" to *Rhetorics of the Americas*, and beyond, set the tone for work on Américan rhetorics. His mentorship and manuscript reviewing likewise made the road we Américan rhetoricians walk on. Writing this chapter, I went back to look at a review of one of my manuscripts that I now know came from him. Reading that review, I was struck by how his words enabled, challenged, and guided me in ways that continue to resonate in my scholarly approach. He commented about when and how to use Spanish. He asked hard questions, pointing out failed moves and short-circuited arguments, but those pointed inquiries were infused with palpable warmth. He noticed small details about history and culture and pointed toward their larger implications. Throughout, he expressed hope for the work and what it could be. I know that I am not the only scholar writing about América who benefited from such guidance, anonymous or not. The pages of this collection are filled with testimony to that effect, particularly from those (like Miriam L. Fernandez, Laura Gray-Rosendale, Victoria Houser, and others) who had the privilege of being Villanueva's students.

Along with that general recognition of Villanueva's critical generosity and leadership, my purpose in this chapter is to highlight three specific orientations that he provided for the study of Américan rhetorical history. These orientations, I argue, have made the subfield what it is and point us toward work yet to do. They are fundamental and expansive: (1) Villanueva ensured that rhetorical scholars looking toward Latin America went through, not around, the realities of colonial violence; (2) his model required subsequent scholars to linger in—not skirt—racialization; and (3) he built frameworks that connected Latinx and Latin American rhetorics without collapsing them, implicating all of us residing in the hemisphere within Américan complexities. In the remaining words of this chapter, I expand on those foundations. I also show how they might ground new projects and facilitate further engagement.

"ON THE DISCOURSE OF COLOR": REMEMBERING RACE

There was a stretch of time in the 1990s when nearly every special issue about race and composition or race and rhetoric on the English side of rhetorical studies included a contribution from Victor Villanueva. His persistent presence not only speaks to his scholarly standing—Villanueva's has long been a pivotal voice—but also to the phenomenal whiteness of the field at that time: he was too often asked to shoulder Latinx representation on his own. That persistent presence ought to also remind us of how foundational Villanueva's thinking about race has been for subsequent scholarship in the field. And, more specifically, because Villanueva was publishing about Latinx, Latin American, and Caribbean contexts in composition and rhetoric spaces before there was a recognizable turn toward

Latin American rhetorics, his thinking about race and racialization also became the bedrock for Américan rhetoric.

Given how thoroughly racialized Latinxs and Latin America are in the US imagination, it might seem impossible that Américan rhetoric could have avoided race. But it could have, especially given the privileging of white scholars such as myself and the early attention to Spanish colonial religious rhetorics. The subfield that emerged could have been framed more hermetically as "Latin American rhetoric." That counterfactual subfield could have positioned itself as disconnected from US rhetorics and as having little relation to Latinx pasts, presents, and futures. Doing so, the subfield might also have cut itself off from the critical cultural studies orientations that predominated in Latinx studies at the time. The field could easily have grown primarily from the work of Don Abbott and, in the process, could have prioritized a timeline beginning with Spanish colonization and emphasizing dominant forums for political rhetoric and rhetorical education. In that more isolated subfield of "Latin American rhetorics," there might have been pressure to start from "the basics" and emphasize the rhetorical practices of those with the greatest power: to tell stories of nation formation, political authority, and "good men speaking well" in the various Latin American countries. But instead, Américan rhetoric became the primary nexus for conversation, and therefore many scholars publishing in the subfield have started from frameworks of racialization and resistance. Victor Villanueva's influence was pivotal to that disciplinary orientation.

As I discuss further in the next section, it matters that Puerto Rico was one of Villanueva's—and therefore the field's—primary entry points into a wider América. "Colonial Memory and the Crime of Rhetoric" is—I believe—Villanueva's first publication taking an Américan orientation alongside a Latinx one. But well before Villanueva was writing explicitly about the rhetorical histories of Puerto Rico—the island—and treating it as a site of racialized Américan rhetorics, he was working in that frame. Starting from Puerto Rico's simultaneously US, Latinx, Caribbean, and Latin American condition and its complexly racialized history helped prioritize attention to what Villanueva termed racial *Memoria*—those threads of shared experience, story, and resistance that keep viscerally present worlds and words that might otherwise be effaced by domination, assimilation, and whitewashing (Villanueva, "*Memoria*").

"Of course the Puerto Rican is colored," Villanueva writes in *Bootstraps*, "what with *el morro*, and the West African, and Columbus's Indians; what with my grandmother, Mama Pina, looking like the stereotypical American Indian; what with my brown-skinned, curly haired sister, and my brown daughter, and my Spanish surname. Octorican" (xii–xiii). Puerto Rico and the Puerto Rican diaspora, Villanueva repeatedly reminds us, are always racialized in white dominant US imagination. Yet Puerto Rico is also perplexing for white, mainland US audiences that aren't ever sure which box to check to locate light-skinned Puerto Ricans within their racialized hierarchies, just as those white, mainland US audiences are perpetually "confused" about Puerto Ricans' birthright US citizenship. "Language is also race in America. Spanish is color," and Spanish is foreign-ness made racial (Villanueva, *Bootstraps* xii). From the beginning, then, Américan rhetoric as encountered through Villanueva had to be aware of its own racialized complexities and ambiguities, and it had to be cognizant that ethnicity, class, language, and location are racialized and racializing. The boundaries of Latin- [x, America, idad] are always drawn in racialized terms.

It is also worth noting, however, that the foundations Villanueva laid were incomplete, or at least incompletely taken up. For good reason, the racialized story of Américan rhetoric that Villanueva told centered on the racial ambiguity of Puerto Rican Latinidad (and in particular his own racialized position: white in *el barrio* and "ethnic" elsewhere, yet always "of color"). Scholarship in Américan rhetoric, in parallel, has most frequently equated Américan racialization with mestizaje. We work, primarily, in the framework of hispano-hablantes and the ongoing encounter between whiteness and Brownness. As José Cortez has recently argued, Blackness, in particular, has been systematically occluded from the purview of

Américan rhetorical studies. Now, Villanueva is not responsible for that occlusion. Indeed, careful readers of *Bootstraps* and his other work should have been cognizant of Puerto Rico's Blackness, as Villanueva himself is. The roots of Américan rhetoric's "mestizo-centric" tendencies reach deeper than any single scholar and are equally extensive in Latin American and Latinx studies (Soto Vega and Chávez). But in those first 1990s-era special issues when composition and rhetoric began to grapple with race more directly, we see the omission taking hold. Villanueva represented Latinidad for the field. Others—Royster, Smitherman, Gilyard—spoke to Blackness. A divide opened up, and scholars in Américan rhetoric and in composition and rhetoric more broadly are only beginning to bridge it. In this moment, Américan rhetorics must reconsider its orientations toward race and racialization, must take stock of its occlusions, and must recommit to the lesson Villanueva started us from: remembering race in all its complexities across all of América.

"THE CRIME OF RHETORIC": FOR ANTICOLONIAL COMMITMENT

Instead of starting from an imagined temporal beginning (in the late fifteenth or early sixteenth century), Américan rhetorical studies began from multiple spatial choques thanks, in large part, to Villanueva. That spatial rather than temporal orientation helps ensure that Américan rhetoric highlights coloniality as an ongoing process. The first scholars writing about Américan rhetorics beyond the Anglo-American frame wrote most often from within two critical "contact zones" (Pratt) where the United States and Latin America collide: Puerto Rico and the US–Mexico border. Villanueva's Américan work, as we know, centered on Puerto Rico, but he also played crucial roles in sponsoring Américan rhetorical scholarship located at the US–Mexico border (e.g., in his coeditorships of the *College English* special issue "Writing, Rhetoric, and Latinidad" and the collection *Rhetorics of the Americas* and also in his mentoring relationships, supporting the work of emerging scholars writing about the border). Both those places are sites of intense colonial violence and perpetually renewed anticolonial activity. Indigenous communities then and now stood in the face of settler greed and regularly foil[ed] it. Black and Brown people on the border and the island find their citizenship undermined, denied, and curtailed yet build political and communal power to confront and overcome oppression. Diasporas spreading across all of América, likewise, cultivate power and possibility in the face of displacement. The starting places of Américan rhetoric that Villanueva has nurtured, in other words, are places that require scholars of Américan rhetoric to grapple with colonialism as a constitutive and persistent Américan feature.

So, Puerto Rico's early place in the emergence of Américan rhetorical studies has had significant consequences. It helped ensure that critique of coloniality—in its many forms and ongoing realities—would be of central importance. And the particular colonial situations of Puerto Rico, likewise, gave shape to the field's understanding of Américan rhetorical coloniality. Coloniality, for Villanueva, is the ongoing heritage of the Americas. That heritage, as Villanueva tells it, begins in the Caribbean with the "First 'Indians,'" the Taíno, who bore the first assaults of European coloniality—guns, disease, religion, and greed. It continues—in Puerto Rico—in the bodies and experiences of the Taínos's descendents and the Black, mestizo, and criollo descendants of others who now live on what was once Taíno land. They, Villanueva argues, keep pieces of Taíno memory and language alive in Boricua ("Rhetoric" 15).

Colonialism, Villanueva demonstrates, defines the Américan experience of Puerto Rico in consistent yet always changing fashion. Almost everything known today about the Taíno is known through European filters. Even their history has been colonized because European ways with words could not fathom nonalphabetic ways with words, just as they could not fathom ways with civilization, religion, government, gender, or race other than their own ("Rhetoric" 19). Even to tell Taíno stories or use Taíno words requires grappling with colonial violence, Villanueva explains. And yet, he maintains, the Taíno endure in language and in bodies today.

Villanueva's discussions of more recent Américan rhetoric also keep colonization and resistance in the foreground. "This might be the postcolonial era," he notes, in his essay about Pedro Albizu Campos, "but here remains the colony" ("Colonial Memory" 631). Puerto Rico's clear yet ambivalent colonial position vis-à-vis the United States becomes illustrative of the twentieth- and twenty-first-century tangle of Américan rhetoric for Villanueva: "Puerto Rico is a free, autonomous, dependent, protected, neocolonial, colonial state with postcolonial identity problems" (633). To speak of Puerto Rico within América is to grapple with Spanish and US imperialism, with racial colonialism and colonial racism, with the choque of American borders where language is nationality and language is race and language is colonization (637).

Study of Américan rhetoric beyond Villanueva's own work has persistently maintained his attention to overlapping colonialisms. Inspired by Anzaldúa's new mestiza rhetoric, the first generations of Américan rhetorical scholarship drew connections between the ongoing survival of pre-Colombian cultures, the long-standing Latin American refusal to accept US dominance, and consistent resistance to white Anglo hegemony throughout the Americas (see, for example, Baca, "te-ixtli"). The most recent scholarship melds theories of coloniality drawn from Latin American studies and Indigenous studies to add even more complexity to the histories of colonialism and refusal that continue to shape América (see, for instance, Mignolo and Tuck and Yang). This most recent work points out that while critiques of colonialism and coloniality have been central to studies of Américan rhetoric, its starting places have frequently privileged mestizx stories and occluded Indigenous communities' ongoing resistance to colonialism. The spatial and temporal colonial choques defining much Américan rhetorical scholarship can sometimes imply that colonialism and coloniality then/there (in the colonial period/in Latin America) were about a collision between Indigenous peoples and Spanish conquistadors, while colonialism and coloniality now/here (in the last 150 years/in and around the borderlands and territories) are about the rapacious power of the United States and its racialized others. In the process, such scholarship tends to place Indigeneity in the past and center mestizxs as the primary descendants and recipients of colonialism ("And so we all became mestizo. . . . We all became mulato. We are mulato, mestizo, Taíno" [Villanueva, "Rhetoric" 18]). As we work toward ever more robust critiques of colonialism, Américan rhetoric needs to follow the lead of scholars like Gabriela Ríos and grapple with the overlapping colonialities and ongoing anticolonial practices of Indigenous peoples throughout América. Such a turn would require more invested conversations with colleagues working within Indigenous and Native rhetorics in the spaces now settled as the United States, with scholars of critical Latinx Indigeneities who highlight the multiple colonialities experienced by Indigenous migrants from Latin America, and with Indigenous scholars across the continent(s).

"MAYBE A COLONY": ON BEING IMPLICATED

Scholarship in Américan rhetoric is implicated in the stories of race and coloniality that we tell. Of the three orientations I'm sketching here, this last is the one US-based Américan rhetorics have, I think, been most reticent to engage, maybe because Villanueva has made it less explicit with regard to Latin America or maybe simply because it's the least comfortable for most of us. I know that I've struggled to pay it more than lip service in my own writing.

Villanueva is famous—as famous as composition and rhetoric scholars get—for his critiques of coloniality and for his insistence on the pervasive importance of race. He ought also to be famous for his persistent and, let's admit it, uncomfortable rumination on complicity. Villanueva's scholarship is rich with reflection on his own ambivalent, never-quite-complete access to whiteness and his always-contingent assimilation to the middle class, the US mainland, and the bureaucracy of higher education (see, for example, Gil-Gómez and Villanueva, "*Memoria*"). In his 2017 contribution to a *College English* special issue titled "English and Leadership Studies," Villanueva chronicles his path through bureaucracies: first the Catholic Church, then the Army, and finally the US academy ("'I Am'" 483–84). He tells of his long-standing, uncomfortable, but also generative place within those bureaucracies and does not shy away from what that attenuated complicity means for him and for composition and rhetoric more broadly. If we follow Villanueva's mapping, and I believe we should, we will notice that coloniality in América—and therefore coloniality in the study of Américan rhetoric—follows a similar route: the organizing, hegemonizing, repressing, controlling power of the church, the military, and the school threads through Américan rhetoric and the work of Américan rhetoricians.

Rhetoric scholars on the English side, trained as we are in the pedagogical investments of writing studies, have recognized this overlapping trio as a historical fact (see, for instance, Bokser, Romano, and Romney, "Indian"). Even Abbott's rather conservative *Rhetoric in the New World* recognizes the confluence of conquest, conversion, and education. But Villanueva does not merely invite rhetoricians to study others' histories of participating in racism and colonialism. Rather, he invites readers and colleagues across a range of subject positions to see ourselves implicated in those histories and their ongoing presents. Those—like me—who hold uncontested access to whiteness must be particularly conscious of our complicity, but Villanueva also suggests that any of us who carry a US passport on our journeys participate in the bureaucracy of colonialism and racism. Whether our passports are literal or metaphorical, whether they take the form of birthright citizenship, naturalization, permanent residency, or even "just" a job at a US institution of higher education, US-based rhetoricians writing and teaching about rhetoric and Latin America are always implicated in the colonialism and racism that the white settler United States of America wields against the Other Americas, including the Other Americas within the United States. And we would do well to continue to learn from Villanueva's persistent reflection, storytelling, and memory in this regard.

Now, I would argue that Américan rhetoric scholarship has at least implicitly kept cognizant of this fact. Its very name, "Américan" presumes that the United States has always been in relationship to a larger America. That name also seeks to turn the presumed preeminence of the United States upside down, or at least sideways. Likewise, though I began this essay by recognizing how white settler Anglo gringos (myself included) had early, privileged access to publication venues, Villanueva's model urges me to foreground another genealogy for Américan rhetoric, one led by scholars of color. That genealogy includes, among others, instigators such as Villanueva, Raúl Sanchez, Jaime Mejía, and Lisa Flores; a middle generation of now established scholars such as Damián Baca, René De los Santos, Darrel Wanzer-Serrano, Christina Ramírez, and Christina Cedillo and a number of emerging scholars such as Karrieann Soto Vega, José Cortez, Miriam Fernandez, José Ángel Maldonado, Ana Milena Ribero, and Gabriela Ríos (see, for instance, Baca, "*Mestiz@,*" Cedillo, Cortez, De los Santos, "Future," Fernandez, Ramírez, Ribero, Ríos, Soto Vega, and Wanzer-Serrano). It is notable that Baca, Fernandez, and Ribero all contributed to this collection, part of a powerful, interconnected community of scholars. These names are just a hint at possible lists and are joined by more every time I sit down to write. Villanueva's insistence on generous mentoring, in particular, gives me hope and guidance in this regard. One thing that is abundantly clear to me: if I want the study of Américan rhetoric to embody an ethical stance toward its subjects, its histories, its self, and its entanglements, I must follow in Villanueva's footsteps, working consistently and extensively to acknowledge and support individual emerging scholars of color and to reshape disciplinary spaces so that their goals and purposes are sustained. As Américan rhetorical studies moves ahead along new routes, it can also draw from its roots. The lessons of Villanueva's careful, extensive, and ongoing self-reflection are there for the learning.

From my own position as someone with a great deal of unearned privilege and modicum of disciplinary standing, I recognize the risk and the opportunity in Villanueva's model of ambiguous implication. After all, though he ultimately rejects the label, Villanueva admits that James Sledd was correct—in a way—to call him one of the "Boss Compositionists" (qtd. in Gil-Gómez). Likewise, Villanueva tends to begin from a place of institutional good intentions, a tendency I share. Even when he critiques actual practice and highlights the precarious position of scholars of color within academic institutions, he (and I) maintains some optimism for what those institutions can do ("'I Am'" 482). Yet Villanueva's hopefulness about institutions, about his colleagues, and about the roles he can play is anything but ostrich-like, and here too I take a lesson. Villanueva's head is up. He's been in the inner circles, and he knows that intentions count for something in those "fine places so far from home" (482). He also knows that good intentions do nothing to extricate him—or any of us—from the belly of the beast. This, especially, is a lesson I take with me into the future of Américan rhetoric. To the extent that we work within the bureaucracy of US higher education, he, I, and all of us are implicated in Américan coloniality and racism. We perpetuate them unless we proactively work against them through our leadership, our teaching, our scholarship, and our mentoring. Once again Villanueva offers a powerful model.

So here is my final challenge for writers and teachers following the paths of Américan rhetoric that Victor Villanueva set before us: that we do more to incorporate our own Américan complicities and complexities—as individuals, as participants in wider ecologies, and as (sometimes unwilling) extensions of bureaucracies—into our understandings of Américan rhetorics. These incorporations may appear as first-person narratives or statements of positionality, but I hope they will go further. They need to go further if we are to truly make our way further along the paths that Villanueva started. Like Villanueva, we can allow our complicities and complexities to infuse, inform, and inspire us as scholars, teachers, and mentors.

I have to admit, I'm better at talking this talk than walking the walk, especially in scholarship. Like most other twenty-first-century scholars, I'm usually good at acknowledging my subject positions and sometimes I manage to foreground how my own stories intersect with the stories I'm telling (even so, Asao Inoue had to nudge me before I did so in this very chapter). But for myself and for the larger subfield of Américan rhetorics, I believe there is more to do. In particular, we (I) can and should grapple more with how US-based rhetorical studies and rhetorical education are wrapped up in the tales of colonialism and racism we chart. This is not new work; Villanueva has done it for years and so have other scholars of Américan rhetoric—Florianne Jimenez's research on US writing pedagogy in the occupied Philippines comes immediately to mind. Histories of Américan rhetoric have, however, often emphasized the liberatory potential of rhetorical education and rhetorical theory, fulfilling our own investment in having pedagogical practice serve the good (see, for example, Olson and Casas, Romano, and Romney, "Rhetoric"). I don't want us to abandon such hopeful stances. Instead, I hope that Américan rhetorical scholars will recommit to the hard look that Villanueva takes in "Colonial Memory and the Crime of Rhetoric"; the institutional and bureaucratic structures we are part of may be the problem more often than they are the solution, yet we can simultaneously excavate those structures' complicity, reveal the cracks in them, and center the individuals and communities who leverage those cracks for the sake of justice.

Américan rhetoricians need to keep taking hard, hopeful looks at ourselves. We need our memories to build connections without obliterating the implications of our institutional pasts and presents. An Américan rhetoric that would extend Villanueva's tradition of anticolonial critique and close attention to racialization must also be an Américan rhetoric starkly aware of its own colonial, racializing projects. This, I think, is an exciting path, one that scholars of Américan rhetoric can tread alongside neighbors and colleagues in related fields and subfields. Victor Villanueva blazed a trail and set us on good routes. His work continues and encourages us to continue on too.

WORKS CITED

Abbott, Don Paul. *Rhetoric in the New World: Rhetorical Theory and Practice in Colonial Spanish America.* U of South Carolina P, 1996.

Anzaldúa, Gloria. *Borderlands/La Frontera: The New Mestiza.* 4th ed., Aunt Lute Books, 2012.

Baca, Damián. *Mestiz@ Scripts, Digital Migrations and the Territories of Writing.* Palgrave Macmillan, 2008.

———. te-ixtli: The "Other Face" of the Americas. *Rhetorics of the Americas: 3114 BCE to 2012 CE,* edited by Damián Baca and Victor Villanueva, Palgrave Macmillan, 2010, pp. 1–13.

Bokser, Julie. A. "Sor Juana's Rhetoric of Silence." *Rhetoric Review*, vol. 25, no. 1, 2006, pp. 5–21.

Cedillo, Christina. "Unruly Borders, Bodies, and Blood: Mexican 'Mongrels' and the Eugenics of Empire." *Journal for the History of Rhetoric*, vol. 24, no. 1, 2021, pp. 7–23.

Cortez, José Manuel. "Of Exterior and Exception: Latin American Rhetoric, Subalternity, and the Politics of Cultural Difference." *Philosophy & Rhetoric*, vol. 51, no. 2, 2018, pp. 124–50, doi:10.5325/philrhet.51.2.0124.

De los Santos, René Agustin. "La Ola Latina: Recent Scholarship in Latina/o and Latin American Rhetorics." *Quarterly Journal of Speech*, vol. 98, no. 3, 2012, pp. 320–36, doi:10.1080/00335630.2012.692166.

———. "'The Future of Our History': Rhetorics of Transformation and Power in Plutarco Elías Calles' 1928 *Informe*." *Rhetoric Society Quarterly*, vol. 45, no. 3, 2015, pp. 199–211, doi:10.1080/02773945.2015.1032850.

Fernandez, Miriam L. "La Llorona and Rhetorical Haunting in Mexico's Public Sphere." *Journal for the History of Rhetoric*,vol. 24, no. 1, 2021, pp. 54–68.

Gil-Gómez, Ellen M. (2012). "'For Rhetoric, the Text Is the World in Which We Find Ourselves': A Conversation with Victor Villanueva." *Composition Forum*, vol. 25, 2012, https://compositionforum.com/issue/25/victor-villanueva-interview.php.

Jimenez, Florianne. "Echoing + Resistant Imagining: Filipino Student Writing under American Colonial Rule." *Journal for the History of Rhetoric*, vol. 24, no. 1, 2021, pp. 39–53.

Mignolo, Walter D. *The Darker Side of Western Modernity: Global Futures, Decolonial Options*. Duke UP, 2011.

Olson, Christa J., and Rubén Casas"Felipe Guaman Poma de Ayala's *Primer Nueva Corónica y Buen Gobierno* and the Practice of Rhetorical Theory in Colonial Peru." *Quarterly Journal of Speech*, vol. 101, no. 3, 2015, pp. 459–84, doi:10.1080/00335630.2015.1056747.

Pratt, Mary Louise. "Arts of the Contact Zone." *Profession*, vol. 91, 1991, pp. 33–40.

Ramírez, Cristina Devereaux. *Occupying Our Space: The Mestiza Rhetorics of Mexican Women Journalists and Activists, 1875–1942*. U of Arizona P, 2015.

Ribero, Ana Milena. "Drifting across the Border: On the Radical Potential of Undocumented Im/migrant Activism in the US." *Performance Research*, vol. 23, no. 7, 2018, pp. 93–100.

Ríos, G. R. (2019). "Andean Relational Ontologies." *Rhetoric Review*, *38*(4), 384–85. https://doi.org/10.1080/07350198.2019.1654760

Romano, Susan. "Tlaltelolco: The Grammatical-Rhetorical Indios of Colonial Mexico." *College English*, vol. 66, no. 3, 2004, pp. 257–77.

Romney, Abraham. "Indian Ability ('auilidad de Indio') and Rhetoric's Civilizing Narrative: Guaman Poma's Contact with the Rhetorical Tradition." *College Composition and Communication*, vol. 63, no. 1, 2011, pp. 12–34.

———. "Rhetoric from the Margins: Juan Francisco Manzano's *Autobiografía de un esclavo*." *Rhetoric Society Quarterly*, vol. 45, no. 3, 2015, pp. 237–49, doi:10.1080/02773945.2015.1032855.

Soto Vega, Karrieann. "Puerto Rico Weathers the Storm: *Autogestión* as a Coalitional Counter-Praxis of Survival." *Feral Feminisms*, vol. 9, 2019, pp. 5–21.

———, and Karma R. Chávez"Latinx Rhetoric and Intersectionality in Racial Rhetorical Criticism." *Communication and Critical/Cultural Studies*, vol. 15, no. 4, 2018, pp. 319–25, doi:10.1080/14791420.2018.1533642.

Tuck, Eve, and K. Wayne Yang. "Decolonization Is Not a Metaphor." *Decolonization: Indigeneity, Education & Society*, vol. 1, no. 1, 2012, pp. 1–40.

Villanueva, Victor, Jr. *Bootstraps: From an American Academic of Color*. National Council of Teachers of English, 1993.

———. "Colonial Memory and the Crime of Rhetoric: Pedro Albizu Campos." *College English*, vol. 71, no. 6, 2009, pp. 630–38.

———. "'I Am Two Parts': Collective Subjectivity and the Leader of Academics and the Othered." *College English*, vol. 79, no. 5, 2017, pp. 482–94.

———. "*Memoria* Is a Friend of Ours: On the Discourse of Color." *College English*, vol. 67, no. 1, 2004, pp. 9–19.

———. "Rhetoric of the First 'Indians': The Taínos of the Second Voyage of Columbus." *Rhetorics of the Americas: 3114 BCE to 2012 CE*, edited by Damián Baca and Victor Villanueva, Palgrave Macmillan, 2010, pp. 15–20.

Wanzer-Serrano, Darrel. *The New York Young Lords and the Struggle for Liberation*. Temple UP, 2015.

Chapter 7

Re-membering "Memoria": The Value of the Personal within Academic Discourse for Our Contemporary Moment

Laura Gray-Rosendale

> *Memoria* calls and pushes us forward.
> *Memoria* is a friend of ours.
> We must invite her into our classrooms and into our scholarship.
>
> —Victor Villanueva, "*Memoria* Is a Friend of Ours"

VICTOR VILLANUEVA'S MANY WORKS have long impacted me greatly as a teacher, from early on in my graduate school studies during the late 1990s at Syracuse University up to the present moment, shaping the specific ways in which I teach writing to students at all levels—from first-year through advanced graduate students.

Victor's innovative scholarly approaches have also shaped me as a researcher; they have often addressed the subjects that have most captured my heart and that I've tried to tackle within various publications over the years, such as basic writing, literacy studies, as well as memoir and autobiographical writing.

And Victor's personhood has also radically shaped me as a human being in the world—my commitments to issues of social justice as well as to the intersections of racial, gender, and economic equality.

When I reflect on it now, my whole career has been in part about following the paths that Victor himself carved through the landscape, chasing after the long shadows he has just left behind.

After all, when I left graduate school for my assistant professor position at Northern Arizona University (NAU), it would be Victor's vacant faculty line that I filled, coming on board to teach some of his old undergraduate and graduate courses in the history of rhetoric and theories of composition. In those early years of my position at NAU, the memories of Victor were still fresh in the air all around me. I could almost hear his quick laugh, the thoughts of his sharp mind whirring through the hallways, the depths of his caring and compassion still hanging in the warm air.

Victor was larger than life. In no way could I ever begin to fill his shoes.

And just a year after taking that faculty position, I would begin directing the writing portion of the STAR (Successful Transition and Academic Readiness) Program at NAU. This is a program for "at risk" students, all of whom are in economic need and first-generation college, and many of whom are students of color. This is a program that Victor himself directed before me, a program that he threw his heart and soul behind, a program that he wrote and published crucial work about, a program that—though I have made many of my own unique changes to it, though its student population has also changed in certain ways since his time here—nearly twenty-five years later still bears Victor's indelible mark. Every time I work with a STAR student—teach a class, go over a particular paper, discuss the future of their education, their life, their career—Victor's voice and his contributions speak to me, whispering from the back of my mind.

What would Victor say to this student right now? How would he approach mentoring and advising my students from economically disadvantaged backgrounds, my first-generation students, my students of color? How would he approach *his students*?

Victor's intellect and empathy have long shaped how I approach the specific curriculum I have designed for these students, one based on a course I created titled English 110: Rhetoric in the Media. These traits Victor exhibits have also impacted other sorts of choices I make, such as who I decide to hire as instructors and train to teach in this program with me each summer. As a result, many of those I have hired over the years have themselves grown up in economic need, were first-generation college, and/or identify as people of color.

And every time I assign the first assignment I designed, the "iText," a kind of literacy autobiography, I think about Victor's groundbreaking work in *Bootstraps*. Every time I read my students' responses to these assignments, it's Victor's voice that I hear.

Start with what they know.

Begin with where they came from, their cultural backgrounds.

Start with who they are.

Yes. Like so many of us in our discipline, my entire career is in large part the result of the fact that Victor came before me, that he made certain things possible. For these reasons and so many more, it is a tremendous honor to have the opportunity to pause and reflect on all that his work has meant to me personally and to our discipline as a whole.

In this essay, I seek in large part to champion and revisit Villanueva's essential essay published in 2004, "*Memoria* Is a Friend of Ours: On the Discourse of Color." Modeling this chapter on the beautiful and creative format of Villanueva's own essay, my piece moves in and out of my own personal experiences and narrative as well as various academic discourses, making the case for the need to revitalize the personal as foundational to the history and theory of rhetoric, particularly in our contemporary historical moment. I argue that, more than ever, in light of the COVID-19 pandemic, increasing economic unrest, climate change, domestic terrorism, MeToo, Black Lives Matter, and our discipline's, as well as all of higher education's, radical destabilization, weaving together the personal and the academic is what we all need.

It's what our students need.

It's what our scholarship needs.

It's what higher education altogether needs.

And once again it is Victor's work that pulls me, that pulls us all in the critical direction we must go.

RE-MEMBERING VILLANUEVA'S "*MEMORIA*"

Victor's essay "*Memoria* Is a Friend of Ours: On the Discourse of Color" is hard to boil down to just a few key ideas. As other contributors to this collection discuss, community and collective memory are significant themes (see Miriam L. Fernandez, Victoria Houser, and Romeo García). Like many of Victor's crucial works, it is the kind of text that resists the attempt to make easy sense of itself or of readers' attempts to label it, to put it in a neat box on a shelf somewhere. Alternating between prose and poetry, traditional scholarly discourse and the discourse of the personal, Victor makes the case that there needs to be more room in academia for marginalized—particularly people of color—scholarly voices and personal voices to speak with, across, and against one another. He argues that the very best scholarship coming from marginalized folks, people whose voices and histories have been colonized and made Other, is going to move in and out of the personal—because this is a significant place of power from which to speak and write.

Victor also writes about the fact that the appeal to emotion has been stripped from our academic discourse, been falsely positioned in opposition to it. But it is essential that we bring it forward, return to it. He states that

> though Aristotle thought it not right to sway with emotional appeals, he knew that the greatest impact on listeners is in fact emotional. The personal here does not negate the need for the academic; it complements, provides an essential element in the rhetorical triangle, an essential element in the intellect—cognition *and* affect. The personal well done is sensorial and intellectual, complete, knowledge known throughout mind and body, even if vicariously. And for the person of color, it does more. The narrative of the person of color validates. It resonates. It awakens, particularly for those of us who are in institutions where the numbers are few. (14–15)

Here Victor indicates that the most powerful scholarship we can create is going to employ both "cognition *and* affect." It will not choose one over the other. Such scholarship will involve the mind and the body. As Victor notes, for all marginalized people, but particularly for people of color, this kind of scholarly work is going to be especially important for the validation it offers, for its resonances, for the ways in which it awakens as well as validates both self and community.

And Victor takes these ideas further in this essay, speaking directly to the marginalized communities from which he himself comes:

> The narratives of people of color jog our memories as a collective in a scattered world and within an ideology that praises individualism. And this is all the more apparent for the Latino and Latina, whose language contains the assertion of the interconnectedness among identity, memory, and the personal. (16)

As others throughout this collection have also noted, for Victor this new kind of scholarship itself challenges the individualistic nature of American culture and of the academy. Instead it always works toward collectivity and community. And, ultimately, it always works toward fostering and promoting issues of social justice.

Then Victor attempts to bring his own memory and identity together in one of my favorite passages published by anyone ever, any time, any place:

> I am trying to figure this out, somehow: who I am, from where, playing out the mixes within. It isn't a question for me, whether public or private discourses. I am contradictory consciousness. The discourse should reflect that. I am these uneasy mixes of races that make for no race at all yet find themselves victim to racism. The discourse should reflect that. I am American (in every sense—a boy from Brooklyn, jazz and rock 'n' roll, and from the Americas, with an ancestry dating back before the Europeans), an academic, a person of color—an organically grown traditional intellectual, containing both of Gramsci's intellectual formulations, yet not quite his new intellectual. The discourse should reflect that as well. And I am in a wheat field, attempting to pass on a memory as I

> attempt to gather one. Personal discourse, the narrative, the auto/biography, helps in that effort, is a necessary adjunct to the academic. (17)

Creating those possibilities for students and researchers to bring personal discourse together with the academic is exactly what Victor calls for in this illuminating essay, to recognize and celebrate the pluralities of our identities. The task will not always be easy. It is often messy and results in missteps and the need to recontextualize, reidentify, reunderstand, and regroup. It is also subject to the political and social forces at work in the world that would seek to reroute the discourses of people on the margins and even to silence us.

But this is it.

This is indeed where we must concentrate our energies, Victor asserts.

THE "DUMB READING GROUP"

> All can be laid bare through the personal made public. ("*Memoria*" 15)

A story. 1979.

She was seated in the back, her tiny body tightly packed into the corner of the room. This is where all of the purple group members sat.

She looked at the red group up front with deep longing. Oh, to be treated as if you were smart, as if you were capable, as if you were the shining hope of the next generation.

They were all white. They were all middle-upper class. They were the kids of the kids who had been fortunate enough to go to college. Though her grandparents were poor Russian immigrants who never went to college (her grandfather instead losing most of his fingers during an industrial accident; her grandmother, who struggled early on with her English but then went on to become the valedictorian of her high school class), she too was a kid of kids who were fortunate enough to go to college, and even top-notch graduate schools. Her father had a job with a growing computer company. But the family was still struggling financially. She looked down at her thrift shop rainbow top, her flooded, patchy jeans.

They were definitely living at the lower end of middle class.

She knew on some dim level that she was supposed to want to be in the red group, maybe even to some people's minds "ought to be there."

But she could barely read. She could barely write.

She had been in a Waldorf school through her early years of elementary school and learned a bit of stuttering French, how to crochet as though her life depended on it, and how to do her times tables with lightning speed.

But no. She could not really read. And she had absolutely no idea how to write.

And her group members, mainly poor white kids from local, rural New England towns, had the same problems she did. The inability to read and write well. The low self-confidence. The fear of failure. The feeling of being an outsider. And, if they did have brief, fleeting moments of success, they had that other deep fear that never really goes away when you've been in the "dumb reading group"—the fear that you will never in fact alter, let alone transcend, your essential, immutable stupidity.

But they had problems she didn't have too.

Like having fathers who were working paycheck to paycheck as prison guards or as truckers or as construction workers. Like wondering whether they were going to have any dinner on the table that night. Like wondering whether any adult would be home at all, let alone be able to help them with their homework. Like wondering whether, if that adult were home, that adult would be sober and kind and loving, or be some monstrous other person who mainly came out at night.

And they had bigger societal problems to contend with too. Like coming from a family of laborers where school would never, ever be valued in the same way as physical work. Like being from a barely scraping by, first-generation immigrant family. Like having no access to newspapers or televisions, being one of twelve children and responsible for the care of at least six younger siblings. Like the ever implicit and oftentimes explicit racism, classism, and sexism embedded within the educational system itself and therefore within even its most well-meaning teachers.

Like the other terrible ideas that pervaded the air.

Your parents never amounted to anything. Your sister, your brother never amounted to anything. You will never amount to anything either. Years later she'll think it was a sick, strange attempt at a syllogism.

Though she would indeed eventually move into the red reading group, she would always remember what it felt like to be on the outside of academic literacy, to be with her purple group peers who were incredibly intelligent, who were so well versed in many other sorts of literacies that the whole academic system simply did not value.

And so, all those years later, when it came time for her to decide on which subject to write her dissertation, though she had taken her fair share of classes on all manner of critical and rhetorical theories as well as contemporary literatures, it was never really a choice.

Not really.

She would write her dissertation on basic writing (directed by prolific scholar of African American rhetorics and literature Keith Gilyard). Basic writers—those were her people. She would publish various articles on basic writing. And her first book, Rethinking Basic Writing, *would be an extension and a further development of those ideas. In it she would touch briefly on not learning to read until the third and fourth grades. If you blinked, you could miss that part, the details mostly buried in a footnote. And it would be many more years still before she would publish anything about these experiences in detail, in the chapter "Deconstructing 'Dumb Reading Groups': Rural New England Culture, Basic Writers/Readers, and the Question of Standards," which appeared in a book titled* Defining Literacy Standards.

Rethinking Basic Writing *was her first major publication. She felt beyond awkward and scared about putting it out there. Keith would very kindly provide supportive thoughts with which to open the book. And then she would nervously reach out to someone else very well known within the discipline—Victor Villanueva—to furnish the book's closing reflections. When she contacted him for the first time, Victor was deeply gracious, generous with himself and his time. To her amazement, this delightful person whom she had admired her entire academic career would say "yes."*

And thus it began. A heartfelt mentorship and friendship that has lasted nearly a quarter century and continues to this day.

But as she drafted and redrafted that manuscript in preparation for its publication, one idea would come back to her again and again.

No matter what she had achieved, no matter what hurdles she had jumped, she was still one of them. She would always be one of them.

A member of the purple reading group. She would always remember.

Even then it was memory that drove her on.

OF BASIC WRITING STUDIES

> And the precedent is old. *Memoria* was the mother of the muses, the most important of the rhetorical offices. Now rhetorics of writing seem to go no further than invention, arrangement, and style; when delivery is still there, it's a matter of "voice." But memory is tied in as well, surely for people of color. ("*Memoria*" 16)

Many, many years have now passed since I spent those days in the "purple reading group." Returning to my own personal and scholarly roots, recently I guest edited two special issues on graduate education and basic writing for the *Journal of Basic Writing*. In doing this, I was being influenced once more by Victor's "*Memoria*." I was coming back to my own memories, thinking through the many ways in which my personal experiences continued to shape as well as inform my academic ones. And when I thought about whose voices I most wanted to hear on this subject—that everyone in basic writing and literacy studies might want to hear—I knew I had to contact Victor. And immediately.

As overextended as he was, Victor was happy to contribute an essay, he said. But could he write it with his graduate student?

He did not feel comfortable writing about the graduate student experience without dialoguing with an actual graduate student about it.

After all, this is Victor we are talking about.

The finished essay, "A Tale of Two Generations: How We Were Taught, and What We Learned (or Not)," is a lovely piece about the history of rhetoric and composition, really, how Victor had to find his way through basic writing studies as a scholar of color in a relatively new subdiscipline, to literally create the learning experiences he needed in order to become expert in the scholarly arena of basic writing studies. His graduate student and coauthor, Zarah Moeggenberg, taught basic writing for some time, like many of us do, with no formal training in how to do so. She had looked forward to taking courses in basic writing theory and practice when she arrived for her doctoral work at Washington State University, but none were available for her to take by the time she was ready to take them. Instead, Zarah, a self-identified queer scholar, cobbled together her learning about basic writing as Victor had done so many years before her. The difference is that much of her learning came from having conversations and doing independent work with Victor himself.

And by offering the history provided in this essay, there was Victor once again, on the ground floor, essentially rebuilding the discipline from its beginnings before readers' eyes so that future generations might know it. Just as in his "*Memoria*" essay, Victor was weaving the personal and the academic together beautifully, revealing the critical ways in which rhetoric and composition studies as a discipline has always depended on this important interconnection. In bringing his talented graduate student on board the project, he was also giving her a critical window into her own professionalization in the discipline, gently ushering her into that scholarly world, helping her to gain a crucial publication.

Victor was also returning to his memories, his experiences, of being a student of color and then a published scholar of color—of what it felt like to be on the outside looking in. This is something Victor's work has done for so many of us who identify as working from the margins, from places of personal and cultural trauma, whether we are queer, or people of color, or lower class, or women, or some combination.

WRITING MY OWN MEMOIR

> Memory simply cannot be adequately portrayed in the conventional discourse of the academy. I am grateful for the acknowledgment of perceptions that academic discourse

> provides, for the resources the conventions of citation make available, for the ideocentric discourse that displays inductive or deductive lines of reasoning, a way to trace a writer's logical connections. Academic discourse is cognitively powerful! But the cognitive alone is insufficient. ("*Memoria*" 12)

Another story. 1988.

She had been an outsider not only to literacy, however. She knew another kind of trauma too.

She had been silenced in yet another way, a way that far too many women in our culture are silenced.

When she was a junior in college at Syracuse University, a stranger broke into her apartment. After sexually assaulting her and nearly killing her, he was caught at the scene by the police. Only later did she learn who he was—the rich, white grandson of the head of the Board of Trustees at her university. He was from the family who owned the company that paid for the big dome on campus where the Syracuse Orange played basketball every season.

And then began many years of seeking healing and justice.

She would write to the parole board each year, try to make sure that he remained in prison until she completed her doctorate. She and her husband would barely escape town with their PhDs in hand just as the rapist was being released back into the city.

She would leave for an assistant professor job across the country and try to build a new life for herself there near the edges of the Coconino National Forest in Flagstaff, Arizona.

But this story, like the other story of her literacy acquisition, would always be with her.

She knew one day she would have to write it.

It would take her some time to tell this story too. For years she would think to publish other things, a textbook on popular culture, edited collections on alternative rhetorics as well as radicalism and feminism, always knowing that someday it would demand to be written, just like Rethinking Basic Writing, *that she'd have little choice in the matter.*

After years of writing and rewriting, constantly second-guessing her decision to tell her story publicly and not to use a pseudonym, revising it again and again, eventually she published College Girl: A Memoir.

Its publication caused a stir in its own small way. As one of a handful of professors at the time who were willing to speak about their experiences of sexual violence publicly, she would be interviewed by local and national outlets. Journals and newspapers in higher education would want to know how she felt about having been assaulted at a university and then later becoming a professor at one.

I have many students who are survivors too, she would say.

I want them to know that they are not all alone, she would say.

I want them to know that their voices really matter, she would say. I want them to know that there is an after, she would say.

She began traveling to university campuses across the country to give talks based on the memoir, to educate universities about Title IX protocols, MeToo, and campus sexual violence, to sign books and to meet students and faculty, some of whom were themselves survivors. The book won a few awards. And through this process she would gain some confidence that her voice—shaky though it sometimes was when she spoke about that night and its aftermath—needed to be out there.

Ever in contact with Victor, she would of course share with him the book's development and publication, tell him that she would love to see him and to give a talk at Washington State.

And he would invite her to speak there about this book that wove together the personal and scholarly, a book in so, so many ways inspired by Victor's own such publications.

Writing from the margins. Writing about the silenced. Speaking for those too often unable to speak for themselves.

And there it was.

Once again it was memory that drove her on.

"HEARING THE CALL": RELEVANCE FOR OUR HISTORICAL MOMENT

> Looking back, we look ahead, and giving ourselves up to the looking back and looking ahead, knowing the self, and, critically, knowing the self in relation to others, maybe we can be an instrument whereby students can hear the call. ("*Memoria*" 17)

The quote above is in fact the very last sentence of Victor's "*Memoria*" essay—and it is a beauty. In fact, it had a large role in shaping how I thought about writing my own memoir and about the functions of memory more broadly. I had to look back fully in order to look forward. I had to look back with a discerning eye in order to better understand my present and to anticipate my possible futures. In this quote, Victor concludes that reflecting back and looking to the future, examining the self in relationship to the community, would finally enable us as teachers and researchers to "hear the call," a call to bringing the personal and the academic together—fundamentally, a call to action. My memoir was my own beginning attempt at more fully answering this call. Since then, still following Victor's call to us all, I have also felt compelled to work on some book projects that examine MeToo and sexual violence within the academy, as well as the important connections between writers' physical activities, their attempts to heal from trauma, and their writing processes.

We are living at a pivotal historical moment. We are engaged in a world where social justice and protest must be at the very center of all that we do. MeToo is enabling survivors across the country and around the world to be heard, requiring that sexual violence becomes a paramount cause for us all. Black Lives Matter is demanding social justice for a long history of racist atrocities. Major challenges to voter rights and problems associated with voter suppression—ones that disproportionately impact those with disabilities, those who identify as culturally marginalized due to societal racism, sexism, classism, or the like, and those who are elderly—are resulting in a groundswell of support and engagement. Climate activists are taking to the streets to demand political and legislative reforms. Many people are trying to find ways to fight against the growth of domestic terrorist groups in our country, such as the one that stormed the Capitol Building, groups filled with anger and hatred and thoughts of racism and homophobia and anti-Semitism. COVID-19 has resulted in further economic instability. And it has demanded that we change the ways in which we interact with one another, the very ways in which we teach our students, moving us in to levels of virtual teaching that no one could have anticipated. With the help of a democratic president and vice president as well as other vocal political leaders on the left, hopefully we will increasingly see some substantial alterations to the United States' political landscape, changes to what have been many years of conservative, racist practices and policies. We may indeed be on the road toward critical transformations.

This is precisely the time when the personal and the scholarly must be brought together more fully within our discipline.

We can no longer afford to just passively listen. Instead, we must actually heed Victor's call.

But what exactly does this mean for us now, in this historical moment?

It could mean a number of crucial things. And I elucidate just a few here. In the classroom, I believe that it means we need to design new writing assignments that allow our students to be more creative, more self-reflective, and more autobiographical in their approaches. During the pandemic, I found myself teaching courses at the undergraduate and graduate levels that addressed memoir writing, writing that moves quickly and easily between the scholarly and the personal.

As Katherine Mack and Jonathan Alexander argue in "The Ethics of Memoir: *Ethos* in Uptake," teaching and researching memoir can be critical in this regard. They contend that "[a]s a function of the genre, memoir *foregrounds* the meeting of the personal and political in ways that other public genres of life writing—or of public writing broadly—do not" (67). I am teaching an undergraduate senior seminar titled Rhetoric and Memoir this semester (a course I have taught for many years now and in many iterations). In this course, students are creating a range of final reflective projects that accomplish what Mack and Alexander call for—everything from memoirs of their own about memories related to being a park ranger; coping with mental illness; negotiating issues of race, identity, gender identity, and social justice; detailing concerns around intersectionality; cataloging their experiences with Black Lives Matter and queer theory; relaying how cultural difference operates;

as well as struggling with gender and sexual discrimination, to various theoretical, analytical meditations on the rhetorical choices of the memoir genre itself. Throughout the course, students keep moving between creative and analytical writing. And after a while, the creative and the analytic truly become one and the same. Their argumentative analyses of the key rhetorical features occurring within the compelling, contemporary memoirs we read together as a class become just as creative as the memoir-esque and reflective writing they produce. And their memoir-esque and reflective writing becomes just as analytical as those argumentative analyses.

Writing memoir is an important tool that allows for meditation on the self and the self's relationship to society. In Victor's "*Memoria*," a truly gorgeous piece of memoir-esque writing itself, he specifically cites a number of significant authors who work to connect their experiences on the margins of culture to memory, to moving within and between the personal and the academic, and indicates that such actions comport with a set of crucial needs, "the need to reclaim a memory, a memory of an identity in formation and constant reformation, the need to reclaim a memory of an identity as formed through the generations" (12). Writing memoir also engages in the act of universalizing the specific, so that readers who may not have had the same experiences can better understand and appreciate other people's experiences different from their own. As bell hooks stated so eloquently in *Bone Black: Memories of Girlhood* many years ago, in writing memoir, "I gather together the dreams, fantasies, experiences that preoccupied me as a girl, that stay with me and appear and reappear in different shapes and forms in all my work. Without telling everything that happened, they document all that remains most vivid" (xiv). And Luis Alberto Urrea wrote a few years later in his memoir, *Nobody's Son: Notes from an American Life*, that reading and writing memoir is about finding sameness within difference, about recognizing that our stories are strangely similar even within and amidst their differences: "My life isn't so different from yours. My life is utterly alien compared to yours. You and I have nothing to say to each other. You and I share the same story. I am Other. I am you" (58).

More recently, I think of writers such as Kiese Laymon in *Heavy: An American Memoir*, Roxane Gay in *Hunger: A Memoir of (My) Body*, and Ta-Nehisi Coates in *Between the World and Me* who have also contributed important thoughts about the value of the memoir genre to issues of memory and truth, as well as the ways in which memoir can function as a challenge to forms of cultural silencing and marginalization. As Laymon explains the process of writing his memoir, for example, he exposes the crucial ways in which his textual choices shaped both his search for memory and truth as well as his very constructions of them:

> For the first time in my life, I realized telling the truth was way different from finding the truth, and finding the truth had everything to do with revisiting and rearranging words. Revisiting and rearranging words didn't only require vocabulary; it required will, and maybe courage. Revised word patterns were revised thought patterns. Revised thought patterns shaped memory. I knew, looking at all those words, that memories were there, I just had to rearrange, add, subtract, sit, and sift until I found a way to free the memory. (86)

Gay also reveals in her description of her memoir that writing it was a political act, an act of making that which is unseen finally seen, the seen itself reconceptualized: "This is a memoir of (my) body because, more often than not, stories of bodies like mine are ignored or dismissed or derided. People see bodies like mine and make their assumptions. They think they know the why of my body. They do not" (5). Coates's book is a memoir written in the form of a letter to his son—and in writing memoir in this alternative format, he challenges the underpinnings of the very genre itself:

> But all our phrasing—race relations, racial chasm, racial justice, racial profiling, white privilege, even white supremacy—serves to obscure that racism is a visceral experience, that it dislodges brains, blocks airways, rips muscle, extracts organs, cracks bones, breaks teeth. You must never look away from this. You must always remember that the sociology, the

> history, the economics, the graphs, the charts, the regressions all land, with great violence, upon the body. (10)

Much like Laymon and Gay, here Coates does not separate the mind and the mental work of fighting racism from the body, the body that experiences it in countless ways every day. Instead, he forces the reader to feel the effects of racism, to not make challenging racism an analytic exercise alone but instead to feel it as lived, to understand it as constantly experienced. This is incredibly valuable for both people who directly identify with Coates's experiences as well as people who have never had such experiences. And, in writing as he does, Coates forces his readers to confront their own culpability, their own participation in a racist culture.

From the beginning of the course, I ask each student to choose their own approach to their reflective projects.

Our own approach? You mean, we can really do this however we want? they ask.

Yes, within the specific strictures outlined in the syllabus, you certainly can, I say.

As a result, many students bring in visuals (pictures and/or videos) as well as written text in order to accomplish their projects. And in each case, I have seen students develop real passion for what they are creating in the midst of very difficult, trying times. They genuinely care about what they are writing—and this matters more right now than ever.

During the pandemic, I built a new unit into this course that focuses specifically on encouraging creativity as well as building resiliency and fostering empathy. Given how valuable it seemed to be for my students, I have continued assigning it. As Mary Karr writes in *The Art of Memoir*, empathy is a huge part of the memoir genre, and at the same time, "we're all hardwired in moments of empathy to see ourselves in another" (45). Fostering empathy through reading and writing memoir—acts of *Memoria*—are especially critical at this current historical and cultural moment. Engaging in such practices can give rise to important conversations around issues of ethos and truth.

Likewise, as Vivian Gornick writes in *The Situation and the Story: The Art of Personal Narrative*, "Truth in a memoir is achieved not through a recital of actual events; it is achieved when the reader comes to believe that the writer is working hard to engage with the experience at hand. What happened to the writer is not what matters; what matters is the large sense that the writer is able to make of what happened" (91). Establishing truth in memoir is about establishing a trusting relationship, not simply about getting the facts right. It's about engaging in a process of discovery together, about taking wrong turns together, and about arriving at some new knowledge together.

As Sidonie Smith and Julia Watson contend in *Reading Autobiography: A Guide for Interpreting Life Narratives*, reading and writing in the memoir genre is important for its inherent complexities: "This apparently simple act is anything but simple, for the writer becomes, in the act of writing, both the observing subject and the object of investigation, remembrance, and contemplation" (1). The act of writing or reading memoir always involves constant reflecting on oneself and one's relationship to others or community. In "*Memoria*," Victor also makes this significant connection between *Memoria* and memoir abundantly clear when he writes (as quoted earlier) that "the narratives of people of color jog our memories as a collective in a scattered world and within an ideology that praises individualism. And this is all the more apparent for the Latino and Latina, whose language contains the assertion of the interconnectedness among identity, memory, and the personal" (16). After these sentences, Victor goes on to add that "there is a common saying among Puerto Ricans and Cubans: Te doy un cuento de mi historia, literally rendered as 'I'll give you a story about my history': me, history and memory, and a story" (16). Selfhood, history, memory, and narrative are all brought together within the memoir genre itself, always enacting the intricate reciprocities as well as the contradictions between identification and dialogue.

In addition, the reading and writing of memoir allow us to share experiences with one another in especially powerful ways that help readers to reflect carefully on their own thoughts and experiences. Sven Birkerts suggests in *The Art of Time in Memoir: Then, Again*, "For whatever story the memoirist may tell, he or she is also at the same time modeling a way to reflectively make sense of experience—using hindsight to follow the thread back into the labyrinth. Reading their work, we borrow their investigative energy and contemplate similar ways of accessing our lives" (22). Finally, in *Memoir: An Introduction*, G. Thomas Couser too clarifies the value of memoir for bringing oftentimes silenced voices to the fore. He writes that for many people, reading and writing memoir can be an act of "claiming their rights," and he makes specific mention of this being the case with traditionally "marginalized or oppressed populations" (178).

This semester in my class we also engaged in some short creative writing exercises I had never assigned before, all of them aimed at critical self-reflection and promoting greater support for one another. Students not only wrote their own responses but also responded in detail to what their classmates wrote. Even though the course was taught online through Zoom meetings in lieu of face-to-face interactions, students developed a deep comfort around each other and came to know themselves and each other in new ways. Within these short creative pieces students shared their dreams, their hopes, and their fears. They also reached out to one another in crucial ways around the various real political concerns impacting their lives—forms of racial injustice, issues of food insecurity, economic struggles, and gender discrimination issues.

To my mind, these are the kinds of turns we increasingly need to make in our teaching—to weave the academic and the personal together. This is especially important for our students of color. It is very important for our students who identify as coming from other culturally marginalized groups. And it is also important for our students who identify as coming from various positions of privilege too.

And I believe, as Victor urged us to do so many years ago, that we need to shift in this direction in our scholarly work as well. As Victor's "*Memoria*" made so clear back in 2004 when it was published, the false separation of personal writing from academic writing has never held up very well within our discipline. After all, we are a discipline that has supported the writing of beautiful literacy autobiographies, the careful analyses of identity constructions, and the painstaking work of self-reflection. Right now it's a false binary that we can no longer afford to entertain, let alone support.

Now we need to find ways to embrace the play between the two. We need to examine the places where they come together and intermix. These are precisely the sites that will lead to crucial changes in ourselves, in each other, in our discipline, and in our society.

Thank you, Victor, for being the amazing human being that you are, for once again helping us to chart a genuinely positive, political path forward.

Thank you always, Victor, for issuing this crucial call.

Now is the time for us all to once again follow Victor's lead, to more firmly and fully respond.

Now is the time.

WORKS CITED

Birkerts, Sven. *The Art of Time in Memoir: Then, Again*. Graywolf Press, 2008.

Coates, Ta-Nehisi. *Between the World and Me*. Random House, 2015.

Couser, G. Thomas. *Memoir: An Introduction*. Oxford UP, 2012.

Gay, Roxane. *Hunger: A Memoir of (My) Body*. Harper, 2017.

Gornick, Vivian. *The Situation and the Story: The Art of Personal Narrative*. Farrar, Straus and Giroux, 2002.

Gray-Rosendale, Laura. *College Girl: A Memoir*. SUNY P/Excelsior Editions, 2014.

———. "Deconstructing 'Dumb Reading Groups': Rural New England Culture, Basic Writers/Readers, and the Question of Standards." *Defining Literacy Standards: Essays on Assessment, Inclusion, Pedagogy, and Civic Engagement*, edited by Ronald A. Sudol and Alice S. Horning, Peter Lang, 2019, pp. 119–44.

———. *Rethinking Basic Writing: Exploring Identity, Politics, and Community in Interaction*. Lawrence Erlbaum, 1999.

hooks, bell. *Bone Black: Memories of a Girlhood*. Henry Holt, 1997.

Karr, Mary. *The Art of Memoir*. Harper Perennial, 2016.

Laymon, Kiese. *Heavy: An American Memoir*. Scribner, 2019.

Mack, Katherine, and Jonathan Alexander. "The Ethics of Memoir: *Ethos* in Uptake." *Rhetoric Society Quarterly*, vol. 49, no. 1, 2019, pp. 49–70.

Smith, Sidonie and Julia Watson. *Reading Autobiography: A Guide for Interpreting Life Narratives*. U of Minnesota P, 2010.

Urrea, Luis Alberto. *Nobody's Son: Notes From an American Life*. U of Arizona P, 2002.

Villanueva, Victor, Jr. *Bootstraps: From an American Academic of Color*. National Council of Teachers of English, 1993.

———. "*Memoria* Is a Friend of Ours: On the Discourse of Color." *College English*, vol. 67, no. 1, 2004, pp. 9–19.

Villanueva, Victor, and Zarah C. Moeggenberg. "A Tale of Two Generations: How We Were Taught, and What We Learned (or Not)." *Journal of Basic Writing*, vol. 37, no. 1, 2018, pp. 35–55.

Chapter 8

Corporeal Composition: *Memoria* and the Discourse of the Body

Victoria Houser

> Academic discourse is cognitively powerful! But the cognitive alone is insufficient.
>
> —Victor Villanueva, "*Memoria* Is a Friend of Ours: On the Discourse of Color"

A MEMORY, Pullman, 2015:

Two weeks into the Master of Arts in Rhetoric and Composition. I've registered to take Classical Rhetoric with a professor named Victor Villanueva. As I sat in my first lecture with Victor, I was terrified about my inadequacies.

I had learned how to be a good student through college, but this felt different and much more intimate than any college class I had taken. I knew how to speak and write the discourse of the academy, but suddenly I sat around a table with other graduate students experiencing Victor's animated teaching for the first time. I remember Victor's passionate engagement with every text we read. Every lecture was more like a conversation happening between and among people who fiercely cared about language. Nothing from my chaste, Christian education prepared me for the deconstruction of "proper" education that I found myself entering that evening. I had taken classical rhetoric in college, and I had read all of the major texts: Augustine, Quintilian, Cicero, Longinus, Plato, Kennedy, even Foucault and Butler. I loved the work of Kenneth Burke. Burke challenged everything about the world for me. In short, I knew some things about rhetoric.

Victor changed all of that; he took theory and brought it to life. I wrote down everything. I tried my best to transcribe every word from that seminar. This was the way with Victor—one came into his classroom expecting to hear an authority figure speak about the readings, and one always walked away with more questions than answers.

It is impossible to write about Victor Villanueva's scholarship and not speak of how he taught, or to discuss his mentorship and leave out the theoretical conversations that highlight those memories. I start with this memory because it shows Villanueva doing what he does best—which is, of course, teaching, challenging, questioning, probing. So many of his scholarly pieces resonate across contexts, defying hegemonic structures, interrupting tired practices, and opening the writing classroom to possibilities beyond the cognitive. In this chapter, I focus broadly on the impact that Villanueva's mentorship and teaching had on generations of scholars in disparate fields of rhetorical theory. Tracing his impact through the countless students he mentored would be impossible, so I focus rather on the way in which Villanueva taught and mentored as a methodology for embodiment.

Putting my personal experiences of Villanueva's mentorship in conversation with his scholarship, I use concepts from his piece "*Memoria* Is a Friend of Ours: On the Discourse of Color" to situate the practice of corporeal writing in composition pedagogy. First, I examine "*Memoria*" in connection with (and in contrast to) current structures of academic discourse. As Laura Gray-Rosendale notes in the previous chapter, Villanueva's use of the personal intentionally repositions and reimagines academic discourse. Then I turn to look at how this piece informs scholarship in composition theory, resonating across genres and fields. In tandem with this, I also explore the ways in which this piece shapes pedagogical approaches for first-year writing. To conclude, I return to Villanueva's mentorship, that is, the locus of learning that stretched the definitions of academic knowledge writ large. It is here that we learn from Villanueva's work—his scholarship, teaching, and mentorship—that academic writing must continue to extend beyond the exercises of argumentation and logic, as he initially challenged us to do at the end of "*Memoria*" (19). Ultimately, I offer theories on corporeal writing as a continuation of inviting the body, the personal, into our classrooms and our writing.

The fear of allowing personal writing into academic contexts persists because we do not have the tools to critique or correct the personal. *Logos* is easy to adjust and guide, easy to wrangle into a set of rules that will be resourceful for students as they work through their academic careers. Writing on the body, as one example of the personal, is much harder to critique or analyze, as bodies can be incredibly unruly subjects. Yet the corporeal does not need to replace the academic. Villanueva puts it like this:

> The personal here does not negate the need for the academic; it complements, provides an essential element in the rhetorical triangle, an essential element in the intellect—cognition *and* affect. The personal done well is sensorial and intellectual, complete, knowledge known throughout mind and body, even if vicariously. And for the person of color, it does more. The narrative of the person of color validates. It resonates. It awakens, particularly for those of us who are in institutions where our numbers are few. (emphasis in original 14)

While Villanueva's focus here is on people of color, the notion of the personal stretches and sticks in a wide range of writing contexts. In feminist theory, scholars such as Barbara Biesecker, Vicki Kirby, Michelle Ballif, and Elizabeth Grosz question the efficacy of working against arguments that position reason over emotion, driving at the same concerns of logocentrism that Villanueva gestures toward in "*Memoria*." Kirby asks, "[I]s it possible that our vigilant opposition to argument that associates woman and nature has become so automatic and prescriptive that it risks intellectual complacency?" (7). The question itself reveals the valorization of the intellectual (transcendence, mind, reason) over the corporeal (emotion, experience, body).

The argument for the personal presents a funny paradox, arguing against arguing. As soon as one starts to argue for an inclusion of the personal under an umbrella of logocentrism, the weight of the entire system bears down on the process. Villanueva writes, "Academic discourse tries, after all, to reach the Aristotelian ideal of being completely logocentric, though it cannot be freed of the ethical appeal to authority" (12). The persuasive power of language works well to obscure the body, the personal, but it can never fully remove the political elements of the personal from the rational. Instead, a tacit agreement concerning which bodies are allowed entrance (white, abled-bodied, male, affluent, etc.) into the discourse of the academy is formed around the guiding principles of reason. Laboring against the overt and subtle racism, sexism, heterosexism, and ableism of the system requires one to find methods outside the system. In other words, *logos* is not enough. Yet the hope is that "all can be laid bare through the personal made public" (Villanueva 15). The greatest challenge is getting your audience to believe you when you write outside the boundaries.

A memory, Spokane, January 2016:

> *Spokane, Washington. I spent the night at the bus station in Seattle. Flying back from Anchorage, Alaska, I had booked the cheapest flights possible, which meant that I had to make do with a bench for the night. I took a bus in the morning to Spokane where I would take another bus back to Pullman. Exhausting. I was late to board the bus to Pullman, and I was surprised to find it idling in the parking lot. No matter, I got on and went to the only open seat in the back of the bus. Two minutes later, two border patrol officers entered the bus and started working their way from the back of the bus to the front. I gave them my passport and answered their flurry of questions.*
>
> *They moved past me quickly, barely looking at my white face. Two rows ahead of me, they stopped to question another woman. I heard her voice shaking as she told them she was an international student traveling back to Pullman for the start of the semester.*

> *They took her off the bus to be questioned further, marching her past every passenger on board. An hour went by, then another. Everyone was feeling unsettled. When the officers finally allowed her to return to her seat, she sat down in front of me and began to quietly sob while the bus engine started. The driver's voice came over the loudspeaker to apologize for the delay. I still remember his almost cheery voice saying, "Sorry, folks. As you know during these times, we can't be too careful. Border patrol has to act on their hunches." The story clicked. When this young woman boarded the bus, the driver felt uneasy about the color of her skin. So he called border patrol. In Spokane, Washington. The rest of the "inspection" was a charade so they could say, "No, no, we're not racist, we questioned everyone." My body seized in a helpless rage. This was Trump's America. I leaned forward and offered her a napkin.*

The body keeps a close account of the political narratives surrounding it, which is what links corporeality and memory, bodily knowledge, to any writing situation. I hate hearing the old adage, "just don't discuss religion or politics," which really means "keep your mouth shut." Keep your eyes down, keep your ears closed, and follow the rules. Instructions for living in a body. But *politics* means nothing more or less than the practice of caring for where we put our bodies. To be told to not speak about politics is to be told to not speak about what happens around the edges of your body. We've made great progress to create inclusive spaces—well, at least enough to check the diversity boxes. "Yet little things happen that betray the underlying racism that affects us all," writes Villanueva. "No matter how appalled by racism we might be. I read Anzaldúa or hooks or the poetry of Espada or Cruz or Esteves or any other writing of color, and I know I haven't become clinically paranoid" (15). The vulnerability of bodies that fall outside the hegemonic grip of white, male normativity begs the practice of memory: "*Memoria* was the mother of the muses, the most important of the rhetorical offices," Villanueva says, "But memory is tied in as well, surely for people of color. It's as if we have accepted Plato's prophecy that literacy would be the downfall of memory, leading only to remembrance" (16). Do we continue to accept this prophecy by excluding the corporeal? We have the corporeal in feminist studies, but what place does it occupy in our composition classrooms? We have heavy theorization about the body (Butler, *Bodies* and *Gender*, Foucault), but little space for the body in our writing practices or pedagogy.

Pathos without the corporeal is just *logos* by a different name. Scholars influenced by Villanueva's work have begun to build pedagogical practices that invite personal narrative to join academic discourse. For example, Aja Y. Martinez's method of counterstory asks the writer to listen to personal narratives that run counter to or are sublimated by institutional practice. Martinez writes, "For people of color, the personal as related through narrative provides space and opportunity to assert our stories within, and in many instances counter to, the hegemonic narratives of the institution" (50). Martinez extends Villanueva's work on *Memoria* by asking students to consider the myriad possibilities narrative practices offer for countering dominant discourses. We see this work enacted, too, in the chapter Martinez authors with Ana Milena Ribero in Section II of this collection. When I asked my students to compose a counterstory project in one of my advanced composition courses, one of them told me they experienced both shock and joy at the prompting to use personal narrative in their writing. Martinez's work offers a very clear example of how the personal, when done well, resonates and awakens the writer to potential that extends beyond the work of an academic exercise and into the corporeal interstices of their lived experiences.

Memoria is first and foremost about the *way* we write, how we write, and why we write; it cuts to the heart of what scholars and teachers theorize and embody. It is about the roots of selfhood in writing, the knowledge that writing cannot function without the writer and all that the writer carries to the page. Villanueva's call to revitalize memory in rhetoric and writing studies opened academic writing to the potentiality of bodies and lived experiences as central elements of scholarly composition. Feminist rhetorical theory best illustrates the possibilities for a kind of corporeal writing that includes memory as a frame for understanding disparate discourse on the body. Feminist rhetorical theory expands the horizon for corporeal writing through several unique frames, such as invitational rhetoric (Foss and Griffin), archival recovery research (Enoch, Hallenbeck), and materialist theory (Barad, Alaimo and Heckman, Grosz). Many of these scholars discuss the importance of thinking and writing about the body through the body, but there is always the complication of language present. How does one write the body without immediately obscuring the body through nailing it to language? Villanueva gestures to many of his predecessors—hooks and Anzaldúa included as "the standards"—who eloquently expressed the need to "reclaim a memory, memory of an identity in formation and constant reformation" (12). But how does one claim, reclaim, configure, reconfigure the corporeal in writing without also losing the central elements of bodily discourse through situating the body linguistically?

Questions of the corporeal, specifically on writing the corporeal, animate the work of memory and storytelling in the writing classroom. Villanueva's call to move beyond the cognitive function of academic writing, including a stronger use of *pathos* in composition, resonates closely with feminist theories that started to work against phallocentric academic writing. Of course, there are significant problems with second-wave, essentialist-focused white feminism and the discourse of the body; but there is something still to be gleaned from these arguments about corporeal writing and the use of bodily memory in composition. In her critique of *l'ecriture feminine*, Ann Rosalind Jones argues that language is a method used by men to objectify the world, which "reduces [the world] to his terms, speaks in place of everything and everyone else including women" (248).

Without getting into French feminist philosophy, I wish to draw from the argument against phallocentric discourse to connect bodily writing to the practice of reclaiming memory. Reclaiming the body through memory in our writing requires an understanding that language has been utilized in academic writing to control, direct, and obscure corporeality and difference. Using Villanueva's call for the reclamation of memory pushes the borders of the corporeal in composition. *Memoria* moves beyond the cognitive, logocentric discourse replicated throughout the hierarchy of academic writing and makes possible the liminal accounts of bodily experience as central, not peripheral, to resisting oppressive, dominant power norms.

The challenges of writing the body require an unlearning of old habits of writing, habits that were forged through imperialism, colonization, patriarchy, and all well-established forms of violence. We are taught at an early age to remove ourselves from our bodies when we write by getting rid of the pernicious first person, "I." I think, I believe, I argue, I desire, I want—unacceptable in the sphere of *logos*. One could perhaps trace the patterns of racism, classism, sexism, and so on through the removal of "I" until there is no "I" left, except the white man who has been painted as God in our cultural makeup. There is no need for exerting the "I" when every "I" could be assumed male, white, upper-middle class. In my very first composition course, the teacher cautioned us all to never say "I think" because it weakened the argument. No, never *think*, simply assert the tacit knowledge and authority that your audience will assume you have so long as you never reveal otherwise. Of course, composition studies has moved beyond these trite rules, but this is due in large part to scholars like Villanueva who were willing to oppose the structured hierarchy of logocentric academic knowledge.

I am also grateful for the affordances of academic discourse for the processes involved in developing and communicating intricate arguments. But we must ask where these arguments take us and with what force they resist the problems taken up in the writing. Again, "the cognitive alone is insufficient. It can be strong for *logos*. It can be strong for *ethos*. But it is very weak in *pathos*" (Villanueva 12). Corporeality and language present an intriguing dialectic for the material and rhetorical, a dialectic that reveals value systems across discourse. In my teaching philosophy, I explain corporeal writing as a practice in which students are encouraged to dwell on lived experiences through critical assessment of cultural logics as they relate to the body politic. For example, in the traditional visual rhetorical analysis assignment, I ask my students to engage with *ethos*, *pathos*, and *logos* in a way that considers lived experiences, both their own and others, in the context of the visual artifact they choose to analyze. Corporeal writing requires students to conduct archival research on their topic of choice and then synthesize their findings with existing scholarship on the topic. The main goal of a project such as this is to inspire creative, embodied approaches that critically analyze how the rhetorical and material elements of everyday life intersect.

Corporeal writing follows practices of embodiment, but it must extend beyond the immediacy of one's own experience to consider how Other bodies are situated within the narrative. This is the element of *difference* that the French feminist writers loudly proclaim as the hallmark of resistance. But memory, and the reclamation of memory, is short lived when examined in singularity. A major constituent of corporeal writing requires the writer to consider their bodily life alongside *Memoria*, or, rather, in conversation with the bodily experiences of others. Villanueva gestures to the difficulties of preserving collective memories in an ideology that pushes individualism above all else, specifically noting the significance of interconnected identities for people of color (17). Making sense of our corporeality necessitates putting the personal in relation to the collective. Corporeal writing, then, involves both personal and collective memory; it opens the future for possibilities of radical intervention and connectedness. Villaneuva eloquently contends that through looking both to the past and to the future, through "knowing the self, and, critically, knowing the self in relation to others, maybe we can be an instrument whereby students can hear [*Memoria's*] call" (18).

A memory, January 2019:

My hands shook as the Skype dial tone rang cold and clear across my tiny apartment. Waiting for Victor to pick up on the other side so I could tell him that I had changed paths. Of all the people who have mentored me, taught me, guided me, Victor's voice is the one I hear the most. The first feedback I received from Victor read: "You're awfully good at this." He followed his opening sentence with several areas that needed to be revised, but I still think of that opening sentence regularly. How often do we hear words of praise like this from reviewers? From peers? From students? Victor's style has always been unique, though, and his perspective on my scholarship became the one most needed.

So I sat there looking at my screen waiting for the Skype call to connect so I could tell him I wanted to shift my dissertation project from genocide and the rhetorics of mass violence to focus instead on feminist rhetorical theory and violence against women. I told him I planned to write about sexual violence and evangelical purity rhetorics. I told him why. There was a long pause as he processed the sudden shift. I could feel my heartbeat up in my ears. Victor folded his hands and said, "Oh, well of course you must now. This is a matter that comes from the heart. If you wrote about anything else, it would be nothing more than an academic exercise for you, and academic exercise won't sustain you past the dissertation." We have very few moments such as these in our careers—in our lives, for that matter.

A poem by Ocean Vuong:

> In the body, where everything has a price,
>   I was a beggar. On my knees,
>
> I watched, through the keyhole, not
>   the man showering, but the rain
>
> falling through him: guitar strings snapping
>   over his globed shoulders.
>
> He was singing, which is why
>   I remember it. His voice—
>
> it filled me to the core
>   like a skeleton. Even my name
>
> knelt down inside me, asking
>   to be spared.

Carefully peeling the body away from the composing process reinforces a dualistic model that elevates reason (*logos*) over all else, including, and perhaps especially, memory. Writing that takes place around the edges of one's heart, at the constitutive points of one's life, requires an active resistance to the social control of bodies. Susan Bordo makes this point in *Unbearable Weight,* where she writes, "If we do not struggle to force our work and workplaces to be informed by our histories of embodied experience, we participate in the cultural reproduction of dualism, both practically and representationally" (182). Bordo's work joins that of several feminist scholars who fiercely argue against dualistic models that elevate reason and the "mind" over bodily matters. Michel Foucault's theorization of the body is the most circulated work for understanding the myriad ways that culture interacts with bodies as a practical site of social control. Judith Butler's expansion of Foucault's work, particularly on sexuality, carried many of these theories into material feminist thought on the sexual difference and bodily autonomy. Butler's work, especially her theories from *Bodies That Matter* and *Gender Trouble*, brought the theorization of the body and the body politic to the fore in feminist scholarship. While rhetorical feminist theory continues to forge paths for embodiment and corporeality in our scholarship, I wonder if we have seen an application of corporeality and bodily writing in the composition classroom.

Rhetoric has a long-standing concern with the linguistic, the *logos*, the inductive and deductive reasoning that permeate our social sphere through the use of language. Yet Villanueva's call for a return to *Memoria* invites us to consider language through *pathos,* which necessarily includes an understanding of bodily experiences. Many feminist rhetoricians and philosophers examine corporeality through posthuman theory, with examples from Deborah Hawhee, Diane Davis, Lynn Worsham, and Michelle Ballif, who have contributed significant scholarship on animal rhetorics, posthumanism, and bodily movement in writing.

Feminist rhetorics brims full of examples on corporeality and embodiment as central to the writing process, but many of these theories have not yet worked their way to the composition classroom. Perhaps this is due in part to associating the body with weakness, banality, reproduction, and unruliness—significant themes for feminist scholarship. Perhaps the body appears as a lower-order concern in teaching writing. Traversing the cognitive elements of writing remains a top priority for academic discourse, leaving precious little time or space for the corporeal (*pathos*). To disregard or ignore the body in the process of writing removes the need for rhetoric entirely, because bodies are the entire reason for rhetoric in the first place.

A memory, summer 2016:

> *"The mind is a beautiful thing, says the mind." Victor returned to this phrase many times over the years. He still reminds me of this whenever we talk on the phone now. In my second year of grad school, I took an independent study on Burke with Victor. We met weekly to talk through the texts and all the surrounding ideas: materiality, Gramsci (of course), transcendence, the strange use of consubstantiality, and so on. In those meetings, ideas were spilling out over the margins, on to the desk, down to the floor. Those talks electrified my writing. I walked three miles to and from campus to meet with Victor, and on the way home, I could feel my feet skimming the pavement as my thoughts ran through terministic screens, Marx, representative anecdotes, the channels created through language.*
>
> *It was an exciting process, heightened by the fervent walks through the unassuming streets of Pullman, Washington. Often I would get home planning to write, but I needed movement still. I would go back and walk through the wheatfields surrounding my street, processing, internalizing, letting my muscles adjust to the ideas. I gave myself over to a process that involved the circulation of blood, stretching newly formed muscles, exercising old ones, extending my feet and hands out as far as I could to touch the nonlinguistic. "The mind is a beautiful thing, says the mind."*

Academic discourse, in a general sense, requires a certain level of ego, an understanding of certain conventions, and a willingness to submit to these conventions. One of the most esteemed rhetoricians, a foundation to the field, Burke himself said that humans are symbol-using animals, goaded by a spirit of hierarchy (16). From top to bottom, the discourse of the academy functions in an elaborate pattern of hierarchy. The beginning stages, graduate school, feel like a hazing process, during which students learn how to do what they must in order to survive (that is, who to cite, who *not* to cite, how to structure a publication for an academic journal), and the stakes are incredibly high. Yet we do very little in the way of sharing the visceral, relentless reality of the academy.

Of course, if one begins the journey in possession of a sturdy pair of boots, the story is much different. With the boots come the bootstraps, or an entire wardrobe of materials passed down from the people in your family who inherited those things from people in their families who inherited them from across the ocean and so on and so on. But rarely do those concerned with doing the difficult labor of writing against violent structures have a tidy trust fund attached to their name. Memory is in short supply when those doing the canonization do not wonder about whether they will eat that night or be able to feed their families the next day.

A memory, December 2015:

> *In response to my reflection on Aristotle, Victor writes: "Let me put it this way—Augustine is an Aristotelian Platonist most influenced by Cicero." We went back and forth about Augustine, Paul, Plato. I was planning to write about the ordination of women for my final paper in the course. It was the end of my first semester with Victor. I sat on the floor in my cold, one-bedroom apartment, racked with anxiety about the final paper for Classical Rhetoric. I wanted to write about Christianity, but how? There was too much attached to my childhood, to my abusive father and silent mother.*
>
> *I emailed Victor asking to meet, and the next day I sat in the familiar brown leather chair across from him and confessed that I couldn't write about Christianity and I felt lost in the maze of Plato, Cicero, Aristotle, Susan Jarret. "Well, don't write about it then," he made it sound so simple. "Write about Burke;*

we both know that's what you love," he told me. I floated out of his office and back to my home, where I wrote uninterrupted for ten hours straight, and I produced the first draft of my thesis. Victor opened the space for me to write around the edges of the class material to allow a different type of writing altogether. It was the first time I truly understood the rhetorical weight of a course grade and what was possible when the course grade became secondary to the writing.

Memoria provides the frame used to stretch our writing. *Memoria* bolsters up the fabric, the threads of what we create in the field. There is a process to this writing, a process that involves our full selves—our insecurities, limitations, trauma, pain, loss, failure, oppression—and the process of developing the threads depends on the frame we choose to hold the material. We pass these processes down the line to our students and to their students as we continue to invent the university, to borrow from David Bartholomae's notorious work. Since the institution of academic writing is predicated on excluding the marginalized, the acquisition of academic discourse is not enough. To talk of Villanueva's contributions necessitates a reflection on how he taught students to write, or, rather, on how he extended the invitation to write with oneself and with our friend, *Memoria*. Scholars Jennifer Sano-Franchini and colleagues make note of the shifting use of memory in writing studies: "Rhetoric and composition scholars have traditionally associated the rhetorical canon of *memoria* with the act of memorization for rhetorical delivery. . . . Scholars like Victor Villanueva have revised this legacy by presenting memory as a methodological tool for the purpose of community engagement" (7).

The revision of a canon of rhetoric is certainly no small feat, and when Villanueva issued the call for stronger engagement with memory, he opened the potentiality of the field to methods that extend beyond academic exercise. Sano-Franchini et al. write, "*Memoria* is a huge component of doing feminist research in rhetoric and composition because ideals and practices of the past are often used as heuristics for present scholarship" (6). While it is true that *Memoria* has offered much to rhetorical feminist work, many of the dominant rhetorical practices still favor (via publication, tenure, awards, grants, fellowships) the austerity of *logos* over the corporeality of *Memoria*.

In closing:

Villanueva's publications in the field of rhetoric and composition altered the way we teach writing and the way we think about the entire academic system of writing. Of course, this is undeniable and self-evident. Yet I would argue, as I think most of us who sat in a classroom with him would, that Villanueva's contributions extend well beyond citations, books, articles, and scholarship in general. Victor taught me how to live with the trouble. Victor taught me how to let the fire live within myself and how to bring that into my classrooms and into my own scholarship.

The potentialities of language and our dwelling within language create countless hang-ups and heartaches, to be sure. Victor taught me how to hold onto those heartaches without fear, for to sacrifice the matters of the heart on the altar of academia is a lonely fate indeed. So, to echo what Victor told me not so long ago: we must write what lives inside us—inside our memories and inside our bodies—because as brilliant and meaningful as academic exercises can be, they are not the point of this business. What we teach our students certainly matters, but how we teach our students matters far more.

Villanueva taught writing and rhetoric through the connective tissues of experience. *Memoria* listens in the quiet hours of writing to those who came before and to those who will come after. *Memoria* waits for us to catch up to ourselves, waits for the moments when our hands shake and our blood runs hot because we have found what moves us to write. Not only to write, but to write ourselves, to write with our bodies, to write our bodies.

WORKS CITED

Alaimo, Stacy, and Susan Heckman. "Introduction: Emerging Models of Materiality in Feminist Theory." *Material Feminisms* edited by Stacy Alaimo and Susan Heckman, Indiana UP, 2008, pp. 1–19.

Ballif, Michelle. "Re/Dressing Histories; Or, on Re/Covering Figures Who Have Been Laid Bare by Our Gaze." *Rhetoric Society Quarterly*, vol. 22, no.1, 1992, pp. 91–98.

Barad, Karen. "Posthumanist Performativity: Toward an Understanding of How Matter Comes to Matter." *Signs: Journal of Women in Culture and Society*, vol. 28 no. 3, 2003, pp. 801–31.

Bartholomae, David. "Inventing the University." *Cross-Talk in Comp Theory: A Reader*, edited by Victor Villanueva and Kristin L. Arola, 2011, pp. 523–53.

Biesecker, Barbara. "Coming to Terms with Recent Attempts to Write Women into the History of Rhetoric." *Philosophy & Rhetoric*, vol. 25, no. 2, 1992, pp. 140–61.

Bordo, Susan. *Unbearable Weight: Feminism, Western Culture, and the Body*. U of California P, 2004.

Burke, Kenneth. *Language as Symbolic Action: Essays on Life, Literature, and Method*. U of California P, 1966.

Butler, Judith. *Bodies That Matter: On the Discursive Limits of "Sex."* Routledge, 1993.

———. *Gender Trouble: Feminism and the Subversion of Identity*. Routledge, 2011.

Davis, D. Diane. *Breaking Up (at) Totality: A Rhetoric of Laughter*. Southern Illinois UP, 2000.

Enoch, Jessica. "Changing Research Methods, Changing History: A Reflection on Language, Location, and Archive." *Composition Studies*, vol. 38, no. 2, 2010, pp. 47–73.

Foss, Sonja K., and Cindy L. Griffin. "Beyond Persuasion: A Proposal for an Invitational Rhetoric." *Communications Monographs*, vol. 62, no. 1, 1995, pp. 2–18.

Foucault, Michel. *The History of Sexuality, Vol. 1: An Introduction*. 1978. Vintage Books, 1990.

Grosz, Elizabeth. *Volatile Bodies: Toward a Corporeal Feminism*. Indiana UP, 1994.

Hallenbeck, Sarah. "Toward a Posthuman Perspective: Feminist Rhetorical Methodologies and Everyday Practices." *Advances in the History of Rhetoric*, vol. 15, no. 1, 2012, pp. 9–27.

Hawhee, Debra. *Moving Bodies: Kenneth Burke at the Edges of Language*. U of South Carolina P, 2009.

Jones, Ann Rosalind. "Writing the Body: Toward an Understanding of 'L"Ecriture Feminine'." *Feminist Studies*, vol. 7, no. 2, 1981, pp. 247–63.

Kirby, Vicki. "Corporeal Habits: Addressing Essentialism Differently." *Hypatia*, vol. 6, no. 3, 1991, pp. 4–24.

Martinez, Aja Y. "A Plea for Critical Race Theory Counterstory: Stock Story vs. Counterstory Dialogues Concerning Alejandra's 'Fit' in the Academy." *Composition Studies* vol. 42, no. 2, 2014, pp. 33–55.

Sano-Franchini, Jennifer, et al.. "Methodological Dwellings: A Search for Feminisms in Rhetoric & Composition." *Present Tense*, vol. 1, no. 2, 2011, pp. 1–9.

Villanueva, Victor, Jr. "*Memoria* Is a Friend of Ours: On the Discourse of Color." *College English*, vol. 67, no. 1, 2004, pp. 9–19.

Vuong, Ocean. "Threshold." *Night Sky with Exit Wounds.* Copper Canyon Press, 2016, pp. 3–4.

Worsham, Lynn. "Toward an Understanding of Human Violence: Cultural Studies, Animal Studies, And the Promise of Posthumanism." *Review of Education, Pedagogy & Cultural Studies,* vol. 35, no. 1, 2013, pp. 51–76.

Chapter 9

Personal and Collective Memory as Shadow Work

Romeo García

HUMANITY AND SOCIETY REMAIN constellated by hauntings and haunting situations of a modern/colonial and settlerizing archive. To echo Avery Gordon, we are all in this story, the palimpsest narratives of settler sites, haunted/ing communities, and wounded/ing spaces-places.[1] Victor Villanueva understood that. His work was as much about calling out the legacies that haunt the Americas and America's people of color as much as it was an attempt to confront and, dare I say, decolonize an epistemology (constitutive of a *coloniality of being*) that invents, devalues, and dehumanizes others (i.e., a *coloniality of knowledge*). Much of Villanueva's corpus of scholarship, an archive of decolonizing archival impressions, is a testament to a knowledge production that uses the field to advance the cause of unsettling the discipline of writing and rhetorical studies (WRS):

> It happens that sometimes academics use their rhetorical skills not to counter hegemony but to maintain it[,] . . . the colonialism that continues to affect how we go about our literacy practices. ("Literacy" 79)

> When we demand a certain language, a certain dialect, and a certain rhetorical manner in using the dialect and language, we seem to be working counter to the cultural multiplicity [pluriversality] we seek. . . . The demand for linguistic and rhetorical compliance still smacks of colonialism. ("Maybe a Colony" 183)

For me it is a moot point to debate whether Villanueva's readings of postcolonialism, from which the passages above emerge, are accurate. Because what he was getting at—"here remains the colony" ("Colonial Memory" 631)—was much larger than any possible misreading. Villanueva was getting at, I believe, the idea and invention of the Americas, which was both self-serving and the foundation for an epistemological hegemony and its institutions to appear and become consequential within and beyond their immediate settings and contexts. And what the modern/colonial collective (MCC) sometimes assumes as a given in their analysis of Americanity, coloniality, and modernity/coloniality, he centered. Because Villanueva understood it was important to locate, identify, and name the mediums through which these hauntings and haunting situations circulate:

> Rhetoric, after all, is how ideologies are carried, how hegemonies are maintained. (*Bootstraps* 121)
>
> [R]acism has always been tied to language, has always had to be sold rhetorically. ("Blind" 11)
>
> The ideological elements which are necessary to hegemony must be maintained and passed on, reproduced. ("Hegemony" 21)

Some might argue WRS is late to the conversations on decoloniality. But while it is true that it is only within recent years that the MCC's project of a decolonial option and its associated vocabulary has been taken up by Latinx writers in WRS (see Baca, Villanueva and Baca, Ruiz and Sanchez, and Garcia and Baca), it is also true that scholars such as Villanueva have been proactive (rather than reactive) in identifying problems, naming contradictions, and unsettling the settled in WRS. His work speaks to how we are uniquely situated to return to the archive of archival impressions—the accumulation of entries, the deposits of trace marks, initiated by some*thing* or some*one* that enduringly acts upon all our archives—and rhetoricize and contend with the effects and consequences words and ideas have had on land, memory, knowledge, and relationality.

The "we" is not insignificant here. Because Villanueva understood we are all in this story, including white folks. His work made us aware that we cannot decolonize being without decolonizing knowledge—the invisible or hidden side of theology, egology, and (the epistemological regime of) modernity.[2]

Allow me to double down on my praise, if only to better clarify the point I am making. Villanueva did not invoke the vocabulary of hauntings, but in every way he understood what Jacques Derrida did, that so long as hegemony "organizes the repression" of peoples there is a "confirmation of a haunting," because hauntings belong "to the structure of every hegemony" (46). Since the mid-1990s, Villanueva had been locating the making of colonial power in the conquest of the Americas (Americanity); identifying a logic of domination, management, and control that persists after colonialism (coloniality); and naming the unavoidable presence of ethnicity, racism, and newness in and around the world, including Puerto Rico (modern/colonial world and its power differentials). Again, I am not too concerned with whether he asked questions in a proper order: Did racism arise out of a colonial mentality-sensibility or was religious-secular epistemic racism the foundation of and for a colonial matrix of power? I would like to believe that when Villanueva posited, "there is something older at work than racism" ("Literacy" 87), he was getting at the entanglements between the idea of race within a Great Chain of Being model, the ends to dominate, manage, and control all domains of life (land, labor, authority, gender and sexuality, subjectivity), capitalism-marketization, and the rhetorics of modernity (salvation, civilization, progress, development) that would attempt to cloak it all. He understood the macro effects of what he referred to as the *unrelenting ideology of colonization* (90).[3] Villanueva found it imperative to locate, identify, and name its tenets because one cannot decolonize some*thing* or the ideas, images, and ends of some*one* if they do not know how it unfolds.

And at the micro-and-meso level, Villanueva, like Frantz Fanon, Ngũgĩ wa Thiong'o, and Aníbal Quijano, was speaking about the haunting effects and consequences colonization has on people and land. Whether *internal colonialism* is the most appropriate conceptual term is insignificant. Villanueva understood that colonization "includes the deterioration of the cultures and traditions of the colonized" ("Literacy" 89) because it is an epistemic and aesthetic issue (economic, authorial, educational, and political, among others). Enrique Dussel wrote that what was central to the Spanish in the colonization of the Americas was both a warlike and a pedagogical praxis. Because the invention of the *other* and their thingification demanded a process: "The conqueror domesticated, structurized, and colonized the manner in which those conquered lived and reproduced their lives" (45). Villanueva had this to say about pedagogical praxis, which allowed us to see *coloniality of instruction-and-curriculum*—a settler-centered instruction in which actor-agents like the men of letters of the past inform and give form to modern/colonial and settlerizing designs. He understood the *idea of the university* as a pillar for such designs and the classroom as a medium to naturalize its modus operandi, manage the truth-and-knowledge claims on appropriateness-correctness, and control epistemic obedience. Villanueva wrote:

> The University still requires "academic discourse," essentially the same prestige dialect as the standard. So the contradiction: students' own voice is to be voiced in mandated ways. Even the forward-thinking "voice advocates" continue to require linguistic or rhetorical monoculturalism. . . . [T]his has been the traditional way with the colonized. ("Literacy" 93–94)[4]

> A curriculum that conceives of empowerment as enabling access to the middle class [ideological] is fundamentally traditional. . . . At the bottom, there is still hegemony. ("Hegemony" 29)

> [T]raditional ways of teaching literacy have not only forced particular languages and dialects upon America's people of color, but have forced particular ways with language—rhetorical patterns—patterns that help to maintain American racial, ethnic, and cultural stratification, as well as gender and class. . . . [W]e are still colonial schools. ("Maybe a Colony" 184, 188)

Villanueva rarely shied away from critiquing the *idea of the university* and revealing *coloniality of instruction-and-curriculum.* What I am calling the *coloniality of instruction* (preceding a *coloniality of curriculum*) has existed since the humanistic university of the Renaissance and coincided with the rise of a hegemonic model of Man-Human-Rights. It stems from a *coloniality of knowledge* (epistemology) constitutive (and not derivative) of a *coloniality of being* (ontology) inseparable from the *idea of the Americas*—the peddling of a racial matrix and racist worldviews predicated on the pretexts of epistemic and ontological difference, laws of who can be in-common, and subtexts for coloniality of power. If coloniality in part is the desire to dominate information (rationality, reason, truth, and rights), *coloniality of instruction* becomes the medium through which that desire can be filtered as factual and a tool to manage and control epistemic obedience, or appropriateness-correctness. That understanding is exhibited in Hegel's statement that pedagogy is the "art of making men ethical" (*Philosophy of Right* 161) and Kant's affirmation that "[m]an can be and must be educated through instruction as well as correction" (*Anthropology* 240). These are understandings derived from the Spanish Friars and Jesuits. In what Fanon, Quijano, and Thiongo referred to as colonization of the imagination, Villanueva saw the tenets of an assimilationist model (English-only policies, Standard American English) thriving in higher education.[5] His work labored to make visible the effort demanded to change education.

Perhaps Villanueva's corpus of scholarship speaks for itself. But for the unacquainted, before Mignolo would deliver the two tasks—analytical and prospective—of a decolonial option, there was a rhetorician who proclaimed, "I will speak of ideology and hegemony" (Villanueva, "Hegemony" 33). He understood that the modus operandi of (a modern/colonial matrix of power and) hegemony—an epistemic zero point and provenance, doctrines of discovery and rights to land/conquest, divine and natural designs, epistemic and ontological differences, and rhetorics of modernity—was every bit epistemological, ideological, and rhetorical. Because power is in part an epistemic and aesthetic war on information and mediums of its circulation fought on the battlefields of ideas

(Man), images (Human Being), and ends (Rights-to). But current movements in the humanities would like us to believe there is an incommensurability between the uptake of a decolonial option as land repatriation and the unsettling of Eurocentrism as an epistemic and aesthetic issue. Given that Villanueva was a reader of Fanon, I cite below a passage that affirms both projects:

> For a colonized people the most essential value, because the most concrete, is first and foremost the land: the land which will bring them bread and, above all, dignity. But this dignity has nothing to do with the dignity of the human individual: for that human individual has never heard tell of it. (*Wretched* [1963] 44)

Many scholars cite only the first part of Fanon's passage above. I include the entirety to underscore the importance of both land and epistemological work. Knowledge, via the semiotic apparatus of enunciation (actors, languages, institutions), is partially how modern/colonial and settlerizing designs such as land as entities and people as objects spread. John Trimbur, Christa Olson, and I perhaps will all agree that Villanueva saw it as important to bring a critique to bear on the modern/colonial situation that holds a firm grip over Puerto Rico as a colony, to unsettle a hegemonic architecture of knowledge and understanding that has contaminated the *idea of the university* and its disciplines, internalizing racist, sexist, and heterosexist epistemic structures since the Renaissance. The ease with which he would claim to have no solutions to the problems he points out is almost humorous. But that was Villanueva's wit, because he sure as hell had an idea. Whether his use of *multiculturalism* is the most appropriate term is not particularly important when we consider what he was trying to advance within a constellation of ideas that strived to reveal how epistemological hegemony is constituted, ideologies are carried over, and hegemony is expanded-disputed in and through language and rhetoric:

> The ideological elements which are necessary to hegemony must be maintained and passed on, reproduced. ("Hegemony" 21)

> [W]e must break from the colonial mindset. ("On the Rhetoric" 659)
>
> The schools of the colony tend to have curricula that aim at achieving cultural assimilation, a limited assimilation, an assimilation that best serves the needs of those who hold power. ("Maybe a Colony" 188)
>
> "Break precedent!" ("On the Rhetoric" 659)
>
> "A multicultural acceptance of voice would acknowledge different cultures' different ways with discourse, different rhetorics, thereby leaving the long colonial trail. ("Literacy" 93)
>
> [R]hetorical practices . . . can help to bring about substantive social change. ("Hegemony" 18)
>
> Rhetoric, then, would be the means by which hegemonies could be countered. (*Bootstraps* 121).

Villanueva did not invoke the vocabulary of *pluriversality*, an idea that refers to both coexistence and co-worlding. And yet, in his espousal to use WRS—to reclaim rhetoric—to be at the service of an-other set of choices, options, and obligations/responsibilities, he advanced the cause of utilizing rhetoric to engage in antiracist pedagogy and a wor(l)ding otherwise. "We do rhetoric," Villanueva proclaimed ("Blind" 18). And with that statement he challenged us all in WRS, as Sylvia Wynters does by unsettling the referent of human and being, to think of rhetoric not as a noun but as a praxis of seeing and walking the world and interacting and exchanging meaning with others. Villanueva made a simple but critical contribution: if rhetoric has been used to fashion a modern/colonial world or to dehumanize and devalue *others* by the same token, it can be utilized to wor(l)d otherwise—humanity-in-difference. And with that idea he indicted the field of WRS and all its academics for remaining the affective channels of rhetorical transmission of and for a certain epistemology, ideology, and rhetoric at work.[6] What Jenna Hanchey calls "haunted reflexivity" (90, 94) Villanueva framed as breaking precedent and bringing about substantive social change.

I WILL SPEAK OF IDEOLOGY AND HEGEMONY[7]

Who are we if not an archive constituted by the accumulation of archival impressions? An archive approach affords the opportunity to view ourselves as stories-so-far. Stories are never really finished because they are subject to change, always already in the process of being and becoming—an archive in the making.[8] Everyday chance encounters and experiences hold the prospect of the possibilities of new stories.[9] Now, our stories-so-far demand we think about the wreckage of what surrounds us and that has not ceased to be, the catalog of hauntings and haunting situations; the wreckage of modern/colonial and settlerizing designs. Hauntings do not emerge out of the ether, nor are they isolated egregious events, but rather an ongoing structuring principle of settlerizing encounters, interactions, and engagements. They require actor-agents and epistemological, ideological, and rhetorical work—the projects of territorial and epistemological appropriation and expropriation. Our stories-so-far, therefore, also demand we think about their haunted/ing literacies, images, and rhetorics. Because we cannot come to terms with hauntings without coming to terms with the semiotic apparatus of enunciations or the semiotic code of human projects and human work—enunciations, symbols and signs, sound, and discourse. Settler states are constructed, haunted/ing communities are constituted, and wounded/ing spaces and places are maintained by human projects and human work—archival impressions.

That hauntings remain presencing, albeit differently, tells us something important. First, that words and ideas matter because they make an argument, and arguments have the potential to have effect beyond their mere utterance, evolving both into tangible actions and a language and discourse; second, that the epistemic experiment and project of inventing people as shadows and relegating them to spaces and places reserved for shadows, for example, can appear and become consequential beyond their immediate setting and context; third, that modern/colonial words, ideas, arguments, and actions move through the political economies of literacy, symbols and signs, and rhetoric; and fourth, that there is an *association of social interests* rhetorically selling and importing, purchasing and sharing-in, and expanding and/or disputing these experiments and projects over space-time. Hauntings never were meant to be a single event but instead a series of settlerizing encounters, interactions, and engagements.

At the onset of my career, which is still in its early days, I argued like Villanueva that memories call and memories return us back home to a place and a feeling. They demand careful reckonings. I have returned to them, both those of a modern/colonial and settlerizing archive and my own, not out of some nostalgic impulse or for the sake of mere recall. To have nostalgia as an aim or end unto itself is not a luxury afforded to the minoritized, racialized, and marginalized (Browne 216). Furthermore, the task and utility of rhetorical study, especially in the broader context of archived cultural memory, forbids anything less than an excavation of engraved archival impressions and a rhetorical inquiry into the trace marks and/or palimpsests that constitute our archives. To return with intention, whether it is to memories, home, and/or a modern/colonial and settlerizing archive, I elicit the aid today of what Gesa Kirsch and I have termed *deep rhetoricity*—a *doing*, predicated on both an ethos of bearing witness in unsettling ways and a praxis of unsettling the settled, that conceives of our bodies as cultural archives and archival impressions that can be returned to and carefully reckoned with. Villanueva so often exhibited such an ethos and praxis in his own work.

Villanueva argued at a recent virtual event that we cannot counter racism in moments but only in memory. Memory is archival insofar that it leaves behind a materiality of trace marks—archival impressions—that can be excavated, used to generate a public record, and rhetoricized for epistemological and ontological meaning. In "*Memoria* Is a Friend of Ours," he situates the memory of the minoritized, racialized, and marginalized at the nexus of personal and collective memory. He writes, "[O]ur experiences are in no sense unique but are always analogous to other experiences from among those exceptions" (15). The adjective *our* is significant. Not all will know the corporeal experience of being *thrown* into the world of colonial difference nor the corporeal exercises of either being *forced* to learn how to address oneself to hauntings and/or *imperiled* to mitigate a precarious subject position of *becoming a subject* in rather than simply *being a subject* of hauntings. But all are constellated. Because we exist in a cosmos of hauntings and haunted/ing situations—the idea of race, epistemic racism, a logic to dominate, manage, and control. Now, again, Villanueva never did invoke a language of hauntings, nor treat hauntings, inheritances, and dwellings as rhetoric, corporeal exercises of address, or categories of analysis, but surely he did in his own way when he argued that literacy and rhetorical education helps to "maintain American racial, ethnic, and cultural stratification" ("Maybe a Colony" 184). So, as Miriam Fernandez argues in this collection, if power has relied on memory, by the same token and in the same context we can use memory in more productive ways—to unsettle the settledness of its epistemological and ontological experiments.

We cannot overlook the significance of the word *exception* either. Villanueva was not staking out a claim about inherent exceptional qualities in regard to the minoritized, racialized, and marginalized. You see, hauntings are neither removed nor do they cease presencing for the exceptional because they physically leave home. I, for example, inherit and embody "The Mexican," a palimpsest of identity, a branding of Brownness. Making it out of my situation never guaranteed nor prevents but always already marks an (inevitable) return. To be Brown(ed) is to be subjected and forced to *return* to, *carefully reckon* with, and navigate a *becoming* in the vicious and haunting cycles of learning how to address oneself to and mitigating precarious subject positions in hauntings. To be Brown(ed) is to be haunted and not exceptional. Villanueva, rather, was drawing on Gramsci's understanding of exception, those who by *chance* "had opportunities" *others* "could not or did not have" ("*Memoria*" 15). Perhaps the most important lesson I continue to learn today is that in the face of the *wreckage* that surrounds us, "thinking oneself out of the spaces of domination" always already necessarily involves a "collective or communal process" (Alexander and Mohanty xxviii). Therefore, opportunities were not had individually but rather because of the work someone else carried out for another—*shadow work*. And as Fernandez suggests in her chapter here, collective memory is an unfinished rhetorical construction that constrains and shapes us in multiple ways.

Villanueva did not register the term *shadow work* either, but it was what he did and it was there in the language of his work that sought to unsettle the settled. He understood that *coloniality of instruction-and-curriculum* was inseparable from the *idea of the university*. The university remains a space and place not designed for "the exceptions." Twenty years since he wrote "*Memoria*" their numbers remain low in the university. This cannot be chalked up to coincidence. Because let us recall the words of John Henry Newman, who described the university as having the practical ends of "training good members of society," "purifying the national taste," and "facilitating the exercise of political power" (206). The university controls whose historicity matters while *coloniality of instruction-and-curriculum* manages truth-and-knowledge claims on appropriateness-correctness to facilitate epistemic obedience. And at least for those who work in the field of writing and rhetoric, we would be remiss if we overlooked the parallel such rhetoric has with that of the Conference on College Composition and Communication's Octalog sessions, the seeding and promoting of the idea of what constitutes the commonplace of a "community" and a "common good" since 1988. We would be greatly mistaken to think that "members of society"/"community" or "national taste"/"common good" did not already mean ideal archetypes and representations of knowledge, understanding, and humanity. Villanueva understood that the "other" emerges as an ontologization within a modern/colonial and settlerizing archive and is maintained in the *idea of the university* and the raison d'être of writing and rhetorical studies. His *shadow work* came in the form of unsettling the settled-ness of the study and teaching of rhetoric.

Now, Villanueva did not invoke a rhetoric of unveiling, unsettling, decolonizing, and/or delinking. These are central pillars of a decolonial analytic. But his inquiry into systems of *ideas* and *ends* like racism, which he understood as always already tied to language and sold and purchased rhetorically ("Blind" 11), situated us squarely on epistemological hegemony and epistemic projects shared in, imported, expanded, and disputed. And Villanueva surely implicated everyday actor-agents—for the rhetoric(s), language(s), and literacies they enact as human projects in the classroom—as the affective channels of rhetorical transmission for such a system. Uncoincidentally, he argued that the "demand for linguistic and rhetorical compliance still smacks of colonialism" ("Maybe" 183). For more than twenty years, Villanueva claimed to not have any definitive conclusions to the problems he called our attention to, but indeed, he effectively enacted a decolonial analytic by examining *where* power unfolds, *who* its actor-agents are, *what* the enunciations and material exchanges of actor-agents entail, and *how* institutions constitute a locus of enunciation for some*thing* or the ideas, images, and ends of some*one* to manifest (see Mignolo, *Darker Side* 188; Veracini 15).[10] So let us return to the *ideas* and *ends* Newman seeds and promotes, as Villanueva would encourage us to do.

Newman is *doing* and *thinking* from the side of humanitas.[11] In other words, the knowing subject or the observer observing, advancing ideas not necessarily unique to them, but rather, both consubstantial to a logic of management and control and tied to a system of *ideas* and *ends*. Immanuel Kant understood "ideas" as an "architectonic" ("Physical Geography" 446), by which he meant the "art of systems" (*Critique* 691). And systems, he understood, were held together by laws and rules, and relied on the idea of whole to parts and parts to whole (*Logic* 100–101). Now, Newman's three points, regardless of intention, were already a palimpsest of Kant's laws of "Nature's purpose" ("Idea" 40), model of humanitas as masters (43), and a "great league of nations" with "united power" (43). And one might say these are just words and Ideas. But words and *ideas* matter. They make an argument. As Lewis Gordon reminds us, Ideas "dwell across the ages in the concepts and institutions human beings have built" ("Problematic" 137). But they require a foundation, infrastructure, or institution to *appear* and *become* consequential (123). And though a racist and contributor to racial discourse, Arthur de Gobineau understood greatly the role institutions played in ensuring that the settler project perseveres beyond its immediate settings and contexts:

> The institutions which the dead master had invented, the laws he had prescribed, the customs he had initiated—all these live after him. . . . [S]o long as even their shadows remain, the building stands, the body seems to have a soul, the pale ghost walks. (33)

What is the US or the university if not institutions and pale ghosts persevering 500 years later? Now, the decolonial question here is, where did Newman and Kant get their *ideas* from? In recalling the Spanish discovery of the Indies ("los Españoles hallaron las Indias"), Bernardo Aldrete described a people as lacking letters ("gentes carecían de toda suerte de letras"). When Aldrete coordinated "aquella gente" with "la policía que las acompaña," he was not talking about *police* as we know the word to mean today. Here, policía is in reference to what *constitutes* "those people," a connection Aldrete affirms when he yokes "gentes carecían de toda suerte de letras" and "fieras desnudos" (Book 1, Chapter XXII, 34).[12] Juan Ginés de Sepúlveda would expand on the association between a lack of letters and nakedness, arguing that the *other* did not even deserve the name of human being ("apenas merecían el nombre de seres humanos"). According to divine and natural "laws," Ginés Sepúlveda contended, the "perfect" ("que lo perfecto") should dominate ("dominar") over the imperfect ("lo imperfecto"). He argued that war against "The Indians" could be justified if they did not concede ("admitir la dominación") to those who were more powerful ("poderosos").[13] These *ideas* appeared and became consequential over time because of institutions and the actor-agents who were its affective channels of rhetorical transmission. Villanueva's *shadow work* so often came in the form of illustrating the continuance of an intellectual tradition-heritage from the Renaissance to Enlightenment to contemporary eras.

Written genres have played a historical role in the cultural practice of humanitas developing, importing, disputing, and reproducing

Eurocentric ideas. Villanueva argued in "Blind: Talking about the New Racism" that racism "has always been tied to language" and "had always had to be sold rhetorically" (11). The epistemic racism of the sixteenth century would be expanded on by the *knowing subject* in the eighteenth and nineteenth centuries. Immanuel Kant, David Hume, Georg W. F. Hegel, Charles Caldwell, Samuel Morton, Sir William Lawrence, Gobineau, and Josiah Clark Nott and George Gliddon all described national characteristics and ranked people on a Great Chain of Being.[14] This same rhetorical reproduction of race and racism, Catherine Pendergast notes in this collection, continues to circulate in legal and political discourse in the United States and beyond.

The white race, according to the comparative discourse of each of these men, held the highest degree of perfection and a monopoly on beauty, taste, and intelligence. Such comparative work relied on the observation of how close to nature people were. The decolonial analytic I am advancing here grounds such observation in a theologically and secularly structured epistemology of the zero point, or a "non-situated, universal, God-eyed view" (Grosfoguel, "Epistemic" 214). Both Kant's project of geographic racism (i.e., colonial difference) and Hegel's chrono-racism (i.e., imperial difference) situate us squarely on matters of epistemology and epistemic racism. When Hegel argued that Europe "is absolutely the end" (163) and "last stage" in history (*Philosophy of History* 552), he was stripping *others* of their histories and rights:

> In contrast with the absolute right of this nation to be the bearer of the current phase in the development of the world-spirit, the spirits of other existing nations are void of right, and they, like those whose epochs are gone, count no longer in the history of the world. (*Philosophy of Right* 343–44)

Kant's and Hegel's comparative discourse set in motion both the *idea* of epistemic and ontological differences (less knowing, less human being) and an evolutionary and dualistic perspective (savage to rational; primitive to civilized). From here, Gobineau would stake out a theologically and secularly structured claim: "[N]o human race can be unfaithful to its instincts [works of Reason], and leave the path that has been marked out for it by God [works of God]" (53). He would also articulate colonial and imperial differences that Kant and Hegel mapped out: "Civilization is incommunicable, not only to savages, but also to more enlightened nations" (171). Other *knowing subjects* would weigh in.

Both Morton and Gobineau would come to declare that although "European institutions" had surrounded and become good models for the *other*, they were just "not made for science and learning" (Caldwell, 140–41). All this discourse continues to call into question the *other's* rights to their histories, selves, and land. And since the *knowing subject* argued that they alone made discoveries, inventions, and improvements—"time has been computed, space measured" (Lawrence 159)—the rights over land, resources, and people were assumed by them (Gobineau 28). Since the invention of the Americas, a *colonial matrix of power*—coloniality of knowledge, being, nature, and power—continues to be a logical structure of management and control. Villanueva was never shy to speak on this in the context of Puerto Ricans, Puerto Rico, and the institutions that ensured both remain haunted and wounded.

In the context of coloniality, the *idea of the university*, which Hegel referred to as "Institutions for higher cultivation" (*Philosophy of Mind* 187), was architected in the sixteenth century (the universities of Mexico) and refined in the "modern history" of the eighteenth century (the universities of Western Europe). It cannot be separated from the ideas of colonial difference in the sixteenth century and colonial and imperial difference in the eighteenth: the histories of dehumanizing and inventing the *other* because they do not adhere to ideal representations of knowledge (e.g., alphabetic writing systems) and humanity; the histories of partitioning geography according to race and ranking beings on a Great Chain of Being hierarchically linked; the histories of erasure and marginalization of the *other's* histories of civilization and contribution to rhetoric. The university was architected as an institution to support, defend, promote, and reproduce Eurocentric *ideas* and ideals. The decolonial analytic Villanueva was advancing, though not in such terms, was that which targeted

> [t]he hegemonic architecture of knowledge (content of the con-versation) and the principles, assumptions, and rules of knowing (terms of conversation). The option that decoloniality offers delinks, from the options articulated by modernity/coloniality and successfully establishes as the only option. (Mignolo and Walsh 212)

And like the university, the humanities can be separated from these histories. Lest we forget the implications of George Kennedy's claim that "[t]he only fully developed system of rhetorical terminology" has been derived from "Greco-Roman rhetoric" (6). He, like Robert Connors, who would argue for an intellectual tradition-heritage that began with Aristotle (35), was thinking from the side of humanitas. Kant located the beginning of philosophy and reason and the genuine feeling for the beautiful and sublime in Greek history; Hegel situated ideas of freedom, spirit, and unity of the sensuous and rational with the ancient Greeks as well. Both Kant and Hegel advanced a meta-narrative of civilization and rhetoric, which is a "unilinear logic of development [that] imagines 'rhetoric' beginning among the archons of Athens, becoming refined with Roman empire-building, flourishing during European Enlightenment, and reaching the rest of the world thereafter" (García and Baca 39). All this is to reiterate, once more, that it is no coincidence that the numbers of "those exceptions" remain low in the university. This is an institution filled with white(ly) actors that, like other Western institutions with similar actors, both renders the *other* silent and invisible and relegates them to the spaces reserved for *shadows*. Villanueva's *shadow work* in this context so often came too in the form of making an appeal—break precedent.

It is important to return to that which calls—memories—at the macro level of an archive we are all in and part of. Though Villanueva did not speak in terms of a modern/colonial and settlerizing archive, he was indeed initiating decolonizing archival impressions into it—entries meant to unsettle the settled-ness of haunted/ing trace marks and palimpsestic narratives constituting global stories-so-far. And he was a firm believer that rhetoricians were uniquely positioned not just to rhetoricize ideas, images, and ends but to unsettle the past and intervene in the settled-ness of the present. Villanueva's *shadow work* contributed a rhetorically informed decolonial analytic that appealed for the unsettling, decolonizing, and amending of the lies, contradictions, myths, narcissism, cynicism, and denialisms of a modern/colonial and settlerizing archive. An archival approach posits an essential question that Villanueva was most interested in: How do we reposition the contents of archives so that we can position ourselves in relation to them *otherwise*?

A MEMORY CALLS: A RETURN HOME

My own *stories-so-far* have demanded I return home. Making it out of a physical place is much different from making it out of that which lives deep in the bones. Making it out cannot remove a haunted/ing consciousness nor prevent the goings-on of hauntings and haunting situations. Rather, it marks an inevitable set of *returns*, *careful reckonings*, and *enduring tasks*.

Villanueva tells us that baseball is the language of the Taíno ("Rhetorics" 19). After a reading of that chapter in a graduate course I taught, a student asks the class, *What is baseball if not the process of returning home?* They were drawing a connection to the guiding frameworks of the course, which I refer to here as the epistemic principles of *returns*, *careful reckonings*, *enduring tasks*, and *being-and-becoming recognizable—deep rhetoricity*. The idea that baseball is partially about *returning* home struck me as beautifully reassuring and haunting. Beautifully reassuring insofar that we "carry 'home'" on our backs (Anzaldúa 21) but haunting in that a haunted consciousness *returning* home can hurt, be painful, and further cause unsettling. In both contexts, we cannot escape how "we are always already attuned" to and by home (Rickert 9). But Villanueva tells us that memories do not just *call*; they also *push* us forward ("*Memoria*" 19).

Though hauntings call, an *epistemological framework for the haunted* pushes me forward. It emerges despite hauntings and in spite of gaining meaning from haunted/ing situations—an ethic, ethos, and praxis of *thinking, feeling, and being-with* hauntings, inheritances, and dwellings as language, rhetoric, corporeal exercises of address, and categories of analysis. Such a framework is a version of a learning-unlearning-relearning path toward a slow and deep (de/re)composition of *being-and-becoming recognizable* to self(ves), others, and communities *otherwise*. Today, part of writing about my own *returns* home has been my attempt to mitigate the terms by which I am forced to return. I see much of that across Villanueva's corpus of scholarship. I would argue that he was initiating decolonizing archival impressions to underscore how hauntings and haunting situations connect us all. And that truly is the point of an *epistemological framework for the haunted*—that no one group can claim to be from a proper place, speak the proper words, and/or be in possession of the proper signs. By returning to Puerto Rico, as he so often did in his scholarship, Villanueva appealed for an unsettling of the settled-ness of Self and relationality.

I want to continue with my analogy if only to better establish a connection. Home and home plate are starting points. Fanon understood home as a space-place and a feeling. The latter can be heard in his cries: "[H]ere I am at home; I am made of the irrational" (*Black Skin* 123). Fanon depicted a haunted consciousness perpetually returning to be in a vicious cycle of being at home: "My originality had been torn out. . . . I wept a long time, [with tears in my eyes I put its machinery together again], and then I began to live again" (129, 138). He strived to shatter that haunted/ing cycle of being a prisoner of what space-place, history, time, culture, and circumstance have made of him. Fanon had the audacity to reintroduce *invention into existence* and *initiate a cycle of freedom* no longer predicated on binaries but on human relationships regardless of color (229–31). What is life, or even baseball, if not a set of *returns* to home, *careful reckonings* with cycles of being-and-doing, and the *enduring tasks* of struggling to be and do better for one's self, others, and our communities? Sharon Holland argues to let the dead speak from spaces-places familiar to them (4). A memory of home calls. So I close my eyes, as I was taught to do by generations of women. I return to be at-and-*with* home, as Villanueva often exhibited in his own work. Because what are the minoritized, racialized, and marginalized to do but speak from the shadows-and-below?

I once was ambivalent about *home*. Because the haunt lived in the bones: "I was haunted" (Fanon, *Black Skin* 129). I wanted to leave it behind and forget I came from there. But it has always held me tight, not yet ready to let me go. Will it ever? Returns are what it demands. So I find myself *returning home*, to a space where one's "I am," always already wedded to one's "where I do and think," is constituted. To a place: Fanon's "zone of nonbeing" (10) or Michael Taussig's "death space[s] in the land of the living" (4–5, 133), where Anzaldúa's "half dead" (25) and Nelson Maldonado-Torres's people at the "company of death" (257) are relegated to. The immense catalog of poverty, violence (physical and rhetorical), and death that have constructed the settler site, constituted the haunted/ing communities, and maintained the wounded/ing space and place of the Lower Rio Grande Valley (LRGV) are a matter of historical record. I have found that being from the LRGV is felt most beyond it, the ambience of hauntings–recursive containments, monitorization, surveillance, and checking(s)—that continue to attune my *stories-so-far*. I am where I do and think, and that is what Villanueva constantly reminded us of.

The LRGV is a shadowland, a geography of exclusion, a border(ed)land. The suffix *-ed* in border(ed)lander is less about rhetorical effect and more about making visible how we inherit and dwell in our *rhetorics of place*: the internalizing of borders and boundaries encoded with the haunted/ing literacies, images, and rhetorics of recursive containment, monitorization, surveillance, and checking(s). This border(ed)land is not an inevitable nor natural outcome as a border(ed)land but a result of an ongoing structuring principle of modern/colonial and settlerizing designs—the *epistemic murk* of US citizens as white European descendants requiring protection from "the Mexican," not through direct colonization but through coloniality. The LRGV as a shadowland occupies a unique space in the modern/colonial imaginary. It is both a *death-space* and a productive space. The haunted of the LRGV also occupy a unique space in this imagination, an imagination that Sharon Holland and Renée Bergland argue either invents, ghosts, configures the *other* as signs of death, and/or casts the *other* as exploitable-dispensable. It is the result of what Michel de Certeau would call a "discourse of its own" (41, 46, 100). The haunted of the LRGV are proof that there has been no justice and that modernity is but a myth. The haunt that lives deep within their bones alters what it means to *return* to and be at home . . . a place and a feeling. Villanueva never took that lightly.

A STRANGER MEMORY CALLS[15]

Hope and struggle characterize the paradoxical realities of denizens from the LRGV, as it does for many Puerto Ricans. We wonder on the daily: Will I ever make it out? Will I ever stop being haunted? Will I ever have arrived? Ojalá. These are our inquiries without warranty; our rhetorics that can only ever guarantee with certainty possibilities; and our hopes without guaranteed predicate. We make the choice, which is hardly a choice at all but a demand, to have hope. Sara Ahmed writes that hope is not "at the expense of struggle but animates a struggle (*Living* 2). Our struggle is that of hoping the seemingly impossible is merely a possibility that has yet to be worked out in the course of actions we take to break free from the generational cycle of haunted/ing stories-so-far. Sometimes I feel like I am caught in a vicious cycle of wondering, though; will I ever have made it and arrived beyond the borders? So I make returns, so that I can re/search (for) hope within the contents—archival impressions—of my archive.

SARITA, TEXAS. 2005. At eighteen, I boarded a Greyhound bus with a one-way ticket to College Station, Texas. But part of being from a border(ed)land means everyone de ahí (from the LRGV) must get "checked" at the Sarita, Texas, internal checkpoint, one of several checkpoints north of the LRGV. Margo Tamez has referred to this space as a Constitution-free and hyper-surveilled zone (282–85), the effects and consequences of early twentieth-century settlers and law enforcement who argued for a last line of defense against the coming and going of "the Mexican." I close my eyes, and I can still see the checkpoint in sight, the lines of cameras, imaging scanners, and agents. I can hear the agents, their lines of questioning as they step onto the bus: "¿De donde eres?" His decision to speak to me in Spanish was intentional, based on my Brownness (Prieto), palimpsest of identity ("the Mexican"), and out-of-placeness (from the LRGV). The agent continues: "Where are you going?" The switch to English was strategic. They know undocumented people are trained for this moment. The switching back and forth of languages is meant to cause confusion. "¿Y tu papeles?" I handed over my Texas identification card. The agent never really saw or heard me. Will they ever? No! Because we are but perceived disruptions in the flow and circulation of bodies. I was granted conditional inclusion; a domestic inclusion without acceptance, granted from a locus that dominates the doors of the inclusion of difference, manages which stranger enters, and controls who is to be checked. I understood then as I do now that it matters que uno es de ahí (from the LRGV) y no de allá (beyond the checkpoint). The checking of my body at the checkpoint would come to typify my experiences in Gringodemia, where I was conditionally admitted too. Will I ever have arrived?[16]

COLLEGE STATION, TEXAS. 2005. I can still see and hear white students protesting diversity. I can hear a white student announce: "We are not that tree-hugging school. . . . We don't want diversity!" I learned that day that tree-hugging was in reference to the University of Texas, a more "liberal" school. At the dorms it was no different, white students screaming: "Go back home, wetback. . . . Fucking Mexicans." Their friends would laugh and confirm what had already been announced: "Yeah, go back home!" Because power requires not just allies but accomplices. I am not even from Mexico. Did it even matter? They never saw or heard me. Will they have ever? No! Because people like me are but glitch in the (colonial) matrix (of power). A memory called. Before leaving for College Station, a tío had a conversation with me: "Tienes que enseñarles que puedes abrí un libro y leerlo también." The who and why was understood. But both of us failed to understand that it mattered little to them, including my professors, if I could open up a book and read it too. I was already "the Mexican" in their eyes. I did not write or speak "white" enough, and given that I am Prieto, I could not pass as white. In terms of writing, this often meant a sea of red on my papers or being told to go to the writing center to get it fixed. The university is a prism through which to see a *germ of decay*—the projects of territorial and epistemological appropriation and expropriation—a reminder that our civilization remains *sick*. It will always have mattered que uno es de ahí y no de allá. My conditional inclusion meant assenting to the reality that I was always already subject to checkings. Will I ever have arrived?[17]

SYRACUSE, NEW YORK. 2013–2017. Year one. Parking near school. I can still see and hear a white university hotel employee standing in the middle of the street for no apparent reason but to smoke a cigarette getting angry because I honked. I can hear him say, "Don't you fucking honk at me, wetback." My son, at the curious age, asks two questions: (1) Why is he mad and yelling, and (2) What is a wetback? Before I can turn to my son and respond, the white man begins to pound on my window and then tries to open the door. "Go back home, you fuck! Go back to Mexico, boy!" My son begins to cry. I am now trapped between vehicles, the vehicle in front of me that is interested in what is going on and the vehicle behind me that cannot go around or reverse because of other vehicles. I turn to my son and try to comfort him, telling him everything is all right. The white man continues with his rant but gets even more aggressive. Spectators all around. I get out of the vehicle to create distance between my son and the man after he begins to hit my son's window. "What the fuck you going to do, boy, do something, boy, fucking wetback, do something. Go back to Mexico, boy." Ashraf Rushdy reminds me, spectators "are not just guilty of looking but also of feeling, smelling, touching, and creating a sound for the full spectacle" (57). Power requires not just accomplices or allies but learned intellectuals who create the necessary distance between themselves and the haunted/ing spectacle, in turn widening the happening of haunted/ing situations. A memory called. Before leaving for Syracuse, another tío had a conversation with me: "Cuidadito, you are just a 'Mexican' in their eyes." The who and why was understood. One's Brownness does not disappear just because one has made it into a prestigious school. Conditional inclusion always already means our bodies are subject to checkings and violence (broadly conceived).

Year two. Being dropped off at school. I can see and hear a white university employee at the parking booth. I can hear her tell me to stop. "What are you doing!" Puzzled, I ask her, "What do you mean?" She did not like my question. I reaffirm to her that I had already gotten permission to drive up to be dropped off. She tells me to pull over to the side. She steps out of her booth and approaches my vehicle. "What are you doing up here!" I tell her I am being dropped off. "Do you even go to school here?" She asks for an ID. I begin to question whether she would ask for other students' IDs. She does not like my question. I refuse to show my ID and tell her once more I am a student and an employee. "If you don't show me your ID I am going to call the police on you." I tell her once more I am just being dropped off to go to a meeting. She starts yelling, "You don't belong here, you need to turn around!" I confirm to her that I am not turning around and that I am going to a meeting. She continues to yell. "I'm calling the cops on you! You're not going anywhere!" My son is concerned. I can see his face through the window. My wife is used to such treatment of my body. I open the door to try to calm him down. "Why, Daddy?" I try to tell him not to worry. The cops show up. My advisor-mentor Steve Parks shows up. We all know what is going on. The lady denies my accusation that she is being racist and discriminatory. Everyone sees it but her. My son most of all sees it. Power requires mechanisms for the coming and going of bodies even after conditional inclusion is granted after one checkpoint. To be Brown is to be subject to random checkings that are hardly ever random at all.

Year three. Picking up my wife from work. I can still see a car pull up behind us with bright white lights. A man approaches the vehicle, blinding me with his flashlight. I can hear him say, "Roll down the window." I can't see who he is, and there are no police lights on, so I refuse to roll down my window. He taps his flashlight on the window and raises his voice: "Roll down the window now!" My son in the back continues to ask about the man and why he wants me to roll down the window. "I need to see your driver's license, roll down the window!" I do not roll down my window, but I do ask about who he is while displaying my license through the window. "It doesn't matter, you need to roll that damn window down!" Still all I can see are glimpses of a white face. Three police cars show up with their lights on. Each cop, including the white man who still hasn't identified himself, take guard at each side of the vehicle. I am taken out of the vehicle and so is my wife. "Who the fuck do you think you are?" the white man who finally discloses himself as an undercover cop asks. I am searched, placed in handcuffs, and told to sit on the ground. "You all need to go back home! Go back to Mexico or wherever you people come from! You all just bring trouble here!" My son starts crying; he knows exactly what they are saying. They finally release us, but I don't believe my son has ever released them from his mind. Power has always required the police to police the police (the state of being human) of *others*. To be Brown is to have zero rights to question such violence.

Year four. Driving down the Onondaga Lake Parkway. I can still see and hear my son worried after we were involved in a car accident. I can hear him ask, "Is being Brown bad, Daddy?" Presumed guilty. I was taken out of the vehicle forcefully after I called the police officer out for being discriminatory. My head on the hood, he tells all of us, "I am not a racist. You people always think every white person is a racist." I responded with a question: "Why is it that after approaching the car that hit us, a car full of white folks, you come to our vehicle and refuse to hear our story?" Silence. I reminded him that I was the one who called the police. "*I* dialed 911." We were finally allowed to leave the scene. "Is being Brown bad, Daddy?" With hesitation and a pause, I respond, "No." He asks because he can pass as white and sees the difference between white and Brown treatment. "Do you want me to beat up that bad man, Daddy?" Still angry, I tell him again, "No." Power does not unfold evenly, so its effects and consequences are not felt equally. And yet power has always required the idea of race, the play of race in intimidation tactics, and the forceful and violent act of putting fear into an *other* race. The power of power, most of all, is the hate it breeds and the vicious cycle it maintains that is all good for nobody. Will we ever have arrived?

BOULDER, COLORADO. 2017. Attending a conference. I am in Boulder for the Conference on Community Writing. I close my eyes, and I can still see a friend and I order an Uber to take us to a fast-food drive-through. The driver engages in a conversation with us. Laughing. Chatting. Everything is good. We arrive at the drive-through: "Yes, can I order a taco, chalupa, and burrito." The driver turns toward me in surprise. I can hear him ask: "Are you Mexican or Hispanic?" We already know what he means by that question. He continues, "Because just a little while ago you were speaking perfect English and then all of a sudden you were like "chal-ú-pa" and "t-á-co." It was one of the few instances when the way I talk was accepted as perfect English. I wondered in that Uber car, after being told I speak perfect English, at what cost will it all have come. The Uber driver knew we were both Brown from the moment we got into the vehicle. Everything was all right up to the moment at the drive-through, because, as he stated, "perfect English" was being spoken. This means we were both able to "pass" as long as we did not exhibit our Mexican-ness beyond skin tone. This he was okay with. The driver understood us completely, from the moment we first chatted till the moment we ordered. This is clear because he himself repeats what was ordered: "and then all of a sudden you were like "chalupa" and "taco." Only at this point he was no longer comfortable with our identity—"The Mexican." The sophistication of power is that it acquiesces and grants conditional inclusion on the condition that power relations remain codified and that the *other* assents in a way that conforms to the likeness of whiteness; because inclusion in such contexts is more often than not a technology of domination, management, and control. Will we ever have arrived?

BALTIMORE, MARYLAND. 2019. Another Gringo-(con) vention. I am at the Rhetoric Society of America Summer Institute. After listening to a keynote by Lisa Flores, who appealed to the audience to take up the much needed work of social justice and antiracism, and concluding the final day of sessions, a friend and I decided to partake in an organized RSA event. I am always wary of these event parties, with the catered food and the drink tickets. On the way to the event, we speak about some of the themes of a seminar titled "Rhetoric, Migration, and Mobility" led by Lisa Flores and Leslie Harrisy. We debate, as we always seem to do, those very themes . As we get in line, that debate and our counterarguments are put to the test. I can still see and hear that elderly white woman *eavesdropping*. You know the kind, the benevolent who clings to and proclaims rhetorical listening as the sign of their own arrival as an accomplice who has overcome whiteness. I can hear her say, "You don't look like you are supposed to be here." I have heard and experienced similar comments before at other conferences such as the NCTE Convention: "I can't even hear your accent." As much as we claim to be a wrench in the system of academia, our epistemic obedience is on display the moment we hand over our university cards upon request—"Let me see your conference badge or faculty cards." We smile, holding in a reaction that will only ever confirm stereotypes of "Brown" folks to her. We are outnumbered. And she's persistent. We assent to submit proof that we belong, under conditions not of our own making. The power of power is that it has an *association of social interests*—the hegemonic family—who do its bidding (monitorization, surveillance, checkings). Sometimes the benevolent figure is not so innocent, because sometimes the modern/colonial gaze cannot help but legitimize power dynamics and whiteness cannot help but be performed. Will we ever have arrived?[18]

Villanueva understood that to be Brown(ed) is to be constantly *thrown* into a world of hauntings and haunting situations (containment, monitorization, surveillance, checkings). It is to be relegated to spaces-places reserved for the shadows-and-below—*forced* to learn the corporeal exercises of address to/ward inheritances; *thrown* into the interplay between *assent*, demand for something else, and an a/waiting (ojalá); *imperiled* to mitigate a precarious subject of becoming a subject *in* rather than being solely a subject *of* one's dwellings. To be Brown(ed) is to be haunted.[19] Memories call. And they can hurt, be painful, and further cause unsettling. Because returns demand a *careful reckoning* with hauntings, inheritances, and dwellings.

But memories can also push us forward. Today, I write to remember the grounds for going on otherwise,[20] to bring out of the shadows and below spaces, places, and people familiar to me; to prepare a ghostly return of hauntings, the dead, inheritances, and dwellings beyond the border and into the politics of my present. A memory of an *epistemological framework for the haunted* calls—an archival impression. So I return, not as a choice but as a demand, to be at home and what bell hooks calls a *homeplace* ("Homeplace").[21] Though Villanueva's work with archives was limited to several publications such as "Colonial Memory, Colonial Research," his shadow work across his corpus of scholarship contributed to the idea that we ought to take an archive approach to the work we do.

A MEMORY PUSHES US FORWARD: AN EPISTEMOLOGICAL FRAMEWORK FOR THE HAUNTED

While my *stories-so-far* demand I think about the wreckage that surrounds me, it also demands I think about that which pushes me forward—the song, poetry, and language that needed to exist in the demand for something else, the memories of decolonizing archival impressions. I return home therefore because I would not be able to describe my past nor conceive of the work I carry out today without the people in my life who carried out *shadow work* for me—a love, care, healing, and learning ethic. These *scholars* stood at the nexus of my *stories-so-far* and *possibilities of new stories.* They had the audacity to speak of, from, and *with* the modern/colonial arrangements of shadows and the below, introducing an *epistemological framework for the haunted*—a thinking, feeling, and being-with others (living, nonliving, nonhuman) *otherwise.* So, I so often return home to take a critical stance on *scholars* familiar to me who, while being forced to assent, refused to consent to and be a cosigner of their own domination. I do so by creating presence from absence and sound from silence out of memories of enunciations (pa que sepas, aprendes, entiendes, no te dejes) and material exchanges (*shadow work*). Ultimately, an archive approach affords me an opportunity to view the contents of my archive and re/search (for) hope in them.

Memoria, Villanueva writes, "pushes us forward" ("*Memoria*" 19). But from where? For the minoritized-and-racialized, it might be from Aimé Césaire's "shadowy realm" (69), Fanon's "zone of nonbeing" (*Black Skin* 10), and/or Luis Rodríguez's "wreckage of my barrio" (qtd. in Villanueva, "*Memoria*" 18). These are the spaces reserved for shadows and those from below. Forward from what? For the minoritized-and-racialized, it might be from the vicious cycle of being in the shadows-and-below: the cry, the putting back together of self that has been broken to pieces, the coming to terms with how the haunt is too much with us, the contemplation of why go on, the hope that it may be possible to reintroduce invention into existence and struggle to live again otherwise. Villanueva underscores some of this in *Bootstraps*. Grandma would not have identified as a rhetorician, but her rhetorical excellence-prowess in situating me in and *with* an *epistemological framework for the haunted* anticipated Linda Alcoff's argument that we need to relearn how to revitalize reconstructive work in epistemology by making truth claims more responsible to the complexities of reality. Grandma knew there was no making it out but, rather, learning how to dwell in one's Brownness otherwise.[22]

I spent many days at my Grandma's house, a place of love, care, healing, and learning. A memory of being kicked out of my house for the first time calls, which has long pushed me forward too. I can see and hear us at the mesa in la cocina. Grandma that day made the choice to get to work. She spoke the truth so I can know ("pa que sepas"), "En la vida, a veces que todo lo que puedes decir es, ¡así son las cosas!" Villanueva argued, "Simply knowing is a kind of power" ("Literacy" 95). Assent was inevitable. Grandma punctuated that idea with an "¡entiendes!" But then and there she also spoke a truth so I could learn ("pa que aprendes") how to see a new path-grounds for going on: "Pues ¿Ahora que?" The difference between assent and consent lies in this interplay. Because as Grandma would say, "Pero no te dejes! ¡No dejaremos que cualquier cosa o persona nos trate comoquiera. Porque si lo dejas, ya valió!" Grandma would not have identified as a scholar, but her ethic, ethos, and praxis of *thinking, feeling, and being-with* (cualquier cosa o persona) was unlike Derrida's traditional or learned scholar whose spectatorship adheres to distinctions between the un/real, non/living, and non/human. She knew it was not only practical to learn how to address oneself to hauntings, inheritances, and dwellings but also possible to learn how to live otherwise by being-with them as an act of defiance. Like a student, I listened to know and to learn. As Grandma would say, "lo que no puedes aprender en la escuela."[23]

Another memory calls—walking and talking on paths we created together. It too has pushed me forward.

2008. Before she was committed to the hospital, and against doctor's orders, Grandma ventured to walk from Jefferson Avenue to East Van Buren. There are multiple ways to take that walk. But knowing Grandma, she took the less public way. Those who will never have arrived know such paths well. She became a fleeting life blending into the shadows. She needed to see me. A responsibility remained at work, even in the face of one's last breaths. Grandma was terco even as she understood she was walking herself home . . . to be at home, a place and a feeling.

"¿Te asuste?" she asked me jokingly, as I opened the door and hugged her. Knowing she was sick, I was more concerned by her unexpected arrival. "Estoy listo," she said after greeting me. Grandma was brutally honest and truthful in that way because she did not have the luxury of treating me as a little kid when I was younger, nor did I expect it. "Pero, quería verte," she continued. "Pues, Vámonos." I knew what that meant. But unlike before, she asked me, "¿A donde quieres ir?" This question struck me as odd, because I always followed her. As we walked in the silence, suddenly a memory called.

When Grandma and I started going for walks and talks, I was but a boy who did not feel at home in his own home. I called home anywhere I could lay my head. In Mexican and Mexican American families, it is taboo to talk about what happens at home. But Grandma knew. She walked with me many days and sat with me many nights on her couch crying. Grandma had this intuition. "Aunque la vida todo te enseña, todavía tienes que aprender." Another memory suddenly called.

"Vamos/Vámonos." When Grandma and I started going for walks, talking was central. Then out of precaution, my homeplace became mobile; out of impetus, communal; and out of love, deep rooted. From our walks to the cemetery to the old neighborhood, I was being taught to think, feel, and be-with absence and silence otherwise. Her enunciations in this way were more than just words: "¿Qué ves? ¡Mira con tus ojos!" | "¿Qué oyes? ¡Escucha con tus oídos!" | "¡Así son las cosas! ¡Pero no te dejes! ¡No dejaremos que cualquier cosa o persona nos trate como quiera!" She was situating me in an epistemological framework for the haunted through enunciations and material exchanges. I learned with her how to cultivate an ethos of bearing witness in unsettling ways and praxis of unsettling the settled: a seeing without being settled with and doing of plunging into, peeling back layers of, and unsettling what is constituted as legible. This was the foundation both for understanding the idea of no te dejes and introducing invention into existence.[24]

I was brought back to our walk and talk by Grandma's question, "¿Recuerdas?" "Si," I responded. I remembered all the times she told me, "Sácate/quítate eso [giving up] de tu cabeza. Cuando piensas así y lo creas, ya valió." I remembered it was her, comadres, and others who assured me it was possible to see and walk a path of new grounds. "¡¿Entiendes!?" I understand it takes a community to learn how to live again otherwise. "¡¿Entiendes!?" I understand that the work of her work—an epistemological framework for the haunted—will be in how I choose to pass it along and stand at the nexus of an-others stories-so-far and possibilities of new stories. "¡¿Entiendes!?" I understand that something will always remain at work. She was at last ready to be at home. And home she went in December of 2008. In my culture, the passing of a loved one is but an invitation to think, feel, and be-with them otherwise. The nonliving can have a powerful presence in the lives of the living. In that way, a responsibility remains at work. That is the past I choose to describe as enunciation in the present.[25]

That which calls also pushes me forward. So I make returns to take a critical stance on what people do despite hauntings and in spite of gaining meaning from hauntings and haunting situations. Because returns can recenter and resituate in our lives the living and the nonliving, who for me represent a "lineage" and "air" of energy and whose enunciations and material exchanges signify "poetry" and "language." My hope and struggle with such returns is to mitigate the terms by which I am forced to return. So, I return to my walks and talks with Grandma. They were not unintentional, situating me in constellated histories, memories, and stories-so-far of hope-struggle—an *epistemological framework for the haunted.* This framework initiates a slow and deep de-composition of self. To unsettle my Brownness, I had to unlearn it and then relearn how to re-compose Self in a way that would allow me to *be-and-become recognizable* once more. The work of Grandma's work—decolonizing archival impressions—will never have been realized by her. Still, I find comfort, first, in one of Grandma's enunciations, "te lo dije." It reflects a hope and a struggle, an awaiting ("ojalá"), for that which may or may not arrive. And I find comfort in knowing what good are returns and careful reckonings if something does not remain at work (enduring tasks). The work of my work today is that of constantly posing the question, as Villanueva so often did in his own work, how do we reposition the contents of archives so that we can position ourselves in relation to it *otherwise*?[26]

Judy Rohrer tells us that we are "the set of stories we tell ourselves" and "the stories that tell us" (189). We inherit, embody, experience, and practice these sets of stories. How we see and walk the world and interact and exchange meaning with others is largely dependent on and is informed by how memories and stories settle us into our local histories of haunting, inheritances, and dwellings. Villanueva understood this. Within these sets of stories, I believe there are constellated stories of women, abuelitas, and comadres who understood what bell hooks did, that there is a "struggle in language" to "recover ourselves—to rewrite, to reconcile, to renew" (*Talking* 28). Perhaps for no other reason did Villanueva emphasize rhetoric. For Grandma, healing and recovery work was preceded by learning, knowing, and purging what is constituted as settled. Perhaps better than anyone I know besides Villanueva, she understood that if haunted/ing literacies, images, and rhetorics had fashioned our hauntings and haunted/ing situations, by the same token they can be utilized to wor(l)d otherwise. From scholars like Grandma to Villanueva, I have learned that if forgetting and conjuration are essential to hegemony, then a remembering that yokes and calls forth hauntings, inheritances, and dwellings to the politics of our present is most crucial. Neither registered coloniality or decoloniality in their vocabulary, and yet both knew it is unthinkable to decolonize being without decolonizing knowledge.

A THANK YOU?

I will have lost more than I will ever gain out of Gringodemia. I will only ever have been granted conditional inclusion and admittance, a tourist with a temporary passport whose welcome has an expiration date. But along the way, certain colleagues and chance encounters have made it all more bearable. Memories call. And so I make one last round of returns . . . as a thank you to academic scholars, including Victor Villanueva.

COLLEGE STATION, TEXAS. 2008. One year before I was supposed to graduate, I dropped all of my classes. That is a matter of record. This was after a professor called on me during class and asked me to step outside the classroom so we could chat. "I am not sure this major is for you," they tell me. Perhaps they were right. I came into Texas A&M (TAMU) as a conditional admit. And over the years, I went from having an interest in biomedical science to psychology to general studies to English. I did not know whether I belonged at the university, much less whether "English" was for me. "I think you should drop," they continued. I had heard these words before from many "English" instructors, who often sent me to the writing center to "fix" my "issues." Neither writing pedagogy nor the writing center then was how they make it out to be today. In fact, what did not make it into my article "Unmaking Gringo-

Centers" was how my first time visiting the writing center at TAMU was marked by bright white lights, whitish narrow cubicles, and a white consultant who would rather correct my essay than actually talk to me about it. I did drop, and I was not sure whether I was going back. This was especially the case given that Grandma had passed in December of that year.

I am sitting in my predominantly white class as a conditionally admitted student. I was already haunted by how the introductions had gone at the beginning of the semester. Each one of my classmates came from good high schools and had read the books that were assigned for the course. It is time for group work. I make eye contact with one white student. They nod, allowing the words "I guess" to slip out. "You clearly do not understand the book, so I will be the leader of this project." They may or may not have been correct. It was the first time I had encountered such literature and poetry. They will never know that I would come to greatly enjoy and be moved by the works of John Milton and John Donne. But in that moment, it meant little that I could open up my book and read it too. As a conditionally admitted student, I struggled to find my voice. Every time I had to speak or write, I was haunted by the idea that they thought I could not speak or write whitely enough. They will never know how I assented in the form of an awaiting: one day I will read, write, and present myself whiter (ojalá). As I struggled to speak and write white, I hoped one day I might arrive among these "scholars," that one day they might be able to see and hear me as a "scholar" in Gringodemia, even if not in my own voice. It will have come at a cost.

2009. I graduated with a 2.572 GPA. That is a matter of record too. I applied to graduate school knowing that an acceptance letter probably would not come my way. In July 2009, I began conversation with a person I did not even know, Professor Cristina Kirklighter, the graduate coordinator at Texas A&M University-Corpus Christi (TAMUCC). I can recall having concerns about my recommendation letters. I even emailed her, saying, "It might not be an excellent recommendation." That being said, I know that

Professor Donald Dickson from TAMU wrote me a recommendation letter. Even if it was not "excellent," till this day, his courses and pedagogy remain one of the best experiences I had at TAMU. Because while my classmates hesitated to work with me because I had never read John Milton or John Donne, and while other professors encouraged me to "change my major," he took the time to help me cultivate my reading and writing. A thank you to Professor Dickson.

In October, I received a conditional acceptance letter to TAMUCC. Professor Kirklighter vouched for me. To this day, I am not sure why. Soon after, my partner and I began living on Elizabeth Street, a low-income neighborhood marked by homelessness, drugs, gangs, and murder that was in the shadows of both the houses on Ocean Drive and "society." Six hundred dollars a month was all we could afford. But with little to no help or assistance, it would do because we knew how to make do, just like many of the minoritized-and-racialized from Corpus Christi to the LRGV.

We lived among many "scholars" on the block who will *never have arrived*. There was the "scholar" of addiction and recovery. They recalled for me many times a memory of near-death experiences and a *cry* that continued to call and push them forward. There was the "scholar" of a serious mental health problem. They would apologize every morning, recalling for me a recurring memory of not knowing whether one was living in the past or in the present. A memory of a *cry* called and pushed them forward to the next day. There was the "scholar" of the streets, who smoked and slanged a little dope. Every morning they would remind us they were taking care of the neighborhood. Sporadically, they would recall a memory for me of wanting to go to school to get my degree. I would end up taking their baby momma to see them one last time because they were on the run from the police. Elizabeth Street was a scary street to live on at first.

When we first moved in, a person down the street was murdered, and later on another person was murdered. Though we all lived in the shadows, we all called Elizabeth Street home. We were "scholars" among "scholars." Every year, after making it out of that neighborhood, when we drive down to Texas, we stop in front of that old blue-and-white house. Because my wife and I know that making it out never guarantees or prevents but always already marks an inevitable set of returns. It is a memory of our struggle there on Elizabeth that calls and pushes us forward today. I cannot speak of graduate school without mentioning this *home* and these "scholars" I came to call friends.

2010. I struggled to see myself belonging, both at the university and in the graduate program. I was always behind, always playing catch-up. I struggled to pass my classes, to secure a position at the writing center, and to be competitive for assistantships. My tío long ago told me, "Tienes que enseñarles que puedes abrí un libro y leerlo también." I was not failing at opening up books and reading them; rather, I was "failing" at reading and writing white (I would "fail" my comprehensive exams too). I was "failing" at accepting every word the "scholars" and my "professors" spoke. Grandma's questions kept calling: "¿Qué ves?" | "¿Qué oyes?" | "¿Entiendes?" | "¡Entiendes!" On March 10, 2010, Professor Kirklighter sent out an email about a visitor coming to campus and the opportunity to eat breakfast with him. I did not respond, because I was on the verge of dropping out of school. But then on March 17, she emailed me to say, "I hope you'll be able to go to the graduate breakfast with Victor Villanueva. . . . I think you'll like him." Later that night, after getting out of my kitchen job, I returned to the email with his flier and to the email Professor Kirklighter had sent out with recommended readings.

I did not know what linguistics was, much less what rhetoric was. So it did not amaze me that he was the "1999 Rhetorician of the Year." At that time, I did not even know what a Regents Professor or what the Conference on College Composition and Communication was. What caught my attention were the words *Memoria*, *journeys*, and *racism*. I began to read. I read *Bootstraps*. I could not put it down. And then I read "*Memoria* Is a Friend of Ours." A few days later, I emailed Professor Kirklighter both to express interest in accompanying Victor at breakfast and to volunteer to pick him up at the Hilton Garden. On April 1, I attended his talk. It was a difficult choice to make because my full-time kitchen job did not want to give me time off. I decided not to go in to work. I did not want to miss this opportunity. I sat there in the second row listening to a "rhetorician" talk about "*Memoria*" for about an hour. Then and now, his work and his words continue to do *shadow work* for me. The memory of this day calls and pushes me forward from the shadows where people like me are rendered silent and invisible for one reason or another. A thank you both to Professors Kirklighter and Villanueva!

Figure 9.1

AND I'LL TELL MY STORY . . .[27]

In "On the Rhetoric and Precedents of Racism," Villanueva wrote, "[W]e must break from the colonial mindset and learn from thinkers from our own hemisphere" (659). Today, decoloniality has given me a language to talk about a praxis of *shadow work* that took place in the hemisphere of the shadowlands I call home. Yes, I am *forced* to recognize and acknowledge that coloniality is the primary condition of possibility for *shadow work*. "Break precedent!" Villanueva encourages us (659). I may be what hauntings have made of me, but *shadow work* has constantly reminded me that I am not contained by it. Grandma, Professor Kirklighter, and Victor Villanueva were all doing *shadow work* for me. Grandma taught me "siempre hay una/otra manera." Dr. Kirklighter taught me *an-other* way through personal writing. And Victor Villanueva taught me that *an-other* way of critique was necessary. Today, I continue to put Grandma's questions ("¿Qué ves?" | "¿Qué oyes?" | "¿Entiendes?" | "¡Entiendes!") into scholarly practice alongside Villanueva's work. Today, between an "ungraspable call" and a "setting-to-work" (Spivak), I continue the praxis of *shadow work* for *anyone* who passes through the doors of my classroom. A responsibility remains at work because of people who have done *shadow work* for me in the form of decolonizing archival impressions.

Shadow work comes from a space that should not have to exist. It comes from a practice that should not have had to be practiced. *Shadow work* comes from an ethos of perseverance and responsibility that should not have had to be constituted. I say all this in the face of ideas such as racism that haunt us all. "We can't buy into the silencing," Villanueva (2006) writes, "of what we know is still racism" ("Blind" 18). What is even more haunting is that ideas such as racism, from past to present, have needed institutions and actors to be its affective channels of rhetorical transmission in the present. If ideas such as racism have *always* been tied to language and sold rhetorically, the question that remains for all readers is, *How will you choose in the now to constitute yourself otherwise?* This is a question Villanueva has been asking of all "scholars" in the field of writing and rhetoric for decades. It is clear that all of us should return to memories and stories because they stand at the nexus of our personal and collective stories-so-far and the possibilities of new stories. And that grounds, I believe, the exigence to initiate decolonizing archival impressions.

Today, I speak of the demand for something else. As I noted at the outset of this chapter, today I mostly classify my work as laboring toward being recognizable to the people who carried out work for me. Villanueva is one such individual in the academic context. As Laura Gray-Rosendale reflects in this collection, he so often returns to memories to provide a glimpse of what it might mean to be on the outside looking in. To echo Villanueva in my context, I have and will continue to tell my story of how a PhD made it out of being homeless. But not alone. Today I tell my story of how a university professor remains critical. But not alone.

83R29122 STE-D

By: Herrero H.R. No. 2751

R E S O L U T I O N

WHEREAS, Romeo Garcia, a master's student at Texas A&M University--Corpus Christi, has been awarded a full graduate fellowship to the Composition and Cultural Rhetoric doctoral program at Syracuse University; and

WHEREAS, Once a homeless teenager in Harlingen, Mr. Garcia caught the attention of a caring high school guidance counselor who not only helped him with practical necessities such as food and clothing, but also persuaded him that success was attainable; she encouraged him to pursue his education, and he became the first member of his family to graduate from college when he earned a degree in English from Texas A&M University; and

WHEREAS, Mr. Garcia subsequently enrolled in the rhetoric, composition, and borderland studies program at Texas A&M University--Corpus Christi, where he also teaches composition to freshmen who face many of the same challenges he once did; he has garnered professional recognition for his research and won awards for his writing, and he received the 2012 Early Career Teacher of Color Award of Distinction from the National Council of Teachers of English; and

WHEREAS, Deeply committed to improving the lives of his students, Mr. Garcia has focused his research on using writing to increase retention and participation in college, especially among Mexican Americans; he knows firsthand the empowering experience of effective communication and hopes to inspire others to develop the skills to contribute their voice to community concerns; and

WHEREAS, Romeo Garcia's passion for teaching and scholarship shows the promise of a bright future, and it is indeed a pleasure to honor him for his outstanding accomplishments thus far; now, therefore, be it

RESOLVED, That the House of Representatives of the 83rd Texas Legislature hereby congratulate Romeo Garcia on earning a full graduate fellowship to Syracuse University and extend to him sincere best wishes for success in all his future endeavors; and, be it further

RESOLVED, That an official copy of this resolution be prepared for Mr. Garcia as an expression of high regard by the Texas House of Representatives.

Figure 9.2

Today, to echo Villanueva, I speak of ideology, hegemony, and contradiction ("Hegemony" 33). But not alone. No! Always in and with those who stood at the nexus of my stories-so-far and possibilities of new stories. That is what constellation means to me: the connection between what is, eventually will be, and/or can be. That is the story I choose to tell, here and now. We tell our stories, as Villanueva has done, because we need to know where we have been in order to imagine an *elsewhere* and *otherwise*. But as he so astutely understood, we are all in this story of hauntings and haunting situations, and therefore, the work of our work cannot be siloed but must involve all people. An archive approach affords such possibilities.

NOTES

1. See Karen Till, "Wounded Cities: Memory-Work and a Place-Based Ethics of Care." *Political Geography*, vol. 31, 2012, pp. 3–14.

2. See Mignolo and Walsh (136); Mignolo (*Idea* 151).

3. See also Villanueva ("Hegemony" 21).

4. See Spivak (61).

5. See Mignolo ("Role" 1240–42; "Literacy" 59; "On the Colonization" 303, 314).

6. See Mignolo and Walsh (212, 223); Grosfoguel ("Structure" 87); Mignolo ("Racism" 1740); Villanueva ("Hegemony" 20, 24).

7. This is a play on one of Villanueva's statements ("Hegemony" 33).

8. See Kevin Browne, "A Douen Epistemology: Caribbean Memory and the Digital Archive." *College English*, vol. 84, no. 1, 2021, pp. 33–57.

9. Stories-so-far is a phrase adapted from Doreen Massey. When she spoke of liberating spaces as the "product of interrelations" and "coexisting heterogeneity" (9), the "simultaneity of stories-so-far" always already stood at the nexus of a process of becoming and possibility (9, 12). The possibilities of new stories is a phrase adapted from Judy Rohrer. When she spoke of the stories "we tell ourselves, the stories that tell us, the stories others tell about us," everyday chance encounters and experiences always held the prospect of the possibilities of new stories (189).

10. Cf. Mignolo (*Darker Side*); Mignolo and Walsh (171).

11. Nishitani Osamu describes the anthropos as those who cannot "escape the status of being the object" and humanitas as those "who possess 'civilization'" (260).

12. This is echoed in the eighteenth and nineteenth centuries too (see Hegel, *Philosophy of Mind*; Nott and Gliddon; Gobineau).

13. Ginés de Sepúlveda (83, 109, 133, 153, 161).

14. For more insight on the Great Chain of Being, see Arthur Lovejoy, who describes the prominent characteristics of this hierarchical configuration as order, plenitude, continuity, and linear gradation.

15. This is a direct reference to Sara Ahmed (*On Being* 2).

16. See Ahmed (*On Being* 163); Derrida (217–19); Mignolo (*Darker Side* xv, 250).

17. See Grande (48); Césaire (39); Fanon (*Wrecked* [1963] 249; *Wrecked* [2004] 157, 181); Mignolo (*Darker Side* 141).

18. See Krista Ratcliffe (105).

19. See Lyons (1); García and Cortez (105–6); Mignolo ("Decoloniality" 377); Holland (3).

20. See Kevin Browne (172).

21. See Fanon (*Black Skin* 12); Alexander and Mohanty (xxviii); hooks ("Homeplace" 384–85); Arellano et al. (31); Quijano (177).

22. See Fanon (*Black Skin* 129, 138); L. Gordon ("Existentia" 15); Alcoff (15); Royster (11, 43).

23. See Derrida (11–14).

24. See Fukushima (14–15); Fanon (*Black Skin* 229).

25. See Perez (27).

26. See Barthes (80, 103, 110); Lorde (24).

27. This is a play on another of Villanueva's statements ("Hegemony" 33).

WORKS CITED

Ahmed, Sara. *On Being Included: Racism and Diversity in Institutional Life*. Duke UP, 2012.

———. *Living a Feminist Life*. Duke UP, 2017.

Alcoff, Linda Martín. "An Epistemology for the Next Revolution." *Transmodernity*, vol. 1, no. 2, 2011, pp. 67–78.

Aldrete, Bernardo. 1606. Del origen y principio de la lengua castellana: ò romance que oi se usa en España. No publisher, 1674.

Alexander, M. Jacqui, and Chandra Talpede Mohanty. "Introduction: Genealogies, Legacies, Movements." *Feminist Genealogies, Colonial Legacies, Democratic Futures*, edited by M. Jacqui Alexander and Chandra Talpade Mohanty. Routledge, 1997, pp. xiii–xlii.

Anzaldúa, Gloria. *Borderlands/La Frontera: The New Mestiza*. 2nd ed., Aunt Lute Books, 1999.

Arellano, Sonia, et al. "Shadow Work: Witnessing Latinx Crossings in Rhetoric and Composition." *Composition Studies*, vol. 49, no. 2, 2021, pp. 31–52.

Baca, Damián. *Mestiz@ Scripts, Digital Migrations, and the Territories of Writing.* Palgrave MacMillan, 2008.

Baca, Damián, and Victor Villanueva, editors. *Rhetorics of the Americas: 3114 BCE to 2012 CE.* Palgrave Macmillan, 2010.

Barthes, Roland. *Camera Lucida: Reflections on Photography*. Hill & Wang, 1982.

Bergland, Renée L. *The National Uncanny. Indian Ghosts and American Subjects*. Dartmouth College P, 2000.

Browne, Kevin Adonis. "Moving the Body: Preamble to a Theory of Vernacular Rhetoric, or How a Caribbean Rhetoric[ian] Is Composed." *Rhetorics Elsewhere and Otherwise: Contested Modernities, Decolonial Visions*, edited by Romeo García and Damián Baca, Conference on College Composition and Communication/National Council of Teachers of English, 2019, pp. 196–222.

Caldwell, Charles. *Thoughts on the Original Unity of the Human Race*. E. Bliss, 1830.

Césaire, Aimé. *Discourse on Colonialism*. Translated by Joan Pinkham, Monthly Review Press, 2000.

de Certeau, Michel. (1988). *The Writing of History*. Translated by Tom Conley, Columbia UP, 1988.

Connors, Robert. "Dreams and Play: Historical Method and Methodology." *Methods and Methodology in Composition Research*, edited by Gesa Kirsch and Patricia Sullivan, Southern Illinois UP, 1992, pp. 15–36

Derrida, Jacques. *Specters of Marx: The State of the Debt, the Work of Mourning and the New International.* Translated by Peggy Kamuf, Routledge, 1994.

Dussel, Enrique. *The Invention of the Americas: Eclipse of "the other" and the Myth of Modernity.* Translated by Michael D. Barber, Continuum, 1995.

Fanon, Frantz. *Black Skin, White Masks*. Translated by Charles Lam Markmann, Pluto Press, 1986.

———. *The Wretched of the Earth*. Grove Press, 1963.

———. *The Wretched of the Earth*. Grove Press, 2004.

Fukushima. Annie Isabel. *Migrant Crossings: Witnessing Human Trafficking in the U.S.* Stanford UP, 2019.

García, Romeo. "A Settler Archive: A Site for a Decolonial Praxis Project." *Constellations*, *1*(2), no. 2, 2019, n.p.

———. "Unmaking Gringo-Centers." *Writing Center Journal,* vol. 36, no. 1, 2017, pp. 29–60.

García, Romeo, and Damián Baca. *Rhetorics Elsewhere and Otherwise: Contested Modernities, Decolonial Visions.* Conference on College Composition and Communication/National Council of Teachers of English, 2019.

———., and José M. Cortez. "The Trace of a Mark That Scatters: The Anthropoi and the Rhetoric of Decoloniality." *Rhetoric Society Quarterly*, vol. 50, no. 2, 2020, pp. 93–108.

———, and Gesa E. Kirsch. "Deep Rhetoricity as Methodological Grounds for Unsettling the Settled." *College Composition and Communication*, vol. 74, no. 2, 2022, pp. 229–61.

Ginés de Sepúlveda, Juan. (1987). *Tratado sobre las justas causas de la guerra contra los indios.* 2nd ed., Fondo de Cultura Económica, 1987.

Gobineau, Arthur de. *The Inequality of Human Races.* 1854. Translated by Adrian Collins, G.P. Putnam's Sons, 1915.

Gordon, Avery F. *Ghostly Matters: Haunting and the Sociological Imagination.* U of Minnesota P, 2008.

Gordon, Lewis R. *Existentia Africana: Understanding Africana Existential Thought.* Routledge, 2000.

———. "Problematic People and Epistemic Decolonization: Toward the Postcolonial in Africana Political Thought." *Postcolonialism and Political Theory*, edited by Nalini Persram, Lexington Books, 2007, pp. 121–41.

Grande, Sandy. "Refusing the university." *Toward What Justice? Describing Diverse Dreams of Justice in Education*, edited by Eve Tuck and K. Wayne Yang, Routledge, 2018, pp. 47–65.

Grosfoguel, Ramón. "The Epistemic Decolonial Turn: Beyond Political-Economy Paradigms." *Cultural Studies*, vol. 21, no. 2-3, 2007, pp. 211–23.

———. "The Structure of Knowledge in Westernized Universities: Epistemic Racism/Sexism and the Four Genocides/Epistemicides of the Long 16th Century." *Human Architecture: Journal of the Sociology of Self-Knowledge*, vol. 11, no. 1, 2013, pp. 73-90.

Hanchey, Jenna N. *The Center Cannot Hold: Decolonial Possibility in the Collapse of a Tanzanian NGO.* Duke UP, 2023.

Hegel, Georg Wilhelm Friedrich. *Hegel's Philosophy of Mind.* Translated by William Wallace, Clarendon Press, 1894.

———. *Hegel's Philosophy of Right.* Translated by S. W. Dyde, George Bell & Sons, 1896.

———. *Philosophy of History.* Translated by J. Sibree, American Home Library, 1902.

Holland, Sharon Patricia. *Raising the Dead: Readings of Death and (Black) Subjectivity.* Duke UP, 2000.

hooks, bell. "Homeplace (a Site of Resistance)." *Available Means: An Anthology of Women's Rhetorics*, edited by Joy Ritchie and Kate Ronald, U of Pittsburgh P, 2001, pp. 382–90.

———. *Talking Back: Thinking Feminist, Thinking Black*. South End Press, 1989.

Hume, David. *Essays and Treatises on Several Subjects.* Vol. 1, J. Jones, 1822.

Kant, Immanuel. *Anthropology from a Pragmatic Point of View*. Translated by Victor Lyle Dowdell, Southern Illinois UP, 1996.

———. *Critique of Pure Reason*. Translated and edited by Paul Guyer and Allen Wood, Cambridge UP, 1998.

———. "Civilization and Enlightenment: Idea for a Universal History from a Cosmopolitan Point of View." *Classical Readings in Culture and Civilization*, edited by John Rundell and Stephen Mennell, 1998, pp. 39–47.

———. *Logic: From the German of Emmanuel Kant*. Translated by Jonn Richardson, W. Simpkin and R. Marshall, 1819.

———. *Observations on the Feeling of the Beautiful and Sublime and Other Writings*, edited by Patrick Frierson and Paul Guyer, Cambridge UP, 2011.

———. "Physical Geography." *Natural Science*, edited by Eric Watkins, translated by Lewis White Beck, Jeffrey B. Edwards, Olaf Reinhardt, Martin Schönfeld, and Eric Watkins. Cambridge UP, 2012, pp. 434–679.

Kennedy, George A. *Comparative Rhetoric: An Historical and Cross-Cultural Introduction*. Oxford UP, 1998.

Lawrence, William. *Lectures on Comparative Anatomy, Physiology, Zoology, and the Natural History of Man*. H. G. Bohn, 1848.

Lorde, Audre. *Sister Outsider*. Penguin, 2020.

Lovejoy, Arthur O. *The Great Chain of Being: A Study of the History of an Idea*. Harvard UP, 1933.

Lyons, Scott Richard. *X-Marks: Native Signatures of Assent.* U of Minnesota P, 2010.

Maldonado-Torres, Nelson. "On the Coloniality of Being." *Cultural Studies*, vol. 21, no. 2-3, 2007, pp. 240–70.

Massey, Doreen. *For Space*. SAGE Publications, 2005.

Mignolo, Walter D. *The Darker Side of Western Modernity: Global Futures, Decolonial Options*. Duke UP, 2011.

———. "Decoloniality and Phenomenology: The Geopolitics of Knowing and Epistemic/Ontological Colonial Differences." *Journal of Speculative Philosophy*, vol. 32, no. 3, 2018, pp. 360–87.

———. "Literacy and Colonization: The New World Experience." *1492–1992: Re/Discovering Colonial Writing*, edited by René Jara and Nicholas Spadaccini, Prisma Institute, 1989, pp. 51–96.

———. "On the Colonization of Amerindian Languages and Memories: Renaissance Theories of Writing and the Discontinuity of the Classical Tradition." *Comparative Studies in Society and History*, vol. 34, no. 2, 1992, pp. 301–30.

———. "Racism as We Sense It Today." *PMLA*, vol. 123, no. 5, 2008, pp. 1737–42.

———. "The Role of the Humanities in the Corporate University." *PMLA*, vol. 115, no. 5, 2000, pp. 1238–45.

———, and Catherine E. Walsh. *On Decoloniality: Concepts, Analytics, Praxis*. Duke UP, 2018.

Morton, Samuel George. *Crania Americana, or, A Comparative View of the Skulls of Various Aboriginal Nations of North and South America.* Philadelphia: John Penington, 1839.

Newman, John Henry. *The Idea of a University Defined and Illustrated: In Nine Discourses Delivered to the Catholics of Dublin*. 1852. Project of Gutenberg, 2008.

Nott, Josiah C., and George R. Gliddon. *Types of Mankind: Or, Ethnological Researches Based upon the Ancient Monuments, Paintings, Sculptures, and Crania of Races, and upon Their Natural, Geographical, Philological, and Biblical History*. Lippincott, Grambo, 1854.

Osamu, Nishitani. "Anthropos and Humanitas: Two Western Concepts of 'Human Being'." *Translation, Biopolitics, Colonial Difference*, edited by Naoki Sakai and Jon Solomon, Hong Kong UP, 2006, pp. 259–73.

Perez, Emma. *The Decolonial Imaginary: Writing Chicanas into History*. Indiana UP, 1999.

Quijano, Aníbal. "Coloniality and Modernity/Rationality." *Cultural Studies*, vol. 21, no. 2-3, 2007, pp. 168–78.

Ratcliffe, Krista. *Rhetorical Listening: Identification, Gender, Whiteness*. Southern Illinois UP, 2005.

Rickert, Thomas. *Ambient Rhetoric: The Attunements of Rhetorical Being*. U of Pittsburgh P, 2013.

Rohrer, Judy. *Staking Claim: Settler Colonialism and Racialization in Hawai'i*. U of Arizona P, 2016.

Royster, Jacqueline Jones. *Traces of a Stream: Literacy and Social Change among African American Women*. U of Pittsburgh P, 2000.

Ruiz, Iris D., and Raúl Sánchez, editors. *Decolonizing Rhetoric and Composition Studies: New Latinx Keywords for Theory and Pedagogy*. Palgrave MacMillan, 2016.

Rushdy, Ashraf H. A. *The End of American Lynching.* Rutgers UP, 2012.

Spivak, Gayatri Chakravorty. "Responsibility." *Boundary 2,* vol. 21, no. 3, 1994, pp. 19–64.

Tamez, Margo. "'Our Way of Life Is Our Resistance': Indigenous Women and Anti-Imperialist Challenges to Militarization along the U.S.-Mexico Border." *Invisible Battlegrounds*, vol. 29, no. 57/58, 2011, pp. 281–318.

Taussig, Michael. *Shamanism, Colonialism, and the Wild Man: A Study in Terror and Healing.* U of Chicago P, 1991.

Thiong'o, Ngũgĩ wa. *Decolonising the Mind: The Politics of Language in African Literature.* East African Educational Publishers, 2004.

Veracini, Lorenzo. *Settler Colonialism: A Theoretical Overview.* Palgrave MacMillan, 2010.

Villanueva, Victor, Jr. "Blind: Talking about the New Racism." *Writing Center Journal,* vol. 26, no. 1, 2006, pp. 3–19.

———. *Bootstraps: From an American Academic of Color.* National Council of Teachers of English, 1993.

———. "Colonial Memory and the Crime of Rhetoric: Pedro Albizu Campos." *College English,* vol. 71, no. 6, 2009, pp. 630–38.

———. "Colonial Memory, Colonial Research: A Preamble to a Case Study." *Beyond the Archives: Research as a Lived Process*, edited by Gesa E. Kirsch and Liz Rohan, Southern Illinois UP, 2008, pp. 83–92.

———. "Hegemony: From an Organically Grown Intellectual." *Pre/Text,* vol. 13, no. 1-2, 1992, pp. 18–35.

———. "Literacy, Culture, and the Colonial Legacy." *Reflections on Multiculturalism*, edited by Robert Eddy, Intercultural Press, 1996, pp. 79–99.

———. "Maybe a Colony: And Still Another Critique of the Comp Community." *JAC,* vol. 17, no. 2, 1997, pp. 183–90.

———. "*Memoria* Is a Friend of Ours: On the Discourse of Color." *College English*, vol. 67, no. 1, 2004, pp. 9–19.

———. "On the Rhetoric and Precedents of Racism." *College Composition and Communication*, vol. 50, no. 4, 1999, pp. 645–61.

———. "Rhetoric of the First 'Indians': The Taínos of the Second Voyage of Columbus." *Rhetorics of the Americas: 3114 BCE to 2012 CE*, edited by Damián Baca and Victor Villanueva, Palgrave MacMillan, 2010, pp. 15–20.

Wynter, Sylvia. "Unsettling the Coloniality of Being/Power/Truth/Freedom: Towards the Human, After Man, Its Overrepresentation—an Argument." *CR: The New Centennial Review,* vol. 3, no. 3, 2003, pp. 257–337.

SECTION II: *MEMORIA* OF MENTORING

THE CHAPTERS IN THIS SECTION center on Victor's mentoring. The authors share their experiences with and appreciation of Victor's mentorship, describing its substantial impact on themselves, on others, and on the field more broadly. Some contributors recount how Victor's mentorship has contributed to their own development as scholars and teachers, and others show how his mentorship has impacted their own research and scholarship. These chapters explore the ways mentoring can be differently embodied and practiced, as well as its importance in cultivating and sustaining alliances across generations within our field.

By way of exploring and reflecting on mentoring, the contributors here engage with multiple of Victor's publications. In addition to "*Memoria* Is a Friend of Ours: On the Discourse of Color," two publications are referenced often across these chapters: his monograph, *Bootstraps: From an American Academic of Color,* and his article "On the Rhetorics and Precedents of Racism." Collectively, this engagement highlights the importance of mentorship for individuals, both mentees and mentors, by exploring how mentorship grows our field's research and the paths we create and enter on as a discipline. As we did in the introduction we provided for Section I: *Memoria* of Rhetorics, we trace some themes across the chapters in this section, posing reflective questions for readers to consider along the way.

In the opening chapter, J. Paul Padilla explores and illustrates the "fictive kinship" many academics of color, like Padilla, engage in, which Victor identifies publicly, using Signithia Fordham's ideas on the topic. But it is Victor's mentoring over twenty years for Padilla that forms the center of this chapter and evokes numerous insights. Padilla concludes that "[k]inship relationships are forged through truth, trust, and togetherness over time," while also observing that "the trial of a writer of color who addresses racism is to speak when silence is sold as the secret to both success and survival" (p. 230). Invoking Victor as one example, Padilla asks: "Are we willing to serve those writers of color as kin, with the same love and empathy and uncertainty that they show in their courage to transform their silence into language and action earnestly and critically, to address racism sympathetically and frankly?" (p. 235). In doing so, Padilla motivates us to think through how we mentor, and how one does this kind of mentoring, this kind of serving. In the final touching section, Padilla distills his mentoring experience with Victor, boiling it all down to "care, community, kinship, [and] courage." Given Victor's example as captured by Padilla, we ought to consider the following as a field: How do we, as mentors all, embody care, community, kinship, and courage?

In the second chapter of this section, Morris Young ruminates on Victor's mentoring of academics of color through his example and his published words. Young discusses the impact "On the Rhetoric and Precedents of Racism" had on him, and how it continued the work he read in *Bootstraps*. The article was the published version of Victor's 1999 Conference on College Composition and Communication Chair's Address, which Young attended and recalls. He considers how important Victor was as a prominent scholar of color speaking about racism and colonialism in the academy at the time. Reflecting on Victor's impact, Young reminds us to consider why representation is still important today and how racism in the US has sustained itself over the last twenty-some years. He asks, how do we move forward, make progress, or understand the ways racism and our colonial sensibilities are deeply knitted in us? The mentoring we see most illustrated in Young's discussion is not a direct mentoring, not a one-on-one in an office kind of mentoring, not even years-long email exchanges; rather, it is a subtle mentoring of example and representation, which we all may not be called to do but can notice and consider.

Robert Eddy (Salah Al-Din) considers his three-decade-long friendship with Victor and likens him to Zhuangzi's figure of "the happy wanderer," whom he explains embodies "quiet attentiveness to everyone's full humanity that invites experiences of crossing boundaries, of movement amidst conflict, contestation, and even among competing fundamentalisms" (p. 257). Eddy considers the way Victor embodies mentoring and caring in his relationships and his antiracist work. Ultimately, he asks how Victor can remain the happy wanderer in "racist structures and environments"? Perhaps, as Eddy suggests, part of the secret lies in love. Echoing Padilla's discussion of fictive kinship, Eddy juxtaposes two images that Victor himself has chosen to represent his own vision of himself as a young man and an older one, revealing not just the kinship Victor imagines with globally distant uncolonized peoples, but also his "wandering" nature and his own sense of connection. Eddy sees in Victor an "Islamic Spanish pluralism of Ibn Hazm, [who is] multiracial, multicultural, multireligious, and all in service to resisting human oppressions by dominant groups" (p. 264).

In a more personal account, Octavio Pimentel recounts his own educational journey and his family's work as "trabajadores del fil" in California, Oregon, and Washington. He connects his own story to Victor's "cuento" given in *Bootstraps*, a central text that he returns to throughout the chapter. While Pimentel's family comes from Ecuandureo (state of Michoacán) and Zapoltiltic (state of Jalisco), both in Mexico, Victor's articulation of the structural racism in the US, particularly in schools, is part of Pimentel's refrain. Eventually he finds a mentor in Victor, "El Jefe," centered on his reading of *Bootstraps*. But it's the tension in Pimentel's narrative that readers might notice, a tension with the field of rhetoric and composition as much as with educational systems more broadly. And yet, despite these messages, he says, "I did not listen to this rhetoric because I knew I was better than that. I knew that my educational experience was something that the academy needed to hear. *Y aqui estoy* and don't plan on going nowhere" (p. 285). In light of Pimentel's personal account, we might ask: What does it mean that some (many or most) BIPOC students and scholars must *not listen* to the rhetoric around them in order to participate, or even be present in, the field or to persevere in schools? In a field where listening seems vital, central even, what lessons are there in Pimentel's refusal to listen to the rhetoric around him? And what roles do mentoring and representation play in that nonlistening?

In her chapter, Lauren Rosenberg tells the story of Victor's mentoring over several years as she writes a book that considers four adult language learners who become organic intellectuals in the way that Gramsci explores. The book changes dramatically, just like her own career. Rosenberg's disciplinary roots are in fiction and storytelling, but she moved into rhetoric and composition at this moment in her career. Victor is there to help, mentor, and encourage her. She shares in the chapter drawings and emails that develop the book, showing how they reveal the kind of collaborative mentoring that the other chapters in this section suggest about Victor. Once the book is done, Rosenberg recalls her dilemma: "All our rich thinking, talking, writing—would it now end? I was at a loss at the end of the editor–author collaboration" (p. 303). Mentoring can result in loss, a paradox for sure, but it can also change and grow. As Rosenberg goes on to share, her mentoring relationship with Victor continues in some ways, but it also developed into an ongoing friendship. Her chapter reveals not only a rich and collaborative mentoring relationship but also a dramatization of the generative potential of mentorship, one that can be asked only at the end of a mentoring that is deep, rich, full of life and ideas and words.

Finally, Ana Milena Ribero and Aja Y. Martinez end this section with an allegory/fantasy counterstory that puts the authors in conversation with Victor in the late 1990s, around the publication of "On the Rhetoric and Precedents of Racism." The dialogue focuses on the various ways that racism today in the third decade of the twenty-first century is remarkably similar to the racism of the 1990s. The two questions that Ribero and Martinez pose through Victor near the end of the discussion are fitting for students and scholars today, particularly ones in mentoring relationships: "How will you work to dismantle the white supremacy of knowledge? How will your actions break the rhetorics and precedents of racism?" To answer such questions, we will most likely need to take *Memoria*'s hand, turn as she turns, dig with her, and bravely take on the future as our present becomes our past. But as each chapter in this section illustrates in various ways, we all also need, perhaps even yearn for, mentors and mentoring that can sustain us in difficult and joyful times. Dismantling white supremacy very likely requires the kind of compassionate mentoring that Victor embodies and that is discussed in this section's chapters.

Chapter 10

Cuentos de Mi Historia con Nuestro Hermano Victor Villanueva: Fictive Kinship to Support Writers of Color Addressing Racism

J. Paul Padilla

A MEMORY. Milwaukee, fall of 2000.

Victor Villanueva agreed to meet with a young writer, a recent graduate of Marquette University, privately at the NCTE Annual Convention titled "Teaching Matters." Reed Magazine, *published by San José State University, informed the writer that his essay would be published in the spring. So insecure and naive was the writer that he published under a pseudonym, and he feared requesting his contributor's copy. (In 2011 he finally did, learning that "Noel Vidal Garcia" was one of a handful of contributors without an MFA or a PhD.)*

The writer, in his mind, was not a writer. James Baldwin, Audre Lorde, bell hooks—they *were writers.*

"Just an essay from Dr. Ratcliffe's Advanced Composition class," the writer remembers telling Victor.[1] *"Just luck, really."*

"No," the writer remembers Victor saying, "you got some serious skill."

Of everything Victor said in that hour, the writer carried with him more than was said in that hour, the writer carried with him more than Victor's words. He carried a sense of care and community that gave him the confidence to believe that, maybe, he is *a writer. That sense started with Kris Ratcliffe, the writer's*

English major mentor and professor for contemporary rhetoric and advanced composition courses. Kris encouraged him to see his future not only as a writer, but also as a scholar in rhetoric and composition studies. One day, he confessed his exasperation to her: "The only Latino writer we ever read (at Marquette) is Richard Rodriguez—and as the *model of, and for, Latinos." Kris introduced the writer to Victor's writing, then to Victor himself.*

. . .

That evening, the Number 80 bus took the writer from the convention site in downtown Milwaukee to his lifelong home in a neighborhood the city labeled "Historic Mitchell Street" and Milwaukeeans called the ghetto.

On the Number 80, he reconciled that sense he carried with the reality he faced. His "gap year" reflected more than the time for a first-generation student of color to decide between law school or graduate school. His gap reflected a particular tension. On one end, the choice to escape poverty to help his aging parents (and perhaps transcending racism, the subconscious hope of a person racialized and minoritized for his dark skin and physiognomy). And on the other, the choice to live as a writer, writing as he had in his essay and as Victor encouraged writers like him to do: addressing matters concerning racism sympathetically and frankly ("On the Rhetoric" 652). Victor understood that tension, but he seemed to transcend it. Victor was the first writer he ever met—un hermano—who addressed racism earnestly and critically without the fate others racialized as people of color faced: silencing, ostracization, vilification. That, somehow, scared the writer.

The writer stared beyond his reflection in the passenger window, staving off tears as the Number 80 reached his stop.

That day, writing ended for me, but being a writer, strangely, began. A decade filled with milestones, transformations, and grief passed before I realized this. Once I did, I realized that writing may happen in solitude, but a writer needs community.

A reminiscence:

"At least Victor agreed to read it," I told myself, "even if he doesn't remember you from the NCTE Convention."

A victory in itself. In the last nine months it had proved nearly impossible to just talk to another writer, let alone fulfill my 2012 New Year resolution to find community. While I could imagine the volume of messages like mine that writers received, I felt that my work held promise, supported by Chimamanda Ngozi Adichie's selection of my sudden fiction for NPR.

"It's your subject," an old college friend told me. "That's the problem."

My fiction addressed racism in the United States, specifically anti-Latino and intercultural Latino racism through second-person perspective narratives. Despite my Juris Doctor degree from a top-tier law school and my in-house counsel role for Fortune companies, I lived as a dark-skinned man in post-9/11 "'Murica": no longer a citizen, no longer "white" by law (I am Mexican American)—a cisgender man racialized often as Muslim, sometimes as Black, once in a while as Hispanic, alive in the American Imagination as the immigrant, the alien, the threat.

How many stories did I have of traveling for work, professional conferences, and continuing legal education courses where I found myself the target of anger, aggression, hate, or law enforcement? How many stories did I have of much worse happening to loved ones and friends still in Milwaukee? These stories were generational, cyclical. 9/11 was my generation's event, but every generation has its own passive revolution. I knew, but I was silent. My silence reflected, in sum, a naïve investment in the hope of transcending racism, a hope that became a species of racelessness I never intended. With the birth of my only child and the passing of my parents, I felt the need to transform my silence into language and action. I felt Victor would understand.

Victor promised to reply in two weeks. Days later, he sent me this:

I've walked the streets of Pilsen. I've taken the El from Pilsen to get off at the Loop to the comfort of the Palmer House.

So do you have an agent? You might want one. I think your writing is absolutely lovely, tender, powerfully quiet.

Let me get over my crisis, then let's chat. I thoroughly enjoyed reading those pieces, especially the first one.

Email me in a week or so, please, so that we can set up a time to Skype. victor.

And so a four-year writing relationship began. Much of Victor's teaching remains invisible to the readers of my texts—not just the feedback on drafts, but the talks and the patience and the forgiving and the trust that forges the courage to examine the contradictory consciousness through critical consciousness. That invisible labor often defines writing for those writers of color who address racism.

Those four years were productive. Thirteen stories constituting the forthcoming collection titled *Si Dios Nos Presta Vida.* Scores of sudden fiction and longer short stories. Essays. Awards. Publications. Many rejections. Many, many failed texts.

Victor's teaching also informed my community service, a practice of servant leadership that grew at the University of Wisconsin Law School. My service ramped up as I wrote under his guidance and I raised my son as a single parent, all while practicing law. Yet something haunted me, something that I couldn't reconcile:

"Shit, 'mano*—keep practicing law and you'll have a heart attack at fifty. [Laughter] You're a writer. You're meant for academia. Here, they'll appreciate what you do in the community. [Laughter]"*

This is how I remember the many pitches Victor made to me to leave law and pursue a PhD in rhetoric and composition studies. (And his wonderful laughter! The laughter that anyone who knows Victor knows well.) He and I came full circle in 2015. His pitch to me in 2000 was serious, but the same at its core. And I knew my truth as I stared beyond my reflection on the Number 80: how long would I go staving off my whole Self?

I am a writer.

He knew this, but he stood by me until I knew. A part of me still wonders why someone so accomplished would be so invested in a nobody like me?

Working with me meant invisible labor for him—much more than feedback on drafts. A writer addressing racism meant the work of addressing reality; institutions, along with those invested in those institutions, try to publicly shape dominant narratives that separate race from hierarchy of power—in essence, race from racism—and privately smother any effort, small or large, contrary to their narratives, which includes silencing anyone deemed "aloof" or "trouble." And that reality meant dealing with the heavens and the storms of the writer. Behind my writing, community service accomplishments, writing and service accolades, leadership programs and awards, was a person with a heart trying to succeed "despite." Even when I decided, at Victor's suggestion, to attend the University of Arizona for my doctoral work instead of Washington State University, he understood the many personal and professional reasons I feared that Pullman would be just another Bloomington-Normal, a small conservative white contact zone.

"Wherever you are," Victor told me, "I'll see you through the end."

Victor was right: "Memory simply cannot be adequately portrayed in the conventional discourse of the academy" ("*Memoria*" 12). Had I relied solely on logos to explain the theme of these memories, so much would have been lost. These memories—*cuentos de mi historia*[2] *con nuestro hermano*—represent something of me as a student and a writer, that which is individual, vulnerable, earnest about the choice of language and action over silence. And *estos cuentos* represent something more, as memories always do, where the analytical and the argumentative, present in the invention, arrangement, delivery, and style of memory, reflect the focus on the experiential and the autobiographical to critically examine the political—ideology and hegemony (Villanueva, "Hegemony" 32–33 and *Bootstraps* xvii–xviii, 140–43). The "I" symbolizes me and so many, with each being a tessera in the mosaic of truth about writing. Here, *estos cuentos* represent tesserae in such a mosaic about writing and about Victor—a few truths about kinship and courage.

In what follows, I explore the importance of kinship, namely, fictive kinship, from writing teachers like Victor to support students of color who address matters concerning racism sympathetically and frankly as writers in communities and in academia. The first section, "On Kinship," speaks to the importance of fictive kinship through an understanding of the challenges faced by writers of color who address racism and the role of a kinship triad to support such writers. The second section, "On Courage," speaks to the challenge of teachers and administrators to provide genuine kinship to writers of color who address racism. The last section, "Onward," speaks to considerations for teachers and administrators in light of Victor's retirement.

ON KINSHIP

I start this exploration about the importance of kinship here, with the challenges faced by the writer of color who addresses racism.

Consider these words from James Baldwin about writing:

> When you're writing, you're trying to find out something which you don't know. The whole language of writing for me is finding out what you don't want to know, what you don't want to find out. But something forces you to anyway. (qtd. in Elgrably)

These words resonate with me not only as a writer, but also as an individual racialized as a person of color in the United States, and given who Baldwin was as a writer and an individual. Baldwin, for those who may not know, was a twentieth century gay Black man from Harlem whose work as a writer and a public intellectual centered upon the moral crisis of racism in the United States, resonating with Americans as powerfully in our time as in his. Perhaps Baldwin meant his words to speak about writing as an art generally. That said, I cannot help but feel his words more deeply, as all of his work addressed racism. He wrote: "I have not written about being a Negro at such length because I expect that to be my only subject, but only because it was the gate I had to unlock before I could hope to write about anything else" ("Autobiographical Note" 8).

To me, Baldwin's words speak to challenges certain writers of color face given their own position in space and time. I mean "certain" in fairness, really. We must recognize that not all writers of color, like not all people deemed to be "people of color," address racism in their writing, personally or publicly. And for some, writing is a conscious act of community, reserved for communities with whom the writer identifies. For those writers who address racism through their work, the compulsion to find out the unknown involves a journey—challenges, struggles, revelations, reconciliations, and stays—at times, conflicted or confused or contradictory—in knowing that racism, as the primary hierarchy of power that defines coloniality in the United States and in every epicenter of coloniality throughout the Americas,[3] is *the* barrier to knowing one's Self and one's relationship to others.

The aforementioned appears lost to many, or so it seems. *Lost* may not be the word. And I think of some in our field of rhetoric and composition studies as I search for the right word.

A salient reminder for me was the receipt of the July 8, 2020, *Newsweek* opinion article "Why I Still Talk to White People about Racism" by Erec Smith, associate professor at York College of Pennsylvania. Smith argued, in short, that people of color in the United States need to embrace their ethical and civil responsibility to educate white Americans about racism after the May 2020 murder of George Floyd, despite trauma, anger, suffering, or grief. While framed in a white/Black binary, his argument entailed specific ideas about people of color worth noting. On knowledge of racism: "We all have doctorates in 'experiencing racism,' and our expertise is needed" (par. 6). (What is the other side of this binary for Smith? White people have doctorates in "exhibiting racism"? In his words: "Yes, racism as we know it was created by white people" (par. 6). On self-care, community-care, and trauma for people of color: "Take whatever metaphorical DayQuil you need and take advantage of this unparalleled moment in time" to educate whites about racism (para. 5). On our ethical and moral responsibility to use our doctorate in experiencing racism to educate whites: "Otherwise, we are hypocrites as we demand white people listen to us and, in the very next breath, tell them they need to stop talking to us" (para. 6). As for Smith, "It's raining woke white people, and you're grabbing umbrellas or running for shelter. I'm dancing in it like Gene Kelly" (para. 5).

I note the receipt of the article as well. A professor sent it to all of us, students and faculty in the Rhetoric, Composition, and the Teaching of English (RCTE) program at the University of Arizona. That is, he sent a link to the article without any statement on it. More on this in "On Courage." For now, it may go without saying that the sending of this article, as well as the article's message, was a response to, and a reminder for, the few students like me left in RCTE.

The right word may never come to mind, but a parallel does. And this parallel speaks to popular beliefs about the role of people of color and, among them, writers of color. Victor noted that the popularity of writer Richard Rodriguez with educators extended beyond Rodriguez being "a fine writer" ("Whose Voice" 17). Rodriguez's popularity reflected the popularity of his message: the duty of so-called minority to assimilate to the American ideal of citizenship, whiteness, with an implied—and questionable—promise of "subtly changing what it means to be American" (Villanueva, "Whose Voice" 17) by "becoming part of America (17). I think this point extends to the ideas of Smith if we see both Rodriguez and Smith as capturing public as well as academic imaginations through the affirmation of a particular destiny for people of color in service of American ideals of whiteness. Some in our field may not hold Smith's ideas. True. But some do—and much more than anyone would admit publicly, I wager. Still, there is something to be said.

As a writer and an individual, I will say this: Smith's ideas—the presumptive duty of people of color to serve whites as top priority; the innate and complete knowledge that people of color should have about racism; the denial of self-discovery and critical consciousness; the degree of shaming, insensitivity, and silencing; the oversimplification of racism's intellectual, psychological, and sociological complexity; the essentialization of racial identities and related forms of racism; the majoritarian narrative of white ignorance, innocence, and simplicity; the flawed notion of shared community—all of these, well . . . these are not uncommon.

Baldwin's perspective about writing parallels Victor's with respect to writing on matters concerning racism sympathetically and frankly. It may be broad, but not unfair, to say that Victor understood that force that drives people of color to explore the unknown about racism. Throughout his scholarship, Victor encouraged those who did explore to do so honestly and earnestly, to face the legacy of colonialism and coloniality, the work of claiming and reclaiming identity through memory and narrative, and the challenges of one's own contradictory consciousness, as Victor himself did in his writing. And Victor did so through a distinct genre in the field of rhetoric and composition studies, the "mixed genre" or "critical autobiographical," as he calls it. With Aristotle's definition of *episteme* in mind—that which is teachable, learnable—Victor stated in an interview the following about his genre:

> We're talking about something else. How we come to know is directly tied to our use of language. So if how we come to know is directly tied to our use of language, that means that the experience and language are tightly intermeshed. So why not make that public?

Even if a writer of color uses a different genre, there is the element of one's own experience in our use of language. Baldwin stated the following about experience and writing:

> One writes out of one thing only—one's own experience. Everything depends on how relentlessly one forces from this experience the last drop, sweet or bitter, it can possibly give. This is the only real concern of the artist, to recreate out of the disorder of life that order which is art. The difficulty then, for me, of being a Negro writer was the fact that I was, in effect,

> prohibited from examining my own experience too closely by the tremendous demands and the very real dangers of my social situation. ("Autobiographical Note" 8)

What Baldwin stated about his experience as a Black writer, I believe, holds true for the experiences of writers of color who address racism. The deep, determined drive of the writer and the demands and dangers of the writer's social situation exist intertwined, a reality with which writers of color live.

For as much as I hear about the writing classroom, I, as a writer and a writing teacher, know that most academic writing does not occur within the walls of a classroom or during the time of a class session. (And, from what I know, there are those writing teachers who steer away from the word, and the reality of, "racism" in the writing classroom, let alone in major writing projects addressing racism in the United States.) While the force of which Baldwin speaks will drive writers of color to persist against the odds and address racism, alone if necessary, I cannot help but think of the larger implications of the words Eduardo Bonilla-Silva shared with me in the fall of 2020: "You cannot do this kind of work alone," he said with respect to my work on racism. "You'll go crazy."

Some of us have no choice. This was the first thought that came to mind.

Bonilla-Silva is right, of course. This is where I believe kinship is so important for writers of color who address racism, especially in light of the reality they face.

What do I mean by "kinship" itself? I point to definitions from Signithia Fordham and Victor to define a variation of fictive kinship important to certain writers of color.

Citing the established definition among anthropologists, Signithia Fordham defined *fictive kinship* as "a kin-like connection between and among persons in a society not related by blood or marriage, who have maintained essential reciprocal social or economic relationships" (56). She focused specifically on the tension between the cultural, political, and economic functions of fictive kinship for identity formation within the African American community and the implicit expectation of "racelessness"—code for the invisible normativity of whiteness—in education institutions (54–55).

Fordham herself neither created the definition of fictive kinship nor limited the definition to African Americans. However, some in academia interpret her essay in that manner, or so it seems. Of the few who have addressed fictive kinship in rhetoric and composition studies, the majority seem to speak specifically to work involving African Americans.

Victor spoke to the concept of fictive kinship in "Of Kin and Community," embracing a broader, interpretative definition and applying the concept to a particular group identity, like Fordham (108–11). Victor explored several variations of "fictive kinship relationships" (108) through his journey from graduate student to scholar within the National Council of Teachers of English (NCTE), the Conference on College Composition and Communication (CCCC), and rhetoric and composition studies more generally. Victor expanded on Fordham's definition, stating the following:

> Although Fordham is writing of African Americans, it is a situation that obtains whenever our numbers are few. We all do it. Hispanics in an overwhelmingly white organization will gather together, women of whatever "race" in male-dominated situations, poor people among the middle class. We all do it. We find those with whom we believe we have a cultural or economic kinship and act accordingly. We bond. (108–9)

The kinship that Victor ultimately identified was one with English teachers, a bond that involved ties to "the principal language of this nation" (109) and unity by a common goal despite differences of opinion, "the linguistic and rhetorical success of our—all of our—youth" (110) with respect to literacy. "We are a community," Victor wrote, "bound by a love of language, through reading, writing, and rhetoric (the effective use and interpretation of what is written and read)" (110).

It is fair to say writers of color who enter rhetoric and composition studies share in that love of language, that goal of literacy, and that tie to the English language, and imagine being part of that community and sharing in that kinship. But one of the very real demands and dangers of being a writer of color addressing racism is the threat of such an identity and such work to kinship in that community. Fordham reminded us that kinship involves a fundamental choice of a community: who is welcomed and who is not. There may be an irony in me stating this point after citing our top scholar on racism for his identification of kinship among English teachers. Yet even Victor identified squabbles over differences among those united in community by fictive kinship ("Of Kinship" 110). I think it is also fair to say that there is more to it. Scholars in rhetoric and composition studies often cite Catherine Prendergast's words about the "absent presence of race" in rhetoric and composition studies—Victor addressed the "return to the question of racism, the 'absent presence' in our discourse (Prendergast)" ("On the Rhetoric" 648). But Prendergast, whose work also appears in this volume, addresses racism separately as the "absent absence" (36), which is a significant difference that speaks for itself. Her words, though published over twenty years ago, carry a certain weight during these times that many would concede.

As I see it, Victor gave writers like me the gift of a fictive kinship that sprang from that community and kinship of English teachers with whom he identified. This gift was truly unique, for the kinship we shared wasn't about misgivings regarding *Latinidad*, but about ideals on addressing racism. He and I never discussed those ideals. I think those ideals are visible throughout his work.

Here, let me focus on four examples—two essays, one talk, and one book—that I feel capture what I mean. In his essay "*Memoria* Is a Friend of Ours: On the Discourse of Color," Victor emphasized the importance of memory to students of color, especially Latinx, for memory, reclamation, formation, and reformation of identity individually and collectively shaped by racism of colonialism and coloniality (12), even identifying himself as having a "contradictory consciousness" (17). Because of this importance, he called on us to remember and invite memory as pathos, along with logos, into our classroom and scholarship (19). In his essay "On the Rhetoric and Precedents of Racism," he underscored the importance of "people of color writing frankly, sympathetically about matters concerning racism" (652), not only for journals in rhetoric and composition studies but also to address the legacy of racism, breaking from our colonial discourse that continues an unchecked hegemony that results, in part, from the failing of multiculturalism, hybridity, and plurality. In a 2015 talk called "Writing as a Way of Doing," he shared this: "How we come to know (epistemologically and ontologically)—how we make sense of our experience in the world—is by way of language." As I shared in the introduction, focusing on the experiential and the autobiographical is to critically examine the political—ideology and hegemony (Villanueva, "Hegemony" 32–33, and *Bootstraps* xvii–xviii, 140–43). Combined, these can be viewed as one's exploration and analysis of the experiential in, and with, the world, defined by the presence of colonialism and coloniality in racism through language and action to understand epistemology, ontology, and axiology. And these are akin to Baldwin's points on writing.

As with racism or writing, something so intimate, personal, and complex as kinship could never be addressed meaningfully in a how-to manual. Kinship relationships are forged through truth, trust, and togetherness over time, hence the nature of "kin-like connection."

What I can offer is an understanding of critical points of support for writers of color addressing racism, an understanding that I view as a triad of support in the form of care, community, nurturing, and security. The first point of the triad involves writing as discovery—support for the writer to have the safe space and latitude to recognize, reckon with, and write about the complex reality of racism for themselves. The second point of the triad involves writing as community—support for the writer to gauge and grapple with the drive, demands, and dangers of addressing racism through the public act of writing. The third point of the triad involves writing as flourishing—support for the writer to follow that force and drive into the unknown and, through invention, memory, arrangement, style, and delivery, create writing that moves the Self and communities closer to the known. At the center of the triad is the principle of genuine investment. This investment is not just in ideals about addressing racism; this investment is in the individual who comes to identify as a writer. Part of that idea of genuine investment involves a variant idea of *confianza*, about which Steven Alvarez wrote. The term *confianza* translates from Spanish to English as "confidence" literally, but it connotes more than that. Alvarez describes *confianza* as a "dialogical trust, acceptance and confirmation between researchers and communities" (220). Referencing the work of Leslie Bartlett and Ofelia García, Alvarez explains that confianza involves a practice that "means reciprocating a relationship where individuals feel cared for" and a "humanizing process centered on local communities, which involves exchanging mutual respect, critical reflection, caring and group participation" (220). I see *confianza* as existing more broadly in different dynamics. Between a writer and a teacher or mentor, *confianza* is that feeling of a deep, reciprocal trust earned through giving, authenticity, and integrity toward the identity and ideals of humanity that drive writers, and those who support such writers, to address racism.

Talk with Victor for fifteen minutes about addressing racism through writing. That time tells a writer what they need to know about him as a teacher, a mentor, and an individual—I know that is how I felt when I first spoke with him at the NCTE Convention in Milwaukee. His kinship shows his investment. Always there. Always engaged. Never a word about inclusion, intrusion, or invisible labor. That means so much.

In knowing Victor for over two decades, in working with him over the last decade, in becoming more than just a writer to my own students and mentees over the last half decade, I gained perspective and appreciation for that which is essential to establish fictive kinship with the individual who decides that they, too, are a writer: courage.

ON COURAGE

There may be a lingering question about fictive kinship relationships with writers of color who address racism in their work. I imagine it as a rhetorical question by teachers and administrators, rooted in a concern about exigency: *What about those of us who promote diversity/plurality/hybridity/multiculturalism/antiracism in our approach to teaching or administration?* However this question may be stated, the core remains the same: *we know it because we do it.* Maybe. Maybe not. It depends. Who is asking? Who is asked? Who can answer and who will be heard?

The challenge of the writer of color who addresses racism, as well as the teacher with whom they share fictive kinship, is the challenge of transforming silence into language and action earnestly and critically. The will to transform is a question of courage. This is particularly true for academia in our nation, I believe. Trumpeted public signaling often belies a troubling private reality—a secret everyone seems to know but fears to speak.

Another memory. Summer of 2020.

> *"I hope this email finds you well," the program head's July 14 message to the writer began. "I'm writing because the faculty is planning some talks around race and identity in the coming weeks."*
>
> *Their message goes on to ask him to join others to educate the program's faculty, most white, on—"race and identity."*
>
> *The writer shook his head.*
>
> *Throughout the national crisis on racism, the writer had not received any messages from the program head or faculty directly. The program's messages exacerbated matters. The writer's conversations with his dissertation co-chair inspired her to write to the program about one of the writer's central concerns on June 6: "Sometimes even well-meaning messages of support are still only directed at the white audience, missing a chance to say that you matter." Nothing changed. On July 8, a professor sent the Erec Smith Newsweek link to all in the program, without a statement. None was needed, ironically.*
>
> *For the writer, the terror and trauma of the times was communal, intergenerational, personal, profound.*
>
> *The writer had many stories of his own, including as a grad student. A story of the CCCC Convention and Portland and anti-Muslim experiences at his hotel, around town, and with the TSA. A story of the day of his oral comp exam, of police*

surrounding him because a white woman, in tears, feared that the writer was trafficking his white-passing son as he picked him up after school. And more. Stories faculty knew. Some gaslit. One, maybe two, empathized. Most ignored, as they ignored his work, despite numerous publications on racism. And overlooked micro-aggressions. And dismissed racial trauma. And never reached out after his near-fatal heart attack, his related health issues, or the loss of loved ones over the last year. Some have yet to say "hello."

The trial of a writer of color who addresses racism is to speak when silence is sold as the secret to both success and survival.

"Over the past eight weeks during this time in our nation's history," the writer's response to the program head began, "(the Program's) public communications on BLM, race, and racism have focused primarily on the education of White students and faculty, with only one faculty member speaking publicly to the considerations of students of color in an effort to encourage others."

His response went on, addressing concerns earnestly and frankly about the lack of care shown toward communities of color during these times, about the choice of each person of color to serve those with whom they have community, about the overarching problem in the program now and over the past four years. His response was followed by others as the Program Head tried to do what they have done to him before: control the conversation paternalistically.

Control means speak only to the extent they allow. After a summer of their numerous long emails on educating whites, the program head decided "long e-mails are not productive or healthy" when the message on racism was the writer's. Control also came with a backhanded comment contextually.

"I also have a right to my own professional and personal well-being."

The writer shook his head.

This is not kinship. And for many students of color in higher education across the nation, this, well . . . this is not uncommon.

The national crisis on racism removed the gag from many silences that, for generations, students of color were conditioned to keep as the price of the ticket into academia. From conversations of support to publications in popular and academic periodicals, more and more stories have addressed this given the predominance of white-centered responses to the crisis. Yet there was, and still is, the expectation to keep our silence—the secret to success and survival. How often have we, as students of color, been reminded of the relationship between silence and success in those private talks about "our future"? How often have you, as a well-meaning figure, reminded students of color of this relationship through coded whispers of strategy, self-preservation, or political appetite? It is perhaps the most open of secrets that those of us in institutions, academia or otherwise, carry. Where race is the absent presence, racism is the absent absence. *Racism* is a word that some teachers and administrators refuse to state even during one of the most pivotal periods in recent United States history, the national crisis on racism.

While many cite Signithia Fordham's essay "Racelessness as a Factor in Black Students' School Success: Pragmatic Strategy or Pyrrhic Victory?" for the idea of fictive kinship in Black communities, fewer, so it seems, cite her essay for her discussion of racelessness in education. Her focus, as I understood it, was the concern about the sacrifice of fictive kinship in one's racial community for the promise of success through "racelessness," code for the institutionalization of whiteness as an invisible cultural norm. That normative whiteness is still present—and another open secret we are expected to keep for the sake of success and survival. But our silence comes in a different way. It comes in the expectations of the adoption of an etiquette, a knowledge of how to speak about race and racism in a way that preserves racelessness.

Erec Smith's call, which I addressed in the section "On Kinship," is one side of a two-headed coin. The other side is liberal white supremacy, a concept that Tsedale M. Melaku and Angie Beeman address in their article "Academia Isn't a Safe Haven for Conversations about Race and Racism." The authors include Beeman's definition of liberal white supremacy as

> the tendency of white people to constantly place themselves in the superior moral position. This takes many forms. Some want to compete for the title of most "woke" progressive. Some show up to insert themselves in conversations about racial and economic inequality only when it becomes popular or high-profile to do so. (para. 12)

As Melaku and Beeman state, "When discussions of systemic and institutional racism do happen, white people often want to run the conversation" (para. 12). Since whiteness is ideological, I would reframe "white people" as "those possessively invested in whiteness." I would also reframe "run the conversation" to "control the conversation."

While controlling these conversations involves many strategies, I see two dominant, intertwined strategies: what Melaku and Beeman call "racism-evasive rhetoric" and what I call "racism-reimagined rhetoric." Melaku and Beeman describe racism-evasive rhetoric as follows:

> Racism-evasive rhetoric denies naming and addressing the significance and realities of racism. Examples include: emotional responses, such as crying, to deflect from hard conversations; using African Americans as color capital; the performance of sending white children to racially diverse schools as a way to deflect from problematic or racist behavior; and claiming special insights due to traveling the world or having intermarried. In Angie's [Beeman] experience, all of these racism-evasive tactics have surfaced in everything from departmental discussions about racism to cynicism and incredulity about her research on the experiences of faculty of color. . . . In line with Angie's research, Tsedale [Melaku] has experienced how white colleagues use racism-evasive tactics to avoid engaging issues that push Black voices from the margins to the center. (paras. 11, 13)

"Racism-reimagined rhetoric" means the rhetoric that seeks to reimagine race as a cultural concept separate from its creation and function as the primary system of dominance and oppression in epicenters of coloniality across the Americas through the centering of whiteness. In the United States, racism-reimagined rhetoric takes many forms. Examples include institutional language of diversity and inclusion as white-defined and white-serving ideals; majoritarian narratives on the promise of progress and cultural assimilation centered on white ignorance and innocence; and performative gestures to abstractions of social justice, including vocal declarations about white privilege in predominantly white academic safe spaces. Together, these provide control to those possessively invested in whiteness over the content, etiquette, and feeling of conversations on racism, which promotes and protects liberal white supremacy.

Perhaps these two types of rhetoric are nothing new. Whereas Victor identified color-blind racism to be the seeming evolution of the same racism as always—that is, the material reality of racism that is not new after all ("Blind" 18), I see liberal white supremacy as the seeming evolution of the supremacy on which bell hooks wrote in her 1989 article "Choosing the Margin as a Space of Radical Openness." Control over our speech and our silence, seeking the voice of people of color to speak only of their pain. I have come to call this "qualified pain," a concept I first explored in my 2019 article "What Isn't Heard: Dyslogistic Silence and Silencing at Candlelight Vigils for the Orlando Massacre."

Qualified pain means pain that speaks to the experience of people of color with racism through racism-evasive rhetoric and racism-reinvented rhetoric absent actual events or actions that implicate whiteness. Where I understand but respectfully disagree with bell hooks is about the margin, specifically the concession of our place there. Whiteness, as a hierarchical construct of power, depends on a position of dominance and centrality, hence its need for those in a position of oppression and marginality. Like hooks and any person of color, I am the center of any space I occupy by virtue of my humanity, even in resistance.

But the writer of color who addresses racism lives with an ever-present existential dilemma. While racism cannot be addressed in half measures, writers of color face the very real demands and very real dangers of their social situation, as the national crisis on racism has highlighted in different ways. In academia, they know the fate of those who breach silence, challenge control, and question care, community, and kinship: silencing, ostracization, vilification. They know because they have been reminded, time and again, by those who reside on either side of the aforementioned coin. They also know these words of Audre Lorde well, even if they had never heard of Audre Lorde: "My silence had not protected me. Your silence will not protect you" (41). And these words, as Lorde meant them for Black women as well as all women, are as meaningful to those racialized as people of color in the United States: *We were never meant to survive* (42).

Lest we forget, Lorde's clarity and courage to transform silence into language and action came from her confrontation with her mortality after a bout with breast cancer. Our silence means complicity and complicity equates not with survival, but death, beginning with the soul. Those who live on the "Other" side of the relational construct of race understand this well. Those who live on the white side, in whatever epicenter of coloniality in which their whiteness is defined, well . . . after centuries, too many still insist that race, which was created as the primary system of dominance and oppression for colonialism and coloniality through a racial hierarchy of power, is somehow not racism and a problem for people of color (or the problem with people of color). It is not and it never has been. Racism is a moral catastrophe, rooted in those most invested in, and most benefited by, a racial hierarchy of power. Ignorance, like innocence, is too often a façade for the preservation of power. For people of color, the choice of language and action toward racism is, at times, the act of last resort for survival.

It is our humanity, not our fear of death, that gives each of us potential for the courage to transform silence into language and action, be it through writing on racism or through kinship with those who write on racism.

Victor's work reminds us, as teachers and administrators entrusted to be servant leaders to writers of color who address racism, that we must think of the questions of fictive kinship as living, not rhetorical. *Are we willing to serve those writers of color as kin, with the same love and empathy and uncertainty that they show in their courage to transform their silence into language and action earnestly and critically, to address racism sympathetically and frankly? Are we willing to love them as kin, to face what they face together? Are we willing to face those writers of color who we serve, knowing that their memory is a mirror to our service and our person?*

No one would answer any of these questions with "no." But I find these questions haunted by these words: "What are the tyrannies you swallow day by day and attempt to make your own, until you will sicken and die of them, still in silence? Perhaps for some of you here today, I am the face of one of your fears" (Lorde 41). Too often, it is my face, and those faces of writers of color, that are feared. This cannot be.

If my memory serves as a mirror, we, as teachers and administrators, must have the courage to be honest with ourselves about our silences in order to have the courage to share kinship with our writers of color. And we *must*, for there are secrets we can no longer keep.

ONWARD

Victor has kept his promise to me: he is co-chair of my dissertation committee, although he is in Pullman, I am in Tucson, and we have never had an "official" student–teacher relationship in any of these twenty-four years. His labor has been entirely voluntary and largely invisible. Better said, his kinship has been the truest of all gifts. Maybe it is just me, but I was surprised by his retirement in 2020. I know that I shouldn't be. A major part of his 2015 pitch to me was the "now or never" talk about his five-year goal for retirement. (I can't help but think of all the jokes about lawyers and math, which can apply to writers too). Maybe it is just that piece of me that cannot—or does not want to—imagine rhetoric and composition studies without Victor Villanueva.

His example of kinship toward writers gives us much to ponder. Doubt is not among these. We could consider the number of the graduate students he has served: 45 directed or chaired PhDs; 41

served or co-chaired PhDs; 75 MAs; Of the 86 PhDs, consider the diversity numbers: 7 Black; 21 Latina or Latino; 4 Asian American; 2 Filipina and Filipino; 1 Afghani American; 8 International. Then consider the number of students who became administrators: 1 vice president for student affairs; 1 vice chancellor; 1 associate dean; a lot of department chairs, even more WPAs. Then there is this number: 2 chairs of CCCC. And these numbers do not capture the many writers like me that he mentored. All of these numbers are impressive. Absolutely. But so much is lost through an emphasis on the quantitative. Like the identity of each writer these numbers represent. And the stories each writer carries. And the people—the kinship—each writer holds dear. And, with all of this, a truth about writing—writing is an art.

Victor reminded me of this truth in October 2020. Given the gravity of the summer of 2020, I suffered perhaps the worst collapse that I had as a writer in my life. He sent me a note that reminded me of what we do as writers in rhetoric and composition studies.

"We're allowed to be artists," Victor began, "And you already are!"

Funny how I had forgotten this. And funny how he knew, through our kinship, the words I so needed to remember. James Baldwin stated this about the writer as the artist:

> The role of the artist, then, precisely, is to illuminate that darkness (of the wilderness of himself), blaze roads through that vast forest; so that we will not, in all of our doing, lose sight of its purpose, which is, after all, to make the world a more human dwelling place. ("Creative Process" 669)

What is worth pondering is what you and I have to offer as our contribution to that mosaic of truth about writing: How will our kinship with those writers of color who address racism help them light darkness, blaze roads, and keep their sights on making our world a more humane place?

There is no greater mirror to the integrity of a servant leader than those who they serve. We carry our memories of Victor. Now, what memories will those who we serve carry of me and you?

One last reminiscence:

Victor and I spoke by phone on December 7, 2020, at his request.

Zoom fatigue, *he explained.*

Pandemic-me empathized.

Our call, scheduled for an hour and slated as a talk about his written feedback on my first dissertation chapter, did what our calls do: it wandered. Fall of 2020 represented for me the first seventeen-week semester of not teaching foundations writing since fall of 2016, and for him the first semester of full retirement outside of a visiting professor gig with Whitman College that ended the week prior.

We talked teaching.

"I dreamed that I was back in the classroom," Victor shared, "With real chalkboards—you know, the blackboards. And I had my hair [Laughter]. . . . Man, I miss it."

Silence.

I couldn't see him. He couldn't see me—and I was glad.

As much as I had thought of myself as a writer by nature and a teacher by occupation, I came to realize that I had changed. I am a writer and, now, I am a writing teacher. Former students stay in touch. Seek mentoring. Share joys. Talk of my teaching in their life. Looked for me when word came out about my heart attack. Care, community, kinship, courage.

On the other end of this line, it occurred to me, is the person who helped to bring that out of me.

"I'm done," Victor laughed, "Done-done."

The words I spoke were just noise to the silence that I kept. The life lesson that I still hadn't learned: the past is indestructible. There is time. Here and now, I have a second chance to break my silence:

> My gift to you would be to change the fabric of space and time to give you that dream. All I have is that wish and these words. You have changed my life. I might have never become a writer without your kinship and your courage. Only each person who worked with you truly knows your impact on them. I know, from the

stories people have shared with me and all of those who have contributed to this collection, you have touched so many lives. Of all the things I wish I could say, of the few things I still hold in silence, I want to say this: I will do my best to share the gift you have given me. I love you, *mi hermano.*

NOTES

1. I note that I break with academic tradition to refer to a scholar by their last name after the introduction of their full name. I do so because of the nature of this essay per se and the nature of the kinship relationship with Victor Villanueva described in this essay.

2. I adopted "cuentos de mi historia" as a nod to Victor's statement about a common saying among Puerto Ricans and Cubans: "Te doy un cuento de mi historia, literally rendered as 'I'll give you a story about my history': me, history and memory, and a story" ("*Memoria*" 16).

3. I provide a brief overview from Chapter 1 of my unpublished dissertation, titled *Sin permiso, sin perdón: Rhetorical Studies on Rhetorics of Race, Latinidad, Decoloniality, and Theory*. Like every nation-state in the Americas, the United States is what I call an epicenter of coloniality. Each epicenter of coloniality has its own history, formation, and existence that involves colonization of a part of the Americas as an effort of imperial rule, independence from imperial rule to form a nation-state, and continuation of certain ideologies of imperial dominance. Of these ideologies, race is an ideology that serves as the primary system of dominance and oppression, as noted by both Aníbal Quijano and Walter Mignolo, defining concepts of citizenship, rights, and humanity.

WORKS CITED

Alvarez, Steven. "Latinx and Latin American Community Literacy Practices *en confianza*." *Composition Studies,* vol. 45, no. 2, 2017, pp. 219–21.

Baldwin, James. "Autobiographical Note, Notes of a Native Son." 1955. *Baldwin: Collected Essays,* edited by Toni Morrison, Library of America, 1998, pp. 5–10.

———. "The Creative Process." 1962. *Baldwin: Collected Essays,* edited by Toni Morrison, Library of America, 1998, pp. 669–72.

Elgrably, Jordan. "James Baldwin, the Art of Fiction, No. 78." *Paris Review,* vol. 91, 1984, https://www.theparisreview.org/interviews/2994/the-art-of-fiction-no-78-james-baldwin.

Fordham, Signithia. "Racelessness as a Factor in Black Students' School Success: Pragmatic Strategy or Pyrrhic Victory?? *Harvard Educational Review*, vol. 58, no. 1, 1988, pp. 54–84.

hooks, bell. "Choosing the Margin as a Space of Radical Openness." *Journal of Cinema and Media*, vol. 36, 1989, pp. 15–23.

Lorde, Audre. "The Transformation of Silence into Language and Action." 1981. *Sister Outsider: Essays and Speeches,* by Audre Lorde, Crossing Press, 2007, pp. 40–44.

Melaku, Tsedale M., and Angie Beeman. "Academia Isn't a Safe Haven for Conversations about Race and Racism." *Harvard Business Review*, 25 June 2020, https://hbr.org/2020/06/academia-isnt-a-safe-haven-for-conversations-about-race-and-racism.

Mignolo, Walter D. "Racism as We Sense It Today." *PMLA*, vol. 123, no. 5, 2008, pp. 1737–42.

Padilla, J. Paul. "Chapter 1. A Letter to My Son Ricardo: On the Question of Self-Identification, Rhetorical Agency, and Decolonial Re-existence." *Sin permiso, sin perdón*: *Rhetorical Studies on Rhetorics of Race, Latinidad, Decoloniality, and Theory* Dissertation. University of Arizona, 2021.

———. "What Isn't Heard: Dyslogistic Silence and Silencing at Candle-light Vigils for the Orlando Massacre—A Response." *Enculturation*, 3 June 2019, http://enculturation.net/what_isnt_heard.

Prendergast, Catherine. "Race: The Absent Presence in Composition Studies." *College Composition and Communication*, vol. 50, no. 1, 1998, pp. 36–53.

Quijano, Aníbal. "Questioning 'Race.'" *Socialism and Democracy*, vol. 21, no. 1, 2007, pp. 45–53.

Smith, Erec. "Why I Still Talk to White People about Racism." *Newsweek*, 8 July 2020, https://www.newsweek.com/why-i-still-talk-white-people-about-racism-opinion-1516309.

Villanueva, Victor, Jr. "Blind: Talking about the New Racism." *Writing Center Journal*, vol. 26, no. 1, 2006, pp. 3–19.

———. *Bootstraps: From an American Academic of Color*. National Council of Teachers of English, 1993.

———. "Hegemony: From an Organically Grown Intellectual." *Pre/Text,* vol. 13, no. 1-2, 1992, pp. 18–34.

———. Interview. Conducted by J. Paul Padilla. 2016.

———. "*Memoria* Is a Friend of Ours: On the Discourse of Color." *College English*, vol. 67, no. 1, 2004, pp. 9–19.

———. "Of Kin and Community." *English Journal,* vol. 101, no. 1, 2011, pp. 108–10.

———. "On the Rhetoric and Precedents of Racism." *College Composition and Communication*, vol. 50, no. 4, 1999, pp. 645–61.

———. "Whose Voice Is It Anyway? Rodriguez's Speech in Retrospect." *English Journal*, vol. 76, no. 8, 1987, pp. 17–21.

———. "Writing as a Way of Doing." *YouTube*, 28 Jan. 2015. WSU Academic Outreach & Innovation, https://www.youtube.com/watch?v=uOmoVtVaz4M.

Chapter 11

On the Rhetoric and Precedents of Representation: Following Villanueva in Challenging Disciplinary and Institutional Racism

Morris Young

A MINOR HISTORY

The scene is the Atlanta Hilton ballroom. It's the 1999 Conference on College Composition and Communication (CCCC) Annual Convention. Victor Villanueva, the chair of CCCC, is delivering his Chair's Address, "On the Rhetoric and Precedents of Racism," to hundreds of scholars and teachers of writing, rhetoric, and literacy about the state of the discipline. He is, in my mind, also speaking directly to me. The chair is instructive, speaking clearly about the consequences of colonialism, the roots of racism, and how these forces exist not only in the explicit violence that causes injury to bodies, minds, and being, but also in the institutions where we work or seek membership (like universities or scholarly organizations), or in our curriculum (What does it mean to teach and learn academic writing? Who is literate?), or in our research (which may exclude, ignore, or patronize those on the margins). I am moved by the energy, the passion, the intellect, the anger. Having heard the words of Victor Villanueva and his interrogation of the relationship between race and rhetoric, how do I respond? I write:

> Let me begin a narrative here. Before I started kindergarten, I often attended story hour at the neighborhood public library,

> where I would receive a handmade program that listed the stories for the day and an animal shaped name tag (artifacts that my mom has saved to this day). I remember when I was about five or six having to go off to some faraway school classroom on a Saturday morning, where a young teacher (I assumed) asked me to identify objects, read a few simple words, and practice my S and T sounds as well as other phonics exercises. I later learned I was being evaluated by a speech pathologist because I did not enunciate my words clearly. On a family vacation when I was twelve, I found myself in New Orleans at an open market looking at some used comic books (my passion at the time) when the burly man who ran the stand looked at me accusingly and said in a gruff voice, "Don't you understand English?" as he pointed aggressively to a "no reading" sign. I only stared at him and thought, "Of course I understand English. Why else would I be looking at the comic book?" I am not sure why these memories stay with me. Perhaps because these were encounters with language, I have internalized them and have become aware of the everyday uses of language and their contexts. Or I recall these experiences now because at the time they occurred I didn't understand their implications. Wasn't story hour just fun? What was a speech pathologist? Did I look as if I didn't know English? Did I look foreign? Though these encounters were not especially dramatic or traumatic life-changing experiences, they were significant because I became aware at an early age of the emphasis our culture places on language. (Young, *Minor* 1).

This writing becomes a book, something important in pursuit of what we have been trained to believe is a "successful" professional career: earning tenure and promotion. But what is also important is unpacking the meaning of literacy and rhetoric in my experience as an Asian American and to make visible these ideas to others since I had not seen myself in the scholarship of composition and rhetoric. But Victor Villanueva, Keith Gilyard, Jacqueline Jones Royster, and others who have narrated and navigated their lives as scholars of color in composition and rhetoric help me to see that there is a place for us.

A little later at that same conference in Atlanta in 1999, I am at the Scholars for the Dream reception, a celebration of first-time attendees and alumni of the program to connect and reflect, to be acknowledged that they belong. But the setting gives me pause: Trader Vic's, a pseudo-Polynesian tiki lounge filled with stereotypical artifacts such as grass shack walls, tiki gods, and tiki torch lamps. And I write again:

> I wondered if the organizers had thought about what were clearly problematic representations of race and culture in this location. The figurines of Polynesian children on the buffet table with their requisite brown skin, round tummies, flower lei, and island attire did not seem to strike the crowd as exploitative. The idea of the tiki lounge did not seem to remind anyone of a history of Western colonialism in the Pacific, a fact that continues to have a lasting legacy as Native Hawaiians among other Pacific peoples struggle for their sovereignty rights as indigenous cultures. (Young, *Minor* 75)

I look around to see how others are reacting, and I catch Victor Villanueva out of the corner of my eye shaking his head, acknowledging that something is wrong. Here is the legacy of settler-colonialism—implicating my own experience as a settler in the homeland of Native Hawaiians—where the experiences of an Indigenous people continue to be represented and remain in the imagination of people as an uninterrogated tropical paradise for their enjoyment. And I know that his words spoken earlier that day will continue to be important.

IDEAS/IDENTITIES

I reflect on that 1999 CCCC Convention in Atlanta because it has become one of the touchstones in my professional life. It was not my first convention—that was in 1992 in Cincinnati when I could not imagine that just a few years later I'd be an assistant professor at Miami University just about an hour north in Oxford, Ohio—but it was the meeting when I understood how and why representation matters not only in our scholarship and teaching but also in our leadership and organizations. Early in my graduate training, I was introduced to Villanueva through *Bootstraps: From an American Academic of Color*, where I learned the power of narrative and saw in his academic life history familiar themes that helped me to begin to understand what my contribution could be to composition and rhetoric.

Bootstraps was a revelation. Here was a text that used story as theory to interrogate the relationship between race and language through the life experiences of Villanueva. It provided an illustration of a critical practice as Villanueva used narrative to weave together rhetorical theory, cultural analysis, and autoethnography to create a robust portrait of the educational inequity often experienced by students of color, multilingual writers, and first-generation scholars and scholars of color. It moved among the range of theories, ideas, experiences in a way that placed each in conversation rather than trying to simply perform critique for the sake of critique—these theories, ideas, and experiences had consequences for real people and required deliberate engagement not apart from but in relation and as a challenge to the discipline's perceived center. For me, *Bootstraps* was as foundational as *Pedagogy of the Oppressed* by Paulo Freire, or *Woman Warrior: Memoir of a Girlhood among Ghosts* by Maxine Hong Kingston, or "Literacy in Three Metaphors" by Sylvia Scriber, all texts that helped me to understand the power of language and literacy in the lives of people who often experienced the power of language and literacy used against them.

"On the Rhetoric and Precedents of Racism" extended and enacted the innovative critical practice of *Bootstraps*. Here Villanueva cited the work of Michael Omi and Howard Winant whose concept of racial formation had become key to my understanding of race as a rhetorical formation. His use of *Racial Formations/Critical Transformations* by E. San Juan Jr., an important but perhaps less familiar Filipino American cultural critic, signaled to me his awareness of the important work taking place in Asian American cultural studies. As an early career faculty member in a predominantly white institution, I felt valued by my department but often out of place in the rural Midwest. In graduate school, I had been part of a cohort of Asian American graduate students and faculty, among other scholars of color, who created the conditions that not only supported our academic work but also provided the emotional and social foundations that are necessary to do the work.

In those early years of attending the CCCC Convention, I believed I had something to contribute in my attention to writing and literacy in the context of what we called "multiculturalism" back then, but I was still unsure of my place in the discipline's institutions. There was an Asian Caucus, but at the time it focused on second language writing and comparative/contrastive rhetoric. There may have been senior comp rhet scholars of Asian descent (later I would meet Gail Okawa, Min-Zhan Lu, and LuMing Mao), but I did not know who they were then or did not see them easily in the convention programs. What I found myself doing was what I did with my own research, trying to theorize Asian American literacy and rhetorical practices alongside African American, Latinx, and Indigenous discourses on language and rhetoric—by looking to develop a professional identity through observing the experience of other scholars of color who may have differed from me by generation or background but still existed within CCCC and had to navigate institutional structures. Hearing Villanueva acknowledge the experiences of Asians and Asian Americans and cite Asian American scholars was transformative in my CCCC experience because it made me visible to the organization. But I also heard a call to action from Villanueva that was both sobering in its assessment of the US and necessary. In that address, Villanueva recounted the violence experienced by people of color:

- We watched the 1992 beating of Rodney King, watched Alicia Soltero Vásquez being beaten by Border Patrolmen.
- San Francisco, 1997. Two young Latino children are found completely covered in flour. They wanted their skin to be white enough to go to school, they say.

- Oxnard, 1995, Mexican and Chicana women working at a Nabisco plant are denied toilet breaks. They are told to wear diapers during their shift.
- Rohnert Park, 1997, Police kill a Chinese engineer, father of three, who had come home drunk and angry after having put up with racist insults at a bar. He's loud. A neighbor calls the police. Still drunk, he grabs a one-eighth inch thick stick, brandishes it. He's shot. His wife, a nurse, is disallowed to administer care. He's handcuffed. Dies while awaiting an ambulance. The reason for shooting him? The police were afraid he would use martial arts with that one-eighth inch stick (Martinez 10–11). ("On the Rhetoric" 650)

And we should ask, more than twenty years later, what has changed, when we have seen in recent months and years:

- People seeking refuge from violence in Central America and Mexico stopped at the US border, or the separation of migrant families by US agents to detain and deport them.
- A summer of protests in response to the murders of George Floyd and Breonna Taylor by police, the shooting of Jacob Blake by police, the murder of Ahmaud Arbery by three white men, and the murders of many more Black people before them; and then the protesters themselves become targets of state violence and the president of the US.
- A pandemic in which Asians and Asian Americans are blamed for the "Chinese Virus" and face continued anti-Asian violence.
- Indigenous peoples protesting at Standing Rock over the threat to water security and sovereign land rights by the proposed Dakota Access Pipeline.
- An armed attack on the US Capitol by insurgents, whose belief in the "Big Lie" that the US presidential election was stolen from Donald Trump provided them with the exigency to enact their white supremacist ideology under the guise of "patriotism."

And we should also ask, what has changed in our discipline since Villanueva reported in 1999 that CCCC membership was 92 percent white, 5 percent African American, 1.4 percent Chicano or Latino, 1 percent Asian American, and 0.5 percent Native American/American Indian ("On the Rhetoric" 651)? Perhaps we have seen some upward movement in the percentages of people of color in CCCC, but it has not been enough to be transformative, especially when we know our classrooms across the country are increasingly more diverse in terms of language, identities, and experiences. Our discipline and professional organizations need to systematically collect and make visible their membership demographic information so that we can more fully understand who we are and how a discipline that remains largely white by a wide margin has an impact on our scholarship, teaching, and professional lives. While the discipline and our professional organizations may make statements, author policies, and perhaps even take action, we still function within a structure that includes bias, whether unintentional or intentional, that has a profound effect on the discipline.

Since 1991, when I became a member of CCCC, through 2023, there have been thirteen scholars of color elected to serve as chair (including two Asian Americans), and many more have been elected to the Executive Committee or served in other leadership roles. We have also seen many more scholars of color represented and recognized for their scholarship in the awards presented by CCCC. But while recognition and representation matter, how can they also serve to interrogate the structures of power that still shape our research, teaching, and profession? When will research on writing, rhetoric, and literacy by scholars of color that focuses on communities of color be seen as informing our theories, histories, and pedagogies of writing, rhetoric, and literacy *in the discipline* broadly and not simply as work within a subfield? How can this lead to change that matters in addressing equity and social justice and not simply remain an academic question?

AN/OTHER STORY

My department is supportive during my probationary period, and despite pushing the deadlines on getting my manuscript of *Minor Re/Visions: Asian American Literacy Narratives as a Rhetoric of Citizenship* revised and submitted to the publisher, I receive tenure and am promoted to associate professor of English. My book comes out in 2004, and while I told myself that the only audience that mattered were the dozen or so people on the tenure and promotion committee, I am happy it is out in the world. I hear from friends and colleagues who offer congratulations, but it is the messages from other Asian and Asian American colleagues that make me feel as though this is something for all of us. And then a surprise. An email from the editor of *JAC* invites me to their meeting at the upcoming 2004 CCCC Annual Convention for an award presentation. I'm honored to receive the 2004 W. Ross Winterowd Award for the most outstanding book in composition theory. Unexpected and humbling.

And then another humbling experience: a review of *Minor Re/Visions* in a major journal by a senior scholar in the field. But it's not a good review. In fact, it is difficult to read not because it offers critique but because that critique often feels like a misreading of the work, which feels like a misreading of me given the use of narrative to structure the concepts and to form the argument. Or perhaps it's not a misreading; it's simply not listening, not being able to hear why and how race matters as part of the lived experiences explored in the book because it does not align with a particular epistemology, or what Asao Inoue has described as the White Racial Habitus. Perhaps most frustrating is a claim that my analysis elides injuries to others on the basis of gender or social class (or even whiteness) to focus on race (though my analysis examines how and why these injuries inform each other and why anti-Asian violence is centered but not to the exclusion of other oppressions). While confused, even angry with this situation, I am also unsure what to do. Perhaps I should respond, but I let it sit because I'm not sure who would hear me other than those who have experienced the same thing.

Years later I am reading the 2019 Chair's Address, "How Do We Language So People Stop Killing Each Other, or What Do We

Do about White Language Supremacy?" by Asao Inoue, and I feel humbled by Inoue's willingness and courage to make visible the structures of white supremacy that exist within our culture and our institutions, within our teaching and research. We can enter into the field, even be acknowledged in the field, and yet we still exist in a White Racial Habitus, within the logic and violence of white supremacy that will question the research, teaching, and service we do because it is often legible in limited ways within these structures: to celebrate difference or to acknowledge suffering. Twenty years ago, Villanueva called on our journals to publish

> people of color writing frankly, sympathetically about matters concerning racism, and all of us writing about what matters to those students of color. That's what will attract people of color in sufficient numbers to begin to affect racism. We can do better than 7% among our teachers and scholars of color, better than a representation that is statistically insignificant in our journals. ("On the Rhetoric" 652)

In 2019, Inoue speaks directly to scholars of color to "break the steel cage of White supremacy, of White racial bias" (353) and "to commiserate together here in this place because often we may be alone at our home institutions" (354), while asking white colleagues to sit in their discomfort, to reflect on what it felt like "to be talked *about*, and not talked to, to be the object of discussion, and not the subject?" (356). And he asks these white colleagues perhaps most pointedly, "How does it feel to be the problem?" (356), a feeling that many people of color experience when they raise their voices to respond to racism, object to inequality, or claim their place.

And another humbling experience. An essay I submit for a special issue of *College English* titled "Rhetorics of/from Color," edited by Victor Villanueva, is accepted. Of course, there is feedback, often tough and probing, as most contributors to this collection can attest. I'm called out appropriately about what comes across as an elision of another experience of colonialism (which I quickly revise), but the ideas are engaged and the argument is encouraged. It is hard to believe that I am having a conversation with the person I heard speaking to me in that ballroom in Atlanta in 1999.

ON BREAKING PRECEDENTS

In returning to Villanueva's "On the Rhetoric and Precedents of Racism," I have taken the opportunity to reflect on whether much has changed in our broader society as racial violence and other acts of hatred have only increased in their frequency and intensity, or in our educational institutions where the COVID-19 pandemic has only exacerbated issues of equity and access and made highly visible the barriers that still exist for students when they enter seeking the promise of education only to find that privilege remains an educational premise. But we are also in a moment when our world has been turned upside down by a global pandemic; threatened by increasingly authoritarian leaders, nationalist ideologies, and nativist movements; and put at existential risk by a climate crisis that threatens safety, health, food security, and the welfare of future generations. We must break precedent, then, because to continue to act in the same way will only maintain the structures that have already increased inequality and suffering.

We must break precedent in our professional lives as well so that we transform our organizations and the work we do. As Villanueva imagines a future, he also identifies a history we must be willing to challenge:

> Now as I try to think of how this profession can improve on its multiculturalism, do more than assuring that people of color are represented in our materials, more than assuring that people of color are read and heard in numbers more in keeping with the emerging demographics of the nation and the world, I remain tied to the belief that we must break from the colonial discourse that binds us all. What I mean is that there are attitudes from those we have revered over the centuries which we inherit, that are woven into the discourse that we inherit. ("On the Rhetoric" 656)

I began this essay with fragments from a narrative, memories that have haunted me because they put in sharp relief how race and language have informed my life. As I consider years later what I tried to ask and examine in *Minor Re/Visions*, I have had to face the discomfort that despite interrogating US racial discourse and attempting to unpack the uses of literacy and rhetoric for Asian Americans, I am still implicated in the colonial discourse that Villanueva has argued has been at the roots of racism. In arguing for literacy as a rhetoric of citizenship, I have relied on the nation as a formation that identifies people as belonging or not, and I have relied on literacy as a practice that often serves as a proxy for citizenship and promises more than it can deliver to those on the margins.

In a recent project ("Rhetorical Legacies"), I have been examining the *Appeal of the Chinese Equal Rights League to the People of the United States for the Equality of Manhood* written in 1893. This pamphlet was written in response to the 1892 Geary Act, which extended the original Chinese Exclusion Act of 1882 by another ten years and instituted additional requirements and barriers to regulate Chinese who sought to enter the US and those who were already in the US legally. While this pamphlet is an exciting example of the rhetorical work of Chinese in the US in the nineteenth century, I find its closing appeal to be unsettling:

> Treat us as men, and we will do our duty as men, and we will aid you to stop this obnoxious evil that threatens the welfare of this Republic. We do not want any more Chinese here any more than you do. The scarcer the Chinese here the better would be our conditions among you. (3)

How could an organization of Chinese in the US argue for their own belonging and yet be willing to exclude new Chinese immigrants simply to protect their own standing? To somehow see themselves as exceptional and worthy of potential citizenship (and they do identify themselves as "law-abiding citizens in the United States" though naturalized citizenship was precarious and then banned with the first Chinese Exclusion Act of 1882) but then to seek to withhold those same privileges from others (3)? And here is the problem of racism, a colonial discourse that allows for the continued exploitation of difference in service to the accumulation of power.

And here is the legacy of "On the Rhetoric and Precedents of Racism" and Victor Villanueva: in returning to this address and rereading his words, I continue to hear why and how we must attend to histories and theories, to answer a call to action, and to continue to work to transform our discipline. These twenty-odd years later I still value the ideas and arguments that help me to see my own teaching and research in different ways and that move me to acknowledge and engage those histories and theories that I have not seen before.

CODA: WORDS OF INDEBTEDNESS

As I hope this essay has made clear, I'm indebted to the forms, words, and ideas of Victor Villanueva. In an act of *imitatio*, I have tried to reflect on my experiences as a scholar and teacher in composition and rhetoric through Villanueva's "On the Rhetoric and Precedents of Racism" because it has in so many ways helped me to identify the moves, tropes, logics, and, of course, rhetoric that have structured so much of my professional life. I am thankful for his example of scholarship and leadership, and for those moments when we have been able to share some words together.

WORKS CITED

Appeal of the Chinese Equal Rights League to the People of the United States for Equality of Manhood. Chinese Equal Rights League, 1893. Attributed to Wong Chin Foo.

Freire, Paulo. *Pedagogy of the Oppressed.* 30th ed., translated by Myra Bergman Ramos, Continuum, 2000.

Inoue, Asao B. "2019 CCCC Chair's Address. "How Do We Language So People Stop Killing Each Other, or What Do We Do about White Language Supremacy?" *College Composition and Communication,* vol. 71, no. 2, 2019, pp. 352–69.

Kingston, Maxine Hong. *The Woman Warrior: Memoirs of a Girlhood among Ghosts.* Vintage Books, 1989.

Omi, Michael, and Howard Winant. *Racial Formation in the United States: From the 1960s to the 1990s.* 2nd ed., Routledge, 1994.

San Juan, E., Jr. *Racial Formations/Critical Transformations: Articulations of Power in Ethnic and Racial Studies in the United States.* Atlantic Highlands: Humanity Press, 1992.

Scribner, Sylvia. "Literacy in Three Metaphors." *American Journal of Education,* vol. 43, no. 1, 1984, pp. 6–21.

Villanueva, Victor, Jr. *Bootstraps: From an American Academic of Color.* National Council of Teachers of English, 1993.

———. "On the Rhetoric and Precedents of Racism." *College Composition and Communication,* vol. 50, no. 4, 1999, pp. 645–61.

———, guest editor. "Rhetorics of/from Color." Special Issue, *College English,* vol. 67, no. 1, 2004.

Young, Morris. *Minor Re/Visions: Asian American Literacy Narratives as a Rhetoric of Citizenship*. Southern Illinois UP, 2004.

———. "The Rhetorical Legacies of Chinese Exclusion: Appeals, Protests, and Becoming Chinese American." *Nineteenth-Century American Activist Rhetorics*, edited by Patricia Bizzell and Lisa Zimmerelli, Modern Language Association, 2020, pp. 290–303.

Chapter 12

Antiracism, *Zhuangzi's* Happy Wanderer, and Overcoming the Crusades

Robert Eddy/Salah Al-Din

I COGNIZE VICTOR AS AN EXAMPLE of *Zhuangzi's* happy wanderer with the unique ability to heal the Islamophobic dissonances of the Crusades and of the Christian *Reconquista* in Spain in our intense friendship of thirty years. Victor is a Western public intellectual, but our friendship has been mutually interpolated by my conversion to Islam as a teenager under the influence of Malcolm X. The center of gravity in our friendship has been Victor's remarkable ability to peer mentor as radical equality with love, ontological affirmation, and deep epistemological challenges lightly but clearly communicated. Victor's complex ancestral homes, languages, and customs include an important place for Spain (for better or worse, given Spanish rule of the Western Hemisphere), and because of seven hundred years of Muslim rule and culture, Spain is also a key element of my identity landscapes. These ancestral sources pull at Victor and his friends in crucial ways while we as Americans love the idea of the future and what is around the next bend in our individual and collective lives. This chapter centers on Victor's "Rhetorics of Racism" work and what it has meant to his stunning ability to mentor and care.

In 2014, Victor and I published an anthology on representations of race and racism. It includes a translation of the essay by the Tang Dynasty Confucian scholar Han Yu. The title is "How to Define a Teacher." A key passage:

> [I]t is not necessary for students to be less-learned than their teachers; and it is not necessary for teachers to be wiser than their students. What this is all about is that some people have learned *Tao* before you, and some people have learned Tao after you. Everyone is good at something. (Eddy and Villanueva 170)

Here is how Victor comments on perhaps the most complex element of *Zhuangzi's* happy wanderer: what it means to bend and flow with Tao (now the accepted transliteration is Dao):

> The Chinese word *Tao* is impossible to translate. Some would even argue that it's impossible to define. The best we can do is to call it "the way of heaven" or "the way of nature" or just "the way." "Everyone is good at something" because the *Tao* flows through everyone's experience, whether we know it or not. We have a nature, a talent, perhaps, that is allowed to express itself through us if we live in balance. So the *Tao* is not a book; it's a way. Some find it; others spend their lifetimes trying to find it and learn it. (170–71)

It is in this sense that Han Yu can meet someone born after him who can be his teacher. Although Tao is ancient, its wisdom is decidedly contemporary—and has always been. The Spanish rhetorician Quintilian, who worked for the Romans during the first century CE, wrote in his *Institutes of Oratory* that

> as emulation is of use to those who have made some advancement of learning, so, to those who are but beginning and still of tender age, to imitate their schoolfellows is more pleasant than to imitate their master, for the very reason that it is more easy; for they who are learning the first rudiments will scarcely dare to exalt themselves to the hope of attaining that eloquence which they regard as the highest; they will rather fix on what is nearest to them, as vines attached to trees fain the top by taking hold of the lower branches first. (qtd. in Eddy and Villanueva, 23–24)

Although Quintilian still holds to what Han Yu calls "elite teachers," he recognizes the learning that takes place among peers. Mark Twain, in the nineteenth century, is purported to have said that he never let his schooling interfere with his education, an argument not against schooling necessarily but for recognizing the vast universe of learning: the Tao. And in the early twentieth century Antonio Gramsci wrote that "*homo faber* cannot be separated from *homo sapiens*" (qtd. in Eddy and Villanueva 9)—the one of skills cannot be separated from the one who knows. To Gramsci, all of us are intellectuals, which sounds much like Han Yu. The "teacher," then, is she or he who understands the balance of things, the yin and yang (also an element of Tao). We all stand to learn from those who follow their natures in balance and peace (Eddy and Villanueva 170–71).

My reading of Victor's writing, of his antiracism work, of his mentoring of undergraduate and graduate students and his equally crucial mentoring of faculty peers in our shared department the last twenty years, is the last sentence above, which is his: "We all stand to learn from those who follow their natures in balance and peace." This sentence and its last word are the heart of Dao, the heart of *Zhuangzi*'s happy wanderer, and the heart of Victor in his antiracism work and in his relationships at work and in friendships. Victor's distinctive influence invites self and others to "follow their natures in balance and peace" and is the heart of his antiracism work because systemic racism/white supremacy is routine and institutionalized political-economic violence, the complete opposite of peace and human balance.

Zhuangzi's happy wanderer suggests, perhaps especially to Western readers, that moving about in the natural environment, particularly in one's preferred terrains of mountains, or forests, or open spaces, or deserts, or marshlands, or other waterways, is what the happy wanderer does. But *Zhuangzi*'s happy wanderer, as Victor demonstrates, is especially engaged with the built environment and social spaces, especially contested contact zones. In both natural and built environments, a happy wanderer evinces a quiet attentiveness to everyone's full humanity, which invites experiences of crossing boundaries, of movement amidst conflict, contestation, and even competing fundamentalisms. A key to understanding Victor's antiracism scholarship and remarkable peer mentoring is noticing how he is the happy wanderer amidst racism and its intersecting oppressions. Here is how Livia Kohn describes the happy wanderer:

> To reach a happy medium between beta and transcendent consciousness, creative people have to combine various antithetical traits and live in a dynamic state of ongoing dialectical tension. Such traits include great physical energy and the need for restful quietude, being both smart and naive, playful and disciplined, imaginative and profoundly realistic, as well as socially engaged and happy in solitude. Creative people are both extroverted and introverted, humble and proud, masculine and feminine, rebellious and rule-bound, independent and domain-trained, passionate and objective, as well as suffering and joyful. (*Science* 223)

This paragraph functions for me as the best description of Victor's writing and ways of living that I have encountered.

How has Victor's happy wandering in contact zones of contested racializations affected his writing? His writing about racism demonstrates a vivid attentiveness to the routinely miraculous quality of everyday life. His racism writing is where he sees and presents everyone as 100 percent human. Here is Victor's English translation of a poem by his father in Spanish that Victor found by accident after his father's death:

A POEM: VICTOR VILLANUEVA Y HERNÁNDES

Triste lucha la del árbol con espinas	Sad struggle of the tree of thorns
Fuerte ardor que solo a su alma se cobija.	Fierce feeling covered solely by your soul.
Vano empeño para el ser que vive,	Vain striving for he who lives,
En tratar de comprender su propia vida.	In trying to understand his own life.
Muy dulce es percivir de la noche sus caricios;	So sweet to see your caresses in the night;
Pero es terrible saber	But so terrible to know

Que más tarde en la madrugada
Agonizando todos ellos quedan. . . .
Triste lucha del árbol con espinas
triste lucha la del que ya un poquito
tarde,
Ni siquiera el más leve suspiro
su alma alienta.
Triste e interminable lucha
esta que jamás se aleja
¡Oh, que triste lucha ésta
que a mi pecho
Tanto apena!
¡Triste lucha . . . triste lucha!

—*"En el pasado versa tu presente"*
19 de enero 1951

That later in the light of day
All the agonies remain. . . .
Sad struggle of the tree of thorns
sad struggle of that which is already a
little late,
Without even the lightest sigh
your soul's breath.
Sad and interminable struggle
that which will never leave
Oh, how sad this struggle
Weighing so on my chest!

Sad struggle . . . sad struggle!

—*"In the past turns the present"*
19 January 1951

(Eddy and Villanueva 319)

Victor, with a lifetime of endlessly resisting systemic racism, does so by being the happy wanderer within the midst of multiple oppressions. How does he act and remain the happy wanderer amidst racist structures and environments, with no blinking away horrors, no justifications, and no avoidance, but instead full engagement, full resistance?

Overview answer: in every room I have been in with Victor, including large rooms at rhetoric and composition conventions but also smaller rooms and digital spaces, he is usually the human center of that space, especially, which is often the case, when he is perfectly silent but fully attentive. Victor is a brilliant, often fully open listener. He is an important wanderer in racist spaces because he never loses his humanity and he never dehumanizes other people, even white supremacists when they are dehumanizing themselves. His present, spontaneous, and compassionate smile is a powerful critique of all fundamentalist, binary acts of verbal and visual warfare. Whether he is translating his father's love poem as private utterance to the beloved but also as social protest document of the "Sad and interminable struggle" against ambient racism, or articulating the equally crucial need to confront the absence of "balance and peace" in the discipline's language and antiracism policies and practices, Victor's deeply human smile, which he manifests at times of maximum epistemological confrontation, is his practice of peace while truth-telling, with others invited to do the same. He confronts routine racism issues and effects with a loving smile while fully pointing to epistemological points and places of violence. Crucially, what I am describing is the happy wanderer as "centered stillness" which "leads to a powerful life of authentic, non-alienated, and productive activity" (Kohn, *Zhuangzi* 151).

> Ibn Hazm's insistence that the Quran and Sunna be interpreted literally has frequently led modern scholars to conclude that he is a conservative or dogmatic thinker. In fact, he is neither. Ibn Hazm's Zahirism emphasizes the limited scope of Islamic law and attempts to curtail the claims made by Muslim jurists to speak on behalf of God's law. This method leads him to support rationalism, individualism, and anti-clericalism. Ibn Hazm argues in favor of these principles consistently in his works on Islamic legal theory. . . . This approach promises to undermine the whole madhhab system, which explains the negative response it received from the religious establishment. In place of the madhhab system, Ibn Hazm seeks to assert the individual responsibility of each Muslim to obey God's law as it is clearly revealed in the sacred texts of Islam. (Sabra 7)

Like Ibn Hazm, Victor's writing, teaching, and living affirm rationalism, individual personhood, and anti-clericalism. I want to be clear on the matter of Victor's commitments—he rejects individualism. He has written and taught against individualism repeatedly because it is at the root of the dominant Western political economy's liberalism. His view is clear that the penchant for liberalism's individualism keeps us from forming collectivities of resistance to oppressions. He has made this point often. So individualism, no; individuality, yes.

Ibn Hazm (994–1064 CE) was an example of tenth-century Islamic Spain's remarkable multiracial, multicultural, and multi-religious commitments (Vilchez 4–24). He was fully committed to pluralism in rhetoric and in teaching and learning relationships (Pluralism Project). Neither Victor nor I believe in reincarnation, but *Zhuangzi's* happy wanderer is based on Daoist reincarnation. If Daoism is right and reincarnation is real, there is good reason to believe that Ibn Hazm is an earlier incarnation of Victor. The multiple identities, pluralist roles, and commitment to shared fate that the polymath Ibn Hazm demonstrated offer a rich comparison to Victor's life and work.

Ibn Hazm was a rhetorician, a theoretician of Zahirism, and the celebrated author of *The Ring of the Dove.* His best-known work is a rhetorical treatise on love (Ghazi Bin Muhammad 6), and we should remember that Victor begins *Bootstraps* with a crucial affirmation about the centrality of love: "Che' Guevara believed revolutions begin with love. Maybe loving a country and its peoples can provide for revolutionary change—more than mere reforms: true equity. Maybe. And loving brings me full circle." (ix–x).

If we understand fundamentalism as the imagined certainty that one's race, religion, or political group has 100 percent of the truth and that anyone outside your group is in error and therefore less than fully human, then Ibn Hazm was a dynamic voice for pluralism. He regarded Judaism and Christianity and its prophets as fully legitimate versions of the one Abrahamic religion that includes Islam. His pluralism is an openness to unassimilated otherness, and it is the heart of his desire to wrest power from Islamic legal scholars and return it to individuals. The line of scripture that Ibn Hazm quoted most often was this verse: "O Humankind! We have created you from a male and a female, and we made you nations and tribes that you may come to know one another" (Qur'an 49, 13). Like Ibn Hazm, Victor's writings and relationships provide alternatives to fundamentalist monologues of totalizing claims to absolute knowledge. Victor often constructs these alternatives to fundamentalist monologues of hermetically sealed imagined pure identities with reference to complex ancestries and the absurdities of racism. Here is a key example from the prologue to *Bootstraps,* in which Victor is referring to himself:

Shakespeare saw Othello as black. Othello the Moor, *el morro.* There's a U.S. army base in Puerto Rico called *El Morro. El Blancito,* the white one in Brooklyn, not white elsewhere, is more the Moor than the Puerto Rican Boricua Indian or the West African black apparently, a hint of some ancient Islamic strain. . . . He's just not typical of the stereotypical. So many subtleties to the absurdities of racism. (xi–xii)

One of Victor's children recently surprised him with the gift of his DNA ancestry. Victor is profoundly aware of all the ways such constructed data can be misused, misapplied, abused, and used for adult fantasies of being special or for routinely racist purposes. Victor as happy wanderer takes the claimed ancestral data both playfully and seriously. Playfully as adult childlike imaginings and seriously as potential occasion for increased sense of shared fate with additional human groups. With his permission, here is the overview:

	Puerto Rican	**Victor**
Southern European	48%	22%
Western & Central African	26%	25%
Native American	17%	8%
Western & Central Europe	6%	30%
Northern Africa	3%	8%
Arabia	0	2%

Western, Central, and Northern African elements of Victor's genome combined are 33 percent. Native American and Arabian together are 10 percent. Southern, Western, and Central Europe are 52 percent. Notice that the math for Puerto Rico adds up to 100 percent but for Victor only 95 percent. Happy wanderer indeed. What of the other 5 percent? The missing 5 percent is a statistical admission that DNA results by any company of any individual are based on "reference populations" populating company databases and are estimates of which populations in their database are most like the genetic markers an individual carries. Each DNA-ancestry company claims that their results do not necessarily mean that an individual belongs to such human groupings but *likely* might because of a similar genetic match. An editor of this volume, in requesting revision to an earlier form of this text, reminds us all that

1. these are norm-referenced results; and
2. they do NOT tell us about our ancestors. They tell us about groups of people with similar genetic makeup who have submitted to this particular company's test of DNA. Such tests can say nothing of our own pasts, nor anything direct about the groups referenced, only about those who have submitted to the test and where they currently reside. The biases in these DNA tests are numerous, one being the assumption that people don't move from where they are or have been. Take the Japanese. After World War II, the largest population outside of Japan can be found in Brazil. My brother's DNA test said that he (and presumably me, since we are identical twins) is 50 percent Japanese. So does this locate our ancestors in Brazil or in Japan? Does it make some of our ancestors Brazilian, Indigenous Brazilians, or Japanese from Japan? Hmmm. And we already know that our father's family came to Hawaii from Japan just two generations back, but a DNA test can't tell us that. So what exactly can this kind of test tell us? Adult fantasies? Maybe. Still, really interesting, or to use Victor's likely word: *funny*.

These possible or likely ancestral sources pull at Victor in crucial ways. Trying to imagine and understand these probable genetic facts, he tries to unify the varied appearance of his likely identity groups that the DNA report suggests. The power of one's imagined collective face in a mirror of constructed multigroup humanity. I wanted Victor to seriously play with the company's claimed version of the multiracial sources of Victor's genome by selecting an image of what his blend of multigroup humanity might look like at this point in his life, and then select another image of what he might have looked like as a young adult given the implied affinity groups in his DNA report.

I wanted the current image and the image of him in his youth that he chose to be as close to uncolonized by the ambient white supremacist gaze as possible. Victor selected an Internet image suggestive of himself in the present, with a white beard similar to his own and an accurate and comparable physique, as confirmed by his life partner, Rochelle, with only one inaccurate visual feature: Victor no longer has hair on the top of his head. Victor sees himself in this image with startling clarity and accuracy. It is an image not of a person from Puerto Rico but from the people called Guanche from the Canary Islands, the southernmost part of Spain, and located close to Africa. A mirror in which Victor sees his version of multigroup humanity. See the image linked in the first QR code on this page.

The image in which Victor sees himself as a young adult is especially intriguing. He experiences the image he chose as unnervingly similar to his multigroup appearance as a young adult, minus the tattoos and ornaments in the image, which he finds affinity producing. See the image linked in the second QR code on this page, from the Guanche of the Canary Islands. What the images show is how Victor selects and constructs his individual and collective identity as enmeshed with families from different global locations before and outside of white supremacist sorting and objectifying.

Since we are all multiple amphibians living in many worlds at once—race, gender, class, sexuality, and the others—and each of us is almost infinitely complex, and the persons who know us best barely know us, the potentially positive use of a DNA test's posited ancestral group connections is to increase a sense of shared fate and of human connection worth reimagining. Victor demonstrates this positive potential uses of DNA testing, projecting a better kind of imagined community, outside of nationalism, inclining toward inclusion, shared fate, connection. How does Victor perceive these two images as before and outside of white supremacist sorting and objectifying? I see Victor looking for the power of his imagined collective face in a mirror of constructed multigroup humanity where the white gaze naturally recedes, gets revealed as ultimately funny and merely human, not special. As Victor demonstrates in his teaching and mentoring, unanticipated connection is what he does most typically and perhaps naturally, with audiences and with materials. He does not exclude but finds new ways to include, nontrivially. These two images are outside the ambient white supremacist gaze, making whiteness irrelevant, no longer the absent present—whiteness as naturally recessive. In the image of the older collective Victor, we see strength looking down, not in any form of submission but in refusal to dominate. The younger collective Victor is not to be messed with. Yes, there is a collective kindness present, but with no patience to be pushed around; he is a person, a cherished equal. What all of us readers of Victor's work and living commitments might learn about the proper use of DNA testing is that we are potentially connected everywhere where humanness resides and oppressions are resisted. What might we learn about ourselves? That we are vastly complex, barely know ourselves, and we need every other person to learn something essential about self, about each other, and about our potential collective, human survival. This is what we learn from Victor and from one another when we open to each other as Victor's selected two images invited him to resee himself. Each of us is looking for our collective group face.

Victor lives in "ongoing dialectical tensions" between and among beta and transcendent consciousness while evincing movement, a dance of being "playful and disciplined, imaginative and profoundly realistic" (Kohn, *Science* 223) but always attempting to study and open up with those who follow their natures in "balance and peace" (Eddy and Villanueva 171). Victor's contribution is his compassionate smile and centered stillness to those he gifted with a relationship, and his giving of relationship is close to universal. I freely admit that for me Victor has a strong "hint of some ancient Islamic strain" (*Bootstraps* xii) and that vivid strain is the Islamic Spanish pluralism of Ibn Hazm, multiracial, multicultural, multireligious, and all in service to resisting human oppressions by dominant groups.

At the end of his illuminating chapter in this collection on how Victor uses fictive kinship to support, inspire, and challenge writers of color who write about racism to reject being silenced by ambient white privilege, reject being silenced by white comfort, and reject silencing by white fragility, J Paul Padilla asks us, "How will our kinship with those writers of color who address racism help them light darkness, blaze trails, and keep their sights on making our world a more humane place?" (p. 236). This crucial question goes with Padilla's other unavoidable question about those mentored by Victor: "We carry our memories of Victor. What memories will those who we serve carry of me and you?" (p. 236). If the answer for any of us is other than viable, dynamic kinship, the experience of shared fate, then we have rejected kinship and we are ourselves colonized and are engaged in colonizing. Hard truths but realities are better than illusions, even self-induced.

I end with the three Chinese characters at the heart of *Zhuangzi's* happy wanderer and at the heart of Victor's fully open and attentive listening, which is the secret of his legion of mentoring successes with undergraduates, graduate students and peers. All three Chinese characters, traditional, not simplified characters, include the radical - xin - 心 for heart, which implies love through dynamic listening.

First the character for love: 愛

The character for listen: 聽

The character for endure: 忍

To listen with the heart is to endure. To form kinship. Victor listens and helps others to endure and to form coalitions of resistance to racism, resistance to colonial oppressions. As pluralism un-self-consciously demonstrates—Victor as Daoist happy wanderer, as practicing Catholic, as demonstrator of the strong strain of ancient Islamic pluralism with Ibn Hazm—and as a current ancestral voice reminds us through Buddhism, another way to see these three Chinese characters together is in the practice of compassion. To listen with the heart and endure with others—to form kinship—is the ultimate act of compassion (to "suffer with" others).

Salaam.

WORKS CITED

Eddy, Robert, and Victor Villanueva, editors. *A Language and Power Reader: Representations of Race in a "Post-Racist" Era*. Utah State UP, 2014.

Ghazi Bin Muhammad, Prince Ghazi. *Love in the Holy Qur'an*. Islamic Texts Society, 2013.

Kohn, Livia. *Science and the Dao: From the Big Bang to Lived Perfection*. Three Pines Press, 2016.

———. *Zhuangzi: Text and Context*. Three Pines Press, 2014.

The Pluralism Project. Harvard University, https://pluralism.org/.

Sabra, Adam. "Ibn Hazm's Literalism: A Critique of Islamic Legal Theory (I)." *Al-Qantara: Revista de Estudios Arabes*, vol. 28, no. 1, 2007 pp. 7–40. https://doaj.org/article/dfdbba6c7c964960a2e64b8ae17f6a4e.

Vílchez, José Miguel Puerta. "Ibn Hazm: A Biographical Sketch." *Ibn Hazm of Cordoba: The Life and Works of a Controversial Thinker*, edited by Camilla Adang, Maribel Fierro, and Sabine Schmidtke. Brill, 2013, pp. 4–24.

Villanueva, Victor. *Bootstraps: From an American Academic of Color*. National Council of Teachers of English, 1993.

Chapter 13

Dandole Gas: Un Profe con Sangre del Fil

Octavio Pimentel

"El Bloque" . . . pues, ¿qué te puedo decir…? I was a graduate student at California State University, Chico when I was assigned to read *Bootstraps*. It was an eye opener . . . finally something that I could relate to. At that point, I was still a youngster in my twenties, not sure whether I belonged in graduate school—or, in fact, in academics. I, like El Jefe, had grown up tough. My parents and I were *trabajadores del fil,* so we faced many racist obstacles on a daily basis. At best, we lived in extreme poverty, and when things got really tough, *pues a la calle*. Forty-five years later I am a full professor at Texas State University and an author of six books, thirty-plus articles, and hundreds of worldwide presentations. I now live in an almost 4,000-square-foot house in a golf course community and I drive a Tesla. Now my life is much different than when I lived on Second Street with my homie Bobby and my dad drove Chelo Silva (a 1969 Ford truck that was given this nickname because he always listened to Chelo Silva). Now is much different than when I wore my dad's clothes to school or when I had to walk two miles to school with my friends Oscar and Aaron because our parents did not have the gas money nor the time to take us and/or pick us from school. Yes . . . now it is very different. . . .

BOOTSTRAPS

In 1993, Victor Villanueva (aka "El Jefe") wrote a book, more like a *cuento*, that would forever change the life of many Brown people. *Bootstraps: From an American Academic of Color* is a critical autoethnography that offers Villanueva's (a Puerto Rican/Nuyorican) academic *cuento*. The book includes many stories that focus on the countless obstacles and signs of racism Villanueva faced daily. Since its publication, thousands of academic scholars have quoted and/or summarized different parts of the book. The problem with this is that in many cases these academics do this in a superficial way—meaning they cite El Jefe as a success story and an example of what Brown people can achieve. But Villanueva's *cuento* is much more complex than this. El Jefe's *cuento* is not meant solely as an example for Brown people to mimic. Instead, his *cuento* should be used to expose the underlying systemic racism that exists in every aspect of academics.

In *Bootstraps,* El Jefe writes about the different challenges he tackled as he became an academic. When he first attended college, it was not easy for him because he had not graduated with a high school degree and instead was forced to drop out of high school and get his GED. As a result, he lacked many of the academic and life skills that many students come to college with. Although Villanueva had difficulty with most of his community college subjects, his English classes were especially challenging for him. El Jefe had a lot of difficulty in these classes because he did not have the expected writing skills. Although Villanueva struggled with many of his community college classes, he did graduate with an associate degree. Soon after that, he moved on to a university to pursue his bachelor's degree. During this time, Villanueva started excelling in his writing. He accomplished this by impersonating his professors' rhetorical practices. Not surprisingly, even though he was experiencing success in his English university courses, he still felt out of place because he was often the only Brown student. Once El Jefe completed his bachelor of arts, he applied for and was accepted into a graduate program in English—because of his ethnicity, not because of his academic record and test scores. In graduate school, Villanueva discovered the power of rhetoric, learning that it was much more valuable to respond critically than to simply respond to a reading with an expected answer.

As with many other contributors to this collection, *Bootstraps* was a game changer for me. It showed me that there were people like me in academia. Although there might not have been many of us, there were some. Specifically, *Bootstraps* showed me that the ACADEMY had taught me that I had FUCKED UP, or that I was FUCKED UP. El Jefe taught me that this label had nothing to do with me and instead was the academy's way of marginalizing Brown people. What Villanueva's *cuento* taught me was that hatred and racism exist in academics and that labels are a tool commonly used to oppress Brown students. More than this, *Bootstraps* motivated me by showing me that there were others like me who were trying to succeed academically despite the obstacles.

Unfortunately (or not), Brown people relate to Villanueva's story a little too much. By this I mean that way too many *gente* have had similar negative academic experiences of being forced to learn and participate in an academic curriculum that does not value their cultural practices. Somehow, some strong-minded individuals—like Villanueva—make *movidas* to succeed academically. But the big underlying question is: Is it all worth it? *No se* . . . my *cuento,* following, pushes all of us to consider this critical question.

LA CALLE SEGUNDA

My father emigrated from Ecuandureo, Mexico (the state of Michoacán), in 1953 and my mother from Zapoltiltic, Mexico (the state of Jalisco), in 1955 to search for a better life. Through different pathways individually, they migrated to Marysville, California, in early 1964. Soon after, they became a couple and started living together. They did not legally marry until 1979. My parents were both extremely hard workers. Unfortunately for them, they did not have many opportunities to excel. Before they died, we had many conversations on the array of racism they faced.

On most days, both of them worked more than twelve hours in the fields and then worked in the evening at bars or restaurants. *Estaba cabron* for them. . . . In 1967, I was born. We had no money. We had no food. Oftentimes when we were homeless, we lived in our white 1952 Buick station wagon with seats that were not anchored to the car. Since we were a migrant family, we worked up and down the West Coast: California, Oregon, Washington. My family also worked in Arizona, Texas, Kansas, and Louisiana.

In early 1969, things went from bad to worse. While my family was picking apples in Washington, my father fell from a twenty-foot ladder and landed standing up. He was rushed to the hospital, where he learned he had broken several vertebrae in his lower back. A week later, he went in for surgery. He was never the same after that; he always had back pain.

Like the negative rhetoric Villanueva faced, the rhetoric my family faced as *trabajadores del fil* was not pleasant. As migrant workers, we were considered uneducated, lazy people who could not find jobs elsewhere. Additionally, fieldworkers are often thought to be undocumented, which was not the case for my family. We were all documented. In fact, I myself was a US citizen.

Almost on a daily basis I awoke to the noise of my *madrecita* cooking the daily burritos we would take to *Cuatro Esquinas*. Most of the time Mom made bean burritos, but when we had extra money, she would make *burritos de carne asada* or maybe *burritos de gallina*. Those were only special treats, and I knew we would rarely get them. *Ta' bien* though. . . . I liked *los de frijoles* best.

As soon as I could hear Mom cooking, I got up. She was always so happy. Never complaining about making fresh flour tortillas at 3:00 a.m. Never complaining about cooking at 3:00 a.m. for the six of us. No one helped her. Not even me. Sometimes I would stand up and get close to her sanctuary, *la estufa*, and she would tell me: *"Vete a sentar. Te vas a quemar los dedos."* Not wanting to fight her joking but assertive commands, I followed orders. Although I never asked, she always gave me a couple of burritos and told me, *"Toma . . . antes que todos se levanten."*

FUCK THE RHETORIC. My family were all total BAD ASSES. I remember routinely leaving for work between 3:00 and 4:00 a.m. When we got to the fields, it was completely dark. *Pero todo está bien.* We turned the car to face the trees and used its headlights to light the peach trees. We, although mostly Dad and Mom because the rest of us were kids, worked our asses off. I remember looking at them and thinking, "Wow, they are fast." As much as I tried to help, I really didn't help that much. As a 7-year-old, I picked only the peaches off the ground and took them to the bin. In contrast to rhetoric that claims *trabajadores del fil* are worthless, underpaid workers who are willing to do any job for any amount of money, my counternarrative defies every bit of this deficit rhetoric. To me, *trabajadores del fil* were great examples of hard workers. Every so often, I would find an old torn *costal.* When I found one, I would put it on and act like I was a total BAD ASS fieldworker like Mom and Dad. I always wore my *costal* with pride. In my head, I was a *trabajador del fil.* A BAD ASS. Someone who could fill fifteen bins of peaches. Someone who could make $60 a day after working fourteen-hour days. Yes, a BAD ASS. That was my rhetoric.

El Jefe uses language like most others can only dream. He uses words softly and sometimes indirectly to send his messages. Unlike many current rhetoricians who use their emotions, mostly anger, to get their message across, he uses words—but in a subtle way that questions rhetorical practices that most Americans, especially academics, unthinkingly support. Following is an example of how Villanueva talks about the communication flaws between teachers and Brown and Black kids.

> Color isn't always race when it comes to teachers. It's an attitude, more an understanding of where we live than where we're from. We came from many places back on the block. A teacher would have had to go a long way to understand and convey an understanding of all those where-froms. But a teacher could have looked around and known the where-at. Few did, even among those who were racially of color. (2)

I found many similarities between my own academic experience and Villanueva's. When I was in K–12 school, the education system pushed a colorless curriculum, much like it does now, which did not make sense to a 7-year-old and certainly does not make sense to me today as a professor. The K–12 education system preaches that we should not see color. Meaning that a teacher should aspire to not "see" that their students are Brown, Black, Asian, White, etc. Even as a 7-year-old, I did not understand that color-blind mentality. How can you not see that Marcos is Brown or that my good friend Tony is Black? How can you not tell that Gary is Asian?

How can you not tell that Eddy is White? I really thought that the teachers had gone to some special school that had taught them that color did not matter.

As I reflect now as an adult, I have to agree with my 7-year-old self that the teacher did attend a special school. Well, maybe not a special school (in the good sense) but a school that force-fed a rhetoric claiming that all students were the same in spite of their color. Additionally, these same teachers were force-fed the idea that all students have the same opportunities to succeed. They bought into the fallacy of meritocracy. As a result, they viewed students who did not succeed as being LAZY and/or saw students' ethnic identities as holding them back. Simply put—teachers were taught, and are still being taught, that Brown and Black folks are inferior to white folks. Although many people buy into this rhetoric, it is crucial that we scrutinize the sociopolitical aspects of schooling, including the curriculum, pedagogical practices, and standardized testing.

In my case, not only did my teachers refuse to see that I was Brown and that English was not my first language, but they also thought there was something internally wrong with me that could account for my poor academic performance. At no point did the school system consider that my poor performance was their fault. They saw a student who was not doing well in school and blamed it on the student, their family, and their culture. As a result of my not doing well academically and the school's refusal to help, the system simply categorized me as a special education student, which impacted the classes I was in. For example, during my elementary years, I was tracked as a Worm, a low-achieving student: Bees (high achieving), Butterflies (standard achievers), and Worms (low achievers).

> [W]e behave as if the minority problem is the immigrant problem. Two generations of learning the language and the ways of America, and all will be better, we hear. But two generations come and go and all that happens is the minority's native tongue is gone. The African American lost his native tongue two hundred years ago. (Villanueva 19)

As El Jefe clarifies in his writing, it is the school system that perceives students' native languages as problems. Schools conceptualize immigrants as deficient individuals who must be saved by assimilating into American culture, defined as white European American (WEA) cultural norms and practices. That being the case, when a non-WEA student enters the school, in most cases the school system tries to remove their BROWNESS, BLACKNESS, or ASIANESS as soon as possible in an effort to assimilate them into "White Ways of being." The school system pushes this agenda in multiple ways, including using a Eurocentric curriculum that affirms WEA cultural practices. For example, among other false information that glorifies WEA ancestry and ways of being, students learn that Columbus discovered America, that July 4 is Independence Day, and that Benjamin Franklin is a hero. More than this, the school system pushes European ways of being by forcing an English-only agenda through programs such as English as a Second Language.

Yeso es lo que me paso a mi. All I ever wanted was to be a BUTTERFLY. I knew that the teacher would never classify me as a BEE. I worked very hard in school. I visited my teacher after school. I also came early to school to get help from her. I tried to get the teacher to show me how to pronounce words without a Spanish accent. I tried to learn how to like peanut butter and jelly sandwiches. I tried to learn stories like the Three Little Bears, and I tried to get excited about holidays like St. Patrick's Day. *Pero nada.* I remained a WORM. Despite my efforts, I was trapped in a net of racism, and it was not going to let me go.

SAN YSIDRO

San Ysidro really set the foundation for who I am. This environment taught me that I needed to be tough to survive. It taught me to be witty but also compassionate. It taught me to care about people, but to also realize that many people should not be trusted. I arrived in San Ysidro in January 1979, my fifth-grade year in school. We moved into some sketchy apartments really close to the border. But I have to be honest . . . we were sketchy too. Soon after the move, someone broke in and stole a few things, which really pissed us off because we did not have much. Pretty soon we learned who the thieves were, and we walked over and got our stuff back—and more. In this environment, you had to do this. If you didn't, you would become a victim again.

San Ysidro taught me a lot more than to be tough; it taught me to love my culture. The old apartment on Sycamore Street was less than three miles from the border. Oftentimes, especially during the summer, my friends and family would walk to the border to enjoy *unos tacos de vapor* or perhaps a *tejuino*. On other occasions, since it was farther, we would drive to see my *tia Perí* and *primos; Negra, Max, Yiyo, y todos los de más*. Those were cool times.

Ya my *cuento* is different. Much like Villanueva's story, I did not have a pretty, guided story. No . . . I had to learn from my own experiences—all of them. Growing up in an environment like San Ysidro taught me to love my culture, my language, my people. It taught me never to be embarrassed by my Mexican culture and to express it whenever possible.

Flashback to sixth grade. In my sixth-grade ESL class, I was assigned a research project of my choice. It could be on football, the environment, attending a university—the topic was wide open. I chose to do my paper on Mexico. In this project, I showed many different aspects of Mexico, from art, monuments, history, language, historical figures, etc. It was an easy project for me because I wanted to show my sixth-grade teacher how beautiful Mexico was.

Reflecting on this, I can really appreciate the complexity of the rhetorical choices I made to complete this project. Simply put—I was using Mexico, as a subject, to teach my ESL teacher about the attractiveness of Mexico and the Spanish language. As a 12-year-old student, I was making some pretty complex *movidas* that should be appreciated. In my eyes, the school did not like people like me, Mexicans whose first language was not English. So what I did was create a project as a tool to teach my teacher about the many different positive aspects of what she considered a flawed (at best) topic. I showed my teacher that I was a complex young rhetorician, thinking about and explaining contentious topics. Then again, I was still the ESL student who was considered a nuisance because he had not assimilated into WEA culture. And I was still the kid who got into trouble because I could not name any of my so-called "Founding Fathers."

> So what had happened? I was an "A" student, third, or fourth in the class, able with language, Saturdays spent on special classes in preparation for the entrance exam to the college prep high school. Why hadn't I made it? Mom says the Bishop's Fund, but that seems inconsistent with a dollar tuition. Cultural bias in standardized tests is the more obvious answer. (Villanueva 22)

Completing this project gave me the confidence to continue pushing agendas in my school assignments. Although I often did not excel in my assignments because my rhetorical practices and beliefs went against school norms, I still tried my best. This effort pushed me to get moved up to the middle education track in middle school. Yay—I was proud of myself; I was now a Butterfly! A wounded one, but still—a Butterfly. Soon after my eighth-grade graduation, we moved to Marysville, California.

MOVING TO MARYSVILLE

Although I had completed some of my elementary years in Marysville while we migrated with the fruit season, returning to Marysville as a young adult in high school was overwhelming. In San Ysidro I had access to a multicultural world that showed me the beauty of diversity. San Ysidro/Tijuana taught me to be proud of my Mexican heritage. It was a cool environment that expected everyone to speak Spanish. I had access to amusement parks and things to do like trips to Tijuana, Sea World, and Padres and Charger games. In San Ysidro I also had access to the Boy's Club, which provided me with an avenue to relieve my stress.

When I arrived in Marysville, I hated it. Although there were many reasons I hated it, the most obvious was that there were very few people who looked like me. In San Ysidro, 99 percent of the population was Mexican or Mexican American and most of them spoke Spanish. In Marysville, 95 percent of the people were white

European Americans who spoke only English. And worse—most were racist!

As soon as I arrived in Marysville, my parents took me to register for high school. Since my dad did not understand English, he waited in his 1974 yellow Ranchero while my mother walked in with me to speak to the counselor. When I sat down, the counselor told me that college would not be a good idea for me. She then asked if I was handy and added that people who were good with their hands could make a good living. Soon she started clicking buttons on her computer and then handed me a printed schedule from one of those dot matrix printers—the ones that make a lot of noise. When I looked at my school schedule, I discovered that she had enrolled me in physical education, metal shop, welding, basic math, basic English, and basic science. Once again, I was a WORM.

As El Jefe claims so eloquently in *Bootstraps*, racism is deeply embedded in the school system, and as a result, it is interwoven throughout societal practices—hence, systemic racism. Let me explain this. As has been argued before, the US school system rewards those students who are familiar with and practice WEA ways of being and punishes those who are not. More specifically, the Marysville High School counselor disregarded my transcript from San Ysidro and simply viewed me as a recent immigrant from Mexico (which was wrong because I was a US citizen); because I was coming from a nonacademically successful middle school (based on standardized tests), because my family were migrant workers, and because Spanish was my first language, she assumed that college was not an option for me.

What is critical to understand, and much more important to consider, is that these racist practices are embedded in more than that high school academic counselor's thoughts and behaviors. The problem is much more complex than that. In most cases, the historical rhetoric that has established the idea of a potential successful college student has always been biased against BROWN people. If you do not speak standardized English, come from a middle-class family, and do well on standardized tests, you are not often classified as college material. These students, often Brown students, are directed toward working-class, vocational tracks that prepare them for working-class professions. Again, the problem is much more complex than a case of a racist counselor. The reality is, school counselors and teachers are prepared in a racist school system. To be clear, though, I do not have a problem with working-class jobs. The problem I have is that Brown students are overwhelmingly being tracked into these professions and not given the opportunity to choose college as an option.

Unfortunately, because the education system tracked me into the lowest educational track in high school, I followed the negative rhetorical expectations that were established for me. More specifically, since I was being consistently told that students like me did not care about or achieve at school, I listened to them; I stopped caring about school until I discovered basketball. Basketball gave me a reason to maintain a C average.

In high school I became an exceptional basketball player, which led me to receive some college recruitment letters. When they asked about my academic transcripts, however, their interest ended because they learned I was not doing well academically. Simply put, I was a "worm" (and therefore never took any college prep classes) and not a good enough basketball player for them to risk a scholarship. The only person who continued to be interested in me was the coach for the local community college. After I accepted his offer to play basketball for our community college and made my commitment to them, he told me that he had accepted a coaching position at California State University, Chico, or Chico State, as it's often called. I'm not sure whether these incidents were related, but soon after that, I was pulled out of my high school class to meet with an Educational Opportunity Program (EOP) advisor to discuss the possibility of attending Chico State.

In *Bootstraps*, Villanueva writes, "I wanted to try my hand at college, go beyond the GED. But college scared me. I had been told long ago that college wasn't my lot" (66), which is an experience I can directly relate to. Although I was not a returning student like El Jefe, I had been told throughout my educational experience that attending a university was simply not in my future. But the way this message was conveyed was not explicit. Instead, the education system created pathways for me that led to that conclusion. That was sneaky, and as my late *padrecito* would say, *"Que cabrones. Que no tienen los huevos para decirte al chingadaso?"* Although I understand my late dad's asking, "Don't they have the audacity to tell you directly?" it is crucial to understand that my story is not unique. The entire education system is complicit in not identifying people like myself as college material, thus creating obstacle after obstacle for people like me to succeed academically.

THE TALK

When the EOP recruiter pulled me out of class to talk to me about the possibility of attending California State University, Chico, I was thrilled. As I reflect now, that recruiter was the first critical thinking academic person I had met. He told me that he knew from my academic records (not sure which ones) that I had the potential to succeed in college. He also told me that he knew I had faced many different obstacles in my educational experiences that prevented me from taking a traditional path to college. At that point, he invited me to apply to attend a five-week Summer Bridge session that would allow me to prove I belonged in college.

In June 1986, I received my invitation to attend the Summer Bridge program at Chico State. I was so excited, but I had no idea what to expect. I had never been to Chico. When I told my good friends about this opportunity, they laughed at me and said that I would soon return because I was STUPID. My friends never thought I would make it in college, but in all fairness, I had never given them a reason to believe in me. When I told my dad and mom I was leaving for college, they thought it was cool but did not truly understand what it meant. I remember my dad helped me pack my stereo and some clothes and gave me $20. Scared as hell, I drove to Chico State *para ver que era el pedo*.

All my life, machismo is something that I have been expected to embrace. But not in traditional ways, as in the belief that males are superior to females. No, it was much different from that. I had two extremely hard-working parents who served as excellent role models.

Unlike in some *machista's* household where the man worked and the female stayed home, I saw that my mother always worked as hard or harder than my father. By that, I mean that my mother worked *en el fíl* with my dad as well as taking care of the family, which meant that she was the primary cook and housecleaner. Given my mother's hard work ethic, she quickly became one of my primary role models. In no way did my version of machismo teach me to disrespect women or to ever think that men were superior to them. In fact, what I learned was the exact opposite. I learned that women could excel in any job and that they had no limitations. Machismo instead taught me to be brave when facing new challenges. It taught me to have confidence in myself even when other people did not. It taught me to NEVER quit! It gave me the *GANAS* to keep on going.

BECOMING A SCHOOL BOY

> There were failures, of course. One professor said my writing was too formulaic. One professor said it was too novel. Another wrote only one word for the one paper required of the course. . . . School becomes his obsession. There is the education. But the obsession is as much, if not more, in getting a degree, not with a job in mind, just the degree, just because he thinks he can, despite all that has said he could not. (Villanueva 71)

Once I successfully completed Summer Bridge, I was admitted to California State University, Chico, as a special-admit student through the Educational Opportunity Program. After being admitted, I knew I was not going to leave. I remember on many different occasions both my father and mother telling me, *"Recuerdate. . . . Ya que te fuistes del mundo de ignorancia, nunca vas a querer a regresar."* Once you leave the world of ignorance, you will never want to return. For the first time in my life, I lived in an environment where I was surrounded by smart people. And even though—at that time—I might not always have been making the best choices, I knew I was doing something right.

NOT ATYPICAL

A 6'6", 275-pound Mexican with a BRIGHT GREEN MOHAWK walks into a writing classroom. Even though everyone wants to look at me, no one does. They are afraid to make eye contact because they think I may be one of those ASSHOLES who is confrontational. And although that may have been true, the real me was more afraid of them. And when I say I was afraid of them, I do not mean physically, because I knew that even if I got into a physical altercation, the worst they could do to me was cause some external bruising, which was not a big deal. What I was really afraid of was their academic boasting—an arrogance they projected that beat me up emotionally and made me question whether I really belonged in higher education. That was what I was afraid of. Stuff like that is much harder to recover from than a busted lip or a black eye. This inner bruising was tough . . . and I am not sure I could have recovered from that.

Samia Yaqub was my first critical teacher. She was such a cool woman. She was a Brown woman from the Middle East who had overcome many different instances of racism and sexism. She made the perfect teacher for me. She was sensitive to me when I needed that and tough when she had to be. We had a great relationship. She was the first teacher who made me think that I was not a *pendejo*, and that I was smart.

One day while waiting for Samia's class, a 5'6", 140-pound white man with a great smile came up to me and asked, "What's up?" Not knowing who he was, I gave him a half smile and nodded my head. I wondered, Who in the hell is this guy? What does he want?

"My name is Tom—Tom Fox. I am a professor here in the English department. Samia has said a lot of great things about you, and I wanted to introduce myself. I also wanted to meet with you. Let's meet tomorrow at 12:00 p.m."

I agreed to meet with Tom the next day. After buying me a Gatorade, he told me that Samia had mentioned that I was an exceptional writer and that I should really consider becoming an English major. He explained that as an English major I would be able to apply for many different types of jobs. He talked to me about pursuing a master's degree, which would prepare me to become a college teacher—like Samia. Toward the end of our conversation, he told me that he was interested in hiring me as a writing tutor the following semester. Surprised at his proposal, I said yes. Here was another moment that I knew was going to change my life forever. Although this seemed a unique way to be recruited into higher education, it is surprising how many other *carnales/Latinx* have had similar experiences. Below is an interaction that El Jefe had with one of his professors at a local grocery store:

> Victor the graduate student is walking to Safeway one day when one of his professors jumps out of a car to ask if he could be willing to take an academic job. The job is to be a "reader," grading papers for an undergraduate course. The requirements are that the course must have more than fifty students enrolled and that the reader be recommended by the professor teaching the course. He accepts. (89)

It might be surprising that Villanueva and I were recruited into working for the academy in such a similar way. Unlike the traditional way of students applying for academic jobs, directors came looking for us. I guess since we were both nontraditional students, it would only make sense for us to be recruited in nontraditional ways.

Being an English major in the late 1980s at California State University, Chico made me an anomaly. Like Villanueva, I too was often the only student of color in class. During this time, I often questioned why I was an English major. I was learning a subject that really did not acknowledge my culture. In effect, I was learning about a topic that I had little interest in. The only reason I stuck with it was because I had told Samia Yaqub and Tom Fox that I would become an English major, so I was going to stick to my word, regardless of the obstacles (yeah—that was the *machista* mentality). As a way to cope with the pain of being an English major, I also majored in Spanish and Chicano studies. I fell in love with those literatures and histories, and these classes helped relieve some of the pain. Six years later I graduated with my BA in English, Spanish, and Chicano studies.

GRADUATE SCHOOL

Soon after graduating with my undergraduate degree, and with the help of Tom Fox, I was accepted into the master's program in English—me, ANGEL, as I was known back then. At this point, during the summer I was still picking peaches and prunes in the fields. Eventually, I was promoted to working at Sun Sweet Dryers drying prunes (*o en las secadoras* as they are better known), which was considered a "good job" because I worked twelve-hour shifts, seven days a week and therefore made good money.

But now I was a graduate student in the Department of English. Time to be the sophisticated individual that I thought people expected me to be. In *Bootstraps,* Villanueva writes:

> Victor was going to learn—quite consciously—what it means to be white, middle class. He didn't see the exploitation; not then; he was obsessed. There were things going on in his classes that he did not understand and that the others did. He didn't know what the things were that he didn't understand, but he knew that even those who didn't do as well as he did, somehow did not act as foreign as he felt. He was the only colored kid in every one of those classes. (72)

Unfortunately, after dealing with a lot of racism and politics, I was pushed out of the Department of English, which resulted in me graduating with a master's in interdisciplinary studies with a focus in composition studies.

I then left for the University of Utah to study with Susan Miller, a good friend of El Jefe's, to become a *profe.* The PhD experience *estaba chevere.* Don't get me wrong. Although it was not a terrible experience, it certainly was not enjoyable or something I would ever want to endure again. Surprisingly, the Department of Education, Culture, and Society (ECS), the department I was accepted into, was very diverse, which I loved. Roughly half of the professors and about 80 percent of the students were of color. The Department of ECS really pushed me to be critical, and specifically to be super sensitive to issues of race, ethnicity, language, sexism, and many other marginalized topics. Luckily for me, I then transferred these interests to my rhetoric and composition program, which I also belonged to. Unlike ECS, this program had only a few students of color and one faculty member of color, my *Compa* Raúl Sanchez. This was exciting because I was now able to talk and write about issues of race and ethnicity, inequality, and other marginalized topics that were often not dealt with at the time.

Villanueva writes in *Bootstraps* about a similar experience when he pushed the field of rhetoric and composition:

> So he [Victor Villanueva] enters his first research project. He wants to begin by breaking away from the suggestion that students of color are basic writers exclusively. Some do go on. Some students of color are never assigned to basic-writing courses. And he wants to break away from the oral-literate, speaking-writing dichotomy. His initial research question asks how basic writers of color differ from traditional writers of color, and whites, in terms of reliance on oral language features in writing. He looks to writing groups, where speaking, listening, writing, and reading interact. (101)

Like El Jefe, I really enjoyed pushing my rhetoric and composition classes to think about issues of ethnicity. In 2002, Susan Miller asked me to be the director of basic writing for the University Writing Program at the University of Utah, another experience similar to Victor's. I embraced this position because I created a syllabus that was grounded in critical readings that dealt with marginalized issues, and I hired critical, caring teachers. I remember that one of the assignments required students to talk about an incident when they were discriminated against. Their follow-up assignment was to present their papers. These so-called BASIC WRITERS created some of the best papers and presentations I had ever read and seen. And the beauty of this (or not, considering that it was a basic writing class) was that the majority of them were students of color.

It does not take a writing professor, or in fact much intelligence, to realize that the education system is flawed. Most college students are placed in their respective first-year composition class as a result of their SAT scores and/or the university writing placement tests.

These tests, in theory, assess students' ability to write by asking them to choose the thesis statement in a paragraph or to determine which sentence sounds better. In some cases, the assessment asks students to write an essay. Not surprisingly, these tests become vocabulary tests more than anything. For example, a student might be asked to write an essay on the following prompt: Describe a rhetorical situation that has put your peers and yourself in an awkward situation. Some students will not excel at this essay prompt. But as Villanueva has claimed in *Bootstraps* and as I am arguing here, simply because a student does not understand a question does not mean they cannot write a successful essay on that topic. The student might only need a bit of clarification, which could be provided by simply restructuring the question and/or changing the vocabulary.

EL PROFE

2005. Another life-changing moment. Between my wife and me, we had already received six offers, and all included a spousal hire, so we were set. At the last minute, before making our commitment to a completely different school, Texas State University (TSU) called saying they wanted to interview me. I agreed to the interview but told them it needed to be immediately because we already had other universities waiting on us. They agreed. Four days later they flew me in, and by the time I had gotten back to the Austin airport to fly back to Salt Lake City, I had received a job offer.

Although there were many reasons to accept the job at Texas State University, a main reason was that it was on its way to becoming a Hispanic Serving Institution (HSI). And although the University of Utah was cool, it made me realize that I needed to teach at a university that had a large Raza population. TSU was where I needed to be. Although it was not perfect, I knew that it was where I belonged.

> And with fall comes the students. There comes the fun of the performance, expression of the need to pass things on, the learning the students pass on to him, the hope for a better future for all. All he knows again is that the suffering is worth something few enjoy: the children and the students provide a life filled with meaning and possibility. (Villanueva 139)

Being a profe at TSU has allowed me to teach students to be critical. Regardless of the class, I teach the students about inequities. I teach them about the racist curriculum that often marginalizes students of color. For the most part, students are receptive to these topics. I attribute this to the fact that I teach them information and allow them to come to their own conclusions. Only on rare occasions (I hope) do I push a predisposed agenda.

Perhaps what I remember most about this transition into a professor is that people were now listening to me because I had three initials attached to my name . . . PhD. I thought that was strange, because I have been talking about similar issues all of my life and was always ignored, at best. In fact, I had often been looked at as an angry Mexican male who took things too seriously, especially when discussing racism. Now, things were different. Now people were listening to me, and I was being asked to present my work at national and international conferences and universities. But let me be clear—I was still facing racism on a daily basis.

Soon after giving presentations, I started to publish articles. All I was doing was writing about critical issues of race that were significant in the field of composition. Then I started publishing books. I remember when my first book came out—very cool. Then my second, third, etc. Again—nothing had changed—I am still the critical *mocoso* from Cali, just with a PhD.

Clearly, I am different from most professors, who are often brought up in upper-middle-class families and have lived with privilege most of their lives. I was raised on the wrong side of the tracks; I have been shot at, robbed, tracked, kicked out of school, and been called a loser most of my life. Although these messages were constant, I did not listen because I knew I was better than that. I knew that my educational experience was something the academy needed to hear. *Y aqui estoy* and don't plan on going nowhere.

Eighteen years later, six-plus books , thirty-plus articles, hundreds of presentations, things are different. By NO MEANS am I saying that I am a superhero or that I was able to accomplish all of this on my own. *Ni madre*—I had a lot of help. But it was "The Block" that gave me the confidence I needed to feel that I belonged in academics, that made me realize that my *cuento* counted. And for that reason, I say GRACIAS to "The Block" and am especially thankful for all the homies that fueled my *ganas* to succeed.

WORK CITED

Villanueva, Victor, Jr. *Bootstraps: From an American Academic of Color.* National Council of Teachers of English, 1993.

Chapter 14

Writing with Victor

Lauren Rosenberg

LIKE MANY OF US TRAINED IN rhetoric and composition graduate programs, I was brought up on Victor Villanueva's essays and textbook. Conversations about racial justice or educational equity rarely occurred without references to *Bootstraps,* or to his essays on colonialism in composition studies, racism in the writing center, or the value of memory for communities of color. As others have touched on in this collection, I knew to turn to Villanueva for the best described and most precise interpretation of Antonio Gramsci's theory of hegemony. For me, as a literacy researcher studying underrepresented populations of adult learners, Villanueva's lessons were woven into the fabric of my doctoral education and who I became as an academic. Yet it was years into my career before I got to know him off the page.

In this chapter, I tell my story of writing with Victor. It started with some direct and not overly encouraging emails from him. Much later it included ways of knowing, unlearning, relating, and thinking about Gramsci and Gayatri Spivak and how literacy can be self-consciously and purposely counterhegemonic. My purpose is to share my story of Victor's extraordinary mentoring while we collaborated on a book as a way to illustrate how he has encouraged not only himself but also generations of scholar-writers to examine how hegemony can be confronted, often through ordinary acts such as changing one's literacy practices. It is also to show how a friendship developed through our scholarly work. I blend reflection and analysis, storytelling and critique, creative and theoretical lenses in the ways Victor showed me to do when we worked together as editor and author engaged in an extended conversation on the politics of literacy education.

I was well into my career teaching composition and creative writing, having achieved tenure with a few articles out, when my path crossed Victor's. Through a string of professional exchanges about my looming book project, I contacted Villanueva. He was incoming editor of the Studies in Writing & Rhetoric (SWR) series, not yet having begun the gig, and I had been advised that my research on how learners in a community of formerly nonliterate adults confronted power might be of interest to him. From a position of relative naiveté, I sent a query. Villanueva encouraged a proposal; I submitted a hasty one that didn't follow the conventions well because I didn't yet know the process, and it was rejected by the series editor at the time. But the reviewers took the work seriously, and their critical yet helpful feedback caused me to start viewing myself as someone who might one day make an important contribution. Victor will look at it again, I was told by a colleague on the Editorial Board. I didn't understand that my project was part of a conversation as a new editor came on board. I spent my posttenure sabbatical revising furiously, hopefully, and then some months later queried Villanueva (now editor) again, asking whether he remembered the project and me. "Yeah, I remember [you]," he wrote back. A while after I had sent him the manuscript, I got a reply of "sorry to disappoint you yet again," though this time it came with an invitation to meet to talk through one chapter that he seemed to think "carries the day" ("Re: SWR submission").

We met at the Riviera in Las Vegas where the Conference on College Composition and Communication (CCCC) was held that year and sat outside by the pool. It was morning before the conference day got started. I was glad that I didn't see anyone I knew because I thought whoever would see me with Villanueva would assume I had something I didn't have. We didn't talk about my chapter, which I had dutifully printed out and carried with me. "Put it away," he waved his hand, and then we just talked. I remember thinking: I don't know where this conversation is going. I didn't have a sense of Victor yet, didn't know that I soon would, and that our conversations would become some of the most valuable I have ever had. At that first meeting, I knew nothing of him.

The conversation was about my manuscript and me, but it was also about the state of the field. He told me my writing was "stiff," "constipated," words that shocked me because no one had ever called my writing tight or dry. I had been a fiction writer before I got a PhD in comp rhet, and I still considered myself a short story writer first. The problem, Victor said, is that you're trying to do this empirical social science thing that you think you're supposed to do. The greater trouble is with the field's insistence on a certain style of academic research. Later, I understood that he was generalizing about the profession because he was articulating a vision for the SWR series that differentiated it from its focus under a previous editor. He was also criticizing the presentation of academic discourse as it was taught in graduate school, a form he believed led to smart but uninteresting writing (he told me I was bad at it). His advice: "Just simply write." Let everything go. Get off the social science model and write it like a novel. Break off the stiff mold. Trying to do academic research, Victor said, has turned your writing into a "fucking raisin!"

I felt as if my head had spun all the way around like a cartoon character having a moment of realization. What could I do in response besides join Victor in laughing? We sat at the poolside table and laughed together. And then he said, "Okay, let's do this." But I felt like he'd said: "Rosenberg, let's jump off a building." It would take a long time for me to put this scene into perspective; over the course of our conversations, I began to understand that this was exactly the kind of risk taking that marked Victor's intervention in the field. As Ana Mileno Ribero and Aja Y. Martinez state exuberantly in the next chapter, "Victor, you have set a precedent for us to break precedent!" (p. 316). He was committed to making the profession more equitable by disrupting the conventions. He would occasionally remark, I don't have a problem with challenging conventions if it makes good sense. I'm paraphrasing here, but my point is that Victor decided to take a risk with me because he recognized a certain potential to change the kind of writing that was accepted into the SWR book series. He wanted to shift the field by bringing more attention to storytelling as a vehicle for individual and social change. Narrative could be foregrounded as a critical methodology rather than as an anecdotal lead-in to more traditional analysis.

What Victor liked about my manuscript were the stories of four people who were becoming more literate in older adulthood after being marked as "illiterates" most of their lives. "I want folks to meet your folks," he told me soon after we met. He liked the idea of recently nonliterate older adults being the organic intellectuals that Gramsci theorized. He liked that I interpreted their desire to become more literate as intrinsic rather than ideological. And he liked that I understood some of their literate activity as pushing back on the assumptions people (including academics) make about motivations for literacy.

This chapter is not only about my story. Or about Victor's vision for a book series. Or about a field he viewed as constrained by its competing impulses to define and distinguish itself among the disciplines and within English by aligning with the social sciences at the same time that it is housed within the humanities. It is also about the ways that story and memory are personal and political for Victor in his own scholarship, and how they can be revisited, reclaimed, harnessed for social change, and directed toward disrupting oppressive systems. Story gives us a way of remaking meaning; it helps us to live with and through experiences and to craft those experiences into artifacts. Victor writes in "*Memoria* Is a Friend of Ours," "While a good academic piece would help me to remember, rich narrative does more for the memory" (16). Story, the shaping of story, guides our work; it will guide my work ahead in our collaboration. Victor reflects on his own "need to reclaim a memory, memory of an identity in formation and constant reformation, the need to reclaim a memory of an identity as formed through the generations" (12).

Some time after we begin our work together as editor and author, Victor will tell me that "*Memoria*" is his favorite piece of his own writing, and that's when I will begin to understand the extent of his commitment to story as both a means of preserving memories ("And I don't want the past forgotten" (11)) and of theorizing. This is why he insists on changing academic discourse; this is why it has to break "off the stiff mold" so that story can be handled as a vehicle for corrective retelling and knowing differently. He writes:

> Memory simply cannot be adequately portrayed in the conventional discourse of the academy.
>
> I am grateful for the acknowledgment of perceptions that academic discourse provides, for the resources the conventions of citation make available, for the ideocentric discourse that displays inductive or deductive lines of reasoning, a way to trace a writer's logical connections.
>
> Academic discourse is cognitively powerful!
>
> But the cognitive alone is insufficient. It can be strong for *logos*. It can be strong for *ethos*. But it is very weak in *pathos*. Academic discourse tries, after all, to reach the Aristotelian ideal of being completely logocentric, though it cannot be freed of the ethical appeal to authority. (12)

I shared the story of our meeting that night over oysters and cocktails with my grad school buddies. What they wanted to read, they said, was a piece about the process and experience of working with Victor. You can call it "Writing with Victor," they joked. The next day I flew home and started rewriting my book again while also keeping account of the mentoring relationship with an editor that would develop alongside my scholarly writing over the next two years, essentially a quilt of Victor's advice:

> *Do the book as a quilt. Try it. Make a patch. See what it looks like, and then send it. I'll work on it with you. It'll just be you and me working on this, sending it back and forth. We'll see what it looks like. In that way, we'll put together a manuscript. Do the cutting, and then the theory will weave its way back in. Make the patches, and we'll stitch them together.*

This began my process of unlearning a certain kind of academic discourse, guided by Victor.

I started with Lee Ann, one of the participants in my research whose experiences with literacy education became part of the core of the book. Pieces of her story that I hadn't thought about in years resurfaced. My memories of her and bits of transcripts that had never seemed to matter became important again because I was writing about a whole person through the lens of her literacy experiences. The narratives coursed through me, stirring up the material again (the material I'd already been writing about for years) as the accounts of *people's lives* rather than as *data*. I'd write a patch and then send it to Victor.

Then there was so much waiting, and, at long last, his response:

> *Aw, heck, Lauren, you just needed permission to write!* . . .
>
> *I don't know if you've ever read my stuff, especially* Bootstraps *(even though I only became willing to call myself a writer ten years later, with an article titled* "Memoria *is a Friend of Ours" that appeared in* College English*). I mention them because narrative can get really boring after a bit, but I developed an ear for when it's time to break out of narrative. That's what you need, I think.*
>
> *Lee Ann—I was left asking how she swapped real estate, given all of the paperwork that's involved.*
>
> *But there were two places where I thought a break to another genre might have been good: right before "Everybody has a story" and directly after this wonderfully powerful line—"passed on the responsibility of representation"! Damn, that's powerful. That's why you couldn't do this in that stiff academic discourse; you were not being true to that responsibility.*
>
> *victor.* ("Re: Patch")

I study the genre and voice shifts in *Bootstraps*. Then I decide to break up Lee Ann's narrative with a theoretical section on the responsibility of representation by yielding to her insistence that her experiences be told a certain way. Lee Ann's story is not unmediated. She chooses to tell it to me, a white woman from higher ed, because she wants her story to be heard, and she wants it to be retold. She wants me to be a certain kind of representative, to get her story out there to other people like me. In this way, Lee Ann speaks back to power. This is her counterstory, her intervention into narratives that have oppressed her (see Ribero and Martinez in this collection).

I am writing to Victor, my first audience. He is listening. I write the patch on Chief, another participant. Chief's patch takes a shape that surprises me because I get to know him differently, eight years after doing the initial research. Then there is a patch about the teachers at the literacy center that comes as a complete surprise. Again, more sections of interviews that I have forgotten about and that appear to me as brand-new texts. Through this process of writing, reflecting, shifting voice, writing to Victor, reflecting on the words of participants, I learn a new way of listening, a new way of constructing meaning. It is not only Victor's influence that shapes my process, obviously. I also become aware of my confidence building as I write the book I want to write the way I want to write it. As I work through it, I am continuously thinking about the participants' words and what they have told me matters to them most. I think about—and Victor and I discuss—my responsibility to treat the case study participants with dignity. He tells me I am doing a good job of writing through racial differences by upholding my commitment to give participants space to tell their own stories without intervening, and then by interpreting their actions with what he calls an "ethos of compassion."

We talk over Skype. You've got "the threading to do," he tells me. Do the threading; make the quilt. Figure out how the patches fit in. The patches, Victor says, "are discourses from the heart." When you put the patches together into chapters, you will find a third kind of writing, a kind of "friendly academic writing." His encouragement is lovely, but I am apprehensive. Victor is mentoring me to write an experimental book through a process he continually compares to his own experience writing *Bootstraps.* Often, he would tell me his story about how the Editorial Board didn't want his monograph because it was rooted in stories, with much of the critique conveyed through the narrative and shifts in genre. He would tell me about his rejections and about how Michael Spooner, the editor, and Keith Gilyard, who reviewed his work, were his champions, and then he would tie all of this back to the goals of his editorship and what he wanted to do for me as an author.

One of the difficulties I face is figuring out a structure. I share some of my uncertainty with Victor, but he makes it clear that I am on my own with this struggle. When I get stuck writing, I draw some ideas for how to organize the book—literally (Figure 14.1). Send me the sketches, he tells me, and I say I will, but I am nervous that he will laugh at me.

"I laughed!" he admits after he reviews my collection of drawings. But then he tells me he likes the "stars," and I develop the eventual structure based on this model.

For the first time since I began my academic career eight years earlier, I am aware of my creative and academic sensibilities joining rather than competing for validation. Until now, I have been keeping the different disciplines of writing separate. In graduate school, I was trained (with good reason) to write academically, and as part of that process, the creative writer was trained out. I was told to stop telling so many stories, to stay with the analysis. I have been a fiction writer, then an academic writer, and now I find another writer emerging. I let go of my training so I can do something else. Victor helps me to recognize that beneath the surface of the academic writing is a storyteller who knows how to pivot into theory and back. I'm finding out how to incorporate everything I know from different contexts to write in a new way.

Reflecting on his own need to work through experience by layering stories, Victor writes in "*Memoria*,"

> I'm trying to figure this out, somehow: who I am, from where, playing out the mixes within. It isn't a question for me, whether public or private discourses. I am contradictory consciousness. The discourse should reflect that. I am these uneasy mixes of races that make for no race at all yet find themselves victim to racism. The discourse should reflect that. I am an American (in every sense—a boy from Brooklyn, jazz

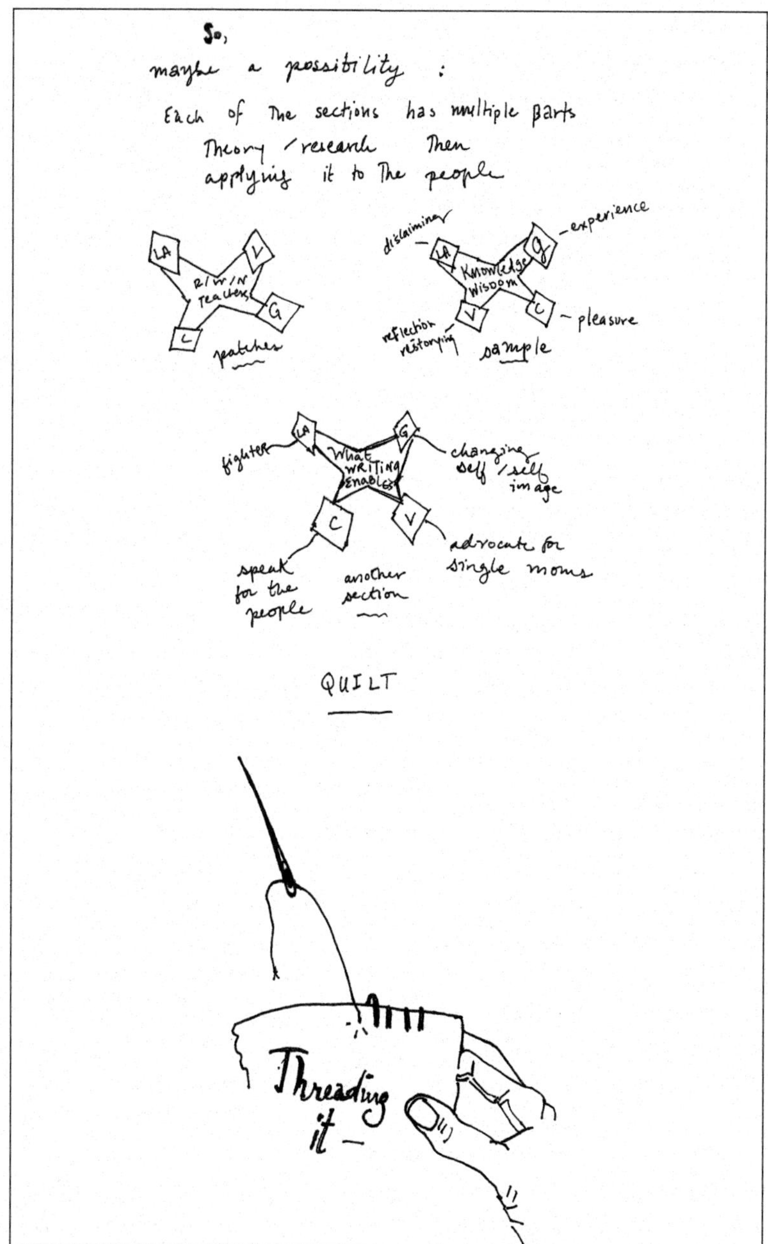

Figure 14.1. A couple of the sketches I shared with Victor as we worked together on a structure for my manuscript.

> and rock 'n' roll, and from the Americas, with an ancestry dating back before the Europeans), an academic, a person of color—an organically grown traditional intellectual, containing both of Gramsci's intellectual formations, yet not quite his new intellectual. The discourse should reflect that as well. And I am in a wheatfield, attempting to pass on a memory as I attempt to gather one. Personal discourse, the narrative, the auto/biography, helps in that effort, is a necessary adjunct to the academic. (17)

His representation of his own identity shows what our stories can make possible. The layers and shifts of genre, the arrangement of one narrative against others, allow us to look at discourses relationally. Victor's best example is himself as he displays the discourses he embodies and that demonstrate his contradictory consciousness. In much of his writing, he describes himself as living with contradictions (of ideology, class, race, politics, education, formations of the intellectual) and working within the muck where collision is uncomfortable, and yet important always. Change is initiated through the contradictions we recognize and confront. "The discourse should reflect that." The shifts of voice, of perspective, show ways of knowing in relation, in reflection. "The discourse should reflect that as well." Academic discourse, as he has written it throughout his career, serves more purposes than simply to advance work. It can be pushed beyond its bounds to combine with other discourses and offset them. In the offsetting, the limitations of the discourse become exposed. Academic discourse can be construed differently to help read experience more deeply, to probe contradictory consciousness. He does it through autobiography. Victor references Gramsci writing about autobiography: "Autobiography can be conceived 'politically.' . . . By narrating it, one creates this possibility, suggests the process, indicates the opening. Autobiography therefore replaces the 'political' or 'philosophical essay': it describes in action what otherwise is deduced logically" (Gramsci qtd. in "Hegemony" 33).

Story matters deeply. For Victor, in *Bootstraps* and in his many essays, there is some autobiography, a story of his experience to warm the theory, to humanize the argument, to remind readers that through rhetoric we make sense of our lives. It is through autobiography, he writes, that we make "the lived live" (Brandt et al. 52). Embedded in autobiography, Victor reveals some of the personal contradictions that have driven his own academic inquiries and kept him in the game, even in moments when he wanted to get out. But they are never easy narratives. Often they illustrate a moment of struggle or unease, sometimes embarrassment, occasionally triumph. In reflecting on the personal, Victor observes in "The Politics of the Personal": "There must be room for elements of autobiography, not as confession and errant self-indulgence, not as the measure on which to assess theory, not as a replacement for rigor, but as a way of knowing our predispositions to see things certain ways, of understanding what it is that guides our intuitions in certain ways. This is the autobiographical as critique" (Brandt et al. 51).

My book is not an autobiography. It is me, a researcher and author, mediating the stories of four people who have their own narratives to tell their own way, so there are different issues with representation for me than there are for Victor. I have to be extremely careful. The way I decide to discuss participants is in terms of the representation they have chosen to offer about themselves. It's tricky. I'm making the argument that the theory resides in the narrative and that the four adult learners discussed in the book become literacy theorists themselves when they restory their narratives. Pulling off the book is a matter of showing readers that they will have to read differently, of convincing them that it is important to read the narratives to get the analysis. I am trying to do something complicated that Victor did in *Bootstraps* and Keith Gilyard did in *Voices of the Self*, something other scholars have also achieved through autobiography, which is to weave together theory and narrative and to convince readers to pay attention to the process.

I am also working across race and class from my subject position as a white, middle-class academic writing about the writing lives of recently nonliterate people who are mostly poor or working class;

three of the four case study participants are people of color. I was constantly aware of my stated objective of retelling the stories of marginalized "others" without appropriation. Even now it is hard to explain the lack of anxiety I felt over this complex navigation. I trusted Victor so much that I knew he would inform me directly if I slipped, or worse, if my privilege made me condescending. We spoke openly, and I knew he was watching my whiteness, but he only called me out once, and that was over the word *people*, which he said might make some readers sensitive. Choosing instead *participants* or *participant authors* took care of the problem.

What I did in my book by sitting alongside the narratives of ordinary adults who were becoming literate and understanding them as experts on their own literacy was to explore Gramsci's question, "What are the 'maximum' limits of acceptance of the term 'intellectual'?" (9). Could nonliterate adults occupy the role of organic intellectuals? This was the larger question that their stories drew out. As Victor tells us in "Hegemony":

> The principal agent in countering the current hegemony . . . is the intellectual—a "permanent persuader," in Gramsci's words (*Notebooks* 10). The intellectual actively seeking substantive social change is a rhetor. But she is not necessarily an academic or someone employed to perform mental labor; "intellectual" has a broader meaning for Gramsci. Everyone is potentially an intellectual. (24)

The question resonates. The multiple roles of Gramsci's intellectual are something Victor wrestles with when reflecting on himself in his early work, though his self-interrogation never truly ceases. Investigating his own position as an American minority functioning in a traditional academic environment remains a preoccupation throughout his career. It is a means of rubbing against, and dislodging, some of the implicit biases of the profession, its hidden restrictions, and always, its contradictions. Even as he views himself as "Gramsci's exception" ("*Memoria*" 15), Victor also recognizes that he is a traditional intellectual born from the peasant classes who embraces the "function of intellectual" while retaining the sensibility, his prior knowledge and the sharpness of critique, of his home communities. Although, as he writes more recently in "'I Am Two Parts,'" "I am not truly *organic*, you see; I've never wanted to go back to the neighborhoods where I grew up" (483). In explaining Gramsci, Victor also characterizes himself:

> Among those who do intellectual work, there are traditional intellectuals and organic intellectuals. At times Gramsci suggests that organic intellectuals are only those who remain intimately tied to the organizations which are part of their class or group, like a Cesar Chavez. At other times, Gramsci describes organic intellectuals as those whose work remains tied to the classes from which they originated, even if they work outside their original communities. That is, organic intellectuals might function within more traditional intellectual organizations, like the university, yet remain organic if the functions they undertake have them conceptualizing and articulating the social, economic, and political interests of the group or class from which they came. Organic intellectuals are involved in a dialectical and rhetorical enterprise: reliance on personal experiences and the experiences of the groups from which they came in order to attract other groups, including traditional intellectuals, to their cause. When the organic intellectual is involved in this enterprise she becomes Gramsci's "new intellectual." She becomes a "permanent persuader," involved "in active participation in practical life, as constructor, organiser" (*Notebooks* 10). She acts as a liaison between the groups seeking revolutionary change and the rest of civil society. ("Hegemony" 24)

In this description of Gramsci, Victor seems to locate himself; yet he continues to slide between the different roles of intellectual, as he still confronts them: "Traditional or organic, traditional and organic, neither one fully. Can't know. Let it go" ("'I Am'" 486). It is from these relative locations that Victor guides me and others like me in navigating our field with an eye toward possibilities for counterhegemony that emerge all around us in actions, in words, in particular slips. He develops that perspective at length in terms of his own experiences in *Bootstraps*. Victor's unique insight into the roles that are potentially available and that can sometimes be embraced—by himself, by other scholars from nontraditional experiences, by ordinary people, including critically astute nonliterate adults—*this* is one of his major scholarly contributions. He helps me to name it in regard to the adult learners who participate in my research and writing, whom I have come to know as literacy theorists through their spoken and written critique.

Even though it is clear to me that the four people I am writing about are intellectuals when they conceptualize literacy through their written and spoken narratives, the manuscript reviewers are not convinced. "You need more of a driving theory," Victor tells me when we go over the reviews. It's time to bring the academic back in. Really good theory, he says, should say "of course." Theory is not this abstract, generalizable thing. But it is, in my view, about people challenging ideas, disrupting them, finding a kernel of something else, something that suggests a different way of looking at things. I struggle with it. The reviewers have complained that the theory is too derivative. One of them says the problem is that the book is too much about the author's story. So? Victor says, why not make it the author's story? *What started out as a research study ended up as an engaged conversation with four people.* Take the insult and flip it. Emphasize the author's voice telling the stories. *I am not apart from, but a part of the stories. It is my story of their stories.*

Here, eventually, is the result:

> What started out as four case studies changed. Initially, I collected the participants' narratives as data, I coded for themes that emerged in their writing, and I reshaped my interpretation based on what they had to say. But the material took on other meanings as I used it for presentations and articles. In each new form, with every rhetorical purpose, the analysis changed. The value of the four people's texts changed. I changed. I continued visiting the center and talking with learners about their writing. What started out as a research study ended up as an engaged conversation with these four

> participants. Even now, when I revisit their transcripts and our discussions of their writing, I can ask myself: What's there that I haven't noticed before? How do I restory the participants' accounts as I continue to shape the narrative of my relationship to them and my own story as researcher, theorist, and teacher? I am not apart *from* but a part *of* the stories. This book is my story of their stories. (Rosenberg, *Desire*, 20–21)

Our conversation that summer as I revised (yet again) turned to Franz Fanon and Spivak, especially Spivak, to how the adults acquiring new literacies in my study were like—no, were—the subalterns seeking a voice in her essay. It began with Victor's critique of a chapter draft, my thirty-five-page revision that he returned with sixteen pages of comments ("I like where this is going, but I think there are ways to thicken the theory, and there are places where there are contradictions, so I'll point all that out" ("Sorry")). And, as always, the encouragement: "So—work on this chapter. Email me every time—every time—something comes up that you don't understand, don't agree with, just want to discuss." ("Re: first chapter"). We spent that July writing back and forth about Spivak.

> Victor,
> You were right: Spivak's essay is just what I need for this revision. I've got a question about something she says that I want to respond to, but I want to be sure I've got it right, especially the complicated first part. The quote is this:
>
> > For the "true" subaltern group, whose identity is its difference, there is no unrepresentable subaltern subject that can know and speak itself; the intellectual's solution is not to abstain from representation. The problem is that the subject's itinerary has not been traced so as to offer an object of seduction to the representing intellectual (285).
>
> It's the "no unrepresentable subaltern subject" that's tripping me up. I *think* that this is about whether the subaltern has the agency to critique her position that has little agency. Since she has been rendered without voice, knowing how/when to

> speak for herself (and with what language) is so challenging. Spivak is not very hopeful about the possibility of speaking. I am pretty clear about what I think about the people getting the space to speak—and also about my own conflicted roles as a first-culture person who both disables and enables that speaking, even in writing the book. But I want to know what you think of this, especially about the very tangled language of Spivak's phrase, all those negatives, which strike me as deliberate. ("a few things")
>
> *Hey, Lauren—*
> *"unrepresentable subaltern"—context: Spivak is in India; she's initially responding to a group of intellectuals called "the subaltern group," telling them to be careful about what they're doing, that they do have a responsibility to represent but that their representation must never be thought of as complete. Part of how she does that is by flipping it—the subaltern has limits herself (many of which are structural to the class system; the caste system is all but moot in India, though Americans seem not to know this). So—you're right in how you're reading this.*
>
> *This is going to transform your book. victor.* ("Re: a few things")

From a letter from me to Victor:

> I recall writing to you from my porch on a Saturday morning and discussing these topics with such intensity: how the notion of *ill*iteracy constructs certain subjects as diseased, my deep concern with retelling the four participants'—the *authors*—narratives without appropriation, and whether it was possible to do that. I worried about taking too much of your time on a Saturday morning, but you assured me that the conversation was not a bother. Afterwards I realized that this is what scholarship looks like, not a smoky scene in a café debating one's already held beliefs, but this exchange of emails on a Saturday morning in summer, this long-distance effort to work through something important and to understand it well enough to make it live in writing. "You've got this nailed," you wrote to me later, "Yes, do move on." (Letter)

I finished writing that fall, but it wasn't until the following February that I received an email from Victor with the subject line, "Time to Go to Production." And then we were done. There was suddenly a hole in my life (and certainly in my inbox) where his voice had been coming through frequently with advice, humor, guidance, story, very real criticism, even disagreement. Once he had written to tell me that one of my participants' (a Puerto Rican woman) poem about the arroz con dulce of her childhood brought back his memory of the recipe his father used to make. Her literacy had impacted his own, he said. All our rich thinking, talking, writing—would it now end? I was at a loss at the end of the editor–author collaboration.

It would have been a different book if I had worked on it with anyone else. Victor drew me out and supported me and kept pressing me to take risks—risks in writing, in genre, in style, in laying out a theoretical book but without a traditional academic structure—in a way that no one else could have done. He taught me to probe academic discourse conventions sharply when it was appropriate, and he showed me how to scrape away at the dominant practices of our field to shine light upon them so that they might be changed. This was what I had admired in Victor's essays before I knew him. I had wondered how he had the bravery to identify and thus to redefine conditions, particularly as they pertained to the positioning of people of color in academia. Through his truthful and generous nurturing of my writing, he taught me to find courage as a writer. I told a friend that Victor transformed me, and she said no, *transformed* is the wrong word. The right word is *released.*

My sense of loss dissipates fairly quickly. By the time the project is completed, we are friends. How could we not be after sharing ideas and writing back and forth for a couple of years? We do the things friends do: talk on the phone and on video, gossip, get together at conferences, develop our own jokes that crack us up. And though Victor is still (and will always be) a mentor, we call upon each other in more balanced ways. I get to write letters of support for him, and I help him work through an institutional challenge. He assists me with an administrative problem that runs out of control and helps with drafting letters to upper administrators and professionals outside the university. Victor coaches me through negotiating a number of contracts, and I learn skills from him that I continue to use to help my colleagues and students. People ask me how I became a good negotiator, and I tell them that I learned from Victor. He remains available and kind, keenly astute and direct, giving to me, and to so many others. No matter the situation, he responds by cutting through the surface to examine the core. He knows so much, and he is so good at figuring out motives and interests and what to expect.

Victor writes in "*Memoria*": "There is a common saying among Puerto Ricans and Cubans: *Te doy un cuento de mi historia*, literally rendered as 'I'll give you a story about my history': me, history and memory, and a story" (16). And so I write this chapter for Victor, because he loves story so much and because of what he sees stories doing to change not only himself, his students, his colleagues, but the profession and the world. *Te doy un cuento de mi historia,* I share my story with you.

WORKS CITED

Brandt, Deborah, et al. "The Politics of the Personal: Storying Our Lives against the Grain." *College English*. vol. 64, no. 1, Sep. 2001, pp. 41–62.

Gilyard, Keith. *Voices of the Self: A Study of Language Competence.* Wayne State UP, 1991.

Gramsci, Antonio. *Selections from the Prison Notebooks.* Edited and translated by Quintin Hoare and Geoffrey Nowell Smith. International, 1971.

Rosenberg, Lauren. *The Desire for Literacy: Writing in the Lives of Adult Learners.* Conference on College Composition and Communication/ National Council of Teachers of English, 2015.

———. "a few things that are coming up as I revise." Received by Victor Villanueva. 20 July 2014.

———. Letter to Victor Villanueva. 16 July 2015.

Spivak, Gayatri Chakravorty. "Can the Subaltern Speak?" *Marxism and the Interpretation of Culture,* edited by Cary Nelson and Lawrence Grossberg. U of Illinois P, 1988, pp. 271–313.

Villanueva, Victor, Jr. *Bootstraps: From an American Academic of Color.* National Council of Teachers of English, 1993.

———. "Hegemony: From an Organically Grown Intellectual." *Pre/Text,* vol. 13, no. 1-2, 1992, pp. 17–34.

———. "'I Am Two Parts': Collective Subjectivity and the Leader of Academics and the Othered." *College English,* vol. 79, no. 5, 2017, pp. 482–94.

———. "*Memoria* Is a Friend of Ours: On the Discourse of Color." *College English,* vol. 67, no. 1, Sep. 2004, pp. 9–19.

———. "Re: a few things that are coming up as I revise." Received by Lauren Rosenberg. 20 July 2014.

———. "Re: first chapter." Received by Lauren Rosenberg. 9 July 2014.

———. "Re: Patch–Lee Ann." Received by Lauren Rosenberg. 27 Apr. 2013.

———. "Re: SWR submission–community literacy study." Received by Lauren Rosenberg. 17 Feb. 2013.

———. "Sorry." Received by Lauren Rosenberg. 8 July 2014.

Chapter 15

Villanueva and We: Breaking Precedents of the Rhetoric of Racism

Ana Milena Ribero and Aja Y. Martinez

IN HIS LANDMARK ESSAY "On the Rhetoric and Precedents of Racism," rhetoric and writing studies exemplar Victor Villanueva quite literally sets several scenes for his audience, transporting us from fifteenth-century Peru (645), to a meeting among graduate students and faculty at a modern-day university (652–53), to the solitude of receiving an insulting rejection from an essay manuscript reviewer (655). Interestingly, counterstory, the Derrick Bell–informed method of fantasy/allegory (Martinez, *Counterstory* 53–79), provides us the tools by which to do the work of historiographic time travel, not dissimilar from the journey we experience through Villanueva's words. Through counterstory as fantasy/allegory, we can transport ourselves and our audiences to otherworldly contexts and dramatized scenarios. As Bell states, his use of allegory and fantasy concerning race—and the methodological use of fiction in general—enables him and his audience to separate themselves from the real and perhaps "see things in terms that are less threatening and confrontational" (*Faces* xxvi). Bell continues, "When the audience reenters reality, messages are left behind that provide a new perspective or set of lenses. It lets them see more clearly what I think I see all the time" (qtd. in Goldberg 57). Specific to rhetoric and writing studies—a field and discipline virtually obsessed with rhetoric's pedagogical effectiveness and applicability—Catherine Prendergast has suggested that Bell's counterstories contribute a "new rhetoric" in the struggle for racial justice (46). Likewise, Adam Banks lauds the value of Bell's "new rhetoric" and attributes his strategic "literacy practices" with creating at least the possibility of a genuine rhetorical situation that demands response and forces dialogue (93).

As a demonstration of this method, our contribution to this edited collection is inspired by and modeled after Bell's first chapter in his book *And We Are Not Saved.* This allegory involves aspects of time travel, in which Bell's much-chronicled heroine-protagonist, Geneva Crenshaw, travels back in time to the Constitutional Convention of 1787. Banks has commented on the scholarship and data for this method of counterstory, and says, "The delegates respond to her arguments as Bell imagines they would, but he does not leave their responses to whims. He bases them instead on the actual words of some of the delegates to the real convention in 1787, and his historical analysis of the general arguments made at the time" (97). Likewise, our own counterstory as allegory/fantasy sends us (Ana Milena Ribero and Aja Martinez) back in time to a fictionalized late-1990s context and places us in conversation with Victor Villanueva on the precipice of his crafting "On the Rhetoric and Precedents of Racism." As we invoke this counterstory method, we transport our audience back in time to a coffee shop in the late 1990s in which we as authors encounter Villanueva mulling over ideas that will serve as his precedent-breaking response to a "Rejecter" (655) of his concepts. We have crafted characters to voice our perspectives in conversation with Villanueva, whose words and concepts represented as dialogue within this essay are directly extracted, quoted, paraphrased, or cited from his words within "On the Rhetoric."

Our aim is to employ the sort of creative, critical, and theoretical storytelling that gestures to Villanueva's distinctive writing style (see Rosenberg's essay in this collection). Readers will notice that the tone of our counterstory is playful, even as we delve into serious discussion about theory, racism, and even death. The tone reflects our intent to help the reader time-travel with us. By making the dialogue sound friendly and conversational, we not only do right by the method of counterstory, but we also invite the reader to join our dialogue, hear our voices, see our gestures, and perhaps imagine themselves taking a seat at the table.

As Martinez has discussed, this particular method of counterstory is pedagogical in intent and is very much written in a way that can facilitate classroom discussion for teachers who encourage their students to engage a text in ways that account for the sociopolitical context of the author (*Counterstory* 57). Through the course of our engagement with Villanueva, we discuss the contemporary state of rhetoric and writing studies, with a few references to our own bodies of scholarship as they have been inspired and influenced by Villanueva's essay. As with Bell's work, Villanueva's contributions to this fictionalized exchange are inspired by his actual words and actions left to us through this published and widely taught and cited essay. Although we undoubtedly associate Villanueva's name with his quoted words, we do so with the understanding that Villanueva as a real person is not static in the beliefs he espoused in this twenty-plus-year-old text. In all, our demonstration of counterstory as allegory/fantasy weaves together citations of Villanueva's historic essay with our own contemporary scholarship and viewpoints, historical cultural references, and characters that represent existing political, social, and racial ideologies.

PART I.

Setting. Spring 2022. Ana Milena Ribero, assistant professor of rhetoric and writing at Oregon State University, and Aja Y. Martinez, assistant professor of English at University of North Texas, are in the Chicago hotel room they are sharing while attending the Conference on College Composition and Communication Annual Convention. While preparing for sleep, they are discussing a topic brought up at a dinner meeting they've just attended.

ANA: I'm definitely going to propose something for that panel about Victor's work.

AJA: Yeah, me too.

ANA: Asao, Siskanna, and Wendy mentioned that each presenter would respond to one of Victor's texts. What text do you think you'll respond to?

AJA [with a thoughtful finger to her lips]: Hm, I don't know. There are so many that I could discuss. One of my favorite texts of his is "*Memoria* Is a Friend of Ours." I really connect with his argument about the role of memory in writing.

ANA: That's one of my favorites too. I also like "On the Rhetoric and Precedents of Racism." I often think about how little things have changed in academia since he published that piece two decades ago.

AJA: Yes! "On the Rhetoric" has been hugely influential for me.

ANA: Maybe we should write something together?

AJA: Responding to "On the Rhetoric"?

ANA: Yes?

AJA: I'd love to. Let's talk more tomorrow over breakfast. It is way past my bedtime.

ANA [laughs]: Mine too. Sleep well, amiga.

PART II.

Setting. Spring 1998. Victor Villanueva, associate professor of English at Washington State University, is seated at a table in a Pullman, Washington, coffee shop. Head down, reviewing an array of both typed and handwritten notes strewn across the table, he is shaking his head, brow furrowed in consternation. Startled to find themselves in the doorway of this coffee shop, twenty-plus years in the past and halfway across the country, Ana notices Victor right away.

ANA [in an audible whisper to Aja]: Is that who I think it is?

AJA [looking around]: Where are we?

ANA [now pointing]: Aja, *look* over there, at the table in the far right corner.

AJA [gasping]: Oh my gosh, it's Victor! But he looks—

ANA [nodding her head and already walking in Victor's direction]: Yes, younger. Let's go say hi.

AJA [hurrying to keep up]: Okay, but Ana, *where* are we?

ANA [over her shoulder, smiling]: I think the question should be "*when* are we"? [Both women arrive in front of Victor]

ANA: Hola, Victor, ¿cómo estás?

VICTOR [distractedly looking up from his spread of papers]: Huh? Well, hello—uh—[clearly searching for a name to this unfamiliar face]

ANA: My name is Ana—Ana Milena Ribero.

VICTOR [nodding and looking over at Aja]: And?

AJA: Oh, yes, my name is Aja Martinez.

VICTOR: Nice to meet you both, have we met somewhere before? [Ana and Aja exchange a look]

ANA: Well, not exactly *before*—

AJA: Yes, more like *later*—in the future it would seem—

VICTOR [a twinkle appearing in his eyes as he decides to play along]: Oh, I see. And how far in the future are we talking about, any flying cars yet?

AJA: Well, I guess that depends on what year it is now—

VICTOR: 1998, of course.

[Again, Ana and Aja exchange a look]

ANA: Victor, this sounds totally crazy. But we are future students of your writing. You've taught us a lot through your published words. I can see you're working on some writing right now, yes?

VICTOR [with a smile]: Ah! Is that right? Take a seat, would you? Join me. [Ana and Aja sit down in the two available chairs]

VICTOR [continuing, with a slight smile]: So, the two of you are making claims to time travel, eh?

AJA: Well, let us explain. There's a method for this sort of travel called "counterstory," and it enables all sorts of things—in particular, the ability to travel as writers to engage other writers within the context in which they crafted landmark texts.

VICTOR [shaking his head in bemused disbelief, then pointing to the spread-out papers on the table]: Such as this mess of texts?

ANA: Well, since you mention the year is 1998, is it safe to assume what you're working out there concerns the rhetoric and precedents of racism?

VICTOR [with a snicker]: ¿Qué es esa brujería? How could you—how do you know that?

AJA: We mean it when we say we're students of your words, and these words you're working out right now become a landmark essay that the magic of counterstory has permitted us the ability to engage, right here, right now, with you, even though we come to you from twenty-plus years in the future.

VICTOR [shaking his head with a congenial laugh]: Okay, mujeres, now I've seen everything. Well, then I'm in! Let's do this counterstory method, engage my words in my context; where should we begin?

ANA: I think it would be helpful if we start by telling you a bit about why we're here, at this moment on the precipice of this text with you—

[Victor nods and gestures for Ana to go on]

ANA: You have been a mentor to many Latinx scholars in the last twenty-plus years—or the future twenty-plus years beyond today [laughs]. And your writing has helped to bring issues of race, racism, and rhetoric to future generations of scholars. I often assign graduate students to read the work you're producing here today in their Introduction to Graduate Studies course so that the moment they are introduced to English studies in general is also the moment in which they are thinking about and critiquing racism in the academy.

VICTOR: ¿Ah si? And what do they think?

ANA: Well, I teach at a predominantly white institution (PWI), and many students are coming to us right after finishing their bachelor's. So thinking about racism and its relationship to rhetoric is new territory for most of them. They are particularly drawn to the opening section of the text: the part in which you provide examples of

Indigenous rhetorics of what is now Latin America during the colonial encounter.

VICTOR: [glancing down to a section of the spread of papers and nodding, acknowledging]: Yes, I've always wanted to do an edited collection about rhetorics of the Americas before colonization.

ANA [continuing]: In the text, you parallel Indigenous rhetorics with classical rhetoric, which students are more familiar with. Through your example, my students see the violence perpetuated by injustice at the lack of recognition of the Aztec's and Inca's rhetorical prowess and then connect it to the lack of recognition of Latin American and Latinx rhetorical and intellectual abilities currently. One of the most cutting lines of the text is when you write [Victor silently mouths the quoted words as Ana recites them], "Now, imagine the phrase 'there is a Mexican philosopher' and compare it to 'there is a French philosopher.' Which carries the greater weight?" ("On the Rhetoric" 658)

VICTOR [nods with a smile]

ANA: I think students—and all readers—answer that question in their heads and confront their biases against nonwhite thinkers, knowledges, and epistemologies.

VICTOR: Exactly. That's why I argue that we don't ignore the concepts, theories, and practices that come from colonized and formerly colonized peoples.

[Both Ana and Aja nod, vigorously]

VICTOR: The field's obsession with enlightenment rhetorics ignores the legacy of racism that some of the most quoted thinkers, like for example Hegel and Kant, bring with them (656).

AJA [jumping in]: Oh, yes! A favorite quote of mine comes from a Cornel West essay, where he takes to task these hallowed Euro-Western Enlightenment figures: [Aja recites the quote with dramatic flair] "The idea of white supremacy is a major bowel unleashed by the structure of modern discourse, a significant secretion generated from the creative fusion of scientific investigation, Cartesian philosophy, and classical aesthetic and cultural norms. Needless to say, the odor of this bowel and the fumes of this secretion continue to pollute the air of our post-modern times" (West 109).

[All burst out laughing as Victor waves his hand in front of his nose as if something stinks]

VICTOR [still chuckling]: And there it is! We, especially those of us doing work on race and racism, must break from the colonial mindset and learn from the thinkers from our own hemisphere—not that we should ignore Europe completely ("On the Rhetoric" 659).

AJA [clutching fake pearls]: Naturally not!

VICTOR [chuckling again at Aja's sarcasm]: The problem of racism is also Europe's problem. But continuing to use these European thinkers as touchstones, without also problematizing how they forwarded racist ideas, is tying the discipline's core to prejudice (659).

[Ana and Aja again nod vigorously]

VICTOR: This not only hurts our discipline, our ability of thinking through bigotries of all sorts, but it also hurts people of color who are in or trying to enter our discipline. We must break from the colonial discourses that bind us (656).

ANA [riffles through the book that has suddenly appeared in her hands, Sara Ahmed's *Living a Feminist Life*]: You are making me think of what Sara Ahmed states about the value of a feminist politics of citation. She argues that "citations can be feminist bricks: they are the materials through which, from which, we create our dwellings" (16). The people we cite affect the kinds of houses we build—the kinds of arguments we make. If we want to relate to academia differently, if we want to build a different sort of academy, we need to build our house from bricks without a white supremacist underpinning.

AJA: Yes! And it's about more than simply *seeking* silenced or appropriated voices. Although some have historically characterized people of color as "'in the margins,'" we know that we've never been marginal—Victor, you taught me that! We've been here all along and have always practiced our rhetorics (Baca and Villanueva; García and Baca). And as answer to Ana's Ahmed metaphor, there is a growing number of projects in rhetoric and writing studies in our time that do the work of unearthing buried minoritized rhetorics, and these are vital and necessary projects (Ramírez and Zeneca; Enoch and Ramírez; Agnew et al. 115–16). These projects undoubtedly bring to voice primary texts as artifacts for rhetorical analysis that would otherwise go uncharted on rhetoric's map (Glenn; Enos et al. 28–30), and I know I'm grateful to the scholars pursuing such important work.

VICTOR [nods approvingly]

ANA: Exactly, Aja! And continuing with what Ahmed says, we need to instead look to "work that lays out other paths, paths we can call desire lines, created by not following the official paths laid out by disciplines. These paths might have become fainter from not being traveled upon; so we might work harder to find them; we might be willful just to keep them going by not going the way we have been directed" ("On the Rhetoric" 15). I like what she says because she recognizes the difficulty of going against the grain in academia. I have a very distinct memory of a professor in grad school telling me that I had to include classical rhetoricians in my comprehensive exam because they represented the history of our field. Now, as I finish my monograph, I don't have a single classical rhetoric citation in it. Not that I don't recognize the merit in those histories of thought. But the kind of rhetorical studies that *I* want to build is not one that could ever be built without the bricks of thinkers and doers in our own hemisphere—particularly of BIPOC women.

VICTOR: BIPOC, ¿Qué significa eso?

ANA and Aja: Black, Indigenous, People of Color.

VICTOR: Ah. A racialized rhetoric and identity term from your time?

AJA: Exactly. And similar to Ana, my own work seeks to centralize minoritized voices through the presentation of counterstories. I am concerned with providing theory, methodology, and methods by which to do this work. If anything, critical race theory (CRT) and its methodology of counterstory illuminate and contribute to the histories and genealogies of people of color who have been practicing rhetoric for centuries.

VICTOR: You mean critical race theory—the work of legal scholars like Derrick Bell and Richard Delgado? Those folks?

AJA: Yes, them and others such as Patricia Williams and Kimberlé Crenshaw, but also some of the folks in education like Gloria Ladson-Billings, Daniel Solórzano, Adrienne Dixson, and Dolores Delgado Bernal. What these folks have collectively offered is a rubric of sorts based on tenets that inform this theory.

VICTOR: Ah, yes, Crenshaw—she wrote that essay on intersectionality?

AJA: Yes, which is a tenet of CRT.

VICTOR: ¡Eso es! I have been thinking about oppression at the intersections. Women of color, for example, carry a double yoke, being women and being of color. And it's a secret to no one that the greatest number of poor are people of color. This is not to say that the eradication of racism—even if possible—would mean the eradication of bigotry and inequity. It is to say that as priorities go, racism seems to have the greatest depth of trouble, cuts across most other bigotries, is imbricated with most other bigotries, and also stands alone, has the greatest number of layers. So, I think if we need to focus on dismantling one form of systemic oppression from our discipline, racism might be the best place to start (648).

ANA: This is exactly why your work means so much to people, to us. You call things out like not many other people do. You advocate for Latinx [Victor raises his eyebrows at this word but doesn't interrupt to question] scholars, particularly for those of us doing work around race and racism. You write about your experiences as an academic of color in order to counter the bootstraps narrative. The first time I read a chapter from *Bootstraps* [Victor smiles and nods] in a "multicultural rhetorics" class during my master's program, I felt *seen*. Like I was seeing people like me in academia and in my discipline for the first time. It was reading your work and seeing you present at CCCC that made me feel I could focus my academic career on issues of race, particularly pertaining to Latinidad. The genre bending and blurring that you did in that text and that you continue to do has contributed to a path for scholars who believe that personal experience is valuable knowledge. I'm thinking about Alejandra Ramírez and Ruben Zeneca, about Romeo García, about your own work, Aja, as well as so many others who incorporate their lived experiences or those of other minoritized populations into their scholarship.

AJA [nodding]: Yes, of course. Victor, you have set a precedent for us to break precedent!

VICTOR [with a wistful smile]: I have always thought that the way to recruit people of color, or as you say, BIPOC, into our discipline is by helping people of color write and publish research about race and racism (652). I am glad to see that I've been putting my money where my mouth is, so to speak.

ANA: It's so important to help grow BIPOC presence in our field and in academia at large. At my tenure-track job, I often feel like the last Latinx unicorn. I'm the only one left.

VICTOR [interrupting]: That word again—*Latinx*—is that "Latin" with an "x" at the end of it? [Ana and Aja exchange a look]

AJA: We can stop to explain it, but from conversations I've had with you in the future, I know you're not going to fully like or support the usage. You'll say to me that "latine (no a)" is a more viable option and is just a matter of knowing Spanish. You think that Latinx is pocho Spanish, and that we can't make it work for Puertorriqueños (Puertorricañx???). You'll say the intention is right with -x, but it isn't necessary, since Spanish does have neuter suffixes (Villanueva, "Re: Chapter 2").

VICTOR [chuckling]: Well, I seem to have it all charted out in your time—I'll wait for this debate, then. In the meantime, Ana, please continue with your story!

ANA [with a bemused smile on her face, picking up where she left off]: I'm a Latinx unicorn—People don't know what to do with me. They are fascinated by me and wonder about my magical powers—the ways that I've navigated whitestream academia—but they don't know or want to understand where I come from and why I do the work that I do. Because there have been very few Latinx and other BIPOC scholars in my department, my well-meaning white colleagues don't quite know how to make the department a friendly place for BIPOC scholars and students. And my not-so-well-meaning colleagues have pigeonholed me, asking me to define "La Raza" for them and wondering out loud if I could teach Latin American literature.

VICTOR [laughing]: A "Latin-Ex" unicorn. That's funny. I think the problem is exacerbated by the disproportionately few people of color being published in rhetoric and composition journals and by the bootstraps mentality that claims that if people of color cannot do better and don't achieve social mobility comparable to our white peers, it is that they are lazy and want to feed off the state. As Latino scholars, we become examples of the bootstraps narrative. Yet the statistics about us in academia are downright depressing ("On the Rhetoric" 649).

AJA [nodding]

ANA: They are not much better twenty-plus years later, let me tell you. Although the number of Latinx PhDs at large has increased minimally, from 5 percent of all PhDs identifying as Hispanic or Latino in 2010 to 7 percent in 2019, we are still disproportionately underrepresented, along with other BIPOC scholars. And the numbers of Latinx folks in rhetoric and composition has actually decreased since your time here in 1998! As Sonia Arellano and I published in 2017, only 1.47 percent of members of the Conference on College Composition and Communications identified as Latino/Hispanic/Spanish (335). In the second decade of the twenty-first century, the structural racism that you are writing about in this essay is still the modus operandi not only in our police forces but also in our institutions at large. As you say, "Racism runs deep" (650).

VICTOR: These numbers are indeed alarming. This is why I have so little patience with the idea of reverse discrimination.

[Ana and Aja nod and sigh in exasperation]

VICTOR: Often the only generalized acknowledgment of racism as structural comes by way of the perception of a reverse discrimination. Attacks against affirmative action cases, for example, ignore the data that shows that white people are still greatly advantaged by our system of higher education in admissions, in access to technology, in knowledge about how to navigate the university, etc. (651).

AJA: Yup! Life. Liberty. The pursuit of happiness. These ideals, these *liberal* ideals, have been and remain color-blind racist abstractions. In the future, as part of my first ever publication—which you, Victor will help me publish [Victor beams]—we will discuss how Eduardo Bonilla-Silva has asserted that the ideology of color-blind racism relies on four frames that function as Burkean tropes:

abstract liberalism, naturalization of race, cultural racism, and minimization of racism (26; Martinez, "The American Way" 588–89).

[Victor and Ana nod]

AJA [continuing]: Abstract liberalism involves ideas associated with political liberalism such as liberty, individualism, and equal opportunity in choice. And applied in an abstract manner, these ideas are used to explain racial matters such as opposition to affirmative action policies because these policies involve supposed preferential treatment, which under the frame of abstract liberalism can be rationalized as a practice opposed to the principle of equal opportunity. However, as you just said, this claim necessitates ignoring the fact that people of color are and have historically been severely underrepresented in most high-ranking jobs, schools, and universities; hence, it is an abstract utilization of the idea of equal opportunity.

VICTOR: That's exactly right! Practices of systemic racism accompanied by the incidents of overt racism that are ubiquitous on our streets and in our campuses make higher education a whole lot more difficult and even violent for folks of color ("On the Rhetoric" 650).

ANA [lowering her eyes and head in sadness]: The violence for our BIPOC communities never ceases. Your litany from the 1980s and the 1990s only pours into the new millennium and hits a peak in our own time when white supremacist police kill BIPOC again and again and again and migrant children from south of the border are separated from their families and sit incarcerated in camps along the border (650). It is so violent for our people. And deadly.

[Victor, Ana, and Aja sit for a moment in silent vigil, remembering the names of those humiliated, dehumanized, injured, and killed for the maintenance of systemic racism in their respective times.]

VICTOR [sighing]: And I suppose in your time as much as in

mine, multiculturalism hasn't improved things much, not even at the sites where students are exposed to such things (650).

[Ana and Aja shake their heads no]

AJA [slightly smirking]: Persuading white folks to love our cultures and food still doesn't quite bring them around to loving us.

[Ana and Victor chuckle derisively]

VICTOR: Well, maybe the relatively low numbers of people of color on our campuses or in our journals—or the high numbers at community colleges with disproportionately few of color among the faculty—reinforce racist conceptions. The disproportionately few people of color in front of the classrooms or in our publications, given the ubiquity of the bootstraps mentality, reifies the conception that people of color don't do better because they don't try harder (650–51).

ANA: Multiculturalism has not gotten us anywhere. The idea that our society can be a "salad bowl" ignores the fact that the lettuce still dominates the salad. Let me stop with this silly metaphor: multiculturalism is a convenient way to think of the US university as, in our time's parlance, "diverse"—but it does nothing to move us toward justice.

VICTOR [his eyes lighting up]: Ah! Justice.

ANA [continuing passionately]: It does nothing to wrest power away from white people and give it to BIPOC communities. In our time, university leadership is *still* overwhelmingly white and cisgender male. In fact, the American Council on Education recently released a report stating that in 2016, 83 percent of college and university presidents were "Caucasian, White, or White American"; women of color are the most underrepresented community, making up only 5 percent of college and university presidents (American College).

VICTOR: [shaking his head]

ANA: Twenty-plus years after the article you're working out

is published, the US is still an unwelcoming place for people of color and specifically for those positioned at the intersection of multiple forms of oppression.

VICTOR: So, tell me some good news! [All laugh in shared exasperation]

AJA: Well, Victor, as you call to action in the conclusion of this article, many BIPOC who you teach, mentor, and inspire have risen to the task of doing work that "writes frankly and sympathetically about matters concerning racism" ("On the Rhetoric" 652).

VICTOR [excitedly nodding]: Yes! Break precedent! Again, in my present era, we are so locked into the colonial mindset that we are now turning to the ex-colonials of Europe to learn something about our own people of color. There again, I'm grateful for the insights. But what are the ex-colonials of the US saying, the ex-colonials of our hemisphere, now caught in neocolonial dependency? I want to call on the research of Puerto Ricans, Filipinos, Chicanas and Chicanos, American Indians, African Americans, as well as Argentines from Mexico—ex-colonials and contemporary colonials of the United States, writing and researching on their colonial relations to the United States. What we know are the writers. And I truly believe we have a great deal to say that we should hear (659). [Looking intensely at Ana and Aja] My question for you is, how will *you* work to dismantle the white supremacy of knowledge? How will your actions break the rhetorics and precedents of racism?

CODA: GRACIAS, VICTOR

Victor, you have continued to serve as our mentor and inspiration—as can be discerned from the content and style of this essay. We have been lifted up and supported by your words, works, and friendship. Victor, you were the first person to *see* Aja's writing and believe there was promise in it, so much so that you reviewed, edited, and published her first ever essay back in that 2009 *College English* special issue. And you're still reading every *papelito guardado* Aja sends your way, with such patience, encouragement, and honesty. As for Ana, you gave her the courage to continue on her academic path when working on her dissertation and now in the interminable process of writing a monograph. Your guidance over the last decade has been invaluable. We are so grateful to you for the time and energy you've put into our projects, and we honestly don't know where you find the time for those of us you so generously commit to and support.

WORKS CITED

Agnew, Lois, et al. "Octalog III: The Politics of Historiography in 2010." *Rhetoric Review*, vol. 30, no. 2, 2011, pp. 109–34.

Ahmed, Sarah. *Living a Feminist Life*. Duke UP, 2017.

"American College President Study 2017." *American Council on Education*, 2017.

Baca, Damián, and Victor Villanueva, editors. *Rhetorics of the Americas: 3114 BCE to 2012 CE*. Palgrave Macmillan, 2010.

Banks, Adam J. *Race, Rhetoric, and Technology: Searching for Higher Ground*. Lawrence Erlbaum/National Council of Teachers of English, 2006.

Bell, Derrick. *And We Are Not Saved: The Elusive Quest for Racial Justice*. Basic Books, 1987.

———. *Faces at the Bottom of the Well: The Permanence of Racism*. Basic Books, 1992.

Bonilla-Silva, Eduardo. *Racism without Racists: Color-Blind Racism and the Persistence of Racial Inequality in America*. 5th ed., Rowman & Littlefield, 2018.

Crenshaw, Kimberlé. "Demarginalizing the Intersection of Race and Sex: A Black Feminist Critique of Antidiscrimination Doctrine, Feminist Theory and Antiracist Politics," *University of Chicago Legal Forum*, vol. 1989, no. 1, article 8, 1989, pp. 139–67.

Enoch, Jessica, and Cristina Devereaux Ramírez, editors. *Mestiza Rhetorics: An Anthology of Mexicana Activism in the Spanish-Language Press, 1887–1922*. Southern Illinois UP, 2019.

Enos, Richard Leo, et al. "Octalog II: The (Continuing) Politics of Historiography." *Rhetoric Review*, vol. 16, no. 1, 1997, pp. 22–44.

García, Romeo, "A Settler Archive: A Site for a Decolonial Praxis Project." *constellations: a cultural rhetorics publishing space*, vol. 2, 2019.

———, and Damián Baca, editors. *Rhetorics Elsewhere and Otherwise: Contested Modernities, Decolonial Visions.* Conference on College Composition and Communication/National Council of Teachers of English, 2019.

Glenn, Cheryl. *Rhetoric Retold: Regendering the Tradition from Antiquity through the Renaissance.* Southern Illinois UP, 1997.

Goldberg, Stephanie B. "Who's Afraid of Derrick Bell? A Conversation on Harvard, Storytelling and the Meaning of Color." *ABA Journal,* vol. 78, no. 9, 1992, pp. 56–58.

Martinez, Aja Y. "'The American Way': Resisting the Empire of Force and Color-Blind Racism." *College English,* vol. 71, no. 6, 2009, pp. 584–95.

———. *Counterstory: The Rhetoric and Writing of Critical Race Theory.* Conference on College Composition and Communication/National Council of Teachers of English, 2020.

Prendergast, Catherine. *Literacy and Racial Justice: The Politics of Learning after* Brown v. Board of Education. Southern Illinois UP, 2003.

Ramírez, Alejandra I., and Ruben Zeneca, "'The Dirt Under My Mom's Fingernails': Queer Retellings and Migrant Sensualities." *constellations: a cultural rhetorics publishing space,* vol. 2, 2019.

Ribero, Ana Milena, and Sonia C. Arellano. "Advocating *Comadrismo*: A Feminist Mentoring Approach for Latinas in Rhetoric and Composition." *Peitho,* vol. 21, no. 2, 2019, pp. 334-56.

Villanueva, Victor, Jr. *Bootstraps: From an American Academic of Color.* National Council of Teachers of English, 1993.

———. "*Memoria* Is a Friend of Ours: On the Discourse of Color." *College English,* vol. 67, no. 1, 2004, pp. 9–19.

———. "On the Rhetoric and Precedents of Racism." *College Composition and Communication,* vol. 50, no. 4, 1999, pp. 645–61.

———. "Re: Chapter 2." Received by Aja Y. Martinez, 21 Oct. 2019.

West, Cornel. "A Reflection on 'A Genealogy of Modern Racism'." *Race Critical Theories: Text and Context,* edited by Philomena Essed and David Theo Goldberg, Blackwell, 2002, pp. 90–112.

SECTION III:
MEMORIA OF RELATIONS

WHILE THE FIRST SECTION OF THIS collection takes up the function of *Memoria* as rhetoric, and the previous section engages Victor's generative mentorship as an overarching thematic, the short chapters in this section offer snapshots and recollections that involve or represent Victor in various ways. And in many ways, these creative works depict a deeper sense of the person Victor is as a scholar, teacher, and mentor. They highlight his humanity. If we think, too, on the breadth of the work we do as academics and teachers, of our interactions at conferences, our email exchanges, our classroom and office meetings with students and others—all these ways we relate to others—as an extension of our scholarship and mentoring, then these chapters are meant to capture some of the living scholarship that Victor has embodied.

These portrayals also show more stories of mentoring: Victor as teacher, as dissertation director, as editor. Jessie Eulalia Padilla takes us into Victor's graduate classroom; Mitzi Ceballos and Wyn Andrews Richards share how they engage Victor's work in their own first-year classrooms. Sherwin Kawahakui Ranchez Sales recounts a mentoring meeting between him and Victor in Victor's office at Washington State University in Pullman. Those of us who have experienced the same can picture Victor's opened laptop on the desk and can visualize the books lining his office shelves, whether at Avery Hall or more recently at the CUE. Tiffany Rousculp and Stephanie Kerschbaum describe how he encouraged them as writers and how he supported the publication of their SWR monographs while he was the editor. Rousculp shares a memorable visit with Victor at Salt Lake City Community College, and Kerschbaum reflects on how he gently nudged her to include more of herself in her writing. Here, too, Asao Inoue shares a poem that speaks to the importance of Victor's mentorship in his own life and disciplinary work, as does Siskanna Naynaha in her description of Victor's presence: his pensive listening, thoughtful silence, easygoing knowledge dropping, and ongoing generosity.

And so the authors here offer some of the relations we all have with Victor. Through these narratives, stories, sketches—through these memories—they demonstrate, too, how *Memoria* can be enacted through our relations with each other.

Chapter 16

How We Know

Jessie Eulalia Padilla

VICTOR ENTERS HIS LECTURES the way he enters his writing—with anecdotes, asides, and personal narrative. Whereas textual conventions indicate rhetorical movement in written works, the transition from Victor's oral narratives to the content of the day's lecture—much like in *Bootstraps* and his many published works—is practically imperceptible. One minute he's telling us about the day's goings-on or a story about his family, and the next he's connected it all to some article he'd recently read in *The New York Times* and the ideological underpinnings of political economy, Burke's master tropes, and the rhetorics of the Global South prior to Europeans colonizing the Indigenous peoples and languages of the Americas.

Most students don't notice the lecture has begun until about twenty minutes too late. It is then that they shuffle around in their bags, searching for a pen or laptop to take notes. As a student and mentee of Victor's, I always began taking notes once he took his seat in the chair at the head of the table. I knew from experience growing up around la mesa de mi familia that a meal began when mis tíos sat at the table and started telling stories. And so it is at Victor's lecture table—the learning happens with story.

ᔕ

I am standing at the kitchen counter of my grandmother's house. She's teaching me how to roll tortillas, an embodied, nourishing art. She speaks little English, and I only broken Spanish, so her hands do the teaching. Strong from a life of farmwork, her hands guide mine as I roll a small dowel back and forth over balls of dough.

Mi papá y mis tíos are at the kitchen table carrying on about local political and social issues and retelling stories of our family's history with the land. They bounce between Spanish, English, and roars of laughter. They'd carry on in this way for hours. That's how they were; that's how I grew up. I was too young to participate in the conversation, too young to sit at the table, but I listened. Just as my fingertips learned to flip steaming tortillas en la comal, I learned the nuanced rhetorics of español—the florid language and repetition of stories that at times seemed to have nothing to do with the conversation at hand, yet always circled back to the crux of the exchange.

❧

Victor is known for his tangential lectures. It's kind of a running joke among the graduate students, one that Victor is in on. But what may sound to some like veering off topic, to my ear, I am in my abuelita's kitchen again. Tangential rhetoric is familiar to me, and I rely on it to make real the extraordinarily abstract concepts we are learning that I would have otherwise lumbered through. Victor's position as an "organically-grown traditional intellectual," as one who treads the borders between el barrio and the ivory tower, between tangents and structure, makes a privileged space for me and students like me where our embodied and storied rhetorics are recognized as valid and essential to the academic conversation. It is those of us who have sat at his table, who also bestride multiple rhetorics and identities, who will continue the legacy of Victor Villanueva's life's work.

Once, after submitting a paper in his Rhetorics of Political Economy seminar, I asked to meet with Victor in his office to discuss my writing. I was ashamed of the quality of my work and wanted to apologize for the amount of personal narrative in my paper. I explained that while I easily understood the complexities in the content of his lectures—Marx and the superstructure; Althusser's ideological state apparatuses; Gramsci's hegemony;

Burke's consubstantiation; Quijano's coloniality and Mignolo's decoloniality—I couldn't write in the way academic text was supposed to be written. Too much narrative. The through lines entangled. Repetitive. Not scholarly.

"You won't easily separate the personal from the scholarly," Victor said, "and I'm not going to ask it of you. We're Latinos, you and I. Story is part of our rhetoric. It's who we *are*. It's how we *know*. If you can't understand this stuff without story, how could you possibly write without it? Write, Ms. Padilla. Your voice belongs here. Write like who you *are*."

Chapter 17

Family

Mitzi Ceballos and Wyn Andrews Richards

WYN

I AM FRIENDS WITH MY BELOVED colleague, Mitzi Ceballos, because of Victor Villanueva. We both came to Washington State University specifically to study with Victor. He paired us together for a group project, which clinched our friendship. Friends for life. Mitzi and I talk every day, and Victor is always there, whether it be in person or in spirit. It comes as no surprise that we both teach English 101 with Victor in the room. We both assign excerpts from *Bootstraps*. We both assign "*Memoria*." We both have rich, sometimes difficult, conversations with our students about racial inequity in English studies as well as in the larger scope of higher education and US society. Mitzi and I both want our students to learn as much from Victor as we have.

It's February 26, 2020. Victor is coming to speak with our students. We decided to combine our classes to meet in a larger space with Victor at the front of the room. As I watch our students come into the room, my heart rate increases. I am excited! So many writers that students read are disembodied shells of humans, but here is Victor Villanueva, in the flesh! Watching our students' eyes, riveted and engaged with Victor, seeing their smiles, hearing their laughs, I know they are connecting not just to Victor the dynamic human, but also to his words that they have already read. One student stayed behind specifically to shake Victor's hand. After this meeting, several of my students tell me they understand why I chose to uproot my family and move across the country to study with Dr.

Victor Villanueva. As I make eye contact with Mitzi throughout our time together, I can see that she feels the same way. In this combined talk with Victor and our students, Mitzi and I are both proud to share our friendship, as well as our mutual love for Victor. As a scholar, teacher, and friend, this is one of my best days.

MITZI

"I was so scared to email him that I made an appointment at the writing center and made the tutor spend a half hour second-guessing every word I wrote." Some of my students chuckle because they think the story of how I introduced myself to Victor as an undergrad is melodramatic. "I actually screamed when I hit send. And get this . . . he responded THREE MINUTES after I sent it!" I pull up the email exchange and show them the time stamp. The whole class laughs when they see I'm telling them the truth.

As a human being, I often wonder what it is I'm giving my students. The teacher-me, the "Ms. Mitzi," as they call me, asks them difficult questions, provides feedback on their writing, and asks more difficult questions. And of course, that's part of why Wyn and I invite Victor into our classrooms. But as a human being, I think, "Let me give you a gift. Let me give you one afternoon of Victor's company." Some of Wyn's Latinx students ask Victor about racism, and I see myself in them. One of my students asks a question and then laughs, relieved, when Victor responds, "Fuck, I don't know." Another student, a Latina like me, says she wants to be like Victor when she grows up. "Don't we all," I respond.

That day we asked a student to take a picture of the three of us. Occasionally someone will ask me if I'm lonely without any family in Pullman, and I remember that picture. "I do have some family here," I tell them. "A small, new family."

Chapter 18

Of Mentors and *Memoria* and Rhetorical Houses in Need of Fixing

Asao B. Inoue

Thinking about memory in my education,
Is thinking about mentors who guided me,
Maybe even saved me,

But surely showed me the way.
It's Chris and Victor, two men
Who went to grad school together,
And ended up somehow both in front of me.

The summer before I began my MA
I read Chris Anderson's book *Edge Effects,*
A beautiful reflection on a forest,
And language, and writing, with just a bit
Of spiritual thinking.
It was exactly what I needed,
the front step to a grand house,
the house of Rhetoric and Composition,
the place I would live for the rest of my life restless
in conditions of success and happiness
struggle and disappointment, but mostly success.

Chris was John the Baptist
in my educational desert—
He'd like that comparison
Given that he's a Catholic deacon

As well as a professor,
Or was—he's retired now.

He told me I was divine,
that I was good enough at language.
Well, not in those words,
But in his methods,
In his kind and gentle ways.
He pointed to the steps,
The entrance to my new home
Before I even recognized it as such,
And waved his hand for me
To come in and stay awhile.

But I couldn't walk through the door.
I tried. Believe me, I tried.
I mimicked his gate and foot-patterns.
The first difficulty was the screen door,
Then the lock with its strange mechanism,
Then the complicated doorknob,
With its particular combination of turns and twists.
And I think there must have also been
A secret password or a handshake
That Chris had neglected to tell me about
Because others got in easily,
Walking right past me, and I was there first,
Fiddling with that fucking doorknob.

But that ain't how things work
in the academy, I guess.
Some call it merit and ability, talent—
Haha, I say that sarcastically, talent.
Talent has to be recognized.
To be recognized, it has to be recognizable,
Something others have the ability to see
As recognizable and as talent.
And what do you think qualifies in a
White supremacist system as talent,

What's recognizable, what does the system
Allow us to be able to recognize as talent?

I'm probably just being bitter,
Too clingy to my grudges,
Too much the tea bag
Left steeping in a hot cup too long.
Strong educational tea, too strong to drink anymore.

It all sounds like secrets of a club you gotta be born into,
A club I ain't never been born into.
They all just surprised I'm at the doorstep.
They didn't know what to do with me.

More memories, this time turned *Memoria.*
Six or so years later comes Victor Villanueva,
Kickin' front doors down.
He says you don't have to open every door by yourself, man.
Who does that?

I enter the big house.
Victor and his *Bootstraps,*
Moved me into my new home.
Victor carried my suitcase in,
Showed me my first room,
Opened things up,
Laid out all my stuff,
Showed me where to sleep,
Which rooms to avoid—For now,
And where the leaky pipes were,
And how to fix them.

This was years,
More like a decade or so of work,
Labors and laboring,
Language and languaging.

And he told me from the beginning,
Some don't want the leaks fixed in the big house.
They like the pipes the way they are.

Some are happy with how things work now,
But they ain't the ones gettin wet.

They room on the second floor,
Meanwhile here we are in the basement,
Slipping around from the drips and leaks,
Everywhere, drips, leaks, water running,
And we are asking,
Shouldn't someone fix that?
It's gonna ruin the house.

Then Victor says, get to fixing shit, man,
And I'll help you.
I'll play lookout
While you are down here
With your wrench and hammer.

I'll bring new pipes in.
I'm strong enough to do that.
You need to do what you do.
Talk your assessment stuff—That's cool.
We need that.
It's really what I've been saying,
Just from a different angle,
Maybe one more accessible to the right white crowd,
Maybe better too.

Don't fuckin' wait for the water to rise.
We'll be a pair of turtles getting everyone wet.
Everybody's gotta get wet
If we gonna fix these fucking pipes, and
Stop all this water from ruining our home for everyone.

Now, some ain't gonna like getting wet
'Cause, well, they ain't been wet before.
They don't like doing the work in the basement.
We are used to it.
This is where we have lived and worked.
We are the foundation.

We are what this house is built on, man.
So get to work—break and fix things.
Some will take all the breaking and fixing personally,
Like our goal was to get them wet,
In a house whose basement is exploding with leaky pipes—
But we're trying to fix everyone's home.
They just can't see it yet, and they may never see it,
But we do, and others like us do, and more tomorrow will.
We all gotta live in this house.

Now, these were not Victor's words exactly.
They are my memories of my mentor, my academic father.
And I hope one day I will be memory too,
To others like Victor is to me,
Mentors should do that, makers of others' memories.

Chris the Baptist and Victor the Father,
Memories, *Memoria*, mentors,
They are friends of mine, of ours,
And we should all be grateful.

Chapter 19

Footprints to Follow

Sherwin Kawahakui Ranchez Sales

FOR A GOOD PART OF MY PhD program, I met with Victor in his office every Monday morning at 8 a.m. During those meetings, we would plan to go over exam reading lists and proposal ideas, but as it goes with Victor, we would get sidetracked a lot. And that never bothered me, especially since we always circled back around to our goals anyway (to which he would say, "See, I know what I'm doing!"). On one particular day, we were discussing something I had written for one of his graduate seminars, in which I had mentioned a funding award I received that was geared toward underrepresented communities. I was, of course, thankful for the award, but the topic of tokenism within academia came up, and I jokingly expressed my discomfort in receiving the financial help, as I believed it called into question how I got accepted into the PhD program as well as the merit of my own work. I said something like, "Am I just a Brown face they can put on their website?" Victor, silent for a second, placed his hands together and looked toward the ground. He responded, "Sherwin. I hate to break it to you man, but you'll be questioning yourself a long time with higher education's tokenism and liberalism."

And he's right. I do constantly question my place in academia, but I also consider myself extraordinarily fortunate that I'm following a legacy Victor has helped create that makes it easier for emerging scholars of color to not feel that pressure as harshly as he did. Throughout my time with him, Victor has shared his experience through his work, in his classes, and when we're just sitting in his office chatting. As he writes in "*Memoria* Is a Friend of Ours," "The narrative of the person of color validates. It resonates. It awakens, particularly for those of us in institutions where our numbers are few" (15). As a new PhD student at the time, I felt invigorated by his guidance, and for all the times I tried something new in my writing, I had confidence in his feedback—even if it was a nudge toward a hard reset, as if to say, "Hey, let's try this again, but let's try it like *this*." His critiques spoke to me: *I see the path you're trying to tread. Hell, those footprints in the dirt you're following are mine.*

I haven't had many teachers like Victor. And I mean that literally. He is one of two scholars of color I've had the opportunity to study and learn from while completing my English degrees. He is the only rhetoric and composition professor of color I've had, and the only one of color to take me under his wing and show me the ropes of this complex thing called academia. He's one of the few teachers that listened to my pie-in-the-sky ideas early on in my program and helped cultivate my confidence and direction. Something I wasn't accustomed to.

On top of all that, though, what I value most are his stories of his journey and how they point us toward the right way. I value how he finds strands of my own narrative and threads it with his so that I understand. I'm following those imprints left marked in the dirt, and as I navigate the challenges that come with working in higher education and doing work that examines race, I know that I'm walking in sturdier boots than I did before, and the straps that previously felt so flimsy seem a bit tougher.

Chapter 20

Blown Away

Tiffany Rousculp

IN SEPTEMBER 2006, VICTOR gave the keynote presentation for Salt Lake Community College's first annual Writing and Social Justice Conference. As he stepped down from the stage, I hesitantly introduced myself, a bit starstruck.

He smiled generously and dropped an f-bomb. With just one word, Victor blew away my fear and put me at ease.

I drove Victor to the Community Writing Center at the Salt Lake City Public Library, one stop on his tour of SLCC's Department of English programs. I showed him around and explained how we developed the center, where we had been, and what we were doing now. His gravelly chuckle turned into full-throated laughter. "You did it," he said when he caught his breath. "Damn it, you did what they've all been talking about."

Late the next day, a real bomb went off at the library, canceling Victor's community discussion scheduled for that evening. A small pipe bomb, hidden in a paper bag on the third floor, blew out a window and evacuated four hundred people. Planted by an angry white man (who drove all the way from Illinois) as retribution for the Salt Lake City Police Department arresting his son for driving drunk.

I drove Victor to the airport the next morning, my 11-month-old son tagging along in his car seat. We talked about family. And people. And different types of bombs. He chuckled until we got to the curb.

As he stepped out of the car, he told me to start writing. Five years later, I did.

When I was done, I sent my writing to Victor, who was then the editor of the Studies in Writing & Rhetoric series. The reviewers weren't sure. Victor was; he encouraged me to blow it up and find the book inside. He believed in the story.

So I did. Started over, and then it was done: "This is a book," he said, the first completely begun and finished within his SWR editorship.

As this book shows, Victor has meant many things to many people. For me, Victor blew away my assumption that someone who went to a community college, who had "only" a master's degree, and who taught at a community college had no business also being a scholar. Victor believed in my story and made it possible, just as he has done for so many others.

Chapter 21

Embodied Engagements

Stephanie L. Kerschbaum

THE FIRST TIME I MET VICTOR VILLANUEVA in person was at the Conference on College Composition and Communication Annual Convention after my book had been accepted for publication in the Studies in Writing & Rhetoric (SWR) series, which he was editing. He'd been patiently, generously, and with charm and grace fielding my anxious first-book-writer-on-the-tenure-track emails for months. My favorite email I got from him during the process of writing my book shared his reflection on how all the rhetorical resources around him as he read in a hospital waiting room mattered to the interactions he had with various staff and employees. He described the incongruity of his physical embodiment, music selections, food choices, clothing, and relationships with others, and how they must confuse everyone he encountered. I loved that he was sharing with me his experience of reading my book and reflecting on his everyday experience of navigating the world.

I meet Victor in a buzzing hotel conference room as part of a panel that he organized for potential SWR writers, complete with a workshopping session for book writers to interact with members of the SWR Editorial Board. Victor stands at the front of the room, pointing and waving at new and old friends. Everyone seems to know—and love—him. I'm beyond excited, but also an incredibly anxious first-book-writer-still-on-the-tenure-track watching everything with intense interest. He's not like other academic mentors I've had; he laughs a lot, is informal, and holds me to the highest standards.

At the end of the convention, Victor invites me to be the author-representative on the following year's SWR panel. When next year rolls around, he introduces me, telling the audience that I was one of the most resistant revisers he'd worked with. I don't know if I love being characterized as a resistant reviser, but he'd prepared me for this, warned me that he wanted me to talk about how I'd responded to two key pieces of feedback from my manuscript reviewers. They'd told me that I had to do more to recognize the significance of identity categories even as I forwarded my theory of marking difference, and that I had to talk about myself more.

Addressing the first suggestion was easier for me than the second. I did not want to talk about myself more. I've been getting—and resisting—this suggestion for years, but Victor was insistent, telling me in no uncertain terms that I had to do this. And I realized who I was resisting this suggestion in front of. Victor's been writing about himself brilliantly, powerfully, for years, emphasizing the importance of bodies, of race, of identity to writing. He enacted this insistence at every turn of the editorial process, including straight up telling me that I had to explain how I work with aural data as a deaf person. More than once, I've belatedly recognized how important that move has been—not just for the book, but for *me*. Avoiding talking about my embodiment and how it matters to my work only made it harder for me to engage with it in my own life.

Considered from the perspective of hindsight, Victor's engagement with me during the editorial process was profoundly humanizing even as he pushed me to grow in the ways he has pushed our entire field to do. In all of my interactions with him, he has followed the exemplar his own scholarship offers, and this is a huge part of the legacy he's built within rhetoric and writing studies.

Chapter 22

Gracias, Viejo

Siskanna Naynaha

I DON'T REMEMBER WHEN IT happened, exactly. When I started referring to Victor as "Viejo"—an honorific and term of endearment in Spanish. It means other things, too, of course, but as with everything when it comes to languaging, context is key.

I do recall sitting in his office, which, at the time, was a small, unassuming space tucked into the corner of Avery Hall on the campus of Washington State University. I was then working on my PhD, and Victor was the chair of my dissertation committee, my teacher (I took every course he taught during my time at WSU), and my mentor. Sometimes we would have formal meetings to discuss one of my dissertation chapters or a paper I was working on for one of his seminars. Sometimes there was political drama in the department that I needed help processing. But often I would just wander into the hallway where his office was located and pop my head in to say hello.

Everyone who's met Victor will tell you he has a presence. He would sit across from me at his desk and lean back in his chair, looking at me over the rim of his glasses, his long, graying beard grazing his chest periodically as he nodded, pensive as he listened. I would usually start with a flood of questions, taking far too long to explain myself and getting way out into the weeds before pausing to see if I'd yet bored him to death. Then he would look at me for a moment in silence, take a breath, and let that knowledge drop. We spoke of everything from political economy to the rhetorics of racism. From Freire to Gramsci to Pedro Albizu Campos. We ruminated on the state of the discipline. We dished about shenanigans at Rico's, the designated local graduate student pub, where my cohort managed to become college-town famous for our passionate, profanity-laced debates. We talked about our children. We both have a kind of booming laughter that can erupt unexpectedly, and sometimes our raucous hooting and guffawing would attract grad students and faculty from the offices nearby.

Victor had unnervingly critical insight on every subject. He didn't always have *the* answer, but he had wisdom and a kind of catholic intellect that could leave you feeling stunned. Throughout the four years I spent at WSU, he was generous with that intellect as well as his time, perhaps almost to a fault. He was busy: busy being department chair, busy giving lectures, busy writing books and articles. But he always made time for me, and for all of the students and scholars he worked with at WSU and far beyond. He gave with his full heart and spirit, which is why I, like so many others, developed a sort of filial tenderness toward him.

And so he became "Viejo" to me. As in, mis viejos, my parents. Father. Others have revealed similar monikers: Dad, Pa, Jefe, Señor, all ways of saying "father." When someone inspires this kind of affection and admiration, it's because they've shared the most precious gift they have to give. Victor says his legacy is us, all the students and scholars he's mentored and taught and nurtured over the years. I say Victor's legacy is love.

Gracias por todo, Viejo. Gracias.

EDITORS

Asao B. Inoue (he/him) is a professor of rhetoric and composition in the School of Applied Sciences and Arts at Arizona State University, where he teaches writing, composition, and assessment theory courses. He has published numerous books and articles on antiracist writing assessment and won numerous national awards for his scholarship. He was the 2019 chair of the Conference on College Composition and Communication. Asao has known Victor since 2001, when Victor was his dissertation advisor at WSU, and has relied on him for friendship and counsel ever since.

Wendy Olson (she/they) is an associate professor of English at Washington State University, where she teaches undergraduate and graduate courses in rhetoric and composition. She serves as the director of Composition and Writing Assessment on the Vancouver campus. She has published on basic writing and composition pedagogy, writing program administration, writing in the disciplines, and feminist rhetorics. A first-generation college student and academic, Wendy is thankful for Victor's guidance as her dissertation director (2002–2006) and for his mentorship and ongoing support since then.

Siskanna Naynaha (she/her) is an associate professor of English in the College of Arts and Humanities at California State University, Dominguez Hills. She serves as the director of Writing Across

the Curriculum, where she facilitates workshops that focus on engaging faculty in antiracist writing pedagogy to improve justice and equity in the teaching of writing in all disciplines. She has published on reading and writing across the curriculum, writing program administration, and Latine students in US higher education. A Xicana and a first-generation college student, Siskanna was inspired by Victor's *Bootstraps* to enter the PhD program in rhetoric and composition at Washington State University in 2002, and he has been a bedrock of support and mentorship for her since.

CONTRIBUTORS

Mitzi Ceballos (she/her) is a PhD candidate in the Department of Writing and Rhetoric at the University of Utah. She teaches first-year writing at the university and at Salt Lake Community College. Her interests include archival research, decolonial theory, and comparative rhetoric. She often emails and occasionally calls Victor in a panic and is always happy and grateful when he answers.

Robert Eddy/Salah Al-Din (he/him) is a professor of English at Washington State University, where he teaches rhetoric courses. He has published six books and a number of articles on the rhetorics of racism. He has known Victor since 1993, when they shared the same panel at the Conference on College Composition and Communication Convention in San Diego. Their friendship has survived the challenge of producing a joint book about racism, including manifestations of racism within the friendship: *A Language and Power Reader: Representations of Race in a "Post-Racist" Era.*

Miriam L. Fernandez (she/her) is an associate professor of English at California State University, San Bernardino, where she teaches first-year composition, writing in the public sphere, multimodal composition, and rhetorical theory courses. Her research focuses on the use of epideictic rhetoric in social constructions of la Malinche/Malintzin and on investigating the rhetorical elements of la Llorona storytelling among Chicanx and Mexican communities. She has known Victor since 2013, when he became her mentor and dissertation advisor at Washington State University.

Romeo García is an assistant professor of writing and rhetoric studies at the University of Utah. His research appears in *College Composition and Communication*, *Rhetoric Society Quarterly*, *Across the Disciplines*, and *Rhetoric, Politics, and Culture*. García is coeditor of *Rhetorics Elsewhere and Otherwise* (with Damián Baca), *Unsettling Archival Research* (with Gesa E. Kirsch, Caitlin Burns Allen, and Walker P. Smith), and *Pluriversal Literacies* (with Ellen Cushman and Damián Baca). Romeo has known Victor since 2010.

Laura Gray-Rosendale (she/her) is President's Distinguished Teaching Fellow and Professor of English at Northern Arizona University, where she teaches undergraduate and graduate courses in rhetoric, writing, and digital media studies. Her research focuses on the history of rhetoric, personal writing, visual and digital literacies, basic writing scholarship, and gender studies. She has published a variety of books, her most recent being *Go Online!* (with Steven Rosendale), an examination of the possibilities and perils of online writing instruction during the pandemic. Currently she is finishing *Basic Writing in the Twenty-First Century* (with Barbara Gleason). Laura has known Victor since roughly 1997, when she was completing her dissertation with Keith Gilyard at Syracuse University. Victor graciously wrote the afterword for her first book based on this dissertation and has been a dear mentor and friend ever since.

Victoria Houser (she/her) is an assistant professor of composition and rhetoric at Methodist University, where she teaches a range of writing and rhetorical theory courses. She researches evangelical purity culture through the lens of cultural, feminist, and queer rhetorics. Her work on purity rhetorics won the Victor J. Vitanza RCID Outstanding Dissertation Award and was a finalist for the Religious Communication Association Top Dissertation award in 2022. Victoria has known Victor since 2015, when he chaired her master's committee at WSU, and she now considers him a lifelong mentor, advocate, and friend.

Stephanie L. Kerschbaum (she/her) is a professor of English and director of the Program in Writing and Rhetoric at the University of Washington, Seattle. She has published widely in writing studies and disability studies and is the author of *Signs of Disability* (2022) and *Toward a New Rhetoric of Difference* (2014). Stephanie first met Victor while working with him on *Toward*, and the lessons learned from his mentorship have influenced her ever since.

Aja Y. Martinez is an associate professor of English at the University of North Texas. Her award-winning scholarship, published nationally and internationally, makes a compelling case for counterstory as methodology through the well-established framework of critical race theory (CRT). In 2008, Victor took a chance on a grad student from the University of Arizona's RCTE program and published her essay "'The American Way': Resisting the Empire of Force and Color-Blind Racism" in a 2009 special issue of *College English*. This was Aja's first-ever publication and gave her sorely needed confidence to continue researching, writing, and publishing her work on the rhetorics of race and racism. Victor would go on to serve as outside reader on Aja's master's thesis and PhD dissertation committees, and, rounding out their years of collaboration, Victor served as development editor for Aja's multi-award-winning book *Counterstory: The Rhetoric and Writing of Critical Race Theory*.

Christa J. Olson (she/her) is Marjorie and Lorin Tiefenthaler Professor of Composition and Rhetoric in the Department of English at the University of Wisconsin–Madison. She teaches courses in rhetorical history, theory, and criticism—often focused on visual and material culture—and publishes research on Américan rhetorical history, visual rhetoric, and public feeling. She learned from Victor the importance of doing formative editorial work to support emerging scholarly areas. Though she and Victor have met in person only a few times, she is immensely grateful for the ways he has mentored her on the page—both through his writing and in responses to hers.

Jessie Eulalia Padilla (she/her) is a PhD candidate in the English department at Washington State University, where she studies rhetoric and composition. Her research areas include the rhetorics, ideology, and political economy of coloniality and the epistemic and existential nature of the relationship between language, rhetoric, and text creation. Upon completion of her program, Jessie will become the first in her family to earn a PhD. She has been a student and mentee of Victor since 2017, and he served as chair of her master's committee. Jessie continues to seek guidance from Victor and is ever appreciative of his wit and wisdom.

J. Paul Padilla (he/him) is a doctoral candidate in the Rhetoric, Composition, and the Teaching of English program at the University of Arizona, where he is completing his dissertation as a Russell J. and Dorothy S. Bilinski Fellow. His scholarship centers on rhetorics of racism, Latinidad, intersectionality, and decoloniality in the United States. His scholarly work has appeared in *Composition Studies*, *enculturation*, *Latinx Writing and Rhetoric Studies*, *Present Tense—A Journal of Rhetoric in Society*, and *College Composition and Communication*. Among his awards and recognitions, he is the recipient of the 2019 University of Arizona Leadership Endorsement and the 2022 K. Patricia Cross Future Leaders Award from the American Association of Colleges and Universities. After meeting in 2000, Victor has become a mentor, a friend, and un hermano, currently serving as co-chair of Paul's dissertation committee.

Octavio Pimentel (he/him) is a professor of rhetoric and composition in the Department of English within the Liberal Arts College at Texas State University. In this role, he teaches courses on writing, composition, language, methods, and technical writing. Octavio has an impressive publication record, with six books and many articles that delve into the realms of writing and the experiences of people of color. It was in 1996, during the Latino Caucus meeting at the Conference on College Composition and Communication in Milwaukee, Wisconsin, that Octavio first crossed paths with Victor.

Catherine Prendergast (she/her) is a professor emerita at the University of Illinois at Urbana-Champaign. She is author, most recently, of *The Gilded Edge: Two Audacious Women and the Cyanide Love Triangle That Shook America.* When she cleaned out her office, she found countless evidence of Victor's support of her career, dating back to the 1990s.

Ana Milena Ribero (she/her/ella) is an assistant professor of rhetoric and composition at Oregon State University. Her research and teaching focus mainly on rhetorics of im/migration, rhetorics of race, critical literacies and pedagogies, and Women of Color feminisms. Her book *Dreamer Nation: Immigration, Activism, and Neoliberalism* (2023) tells the rhetorical story of Dreamer activism during the Obama years. Ana officially met Victor at the CCCC Convention in 2014 when he attended her Scholars for the Dream presentation, although she's been a student of Victor's writing since her entry into academia. Victor served on Ana's dissertation committee and continues to be a mentor.

Wyn Andrews Richards (she/her) is a PhD candidate in English rhetoric and composition at Washington State University, where she teaches Rhetorics of Racism, Everyday Rhetorics, College Composition, and College Composition for Multilingual Writers. Her research interests are rhetorics of racism, antiracist pedagogies, and writing program administration. A very lucky mentee of Victor Villanueva, Wyn assigns his work to all of her students in every course she teaches.

Lauren Rosenberg (she/her) is an associate professor of rhetoric and writing studies and director of first-year composition at the University of Texas at El Paso. She teaches courses in composition theory and pedagogy, critical and community literacy studies, feminist theories and methodologies, and writing program administration. Lauren began working with Victor in 2013 when he served as SWR series editor for her monograph, *The Desire for Literacy: Writing in the Lives of Adult Learners.* An article based on the book, coauthored with Stephanie L. Kerschbaum, "Entanglements of Literacy Studies and Disability Studies," won the 2021 Richard C. Ohmann award from NCTE.

Tiffany Rousculp (she/they) is a professor in the English, Linguistics, and Writing Studies program at Salt Lake Community College, where she teaches composition, linguistics, and writing studies courses and directs the Writing Across the College program. She has published multiple articles and two books on community literacy and WAC. Tiffany is also the founding director of the SLCC Community Writing Center and has worked for three decades to bend assumptions about writing instruction within higher education. She met Victor's writing in 1994 and has known him since 2006, when meeting him changed her ideas of who a scholar could be.

Sherwin Kawahakui Ranchez Sales (he/him/his) is an assistant professor of English and Writing Center director at California State University, Dominguez Hills. He has taught composition, rhetoric, Asian Pacific American literature, and writing center theory courses, and his research follows these interests as his work aims to center discussions of race, particularly as they concern Asian American and Pacific Islanders. He has contributed to journals such as *Rhetoric Review*, *College Composition and Communication*, *Xchanges*, and *The Peer Review*. Sherwin has known Victor since 2017, when Victor was his professor, advisor, and mentor throughout his PhD program.

John Trimbur (he/him) is an emeritus professor of rhetoric and writing studies at Emerson College, where he taught courses on composition theory and pedagogy, transnational Englishes in the Black Atlantic, and literary/political magazines in South Africa and the Caribbean. His most recent book is *Grassroots Literacy and the Written Record: A Textual History of Asbestos Activism in South Africa* (2020). John met Victor in the late 1980s, when Victor contributed a chapter on Freirean pedagogy to *The Politics of Writing Instruc-*

tion, which John coedited with Chuck Schuster and Rich Bullock. They have been friends and comrades ever since.

Morris Young (he/him) is the Charles Q. Anderson Professor of English at the University of Wisconsin–Madison. His work focuses on writing and identity, the intersections of literacy and rhetorical studies, and Asian American culture. His current work considers the generation and function of Asian/American rhetorical commonplaces as a response to exigencies of exclusion, marginalization, and containment. His book, *Minor Re/Visions: Asian American Literacy Narratives as a Rhetoric of Citizenship* (2004), received the 2004 W. Ross Winterowd Award and the 2006 CCCC Outstanding Book Award. Morris first corresponded with Victor for a special issue of *College English* and then as they crossed paths over many CCCC Annual Conventions.

BOOKS IN THE CCCC STUDIES IN WRITING & RHETORIC SERIES

Memoria: Essays in Honor of Victor Villanueva
Edited by Asao B. Inoue, Wendy Olson, and Siskanna Naynaha

The Hands of God at Work: Islamic Gender Justice through Translingual Praxis
Amber Engelson

Queer Techné: Bodies, Rhetorics, and Desire in the History of Computing
Patricia Fancher

Living English, Moving Literacies: Women's Stories of Learning between the US and Nepal
Katie Silvester

Recollections from an Uncommon Time: 4C20 Documentarian Tales
Edited by Julie Lindquist, Bree Straayer, and Bump Halbritter

Transfer in an Urban Writing Ecology: Reimagining Community College–University Relations in Composition Studies
Christie Toth with Joanne Castillo, Nic Contreras, Kelly Corbray, Nathan Lacy, Westin Porter, Sandra Salazar-Hernandez, and Colleagues

Teachers Talking Writing: Perspectives on Places, Pedagogies, and Programs
Shane A. Wood

Materiality and Writing Studies: Aligning Labor, Scholarship, and Teaching
Holly Hassel and Cassandra Phillips

Salt of the Earth: Rhetoric, Preservation, and White Supremacy
James Chase Sanchez

Rhetorics of Overcoming: Rewriting Narratives of Disability and Accessibility in Writing Studies
Allison Harper Hitt

Writing Accomplices with Student Immigrant Rights Organizers
Glenn Hutchinson

Counterstory: The Rhetoric and Writing of Critical Race Theory
Aja Y. Martinez

Writing Programs, Veterans Studies, and the Post-9/11 University: A Field Guide
Alexis Hart and Roger Thompson

Beyond Progress in the Prison Classroom: Options and Opportunities
Anna Plemons

Rhetorics Elsewhere and Otherwise: Contested Modernities, Decolonial Visions
Edited by Romeo García and Damián Baca

Black Perspectives in Writing Program Administration: From the Margins to the Center
Edited by Staci M. Perryman-Clark and Collin Lamont Craig

Translanguaging outside the Academy: Negotiating Rhetoric and Healthcare in the Spanish Caribbean
Rachel Bloom-Pojar

Collaborative Learning as Democratic Practice: A History
Mara Holt

Reframing the Relational: A Pedagogical Ethic for Cross-Curricular Literacy Work
Sandra L. Tarabochia

Inside the Subject: A Theory of Identity for the Study of Writing
Raúl Sánchez

Genre of Power: Police Report Writers and Readers in the Justice System
Leslie Seawright

Assembling Composition
Edited by Kathleen Blake Yancey and Stephen J. McElroy

Public Pedagogy in Composition Studies
Ashley J. Holmes

From Boys to Men: Rhetorics of Emergent American Masculinity
Leigh Ann Jones

Freedom Writing: African American Civil Rights Literacy Activism, 1955–1967
Rhea Estelle Lathan

The Desire for Literacy: Writing in the Lives of Adult Learners
Lauren Rosenberg

On Multimodality: New Media in Composition Studies
Jonathan Alexander and Jacqueline Rhodes

Toward a New Rhetoric of Difference
Stephanie L. Kerschbaum

Rhetoric of Respect: Recognizing Change at a Community Writing Center
Tiffany Rousculp

After Pedagogy: The Experience of Teaching
Paul Lynch

Redesigning Composition for Multilingual Realities
Jay Jordan

Agency in the Age of Peer Production
Quentin D. Vieregge, Kyle D. Stedman, Taylor Joy Mitchell, and Joseph M. Moxley

Remixing Composition: A History of Multimodal Writing Pedagogy
Jason Palmeri

First Semester: Graduate Students, Teaching Writing, and the Challenge of Middle Ground
Jessica Restaino

Agents of Integration: Understanding Transfer as a Rhetorical Act
Rebecca S. Nowacek

Digital Griots: African American Rhetoric in a Multimedia Age
Adam J. Banks

The Managerial Unconscious in the History of Composition Studies
Donna Strickland

Everyday Genres: Writing Assignments across the Disciplines
Mary Soliday

The Community College Writer: Exceeding Expectations
Howard Tinberg and Jean-Paul Nadeau

A Taste for Language: Literacy, Class, and English Studies
James Ray Watkins

Before Shaughnessy: Basic Writing at Yale and Harvard, 1920–1960
Kelly Ritter

Writer's Block: The Cognitive Dimension
Mike Rose

Teaching/Writing in Thirdspaces: The Studio Approach
Rhonda C. Grego and Nancy S. Thompson

Rural Literacies
Kim Donehower, Charlotte Hogg, and Eileen E. Schell

Writing with Authority: Students' Roles as Writers in Cross-National Perspective
David Foster

Whistlin' and Crowin' Women of Appalachia: Literacy Practices since College
Katherine Kelleher Sohn

Sexuality and the Politics of Ethos in the Writing Classroom
Zan Meyer Gonçalves

African American Literacies Unleashed: Vernacular English and the Composition Classroom
Arnetha F. Ball and Ted Lardner

Revisionary Rhetoric, Feminist Pedagogy, and Multigenre Texts
Julie Jung

Archives of Instruction: Nineteenth-Century Rhetorics, Readers, and Composition Books in the United States
Jean Ferguson Carr, Stephen L. Carr, and Lucille M. Schultz

Response to Reform: Composition and the Professionalization of Teaching
Margaret J. Marshall

Multiliteracies for a Digital Age
Stuart A. Selber

Personally Speaking: Experience as Evidence in Academic Discourse
Candace Spigelman

Self-Development and College Writing
Nick Tingle

Minor Re/Visions: Asian American Literacy Narratives as a Rhetoric of Citizenship
Morris Young

A Communion of Friendship: Literacy, Spiritual Practice, and Women in Recovery
Beth Daniell

Embodied Literacies: Imageword and a Poetics of Teaching
Kristie S. Fleckenstein

Language Diversity in the Classroom: From Intention to Practice
Edited by Geneva Smitherman and Victor Villanueva

Rehearsing New Roles: How College Students Develop as Writers
Lee Ann Carroll

Across Property Lines: Textual Ownership in Writing Groups
Candace Spigelman

Mutuality in the Rhetoric and Composition Classroom
David L. Wallace and Helen Rothschild Ewald

The Young Composers: Composition's Beginnings in Nineteenth-Century Schools
Lucille M. Schultz

Technology and Literacy in the Twenty-First Century: The Importance of Paying Attention
Cynthia L. Selfe

Women Writing the Academy: Audience, Authority, and Transformation
Gesa E. Kirsch

Gender Influences: Reading Student Texts
Donnalee Rubin

Something Old, Something New: College Writing Teachers and Classroom Change
Wendy Bishop

Dialogue, Dialectic, and Conversation: A Social Perspective on the Function of Writing
Gregory Clark

Audience Expectations and Teacher Demands
Robert Brooke and John Hendricks

Toward a Grammar of Passages
Richard M. Coe

Rhetoric and Reality: Writing Instruction in American Colleges, 1900–1985
James A. Berlin

Writing Groups: History, Theory, and Implications
Anne Ruggles Gere

Teaching Writing as a Second Language
Alice S. Horning

Invention as a Social Act
Karen Burke LeFevre

The Variables of Composition: Process and Product in a Business Setting
Glenn J. Broadhead and Richard C. Freed

Writing Instruction in Nineteenth-Century American Colleges
James A. Berlin

Computers & Composing: How the New Technologies Are Changing Writing
Jeanne W. Halpern and Sarah Liggett

A New Perspective on Cohesion in Expository Paragraphs
Robin Bell Markels

Evaluating College Writing Programs
Stephen P. Witte and Lester Faigley

This book was typeset in Adobe Garamond and Frutiger by
Barbara Frazier.
Typefaces used on the cover include Garamond and News Gothic.
The book was printed on 50-lb. white, offset paper.